THE ASIATIC SOCIETY
AND THE DISCOVERY OF INDIA'S PAST
1784–1838

THE ASIATIC SOCIETY
OF BENGAL
and the Discovery of India's Past
1784–1838

O. P. KEJARIWAL

OXFORD
UNIVERSITY PRESS

UNIVERSITY PRESS

YMCA Library Building, Jai Singh Road, New Delhi 110001

Oxford University Press is a department of the University of Oxford. It furthers the
University's objective of excellence in research, scholarship, and education
by publishing worldwide in

Oxford New York
Athens Auckland Bangkok Bogota Buenos Aires Calcutta
Cape Town Chennai Dar es Salaam Delhi Florence Hong Kong Istanbul
Karachi Kuala Lumpur Madrid Melbourne Mexico City Mumbai
Nairobi Paris Sao Paolo Singapore Taipei Tokyo Toronto Warsaw

with associated companies in

Berlin Ibadan

ISBN 0 19 565089 1

Typeset at Sri Aurobindo Ashram Press, Pondicherry 605002
Printed at Saurabh Print-O-Pack, Noida, UP 201301
and published by Manzar Khan, Oxford University Press
YMCA Library Building, Jai Singh Road, New Delhi 110001

IN MEMORIAM
A. L. BASHAM
DEB PRATIM BANERJEE

Contents

Plates

Map

Contents

Plates

Map

Foreword

When I visited Calcutta for the Bicentenary Celebrations of the Asiatic Society, I met a young scholar, Dr O. P. Kejariwal, who showed me a copy of his thesis. After reading it, I strongly recommended him to publish it, and I am very glad that he has now done so.

The work of Dr Kejariwal covers the first fifty years or so of the life and activities of the Asiatic Society. Still inspired by the brilliant and enquiring spirit of its founder, Sir William Jones, it numbered among its members a series of devoted and able scholars—men like Wilson, Colebrooke, Prinsep, and the Hungarian Csoma de Körös—who raised the edifice of Indology on the base laid by Jones, so that at the end of the period covered by this book there were professors of Sanskrit in many universities of Europe and the broad outlines of the early history of India were revealed.

Clearly, succinctly and interestingly, Dr Kejariwal tells us of the activities of this small band of scholars who were inspired to reveal India's past. Few if any of them derived any material gains from their work, and most of them appear to have met the expenses of their research out of their own pockets. The main motive in most of their minds seems to have been the study of India for its own sake.

The Society took an interest not only in languages, literature and culture, but also in the natural sciences as they were related to India. The latter interest is still alive in the Society, but nowadays it clearly takes second place. The really important work of the Society has been obviously in the field of the humanities.

The fact, however, that in its early phases many of its members devoted their attention to what was then called 'natural history', has been used by some critics to support their argument that the main motive in the minds of its early members was to strengthen the British hold on India, and views of this kind were sometimes heard in the course of the Bicentenary seminars. It is well known that Warren Hastings was of the view that if the East India Company was to establish a firm and lasting regime in its territories its officers had to gain a sympathetic understanding of the culture and customs of the peoples whom they governed, and it is possible that in giving his blessing to the foundation of the Society Hastings was partly motivated by such ideas—but only partly, for his writings show that his interest in Indian culture went far beyond those of an intelligent administrator.

Whether such ideas played any part in the conscious motivation of the members of the Society is much more doubtful. When Jones translated *Sakuntala* and thus introduced the Sanskrit drama to the western world, are we to believe that he consciously thought: 'I am doing this in order that my country may dominate a subject people'? Could any such motive have been in the mind of James Prinsep, when he deciphered the inscriptions of Asoka? Was Colebrooke inspired in his pioneering work on the Veda chiefly by motives of patriotism? If these scholars had worked to serve their country or the Company in their spare time they could surely have found more effective ways of doing so.

In fact, these pioneer Indologists must have been motivated chiefly, in every case, by the desire for knowledge and understanding — knowledge and understanding of a civilization different from their own, which they recognized as possessing uncharted beauties and unplumbed depths. At the back of all good scholarship is burning intellectual curiosity, a determination to understand—and this the pioneers of the Asiatic Society possessed in full measure.

Moreover, their work indirectly helped to lay the foundations of modern Indian nationalism. If intelligent Indians had not steadily come to realise that their culture had possessed not only profound mystics, but also precious heirlooms like the dramas of Kalidasa and the inscriptions of Asoka, the whole history of modern India would have been very different, and perhaps much more painful. In fact India is greatly indebted to this small band of gifted amateurs who commenced the long and as yet incomplete process of revealing her great heritage. That they happened to be Britishers is perhaps merely an accident of history, but they are none the less worthy of the praise and admiration of posterity of any and every race, for their great contributions to the enrichment of the human spirit.

Therefore I heartily commend Dr Kejariwal's excellent study to discriminating readers throughout the world.

A. L. BASHAM

Preface

'Often, the simplest way of explaining what a book is about and what it aims to achieve', says Gunnar Myrdal in the Preface to his *Asian Drama*, 'is to tell why and how it came to be written.' The observation is especially apt in regard to the present work because it was only a chance incident which made me take up this work on the Asiatic Society. The incident elucidates in a way the scope and aim of this study.

In 1978, during a visit to the National Archives, I idly picked up a book, and, leafing through it, my eyes came to rest upon an article on the Allahabad Pillar. I began reading the article casually but suddenly it held my interest. It was obvious from the article that the author, A. Troyer—whom I had not heard of—was completely unaware of the great Gupta king Samudragupta, whose name he had deciphered in the inscription on the Allahabad Pillar. He was also confused over the identity of Chandragupta, another name that the inscription had revealed: whether it was Chandragupta Maurya or some other king. This in itself was a revelation for me—in an age when every school-child in the fifth class knows of Samudragupta,—the realization that there was a time when Samudragupta was not known at all!

Till this time I had not even seen the title of the book. Now I turned to the title page: it was the third volume of the *Journal of the Asiatic Society of Bengal*, published in 1834. I immediately requisitioned other volumes of the *Journal* and a few volumes of the *Asiatic Researches* which had preceded the *Journal*. I was also fortunate in laying my hands on the *Centenary Review* of the Society, published in 1885.

I still remember that afternoon. It seemed to me that I had launched upon a voyage of discovery. I wanted to devour as many articles as possible since at almost every turn I found a surprise. I discovered that even Asoka and Kanishka, not to mention their dynasties, were unknown names till the Society's work brought them to light. I was thrilled by the account of how Sir William Jones identified the Sandracottus of the Greek texts with Chandragupta Maurya, and

Prinsep deciphered the Asokan script. It was astonishing to see that many of the other dynasties—the Palas, the Senas, the Maukharies, the Valabhis and many others which constitute the core of ancient Indian history today—were unknown till, primarily through the exertions of the Society's members in the nineteenth century, these genealogies took coherent shape.

Then, as I read one article after another—another thought raced through my mind. Here I was faced by the significant contributions British Indologists had made to our history and culture; yet British historians were often made out to be biased and imperialist in their intentions. C. H. Philips' statement that 'Historians who have devoted themselves to the study of the peoples of the subcontinent have shown little awareness, and little tendency to evaluate the work of their predecessors so that the student seeks in vain for even a single published article in which the character of their work is examined', made me wonder if we had not convicted the British historian even before his case was ever brought before Clio. Such thoughts decided the topic of my research for me; and this study is the result.

As the reader will see, the present study works at two levels: one, the institutional, that is the development of the Asiatic Society of Bengal as an institution, and the other, the historiographical, that is, the progress of studies in Indian history and culture together with the factor of the motives of study. The spread of awareness of India's rich philosophical and historical heritage in the west is a third dimension which I have tried to touch upon, although this aspect requires a separate study by a scholar conversant with the major European languages. All these three dimensions could adequately be treated only within a chronological framework, which I have adopted for this study. If this work inspires separate studies on the historiography of different dynasties, ideas or institutions, my labour will be amply rewarded.

Acknowledgements

I consider myself fortunate in having received generous assistance from scholars and institutions in India and abroad in the course of collecting the material for this study. A fellowship from the Indian Council of Historical Research in New Delhi enabled me to free myself from my official duties and take up this study. The British Council made it possible for me to visit London and consult the records there and meet several scholars. I am grateful to Professor Kenneth Ballhatchet who went through parts of my manuscript and gave me valuable advice. Professor Peter Marshall, with his eye for detail, saved me from many pitfalls. My meetings with Professors Ballhatchet and Marshall, besides Sir Cyril H. Philips and Mr J. B. Harrison, were made possible by the late Dr B. N. Pandey whose loss I regard as one of the greatest tragedies in my academic career.

The person responsible for my acquaintance with Dr Pandey is Dr Amit Kumar Gupta, the one man to whom this work owes the most. Right from the time of deciding the subject to practically writing the last line, he has been generous with his time and extremely helpful with his suggestions. Dr B. N. Mukherjee, Carmichael Professor of Ancient History and Culture, Calcutta University, read through the manuscript and pointed out several useful references besides solving problems I had in consulting documents in the Asiatic Society. My guide for this work was Dr J. Kumar of the University of Bihar and presently Member of the Bihar Public Service Commission. He has helped me in this work as well as in administrative matters in the university. I am also grateful to Professors David Kopf, Paramatma Saran and Lallanji Gopal for their kind words of encouragement and advice. Let me add that the responsibility for the views expressed, analyses made and errors that may have crept in is entirely mine.

I am also grateful to the staff of the India Office Library, the British Museum and the Royal Asiatic Society in London and particularly to Mr Richard Pankhurst; the staff of the National Archives and the Nehru Museum in Delhi, and the Uttarpara Public Library in West

Bengal. Sri Sunil Chatterjee, Librarian of the Carey Library, and Dr S. Mukhopadhyaya, Principal of Serampore College, made it possible for me and my wife to stay in the College Hostel and consult the material in their very rich library. I owe a great deal to the staff of the National Library, Calcutta, and in particular to Mrs Kalyani Moitra and Mrs Meera Chatterjee for whom no words of gratitude can be enough.

Others who helped me in one way or another in taking up the project and completing it are Lotika Ratnam of All India Radio, Professors J. P. Singh, and J. B. Bhattacharya, Dr G. Sengupta of the North-Eastern Hill University, Dr Harbans Mukhia of Jawaharlal University; and Mr V. Patanjali.

I am grateful to Mr S. K. Dhawan, librarian in the Publications Division of the Government of India, for preparing the index.

I am deeply indebted to the late Professor A. L. Basham for writing his generous Foreword. He went, in meticulous fashion, through certain portions of the book, offering valuable advice and suggestions.

And finally for my wife, Debleena, all I can say is that this work would not have been possible had she not been constantly by my side and helped me in a thousand ways.

Sir William Jones

H. T. Colebrooke

H. H. Wilson

James Prinsep

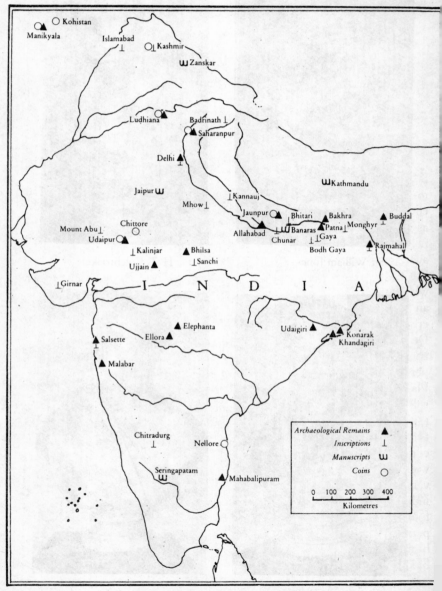

O Kohistan

Manikyala

Islamabad

O Kashmir

Zanskar

Ludhiana

Badrinath

O Saharanpur

Delhi

Kathmandu

Jaipur

Mhow

Kannauj

Jaunpur

Bhitari

Bakhra

Buddal

Mount Abu

Chittore

Allahabad

Banaras

Patna

Monghyr

Udaipur

Chunar

Bodh Gaya

Gaya

Rajmahall

Kalinjar

Bhilsa

Ujjain

Sanchi

Girnar

I   N   D   I   A

Elephanta

Ellora

Udaigiri

Konarak

Salsette

Khandagiri

Malabar

Chitradurg

Nellore

Seringapatam

Mahabalipuram

Archaeological Remains

Inscriptions

Manuscripts

Coins

0   100 200 300 400
Kilometres

Sites of important discoveries 1784–1838

1

The Background

I have travelled everywhere from Bengal to Delhi, but nowhere have I found anything from anyone except oppression of the poor and plundering of wayfarers. . . . The Indian nobles are a set of disorderly inconsistent blockheads who exist solely for ruining a world of people.[1]

Such were the reactions of the French adventurer, Jean Law, as he toured India in 1759. It was a troubled time in the history of the country: the death of Aurangzeb in March 1707 seemed to have acted as a signal for turbulent forces to surface in the shape of 'those nominal sovereigns, sunk in indolence and debauchery, who sauntered away life in secluded palaces, chewing *bhang*, fondling concubines and listening to buffoons.'[2] After Aurangzeb's death, his son Muazzam who ascended the throne as Bahadur Shah, gave a semblance of order and authority to the disintegrating empire, but even this facade crumbled after his death in 1712. His successors on the throne of Delhi were merely puppets in the hands of powerful and unscrupulous courtiers, and were either murdered or deposed. Thus, during the period of fifty years between the death of Aurangzeb and the battle of Plassey in 1757, there were as many as nine emperors, who on average ruled five and a half years each, in contrast to the average of about thirty-five years of each of the five great Mughal rulers. Of the nine, three were murdered and three deposed.[3] Muhammad Shah, who enjoyed the longest reign (1719–48) survived only because he never wielded any real power. Nicknamed the *Rangila* (the colourful), his very weaknesses — neglect of the administration and wanton self-indulgence — ironically helped him retain the throne while his nobles fought and conspired against each other for real power. About the period 1719–39, H. N. Sinha feels that no two decades of Indian history have recorded more intrigues, more crimes and more bloodshed.[4]

Such political instability naturally affected the law and order situation, which in turn affected trade and commerce. While the village economy, self-sustaining in nature, may have continued as before, the general economic situation was dismal. Speaking of the prevailing conditions, the contemporary historian Ghulam Hussain mourned:

> It was in such an enfeebled state of the Empire that there arose a new sort of men, who far from setting up patterns of piety and virtue . . . squandered away the lives and properties of the poor with so much barefacedness that other men, on beholding their conduct, became bolder and bolder and practised the worst and ugliest actions without fear or remorse. . . . From these sprung an infinity of evildoers who plague the Indian world and grind the face of the wretched inhabitants. It is in consequence of such wretched administration that every part of Hind has gone to ruin and . . . life itself is become distasteful to most.'

Recently, however, there has been some rethinking among historians on the character of eighteenth-century India as painted by contemporary historians like Ghulam Hussain, and historians like Jadunath Sarkar, K. K. Datta and Tara Chand who are generally described as 'traditional'. The new school points out that the assessment of earlier historians was based on events occurring in Delhi and that they had ignored developments in the provinces which asserted their independence from Mughal rule.⁶ Thus Murshid Quli Khan and Nawab Alivardi in Bengal, Nizam-ul-Mulk in Hyderabad and Saadat Khan in Awadh were able rulers who brought about political stability and looked to the well-being of the people. George Bearce, on the other hand, tried to assess the motives of historians who painted eighteenth-century India in such dark colours and arrived at the conclusion that they did so merely to serve their own ends.⁷ Other scholars studied the scientific and technological developments of the period and concluded that this was not really the 'dark age' as it had been generally portrayed.⁸

Hermann Goetz, one of the first scholars to challenge the older view agreed, however, that this was a period of 'political and economic decline', marked by 'unscrupulous struggle' for wealth and power.⁹ On the other hand, there have been periods when great art has co-existed with decadent society and unstable political combinations. In eighteenth-century India, provincial governors, having freed themselves from the Mughal yoke, appropriated the funds they ought to have passed on to the centre and spent them in luxuries and beautification of their provinces. This gave an impetus to architecture and new forms of dance and poetry.

The recent rethinking about the pre-British eighteenth century has, however, not been able to obscure the fact that in the field of intellectual creativity, this was a stagnant period. A review of the writings of the period in the major languages of the country would help in clarifying the point.[10]

Sanskrit had lost its vitality even before the advent of Islam. Destruction of the seats of learning and of monastic centres by Islamic conquerors had rendered it practically a dead language. There was a brief revival during the Vijayanagar empire (fifteenth–sixteenth centuries), but Sayanacharya's commentary on the Vedas seems to have been the last intellectual achievement in the language before the Europeans began to take an interest in Sanskrit studies. The seventeenth century witnessed minor works like the *Chitramimamsa* and the *Lakshanavali* of Appaya Dikshita, and the *Shiva Lilarnava* of his nephew Nilakanta Dikshita, but the eighteenth century seems to have contributed nothing of note to Sanskrit literature. Speaking of the state of Sanskrit studies in Bengal, one of the main centres of learning, the eminent Sanskritist Edward FitzEdward Hall remarked in 1868:

> There, notoriously, the *Vaidic* tradition was, for many centuries, virtually in abeyance. . . . Of this position we have satisfactory proof in the writings of Bengal *pundits*. How many among them have commented on the *Veda*, or expounded the *Mimamsa*? Until very recently, the learned of Bengal have long been satisfied, substantially, to do without the *Veda*.[11]

The golden age of Hindi literature had passed by in the sixteenth century, with Tulsidas, Surdas and Kabir. The Mughal court had produced poets like Rahim and Raskhan who were accomplished poets but this creative energy seems to have been drained by the eighteenth century. The one name that comes to mind is that of Bhusana (1613–1712) who eulogised the exploits of Sivaji, but even he can by no means be classed with the saint-poets mentioned earlier.

Urdu perhaps was an exception. The decline of Mughal glory seems to have inspired poets to compose exquisite elegies. Of these, Mirza Muhammad Rafi Sauda (1713–80) is considered the greatest. Besides him, there were Mir Muhammad Taqi Mir (1722–1810), Khwaja Mir Dard (1719–85), and the great folk-poet Wali Muhammad Nazeer (1740–1830). The age, however, belonged to the poets and there seems to be no work of philosophical or scientific depth.

In fact, it was not until the foundation of the Fort William College in 1800 that we find a revival of Urdu prose and subjects demanding serious study.

As with Hindi, Gujarati literature was past its most glorious period, the fifteenth and sixteenth centuries, the age of Narasi Mehta and Hemachandraraya. Although the eighteenth century saw poets like Jinaharsha, Sivanand and Pritamdas, the character of the age left its stamp on the development of the language, rendering it almost barren.

A similar fate overtook Marathi, whose greatest poet was Jnanadeva in the thirteenth century. Eknatha, Ramdas and, above all, Tukaram, wrote some of the most beautiful devotional songs in the language in the seventeenth century. Moropant (1729–94), the one great name in the eighteenth century, is, however not as outstanding.

In the south, turmoil and political instability followed the decline of the Vijayanagar empire, which had been a unifying factor in the region. Kannada literature had survived the fall of Vijayanagar with the patronage of Chikkadevaraja Odeyar (1672–1704), who was himself a writer; but its glorious days had passed with Sadakshardeva's *Rajasekharavilasa* (1657), 'one of the most highly esteemed poems in Kanarese'. With Haidar ascending the throne of Mysore, Kannada literature was in decline till the beginning of the nineteenth century.

An outstanding figure of Malayalam literature, Tuncat Ramanujan Ezhuthachan had produced some of his best compositions by the early eighteenth century. Author of a number of works on Indian mythology, he gave the language a new idiom which is still in use. With the exception of Kunjan Nambiyar, and some compositions for the local style of dance-drama, Kathakali, Malayalam had little of high creative order in the eighteenth century. It was only with European missionaries who compiled dictionaries that a new dimension was given to Malayali prose.

Nor were there signs of much activity in Tamil, except for the works of the Saiva mystic Thayumanavar. Most of Tamil literature consisted of the compositions of court poets who 'lisped the language of banality and futility'. As with Malayalam, it was the western missionaries who began a scientific study of the language by compiling lexicons, and putting out missionary literature in the local language, who helped to standardize the vernacular prose.

The period of the Vijayanagar empire, and especially the reign of Krishnadevaraya (1509–29), had marked the golden age of Telugu letters. After him, Telugu literature reached its nadir, 'the age of despair'. Some of the feudatory nobles were patrons of men of letters, but nothing was written which could equal the productions of the 'eight elephants' of the Vijayanagar court. The only exceptions were Tyagaraja of Tanjore whose musical compositions are still popular and some other compositions in the *Yakshagana* style.

The same tendencies were in evidence in eastern India. Oriya literature showed all the signs of barrenness except for the works of Upendra Bhanja (1670–1720), who set a new trend in lyrical poetry.

Assamese literature had been at its finest in the sixteenth and early seventeenth centuries when Sankar Deb and Madhab Deb gave a new idiom to the Krishna *bhakti* movement. The eighteenth century saw mostly mediocre works in prose eulogising the Ahom Kings.

Similarly with Bengali. Chandidas in the fifteenth century and Chaitanya in the sixteenth had greatly enriched the devotional literature in the language. But the eighteenth-century poets lacked freshness of outlook and doled out 'frivolous niceties on the lines of a vitiated classical taste'.[12] Even Bharatchandra Ray Gunakar, a prominent poet of the period, wrote much that was purely erotic. The only exception to this trend was Ramprasad Sen (c. 1718–60) whose devotional lyrics addressed to Kali are still popular.

To sum up, with the exception of Urdu, the court language, there was little creative vitality of a high order in the major languages of the country. The literature of the period was dominated by court chroniclers or poets who either indulged in eroticism to please the court or who wrote devotional poems in an effort to seek divine help to relieve the people of their misery. The age of intellectual effort seemed to have passed with the Vijayanagar empire. Had Dara Shukoh survived the war of succession, he would no doubt have inspired studies in the ancient Sanskrit texts, but after his execution (9 September 1659), India seemed to have lapsed into a shell of intellectual inactivity. The long and austere reign of Aurangzeb cast a cloud on different forms of creativity, and the country, instead of making progress in its already rich heritage of the arts and philosophy, gradually forgot them.

The situation was worse in the field of historical studies. It seems strange that only about two hundred years ago, even learned Indians were unaware of the existence or significance of such names as Chandragupta Maurya, Asoka, Samudragupta, Kanishka, Harsha and even Buddha—names which form the core of ancient Indian history. Thus we can say that in the eighteenth century, India had a past but it had no history. The past was preserved in the form of archaeological and architectural remains, inscriptions on buildings, stone and iron pillars, copper-plates, buried sites of ancient cities, and coins, but there was no work of history to highlight their importance. This lack of historical perspective made India apathetic to its historical remains. The question whether Indians possess a historical sense has been a question which has exercised historians, both western and Indian. Western scholars writing on the subject have given various explanations of this phenomenon. Lowes Dickinson feels that the geography and climate of India made the Indian psyche apathetic to history.[13] Teilhard de Chardin laid stress on the other-worldly outlook of Indians which made them indifferent to recording and preserving the events of this world and life, which were both in a sense unreal, the creation of *maya*.[14] Perhaps the clearest enunciation of this point of view came from Amaury de Riencourt in his *Soul of India*. According to him:

> Aryan India had no memory because she focussed her attention on eternity, not on time . . . To the Indian, the supreme spiritual reality was a transfiguration of *space* and not of time, of Nature and not of History. . . . since suffering is caused by man's obstinate craving for the unreal, history and suffering are synonymous; suffering can come to an end only when history does.[15]

He adds: 'What sense of history, of the significance of the flow of time can there be for people who use the same expression for yesterday and tomorrow (*kal*, in Hindi?)[16]

Indian historians on the other hand point out the several passages from the *Sastras* which lay stress on the material life and even cite Vatsyayana's *Kama Sutra* to highlight the importance Indians paid to the material aspect of human life. It is pointed out that *Itihasa*, the Sanskrit equivalent of history, was so exalted a science in ancient India as to be considered the fifth *Veda*, and Kautilya considered it mandatory for a good king to regularly listen to *Itihasa*. Dr P. V. Kane points out the recurrence of this word in different Sanskrit texts including the *Upanishads* and the *Brahmanas* to show the esteem in which this discipline was held in ancient India.[17] Other scholars have written about various compositions in ancient India which are close to historical writing and even mention the existence of certain officials under the regime of the Mauryas, the Guptas and kings of other dynasties whose job it was to maintain records of events during the reign of different kings.[18]

In spite of this, it has been generally admitted even by those who

have counteracted the dominant western view, that except for *Rajatarangini* of Kalhana, there is no Sanskrit text in history as we understand
the term today. Why this should be so is again a vital question and
scholars have attempted several explanations including the possibility
of wholesale destruction of ancient historical manuscripts. Discount-
ing this theory on the grounds that it was strange that agents of
destruction should have singled out this branch of literature for their
special favour, R. C. Majumdar sums up the entire question aptly
when he says:

> We have, therefore, to admit that the literary genius of India, so fertile and
> active in almost all conceivable branches of study, was not applied to
> chronicling the records of kings and the rise and fall of states and nations.
> It is difficult to give a rational explanation of this deficiency, but the fact
> admits of no doubt.[19]

There is also little doubt that in general Indians have shown little
evidence of awareness of the importance of historical remains and the
need to preserve and study them. Thus time and again we find the
early British Indologists speaking of the dilapidated condition of
ancient monuments and the difficulties in procuring old manuscripts.
Charles Wilkins noticed the Buddal pillar, which yielded information
about the Palas, when it had nearly been destroyed. Sir William Jones
could not obtain a Sanskrit text of the famous play *Sakuntala*, and in
Colebrooke's time, doubts were expressed about the very existence of
the Vedas. The *Rajatarangini*, the principal historical work extant in
Sanskrit, would have been irretrievably lost had not Wilson and later
Bühler salvaged the incomplete and mutilated texts; and Prinsep's
tenure in the Society was full of achievements in retrieving, restoring
and trying to preserve the ancient historical monuments of the country. Among these were the Sarnath remains and the Allahabad pillar
which yielded such significant information about Asoka and
Samudragupta — two of the greatest monarchs of India, and in fact, of
the world.

The greatest loss was in ancient coins. When discovered by the local
people, they were melted and turned into ornaments and amulets.
Who knows how many coins would have remained for the historian
had not Tod employed people to collect ancient coins, and scholars
like Swiney, Conolly, Burnes and others not taken an interest in
collecting and preserving them? Charles Masson, as we shall see,
amassed nearly thirty thousand coins from the plains of Beghram and

estimated that nearly fifteen million had been lost or destroyed.[20]

In fact, if we compare the ancient coins available today with the number which must have been minted over the centuries, there is little doubt that what we have is almost negligible. Along with the coins, what other valuable historical data must have been lost? When one reflects on this phenomenon, it seems a mere accident that the coins of Samudragupta, Kanishka and other kings came into the hands of the numismatist.

Similarly, valuable manuscripts were lost, inscriptions effaced, and dwellings or towns built over important historical sites. Marauders raided old structures like *stupas* for hidden treasures; and local *zamindars* pulled down ancient buildings merely to collect bricks for their new houses. The remains of Sarnath provide an example. The local Diwan, Jagat Singh, removed the bricks from the Dhamek *stupa* so that the entire structure, standing for centuries, seemed on the verge of collapse. The situation was most vividly described by Alexander Allanson in 1836:

Despoiled by bigots and through time grown gray,
By wretches pillaged for a bauble's worth.
Still do thine iron-bound walls resist decay.
By fame forgotten – in historic dearth.
Whence shall we seek for knowledge of thy rise?
No proud inscription on thy walls proclaim,
Not e'en tradition's lying tongue supplies,
Thy founder's object or thy builder's name.
All save thyself have long since decayed.
The one that ordered – millions that obeyed.[21]

Again, we learn, for example, from Colin Mackenzie's account that there was an impressive *stupa* at Amaravati, but it no longer exists.[22]

As for whatever appeared unusual, only fantastic stories were offered to explain their existence. The Asokan pillars, for example, were widely believed to be the *gada* (mace) of the *Mahabharata* hero, Bhimsen. In Bihar, where there were two mounds near an Asokan pillar, the local inhabitants had this story to relate about the place: once Bhimsen was carrying two hillocks suspended from either end of a tree trunk which he carried across his shoulder, walking with the pillar in his right hand as a means of support. At that place, the tree trunk suddenly gave way under the weight of the hills and Bhimsen left the hillocks as they were and planted his walking-stick there.

Again, the ruins of Mahabalipuram were said to be the remains of an ancient city built by the mythical King Bali, who having visited the Kingdom of Indra, vowed to build a city more beautiful. Indra, in a fit of jealousy and vengeance, demolished the entire city, hence the Mahabalipuram ruins. In such terms did Indians conceive of the past in the eighteenth century.

If the Indians were thus ignorant of their own history, the western world was more so, having been fed primarily on travellers' tales right from Grecian times. In spite of some scholarly works like those of Dio Chrysostom (first century A.D.) who for the first time showed an awareness of the *Ramayana*, Clement of Alexandria (A.D. 220), who is said to be the first writer to mention the Buddha, Hippolytus (A.D. 230) who showed a direct knowledge of the *Upanishads*, and later the realistic descriptions of Marco Polo, the west preferred to cling to the idea of the east as a land of wonders peopled by fantastic creatures. Perhaps nothing shows this better than a description of a book published in 1494, the sale of which almost five centuries later was mentioned in the journal, *Bengal Past and Present*. In its issue of 1930 (January–June), the Editor's note-book carried the following item:

Two sales of Indian interest took place in London during the month of December last. On December 17 a copy was sold at Sotheby's of Giuliano Dati's exceedingly rare pamphlet on India 'Il Secondo cantare Dell' India', which was printed in Rome in 1494. The woodcuts exhibit an extraordinary conception of the inhabitants and fauna of India: there are one-eyed, dogheaded, and headless men, pygmies, men and women with large feet used as parasol, a winged snake, a flying panther and other strange beasts, birds and insects.[23]

The year of this publication—1494—is significant. Work had begun by then on construction of the Portuguese fleet that was destined for India. The following year, King Manuel ascended the Portuguese throne, determined to gain for his country the laurels of finding the sea route to India. When in 1498 Vasco da Gama succeeded in setting foot on Indian soil, he changed the course of history in several ways. One of these was to lend a dimension of reality to the European accounts of India, so that they now changed from the region of the fabulous and the mysterious to that of reality; it was now a land peopled with real human beings.[24]

Writings on India after the discovery of the sea route can be divided into three broad categories: writings based on travel, trade and the exploits of European powers on Indian soil;[25] the accounts by the missionaries; and scholarly writings on India. Besides these, there are numerous references in the literature of the period, for example, in Shakespeare, Milton, and Spenser's writings but these were the result rather than the cause of European awareness of India.

The people who contributed to the first category of writings were the Portuguese, the Dutch, the French, the Danes and the English. Of these, the Portuguese texts outnumbered the others and in Portugal they enjoyed an even wider circulation than religious works.

The first Portuguese to write about India was Tomé Pires, whose *Suma Oriental*, although completed by 1515, was kept as a secret document and not published until 1944. In spite of this, the book was well known as an Italian version had been published in 1510. Pires gave a detailed account of the ports on the west coast of India and the economic situation of Gujarat and Bengal.

Duarte Barbosa's *Livro*, written around 1518, described in detail the political situation, social customs and religious rites of the Indian people.

A valuable source for reconstruction of the history of the early Portuguese in India is Gaspar Correa's four-volumed *Lendas da India*, which brought the story down to 1550. The most popular writer on India was, however, Fernao Lopes de Castanheda (1500-59). His *Historia da descobrimento e conguista da India pelos Porguguezes* (History of the Discovery and Conquest of India by the Portuguese), based on official reports, personal observation, and the testimony of participants in events, was instantly successful. In an age when translations were not common, Castanheda's *History* was translated into French (1553), Spanish (1554), Italian (1556), and English (1582).

Joao de Barros (*c*. 1496-1570) could not be as impartial as Castanheda probably because he was the official historiographer of Portugal, the first European state historiographer on India. Nevertheless, his *Decadas da Asia* in four volumes have earned him the title of the Portuguese Livy.

Barros was succeeded as state chronicler by Diogo do Couto, who had the additional distinction of founding the Archives in Goa (25 February 1595) to which he was nominated the first Keeper. This gave him access to original documents. As a result, his *Decadas da Asia* contains details of every skirmish, every semi-piratical cruise and every Council held in Goa, with the names of many of those involved personally in the events.[26]

Another Portuguese writer of note was Garcia da Orta (1535–1570), perhaps the most learned Portuguese to reside in India during the sixteenth century. His book entitled *Colloquios dos Simples e Drogas* (Conversations about Herbs and Drugs) contained far more than its title suggested. An acute observer, Garcia gave detailed information about the rulers and kingdoms of India 'which are relatively the most exact which are given to us by the Portuguese writers of the sixteenth century.'[27]

No account of Portuguese writers on India can be considered complete without mention of Luiz de Camöens (1542–80), scholar, chronicler, poet and soldier. His is a name which 'alone rescues Portuguese literature from insignificance'.[28] His poem *Os Luciadas* based on his adventures in India is 'the epic poem of the Portuguese fatherland, the autobiography of the poet and an encyclopaedia of all the knowledge of the period.'[29]

Other Portuguese writers of significance like Francisco de Andrade, Damiao de Goes, and the last of the Portuguese official historians, Bocarro, contributed valuable material on India before Portuguese influence waned in the early eighteenth century. In the writings of the Portuguese, we come across kings, kingdoms, customs and places which for the first time can be easily identified. India became a real world for Europe; and even started influencing European life. The change is aptly described by Conde de Flealho who, writing about Garcia da Orta's time, said:

> Thus [in Portugal] India invaded and absorbed the interest of the social life of the higher classes, as well as of the common people. . . . And in those forms of literature which give expression to the most intimate feelings of a people, the Indian touch is never wanting.[30]

Dutch writings on India were neither so prolific nor so scholarly. Philippus Baldaeus, a missionary, wrote on the economic and political conditions on the Coromandel coast and Gujarat, often giving a garbled version of treaties and other events.[31] A more objective account was François Valentyn's *Oud en Nieuw Oost-Indien* (1724–6) in which were reproduced certain contemporary documents of which there is no other record.

Other important Dutch works on India were Pieter van Dam's official history of the Dutch company (1701–3) written at the request of the Company's Directors, and Jan Huyghen vans Linschoten's

Itinerary (1595–6) based upon the author's observations in Goa and its environs.

Abbé Prévost's *Histoire Générale des Voyages* (1741–61), one of the earliest French works about the east, was a mere compilation, in abridged form, of earlier accounts. Abbé Guyon's *Histoire des Indes Orientales Anciennes et Modernes* (1744), on the other hand, was a history of early French activity in India, and the role of the French East India Company and Dupleix in French politics in India. Another account of the French East India Company, its constitution, laws and privileges, was Dufresne de Francheville's *Histoire de la Compagnie* (1746). A still more comprehensive work was the *Recueil ou Collection des Titres, Édits, Déclarations, Arrêts, Réglements et Autres Pièces Concernant la Companie des Indes Orientales de 1664 à 1750* (1751–6) by Dermis who was in charge of the Company's archives.

The most celebrated of these works was Abbé Raynal's, translated into English in 1776 by Justamond as *A Philosophical and Political History of the Settlements and Trade of the Europeans in the East and West Indies.* The interest of the work lies in Raynal's observation that the French should eschew a policy of aggression and appear as the protectors of Indians against English tyranny. In such a case, argues the author, 'the French considered as the deliverers of Indostan, would emerge from the state of humiliation into which their own misconduct had plunged them. They would become the idols of the Princes and peoples of Asia.'[32]

Danish activity in India was neither long-lasting nor very significant, hence there is not much Danish writing on India for this period. The earliest Danish writings on the east was a pamplet giving a brief account of Ove Gjedde's expedition to India in 1618; in 1622 Jón Ólaffson gave a vivid account of an expedition to Tranquebar. A significant Danish work was August Hennings' *Gegenwärtiger Zustand der Besitzungen der Europäer in Ostindien* (1784–6) in three volumes, inspired by the incorrect information about Danish trade given by Raynal in his *Philosophical and Political History.* Hennings pointed out that in spite of the plethora of writing on this part of the world, the actual historical material was scarce. 'We shall never get a real knowledge of this great and important part of the world, and we shall never be able to give a correct judgement of the prevailing conditions as long as our travel-book authors endeavour to capture everything at a single glance."[33]

The British, latecomers on the scene, were nevertheless more deeply involved in Indian affairs than their European rivals. The early history of the East India Company was admirably documented by Robert Orme in *A History of the Military Transactions of the British Nation in Indostan*, the first volume of which was published in 1763 and the second in 1778. Orme was the first official historian of the East India Company and so had access to the Company's records. Although Orme's *History* was perhaps the best written and certainly the best known, there were other accounts of the East India Company by contemporary writers. In 1779, for instance, was published *An Analysis of the Political History of India in which is considered the Present Situation in the East, and the connection of its several Powers with the Empire of Great Britain* by Richard Joseph Sullivan.[34] There must undoubtedly have been several such publications for the catalogue of Orme's books, as prepared by Charles Wilkins after their presentation to the East India Company, listed 'fifty-one volumes, containing one hundred and ninety tracts on the subject of India, and the Honourable Company's affairs, from about the year 1750 down to the year 1788.'[35]

Beside political analysts, there were English travellers like Edward Terry, Ralph Fitch, Sir Thomas Roe, Ovington, Henry Lord and Thomas Coryat, who gave to the English public accounts of the strange land and people they had seen. England also had two great collections of travellers' tales; the first of these was by Richard Eden who published in 1553 *A treatyse of the newe India*, and Richard Hakluyt who published the *Voyages* between 1598 and 1600. The two collectors had their predecessors in the Italian Giovanni Battista Ramusio who had compiled three volumes of *Delle Navigational et Viaggi* published between 1550–3; but with Hakluyt's third and final volume in 1600, he gave to the world the most complete compendium of travel literature of the time and, to the English nation, according to the historian Froude, its national epic.

Before closing this account it is important to mention Ludovico di Varthema, whose *Itinerary* was published in Italian in 1510 and who gave a detailed account of the country around Calicut and the Malabar Coast. The travels of Bernier and Tavernier are too well known to need detailed mention.

Although the literature on travel, trade and contemporary politics was vast, no serious attempt was made by these writers to study or understand India's past or her culture. The official historiographers or those who wrote on European activities in the east confined themselves to European politics as played out on Indian soil. If they mentioned aspects of Indian life or society, it was only because of their strangeness. Similarly, travellers in India noted down everything curious that met their eye and passed it on to a gullible west, which used this data either to project Europe's superiority, or to criticise European institutions by setting it against the idyllic east. These opposing views were based on the author's personal philosophy and beliefs. Thus, though we can fairly well reconstruct the history of India in the fifteenth, sixteenth and seventeenth centuries by studying these writings, they reveal little as to India's philosophy, ancient history, or religion.

These aspects were studied more attentively by the missionaries.

Missionary literature on India can be divided into two categories: the first consisted of letters from Jesuit missionaries to Rome, recording the progress of missionary activity in India. More important for us is the second, the work of missionaries who, while staying in India, made a serious study of the philosophy, religion and culture of the people.

The first translation from a Sanskrit work into a European language was made by the Dutch missionary, Abraham Roger. In his *De Open – Deure tot het Verborgen Heydendom (The Open Door to Hidden Heathendom)*, published at Leiden in 1651, Roger incorporated some two hundred stanzas of the Sanskrit poet Bhartrihari, translated with the help of a Brahman.[16] Although Roger made some observations on the ancient Brahmanical literature, it is evident that he himself did not know Sanskrit or any other Indian language.

The first European to show acquaintance with an Indian language was Father Thomas Stevens, who was also the first Englishman to come to India. Father Stevens arrived in Goa in 1579 and stayed there for some thirty years. With the publication of his grammar of Konkani in Portuguese, Father Stevens became the first European to publish the grammar of an Indian language in a European tongue.

The first European to master the Sanskrit language was the Jesuit Roberto di Nobilii (1577–1658). He personifies all the virtues as well as all the faults of the early scholar-missionaries. So thorough was Nobilii's knowledge of Sanskrit that it is said he could pass himself off as a Brahman and was in fact known to his colleagues as the 'Brahman Jesuit'. He, however, put his formidable scholarship to serve the task of conversion and 'scrupled at nothing to accomplish his end.' The author of the article 'India and Comparative Philology' in the *Calcutta Review* of 1857 regrets that 'learning so great, and zeal so inextinguishable as his, should not have been used at least more honestly'.[17]

De Nobilii also wrote some treatises in the vernacular and Sanskrit, none of which survive. He is better known as the author of *L'Ezour Vedam*, a clever forgery of the Vedas in which he extolled the virtues of Christianity, and which deceived Voltaire into considering it a genuine Sanskrit text.

The missionaries realized that their most potent weapon for conversion lay in their mastery of the local languages. Some time after 1607, Père Vico even applied to Rome for the adoption of Sanskrit as the liturgical language of the Church in India.[18]

Whatever the motive, to acquire proficiency in a foreign tongue requires methodical and dedicated study. This spirit of dedication can be seen in the work of the German Jesuit, Father Heinrich Roth, who like de Nobilii, became so proficient in Sanskrit as to dispute with the Brahmans with ease. Roth was the first European to write a Sanskrit grammar, which however was never published. He died at Agra as the head of the Jesuit College in 1668. Similarly, the Sanskrit grammar prepared by another German Jesuit, Johannes Ernst Hanxleden (who stayed in India from 1699 to 1730), was not published either, but both grammars were used in manuscript form by the Carmelite missionary, Father Paulinus, for his two Sanskrit grammars published in Rome in 1790 and 1804.[19]

According to Winternitz, Father Paulinus was the most important of the missionaries who revealed the early treasures of Indian literature. Born in 1748 in south Austria, Paulinus came to India in 1774 after studying oriental languages. After a fourteen-year stay in India, he carried back to Europe 'a more accurate and perfect knowledge of Sanskrit, and the dialects of the south of India, than any European.'

Among the numerous works he published after his return to Rome was the Latin version of the famous Sanskrit dictionary of Amarasingha[40], and the two Sanskrit grammars. By the time of his death in 1806 he had drawn the attention of the west to Sanskrit and the vernaculars of India, and become a European celebrity.

The most comprehensive review of Indian literature before the foundation of the Asiatic Society of Bengal was provided by the

French Jesuit, Jean-François Pons, in a survey sent to a brother missionary, Père du Halde, in 1740. Père Pons, who must have had some knowledge of Sanskrit, called his letter to Père Halde 'an essay on certain aspects of Indian literature'. The essay divided the entire range of Sanskrit literature into ten sections and dealt with Sanskrit grammar, the dictionaries, treatises on versification and poetry, history, the Vedas, mathematics and philosophy. He regarded Sanskrit grammar as one of the most beautiful sciences that ever existed and was the first European to speak of the six schools of Indian philosophy. Père Pons was also the first European to gather from the Brahmans the fact that, though there was no historical literature in Sanskrit, there were 'several books which were called *natak* and which contained much ancient historical matter without any admixture of fables': a line of enquiry which was later pursued by Sir William Jones and led to the discovery and subsequent translation into English of Kalidasa's *Sakuntala*.

By the mid-eighteenth century, so rich had the Roman archives become in material on India, and so significant was the missionaries' contribution in Indian studies that Cardinal Wiseman remarked with some justification that it was in Rome that the languages and literature of the Hindus were first systematically studied in Europe.[41]

Jesuit scholarship on India has generally been criticised for its motivation — the desire to use it for preaching and conversion. And indeed we often find them ridiculing local customs and religions. Thus the Jesuit missionary Teixeira writing from Goa in 1558: 'Sometimes we spend our time making fun of their gods, of their eating and drinking habits, and of the errors in their religion, so that they will grow less fond of them.'[42] Yet it cannot be denied that there were missionaries like Père Pons, Father Paulinus and Father Stevens, who devoted a lifetime to serious study, and at times their frank admission of the superiority of the Indian languages and literatures suggests that their interest in these pursuits was eventually scholarly.

Besides these missionaries, there were other scholars who pursued Indian studies from a non-utilitarian standpoint. The first of these was the Italian, Fillippo Sasseti (1540–88) who, had he not died so young, would have through his contributions stood a fair rival to many of the illustrious members of the Asiatic Society. Sasseti belonged to a family which in the fifteenth century managed the far-flung enterprises of the Medicis. Fillippo had little taste for business affairs and was a prominent member of the learned Societies of Florence. Later, however, he was compelled to take to business, which brought him to India as factor for the Rovellasca interests. Even before coming to India Fillippo had read widely about Asia and digested the publications of Ramusio, Barros, Orta and Maffei. Once in India, he picked up acquaintance with a Brahman pundit and started learning Sanskrit. During the six years he spent in India (1583–8), Fillippo despatched thirty five letters to Florence containing his observations on Indian affairs. One of these letters, dated 27 January 1585, addressed to Pier Vettori, classified fifty-three elements of the Sanskrit alphabet based upon tongue and mouth movements, pointing out the similarity between Sanskrit and the classical European languages: an observation which made him a forerunner of Sir William Jones on the subject.

It is apparent that the early European missionaries and scholars, with few exceptions, were primarily interested in the religions and languages of India. The people who first spoke of India as having possessed scientific knowledge in ancient times were the French: in fact, the history of early French orientalism is also the history of the re-discovery of ancient Indian astronomy in the modern period. The first information about Indian astronomy, however, reached Europe not from India but from Siam. In 1687 Louis XIV sent M. de la Loubère on an embassy to Siam from where he brought back portions of a manuscript containing rules for computing the places of the sun and the moon. The manuscript was submitted to the celebrated astronomer of his time, Cassini, whom Louis had brought from Italy to be in charge of the Paris observatory. In his memoir published in 1691 Cassini showed how advanced the science of astronomy had been in ancient India. Eight years later, in 1769 Le Gentil came to Pondicherry to observe the transit of Venus and here, with the help of pundits, he acquired and gave to Europe a full account of the principal elements and methods of computation employed in Indian astronomy. Le Gentil's work in turn inspired Jean Sylvain Bailly (1736–93), who tried to reconcile the data of Indian astronomy with the results of the most advanced knowledge of his day and argued that eastern astronomy had been the source of Greek science. Bailly's work at once attracted the attention of other European astronomers and even Laplace remarked on the accuracy of Indian astronomy. Another French astronomer, Joseph de Lisle (1688–1768), procured two treatises on astronomy from India, one being the *Panchanga Siromani*, sent to him in 1750 by Père Patouillet, and the other obtained from Père Xavier du Champs[41] who sent it from Pondicherry to Père Gaubil in China, who in turn sent it to de Lisle in 1760.[43] Soon the English picked up the trail and produced two great scholars of Indian astronomy, John Playfair and Samuel Davis, both of whom will figure in Chapter 2.

Another great French Orientalist was Pierre Sonnerat who, as a student of natural history, was sent by Louis XVI to India on a scholarly tour. Sonnerat's account of his travels, *Voyages aux Indes Orientales et à la Chine* (1774-81), contained an account of the languages, arts, sciences, religion, natural history, and geography of India. The book was published in German at Zurich in 1783, the time when English interest in scholarship on India had begun to grow.[44]

The first Englishman to have pursued Indian studies from a non-religious, non-political standpoint was John Marshall, a servant of the East India Company, employed in the factory of Kasimbazar in Murshidabad district. Not much is known of him, but some time between 1668 and 1677 Marshall did an English translation of *Serebaugabut Pooran* (*Bhagavata Purana*) which was sent to England and deposited in the British Museum.

The labours of Marshall were, however, not followed up since the factors and merchants of the Company 'found a more agreeable occupation in measuring ellas of cloth than in scanning the measures of oriental poetry.' A whole century passed before Indian studies were taken up by the English. The pioneer in this phase was John Zephaniah Holwell (1711-98) better known as the spokesman of the 'black hole' tragedy. Holwell seems to have had scholarly interests, and the new country with its strange peoples and a stranger culture fascinated him. The result was the book with the lengthy title, *Interesting Historical Events, relative to the Provinces of Bengal and the Empire of Indostan. . . As also the Mythology and Cosmogony, Fasts and Festivals of the Gentoos, followers of the Shastah, and a Dissertation on the Metempsychosis, commonly, though erroneously, called the Pythagorean doctrine.* In 1786 was published another book: *Dissertation on the Origin, Nature and Pursuits of Intelligent Beings and on Divine Providence, Religion and Religious Worship.*

Holwell's major contribution to the European view of India lay in two areas: he established the great antiquity of the Indian people and their literature, and secondly he stressed the application of standards other than European to the study of India and its culture. He emphasized that Indian claims to antiquity could not be dismissed lightly, no matter how irreconcilable they might be with the Christian view of world history. He insisted that 'from the premises already established, this conclusion at least may fairly be deduced, that the world does not now contain annals of more indisputable antiquity than those delivered down by the ancient Brahmins.'

Holwell also thought that a different or a new orientation was required when dealing with Indian studies. In his Preliminary Discourse to the *Religious Tenets of the Gentoos* he said:

> Having studiously perused all that has been written of the empire of Indostan, both as to its ancient as well as more modern state; as also the various accounts transmitted to us, by authors in almost all ages . . . I venture to pronounce them all very defective, fallacious and unsatisfactory to an inquisitive searcher after truth; and only tending to convey a very imperfect and injurious resemblance of a people, who from the earliest times have been an ornament to the creation if so much can with propriety be said of any known people upon earth.[45]

Holwell also warned against the dangers of superficial studies of the alien culture:

> A mere description of the exterior manners and religion of a people, will no more give us a true idea of them than a geographical description of a country can convey a just conception of their laws and government. The traveller must sink deeper in his researches . . . His telling us such and such a people, in the East or West Indies, worship this stork, or that stone, or monstrous idol; only serves to reduce in our esteem our fellow creatures to the most abject and despicable point of light. Whereas, was he skilled in the language of the people he describes, sufficiently to trace the etymology of their words and phrases, and capable of diving into the mysteries of their theology; he would probably be able to evince to us, that such seemingly preposterous worship, had the most sublime rational source and foundation.[46]

This is a perfect expression of the thinking among Englishmen in India in the latter half of the eighteenth century which led to the foundation of the Asiatic Society.

Similar sentiments were expressed by Alexander Dow (1735–79), another prominent Englishman to take up Indian studies before the establishment of the Asiatic Society. Dow was primarily a Persian scholar whose *History of Hindostan*, published in three volumes between 1768 and 1782, remained a 'standard work on Muslim India and guided or influenced the researches of his successors' for about sixty years before it was discredited by John Briggs' *History of the Rise of the Mohammedan Power in India*, published in 1829.[47] Dow was also knowledgeable about the Hindu religion and customs as he kept the company of learned Brahmans, and was one of the earliest writers in modern times to mention the Vedas. Like Holwell, Dow tried to provide a corrective to earlier impressions of India and stressed a new orientation to the study of India and its culture. In his *History* he spoke of the difficulties in pursuing Indian studies:

> Excuses . . . may be formed for our ignorance concerning the learning, religion and philosophy of the *Brahmins*. Literary inquiries are by no means a capital object to many of our adventurers in Asia. The few who have a turn for researches of that kind, are discouraged by the very great difficulty in acquiring that language, in which the learning of the Hindus is contained; or by that impenetrable veil of mystery with which the Brahmins industriously cover their religious tenets and philosophy.[48]

About the time the last volume of Dow's *History* was published (1782), a definite change came about in the intellectual climate of Bengal, the prime factor in the change being the personality of Warren Hastings. The first important project which Hastings encouraged and patronized was *A Code of Gentoo Laws* by Nathaniel Halhed. A more academic work of Halhed's was the *Grammar of the Bengal Language* (1778) which made him the first grammarian of Bengali.

Warren Hastings and Nathaniel Halhed are commonly depicted as having designs on strengthening the British hold on India through study of the laws and languages of the natives. *A Code of Gentoo Laws* and to a lesser extent *A Grammar of the Bengal Language* are cited as proofs of the assertion. What is less known, however, is that Halhed, besides being the author of the *Code* and the *Grammar*, translated several ancient Sanskrit texts like the *Bhagavat Purana, Shivapurana, Brahmavaivarta Purana* and even the *Mahabharata* into English. These were done independently of state patronage and were works of pure scholarship.

Another great scholar and orientalist to benefit from Hastings' policy of promoting Indian studies was Francis Gladwin (one of the founder-members of the Asiatic Society), who in 1775 compiled an *English-Persian Vocabulary*. In a letter to the Council of Fort William written in 1775 Gladwin expressed his doubts about the public utility of his work, adding that he had done the work in his leisure hours taking great pains and incurring great expense, and had no objection to printing it provided he did not sustain any loss by its publication. Hastings, however, saw to it that Gladwin was given liberal assistance and his *Vocabulary* was published in 1780 at Malda.

The publication of Gladwin's *Vocabulary* was preceded by his translation of *The Ayin Akbary, or the Institutes of the Emperor Akbar*, published in 1777. Gladwin's attention was drawn to this work, as he tells us in the Preface, 'by the high encomiums which are bestowed upon it by the learned Mr. Jones in his Persian Grammar.' Another work on Indian history to appear in pre-Asiatic Society days was *The Civil and Military Institutes of Timour* (1780), published jointly by William Davy, who was Warren Hastings' Persian Secretary, and Joseph White, Laudian Professor of Arabic at the University of Oxford.

The most prominent member of this early group of orientalists was Charles Wilkins (1750–1836), another founder-member of the Asiatic Society. Wilkins made his mark as a Sanskritist in 1785 with the publication of the English translation of the *Bhagavad-Gita*. His friend Nathaniel Halhed had inspired him to learn Sanskrit but in the days preceding the formation of the Society, Wilkins' main distinction was as a printer of Halhed's *Grammar* for which he acted as 'metallurgist, engraver, founder, and printer', and so he became India's Caxton.

With Charles Wilkins we reach an important stage in the development of western awareness of India. From a series of travellers' tales, and attempts to decry Indian customs and manners, a stage was reached when the west began not only to make efforts to understand, but value India and her culture. In the first stage, scholarship was of little consequence; the emphasis was on the exotic, the mysterious, the fantastic. In the second, although there was no lack of scholarship, it was scholarship with a purpose, and vested interest. But now the western scholar approached India with the desire to learn.

As William Jones observed, to form a correct idea of the religion and the literature of the Hindus it was necessary to forget 'all that has been written on the subject, by ancients or moderns, before the publication of the Gita'.[49]

Although in the Preface to his translation of the *Gita* Wilkins spoke of Hastings' encouragement to the Company's servants 'to render themselves more capable of performing their duty . . . by the study of the languages, [with] the laws and customs of the natives', he was the first non-missionary European to master Sanskrit, a true scholar whose work inspired Sir William Jones, the greatest orientalist of the age.

If the British intelligentsia was ready by this time to study alien cultures, conditions in India were also favourable for such pursuits. It is difficult to agree with Shafaat Ahmad Khan that 'there were no signs in the eighteenth century of that vigorous revival of her energy which has found perfect expression in her wonderful regeneration in modern times.'⁵⁰ The signs were in fact obvious and they were personified in Warren Hastings.

Though the Battle of Plassey in 1757 had provided the English with a foothold on Indian soil they could neither consolidate nor stabilize their administration till Warren Hastings returned to Bengal in 1772. Clive had been content to reap the rich fruits of trade and plunder; it was Warren Hastings who, by ending the 'dual government', laid the foundations of British administration in India. It was during Hastings' time that Englishmen from being 'alien freebooters longing to return home shouldering their bag of riches', changed gradually into administrators responsible for the well-being of the people. A little-known poem published in London in 1773 entitled *The Nabob*, which consists of a dialogue between the poet and his friend, illustrates this point. The 'friend' in the poem is the typical English adventurer of the 'Clive generation' who tells the poet:

> Concerns it you who plunders in the East,
> In blood a tyrant, and in lust a beast?
> When ills are distant, are they then your own?
> Saw'st thou their tears, or heard'st the oppressed groan?
> What others feel, if we must feel it too;
> If for distress, we give the tribute due,
> Not *Heraclitus* could with tears supply
> The constant spring of sorrow's flowing eyes;

To this the Author replies in anger and disgust:

> I hate this apathy; — This *stoic* plan
> Seems sullen pride; as man, I feel for man,
> My country's honour has received a blot,
> A mark of odium ne'er to be forgot:
> A larger country still I boast; embrace
> With a warm heart all Adam's wretched race.⁵¹

Hastings was not merely the product of this consciousness but also a factor who inspired other Englishmen in India. He undoubtedly had British interests at heart but at the same time he 'loved the people of India, and respected them to a degree no other British ruler has ever equalled.'[52] His sincerity in this matter is evident from his Evidence before the House of Commons in which he declared:

> Great pains have been taken to inculcate into the public mind the opinion that the native Indians are in the state of complete moral turpitude, and live in the constant and unrestrained commission of every vice and crime that can disgrace human nature. I affirm by the oath that I have taken, that this description of them is untrue and wholly unfounded.[53]

Further, Hastings saw neither the need nor the desirability of importing English laws and customs and burdening the Indian people with them. He specially enjoined that 'in all suits regarding inheritance, marriage, caste and other religious usages and institutions, the laws of the *Koran* with respect to Mahomedans and those of the *shaster* with respect to *Gentoos* shall be invariably adhered to; on all such occasions the *Moulvies* or *Brahmins* shall respectively attend to expound the law, and they shall sign the report and assist in passing the decree.'[54]

Warren Hastings' encouraging Nathaniel Halhed to compile *A Code of Gentoo Laws* (1776) was merely an extension of this policy. When he found that the *moulvies* and pundits sitting in court took advantage of their exclusive knowledge and sometimes misled the English judge for monetary considerations, he realized the need for English judges to know the laws of the land at first hand.

Hastings' decision to get the Indian laws studied and ancient texts compiled and translated has unfortunately led later historians to conclude that his 'encouragement of Oriental Studies had a practical side',[55] and that 'in British India, Warren Hastings was encouraging the study of Sanskrit for purely utilitarian reasons.'[56] These historians overlook the fact that Hastings, though Governor-General of India, had not only to please the Court of Directors thousands of miles away but also their nominees, the members of the Supreme Council, which had a fair share of Hastings' enemies. The Court of Directors consisted of businessmen whose only interest lay in making their profits swell. Hastings realised this weakness only too well. Thus while recommending the publication of Wilkins' translation of the *Bhagavad-Gita* by the Court of Directors, he wrote to Nathaniel Smith, the Chairman of the East India Company, in 1784:

> Every accumulation of knowledge and especially such as is obtained by
> social communication with people over whom we exercise a dominion
> founded on the right of conquest, is useful to the state: . . . it attracts and
> conciliates distant affections; it lessens the weight of the chain by which the
> natives are held in subjection; and it imprints on the hearts of our own
> countrymen the sense and obligation of benevolence.[57]

A more eloquent testimony of Hastings' practical side — the
awareness of the pragmatic value of promoting oriental studies —
might be difficult to find: on the other hand this letter also testifies to
his love of such studies for their own sake. He thus described the
translation of the *Bhagavad-Gita* as 'the gain of humanity', and added
that the ancient writings of India would 'survive when the British
dominion in India shall have long ceased to exist, and when the
sources which it once yielded of wealth and power are lost to
remembrance.'

Hastings' letter to Nathaniel Smith thus demonstrates both aspects
of his personality: on the one hand, as a shrewd and down-to-earth
administrator and empire-builder; and on the other, as the product of
a liberal education which taught that the study of literature should be
pursued for its own sake and that it diffused generosity of sentiment.[58]

Hastings' approach to oriental studies is indicated by his quoting
the *Gita* in letters to his wife (written certainly, one would hope, in a
more sincere vein than those to the Court of Directors), discussing the
Indian classics with Halhed, and in the midst of troubles on the
political front, learning both Persian and the common dialects of
Bengal.

While Hastings represented the new approach to colonialism,
contemporary scholars who took up Indian studies were products of
the age of enlightenment in Europe and especially in England.

This new climate of opinion was symbolized by the establishment of
the Royal Society in 1660. In 1666 Louis XIV hesitatingly extended
royal patronage to the French Academie Royale des Services, some of
whose members were out of sympathy with the King. It was, however,
in the eighteenth century that the scientific spirit reached its peak.
Learned societies were founded in Berlin (1701), Uppsala (1710), St
Petersberg (1724), and Copenhagen (1743). In 1739 Linnaeus and five

other Swedish scholars formed the Collegium Curiosum; in 1741 this was incorporated as the Kongliga Svenska Vetenskaps-academien, which later became the Swedish Royal Academy. In France provincial academies sprang up in Orléans, Bordeaux, Toulouse, Auxerre, Metz, Besançon, Dijon, Lyons, Caen, Rouen, Montauban, Angers, Nancy and Aix-en-Provence.[59]

Learned bodies, societies and academies naturally gave rise to learned journals. There were said to be seventy-three periodicals in Paris alone led by the *Mercure de France* and the *Journal des Savants*. Germany contributed *Briefe die neueste Literatur betreffend* which had Lessing and Mendelssohn among its regular contributors. The Italian journal *Giornale dei Letterati* carried articles on science, literature, and art, while *Caffè* was a journal of opinion like *The Specatator*. In Sweden, Olof von Dalin made *Svenska Argus* a messenger of the Enlightenment. So strong was the wave of scientific quest that between 1701 and 1762 even the Jesuits published the erudite and liberal *Mémoires pour servir à l'histoire des sciences et des beaux-arts*, better known as *Journal de Trévoux* from their publishing house at Trévoux near Lyons.[60]

In spite of the plethora of scientific societies and journals throughout Europe, we have to look to England for pioneering the scientific movement. With the foundation of the Royal Society and journals like *The Grub Street Journal (1730–37)*, and *The Gentleman's Magazine* (1731), the English were well placed for starting the Asiatic Society and a journal like *Asiatic Researches* in a remote land, with a width of perspective which perhaps none of the other Societies achieved.[61]

This intellectual effervescence showed itself also in the change in historical thought in this century.

Historical thought in the Middle Ages in Europe was largely influenced by Christian theology, and St Augustine's *City of God* dominated historical thinking to the end of the seventeenth century. This Christian view of history was reinforced further with the publication, in 1681, of *Discours sur l'histoire universelle* by Bishop Bossuet, tutor to the French Dauphin. This work stressed two points: that the writing of history was still to be treated theologically, and that now the historian adopted a broader outlook, thinking not only in terms of Europe or his own country, but in terms of universal history. However, Bossuet's history was 'universal' only in name, since it dealt only with four or five non-European peoples who were essential to the history of Christianity. In fact, it was not even history but a sermon in which the biblical text was supplanted by historical subject-matter carefully edited and prepared in the interest of the Church.

The Christian stronghold in historical thinking was first attacked by Bayle in his *Dictionnaire Historique et critique* published in 1697. This was not essentially a work of history; what Bayle had done was to apply the Cartesian method to the study of history and show that the Bible and Biblical tradition, believed to be the only two sources of history, were not empirically trustworthy. This was a revolution in historical thought. As Machiavelli had freed politics, and Galileo physics, so did Bayle free history from the shackles of theology. And this he achieved by demanding that reason refuse to accept a historical 'fact' until it had first been examined.[62]

From this it was but one step to Voltaire, who attacked the theological aspect of history but laid stress on its universal aspect. History, he emphasized, should not be conceived in terms of one religion, one State or one people but in terms of all humanity. Thus in his *Essay on the Manners and Mind of Nations*, Voltaire spoke of the people not only of Europe, but of Japan, Peru, China, and India.

The appearance of the *Essay* prompted philosophers and historians to take into account the empires and cultures of the Islamic lands, India, South-East Asia, and America. The co-existence of several peoples was recognized and in the writing of history, these took precedence over the history of universal empires leading towards the ultimate triumph of Christianity.

In spite of the outward looking view of the European intelligentsia, there was one limitation in their writings, pointed out perhaps for the first time by Carl Becker. It was that even while writing about alien peoples and civilizations, their point of view remained European. It was Europe and Christianity that weighed on their minds even as they wrote about the newly-discovered lands, peoples and cultures.

For example, Raynal's popular *Philosophical and Political History of the Indies* seemed to transport the intellectual of Europe through unknown lands but its main purpose was to demonstrate the admirable native customs of these foreign peoples and the corruption and the misery imposed by their Christian conquerors which 'a philosopher should note and deplore.'[63] In 1739 the Marquis d'Argens published the *Lettres Chinoises* where, through letters written by an imaginary Chinese, he criticized European manners and institutions. Similarly in 1757 Horace Walpole amused his English readers with *Letters from Xo Ho, a Chinese Philosopher*. Montesquieu roamed mentally over the whole world, including India, but only to provide illustrations for his *Esprit des lois;* even Voltaire looked to China and India only to demonstrate the debasement of Europe and Christianity. The eighteenth-century philosophers and historians were thus certainly aware of different lands and continents but for them Europe remained the centre of the earth. Let us see what happens as late as 1784. Johann Gottfried Herder publishes the first part of his *Ideen zur Philosophie der Geschichte der Menschheit* (Ideas for a Philosophy of the History of Mankind) in which he urges the necessity of understanding the cultures of various races of mankind in their concrete historical reality.' Herder himself puts it thus:

> In early life when the fountains of knowledge lay before me in all their morning splendour, the thought often occurred to me whether, as everything else in the world had its philosophy and regulative principles, that which so much concerns us, the history of mankind as a great and entire aggregate, had not also its philosophy and scientific laws.[64]

Yet ultimately we find that in spite of the broadening of vision, and the breakthrough in historical and political thought, Herder's major preoccupation remains the same as Voltaire's and earlier thinkers, i.e. Europe and Christianity.[65]

1784 is undoubtedly, an important year in historical thought because of the publication of Herder's *Ideas*: it is, however, far more significant for an event which, unfortunately, has not received the attention of historiographers and exponents of historical thought. This was the establishment of the Asiatic Society in Calcutta by Sir William Jones. One has only to read the opening lines of Jones's inaugural address to the Society to realize that his vision gave real content to what other historians and philosophers had merely talked about.

Referring to his journey to India on his appointment as a judge in Bengal, Jones said:

> When I was at sea last August, I found one evening, on inspecting the observations of the day, that India lay before us, and Persia on the left, whilst a breeze from Arabia blew nearly on our stern . . .
> It gave me inexpressible pleasure to find myself in the midst of so noble an amphitheatre, almost encircled by the vast regions of Asia, which has ever been esteemed the nurse of sciences, the inventoress of delightful and useful arts, the scene of glorious actions, fertile in the productions of human genius, abounding in natural wonders, and infinitely diversified in the forms of religion and government, in the laws, manners, customs, and

languages, as well as in the feature and complections of men. I could not help remarking how important and extensive a field was yet unexplored, and how many solid advantages unimproved.[66]

This is a remarkable statement from someone yet unaware of the history, philosophy and arts of India and who began his study of Sanskrit only three years later. Jones seemed however to have divined that the centre of the history of mankind lay in the east and he was the first scholar to have looked at the east without a western bias. He realized that the history of mankind could not be written without knowing the east. It was for this reason that he laid greater emphasis on knowing the east itself and not looking to it for material to explain or criticise the west and the western man. Whereas others wrote either to amuse or provide a better understanding of the west, Jones was the first to use his vast scholarship and knowledge of the classical languages to understand the east better. His subsequent discourses on the theory of the common origin of the five principal Asiatic nations (India, Arabia, Tartary, Persia, and China), were proof enough that the history of mankind could be written only after the history of the east was properly known. Sir William Jones thus may be called the Copernicus of history,[67] and with him begins the history of the Asiatic Society, and our present study.

2
The Founder's Decade, 1784–1794

1783. After a period of uncertainty lasting four years, Sir William Jones boarded the frigate *Crocodile* on his way to India as a puisne judge in the Supreme Court at Calcutta. The voyage took five months. One day during the voyage, Jones brooded on the areas of study he would like to explore during his stay in India, and noted down sixteen items in a list which read as follows:[1]

1. The laws of the Hindus and Mahomedans.
2. The history of the ancient world.
3. Proofs and illustrations of Scripture.
4. Traditions concerning the deluge, etc.
5. Modern politics and geography of Hindustan.
6. Best mode of governing Bengal.
7. Arithmetic and geometry and mixed sciences of Asiatics.
8. Medicine, chemistry, surgery, and anatomy of the Indians.
9. Natural products of India.
10. Poetry, rhetoric and morality of Asia.
11. Music of the eastern nations.
12. The She-king or 300 Chinese odes.
13. The best accounts of Tibet and Kashmir.
14. Trade, manufactures, agriculture and commerce of India.
15. Mughal administration.
16. Maharatta constitution.

No ordinary mortal would even think of achieving all this in a single lifetime.

William Jones was born in London on 28 September 1746. His father, after whom he was named, was a well-known mathematician whose friends included Samuel Johnson, Sir Isaac Newton, and Lord Parker, the President of the Royal Society. Jones's father died when his son was three years old, leaving him to the care of his mother, who proved to be an ideal teacher. She aroused in the young William boundless curiosity by always advising him, in answer to his questions, 'Read and you will know.'

Largely because of such encouragement, Jones was quoting from Shakespeare at the age of four. In spite of an accident at about this time which permanently damaged his right eye, so that he was even advised by the doctor to give up school, Jones earned the epithet 'Great scholar' from his schoolmates at Harrow. His school teacher admitted that Jones knew more Greek than himself, and Dr Thackeray, his headmaster, expressed the view that even if Jones were left naked and friendless on the Salisbury plains, he would still find the road to riches and fame. At twelve, Jones knew Shakespeare's *Tempest* by heart and by twenty, was proficient enough in French, Italian, Spanish, Portuguese, Greek and Latin to compose original pieces in them. In his twelfth year, he translated into English several of Ovid's epistles and all Virgil's pastorals. Lord Teignmouth, Jones's biographer, remarked that if Jones's literary achievements were compared with his years, one could find few instances of a more successful application of time and talents.[2] This probably is as true today as it was in 1799, when Lord Teignmouth wrote Jones's biography.[3]

At University College, Oxford, where he was admitted in 1764, Jones distinguished himself as he had done at Harrow. The Master of the College, the Reverend J.H.S. Wild, at the opening session of the Sir William Jones bicentenary celebrations on 2 September 1946, remarked: 'None of the alumni of this college—which will soon be celebrating the seventh centenary of its foundation—has been more distinguished than Sir William Jones.' Jones's first year in college was marked by his study of Arabic. To study the language, Jones employed a Syrian named Mirza, whom he maintained at Oxford at his own expense. Seeing the affinity between Arabic and Persian, Jones also started learning Persian. By 1768 he had acquired such a reputation for oriental scholarship that King Christian VII of Denmark asked him to translate the history of Nadir Shah, the *Tarikh-i-Nadiri*, into French. The *History* was published in 1770. Lord Teignmouth asserts that at that time, Jones was the only person in England capable of producing a work which required a knowledge of two foreign languages, one of which was scarcely known in Europe.[4] So thorough was Jones's knowledge of French that Louis XVI is said to have exclaimed: 'He is a most extraordinary man; he understands the language of my people better than I do myself.'

The *History of Nadir Shah* brought Jones great fame but little money. But his independent nature led him to give up his tutorship to Lord Althorp, which had so far been his means of livelihood.[5] He now turned to the Bar, and was admitted to the Temple on 19 September 1770. By this time he had probably completed his work on the *Grammar of the Persian Language*, otherwise it could not have been published in 1771 with Jones spending all his time and energy in reading for the Bar.[6] At the Bar too, he distinguished himself. His *Essay on the Law of Bailments*, published in 1781, was regarded as a classic at the time. According to the American juristic writer, Justice Story, even if Jones had not written anything else, 'he would have left a name unrivalled in the common law for philosophical accuracy, elegant learning, and finished analysis.' With all his attention devoted to law, Jones's interest in oriental studies might have diminished if he had not been able to come to India. As he wrote to Gibbon in 1781:

> With regard to Asiatic letters, a necessary attention to my profession will compel me wholly and eternally to abandon them, unless Lord North should think me worthy to . . . appoint me to supply the vacancy on the India Bench. . . . If the present summer and the ensuing autumn elapse without my receiving any answer, . . . I shall . . . entirely drop all thoughts of Asia, and, deep as ever plummet sounded, shall drown my Persian books.[7]

In fact, Jones waited for an answer not only in 'the present summer and the ensuing autumn', but for three summers and autumns.

At this point it would perhaps be useful to discuss Jones's attitude to oriental studies. Sir William Jones is primarily known as a great linguist. He knew as many as twenty-eight languages.[8] Jones, however, would perhaps have disliked being dubbed a mere linguist: he considered the acquisition of languages necessary because they held the key to 'the history of the human mind'. Having drunk at the fountains of oriental literatures, Jones realized that they held not only beauty but great wisdom. His desire was to make his fellow Europeans conscious of these treasures. Europe's colonial spirit was at its height in the late eighteenth century. Wherever Europeans went, they found people far below themselves in the 'scale of civilization'. To them therefore, Europe was the biblical centre around which the entire universe revolved. Jones was very conscious of this attitude, and, extremely critical of it.

> Some men [he wrote] never heard of the Asiatic writings, and others will

not be convinced that there is anything valuable in them; some pretend to be busy, and others are really idle. We . . . [are] like the savages, who thought that the sun rose and set for them alone, and could not imagine that the waves, which surrounded their island, left coral and pearls upon any other shore.⁹

Jones, in fact, was one of the first European scholars to break through European prejudices against oriental studies and to widen the horizons of the European literati. Thus he began his *Essay on Education* by quoting 'a celebrated Eastern philosopher'. This in itself was remarkable for an eighteenth-century European scholar, to have taken as his point of departure a quotation, not from any of the classical writers of Europe, but an oriental author.

Jones was, however, not blind to the beauties of the classical languages of Europe; he was in fact convinced that they 'were the standards of true taste'. What he protested against was Europe's absorption with its own literature. Thus in his *Essay on the Poetry of Eastern Nations* he remarked:

> I cannot but think that our European poetry has subsisted too long on the perpetual repetition of the same images, and incessant allusions to the same fables. . . . If the languages of the eastern nations were studied in our great seminaries of learning, . . . a new and ample field would be opened for speculation; we should have a more extensive insight into the history of the human mind; we should be furnished with a new set of images and similitudes; and a number of excellent compositions would be brought to light, which future scholars might explain, and future poets might imitate.

Jones himself showed the path when he composed hymns addressed to nine Hindu deities and even decided to orientalize his proposed epic *Britain Discovered*. Walt Whitman's poem, *Brahma*, and T. S. Eliot using a Sanskrit *mantra* as a refrain, merely follow in Jones's footsteps. His influence in this field was perhaps best summed up by Hewitt when he said, 'Jones altered the English conception of the Eastern world.'¹⁰

For a man who harboured such a broad vision of human affairs and thought in terms of human literature, it was natural that Jones should abhor all forms of tyranny and slavery. This is reflected in his letter to his former pupil, Viscount Althorp, during the American War of Independence:

> Nothing but peace can preserve us, but how can it be attained? . . . There is but one remedy: abandon for ever all idea of American dependence;

declare them independent States, and open a general treaty of pacifica-
tion. . . . Every man among them is a soldier, a patriot—subdue such a
people: The King may as easily conquer the moon or wear it in his sleeve.[11]

As a result of 'his plain speaking, and honest convictions, and the
dishonest whisperings and misrepresentations of his enemies', Jones
not only had to withdraw his candidature for a seat in Parliament, but
also to wait four years for confirmation of his Bengal judgeship. It was
perhaps well for posterity that Jones failed to secure the parliamentary
seat, otherwise he would never have come to India.

The main stumbling block in the way of his Bengal appointment was
the Lord Chancellor, Lord Thurlow, who gave in only when the King
himself intervened. King George III's letter to Thurlow saying that he
would take Jones's appointment in Bengal as a personal compliment
was dated 1 March 1782; on 4 March the appointment was publicly
announced; on 20 March Jones was knighted, married on 8 April[12],
and on 12 April set sail for India.

The *Crocodile* reached Calcutta in September 1783. Jones's fame
had preceded his arrival and great things were expected of him in the
field of oriental studies.

The field of investigation was indeed very vast. The India that Sir
William Jones came to was steeped in a sort of amnesia about its
ancient past. The history and chronology of the ancient period was all
but lost, being inextricable from a mist of more or less legendary
tradition, a great part of which was fantastic, and all of which was
exaggerated or distorted.[13] India's past was preserved in its literature
and architectural remains but its history had been lost. Even the
learned pundits were not aware of the existence of important dynasties
like the Maurya, the Gupta, the Pala and others.

On the other hand, European ignorance about India led even
serious writers in Europe to believe that Malay was one of the most
widely spoken languages of the Indian subcontinent.[14] In fact Jones
himself knew little of India and its culture. His reading on Indian
affairs was more or less confined to Orme, Dow and D'Herbelot's
Bibliothèque Orientale. He conceived of India as divided into three
parts (as did Herbelot in his article on *Hend*), thought Assam was a
part of the Malay peninsula, and Porus an Indian town. Sanskrit was
to be respected rather than studied.[15] His early writings on oriental
literature dealt with Arabic and Persian to the complete exclusion of
Sanskrit. But these views only reflected the general situation in

Europe. 'No Sanskrit manuscripts had been published, and no one had brought back manuscripts, unlike Edward Pococke's seventeenth-century model of transporting hundreds of valuable Arabic and other manuscripts from Aleppo. At best, the literature was unknown to the West; at worst, the land of nonliterate 'black men', as the British colonialists spoke of Indians, had produced little or none.'[16]

Jones, was, however, not only above racial prejudices, but also knew of richness of Asian, if not specifically Indian, culture. This he outlined in his preliminary discourse to the Asiatic Society. Speaking of his train of thought on board the *Crocodile*, he went on to say:

> I could not help remarking, how important and extensive a field was yet unexplored, and how many solid advantages unimproved; and, when I considered with pain, that such inquiries and improvements could only be made by the united efforts of many, who are not easily brought, without some pressing inducements or strong impulse, to converge in a common point, I consoled myself with a hope . . . that, if in any country or community such an union could be effected, it was among my countrymen in Bengal.[17]

Here, in fact, lay the seeds of the Asiatic Society. As soon as Jones overcame his initial problems[18] he devoted himself to the realization of his dream. In January 1784 he sent a circular letter putting forward his plans of establishing a Society to encourage oriental studies.[19] He also discussed his plan with his senior colleague in the Supreme Court, Sir Robert Chambers, who applauded the project and invited men of letters to give Jones's idea a solid foundation.[20]

15 January 1784. Thirty gentlemen—the elite of the European community—met in the Grand Jury Room of the Supreme Court at Calcutta, with Sir Robert Chambers in the Chair, and passed a resolution for the establishment of the Asiatic Society. In this modest fashion was laid the foundation of the great centre of learning, the mother institution of oriental Societies all over the world. No trumpets heralded its foundation, no fanfare marked its first meeting. Yet it was a revolutionary event: for the Society's establishment marked the restoration of learning in and about India. John Collegins commemorated the event in verse:

> Britannia's genius, eager to explore
> The mystic mines of Asiatic lore,

With smiles benign accomplish'd
Jones address'd.
And bid him trace the records of the East.
He came – the heavenly *Gopia* round him flew,
His preference every son of Learning drew:
Then first, ye scholars! met at his command,
The father of the literary band.[21]

Although the Society had a humble beginning, its founder had no doubts that it would grow to full maturity; and cited the example of the Royal Society 'which at first was only a meeting of a few literary friends at Oxford, rose gradually to that splendid zenith, at which a Halley was their secretary, and a Newton their president'.[22]

As to the Society's objects of inquiry, Jones remarked that they would be 'MAN and NATURE: whatever is performed by the one, or produced by the other.' No comparable phrase can so encompass the entire range of human knowledge. However, Jones himself set a limit to the Society's objects of inquiry by suggesting that they should be confined within the 'geographical limits of Asia'. This again was a revolutionary idea, at a time when Europe was supposed to be the storehouse of all knowledge, secular and divine. Jones was for intellectual inquirers what Alexander was in geographical conquest.[23] He invaded almost every branch of learning, as that conqueror did provinces and kingdoms[24] and tried to enthuse others to do the same.

Yet Jones was not simply an idealist perched in an ivory tower. On 22 January 1784 he took the practical step of requesting Members of the Council to accept the title of 'Patrons' of the Society.[25] The Council agreed to the request and also approved and applauded the Society's endeavours to 'promote the extension of knowledge by the means, which your local advantages afford you in a degree, perhaps, exceeding those of any part of the Globe'. The Society's move to confer the title of President on Warren Hastings, was, however, as much a practical move to secure the blessings of the Head of Government as the recognition that Hastings was a great patron of oriental learning.

Hastings' reply to the Society's offer is a model of humility and the propriety of giving the deserving person his due:

From an early conviction of the utility of the institution, it was my anxious wish that I might be, by whatever means, instrumental in promoting the success of it; but not in the mode which you have proposed. . . . I have not the leisure requisite to discharge the functions of such a station; nor, if I did possess it, would it be consistent with the pride, which every man may be allowed to avow in the pursuit or support of the objects of his personal credit, to accept the first station in a department, in which the superior talents of my immediate followers in it would shine with a lustre, from which mine must suffer much in the comparison. . . . On these grounds I request your permission to decline the offer which you have done me the honour to make to me, and to yield my pretensions to the Gentleman, whose genius planned the institution, and is most capable of conducting it to the attainment of the great and splendid purposes of its formation.[26]

This letter from Hastings was read to the Society at its meeting held on 5 February, after which the Society thanked the Governor-General in a resolution and requested Sir William Jones to become President of the Society.

In his Preliminary Discourse to the Society Jones had promised that if during his intellectual excursions he was 'so fortunate as to collect, by accident, either fruits or flowers, which may seem valuable or pleasing', he would offer his humble *nezr* to the Society.[27] His first contribution came at the Society's meeting of 19 February in the form of 'A Dissertation on the Orthography of Asiatic Words in Roman Letters'. It is most significant that Jones's first contribution should have been on this subject, for no scientific research on alien languages could make much progress unless there was a uniform system of transliteration. Without this, different meanings could be read into the same passage. Thus Jones described a personal experience at Oxford when he came across a couplet of the celebrated poet Ibn Zaidun transliterated into the Roman alphabet and requested the well-known Arabic scholar Dr Hunt and two or three others to put the passage back into Arabic. To his dismay, all of them wrote differently, and, in his opinion, erroneously.[28] Jones pointed out that almost every writer had a method of notation peculiar to himself and none appeared to be a complete system. In India itself two earlier scholars, Charles Wilkins and Nathaniel Halhed, had tried to evolve systems of orthography, but their use was confined to their works alone. Jones mentioned the deficiency in the earlier systems and set out to expound each letter of the Devanagari[29] alphabet, giving its equivalent in Roman characters. While at this exercise Jones became aware of the deficiencies of the English alphabet. 'Our English alphabet and orthography', he said, 'are disgracefully and almost ridiculously imperfect; and it would be impossible to express either Indian, Persian or Arabic words in Roman character.'[30] The Devanagari on the other hand was 'precise' and 'clear' and 'more naturally arranged than any other'.

Jones then made the Devanagari alphabet his standard, and devised a system of transliteration which, with a few changes, still remains valid.

Mukherjee, in his book on Sir William Jones, dismisses Jones's contribution to the standardization of transliteration as 'minor'. Scholars who have devoted a lifetime to oriental studies over the years do not seem to agree. In the special centenary meeting of the Asiatic Society in 1884 it was said, 'If Sir William Jones had done nothing else but translate the laws of Manu and invent a system of transliteration which forms the basis of that now adopted by all scholars ... he would have immortalised his name; but he was what in Sanskrit we call *nana-sastra-visardah*.'[31]

Professor Monier-Williams, the Boden Professor of Sanskrit, devoted a whole lecture to Jones's system at the International Congress of Orientalists held at Berlin in 1881. He pleaded 'for the universal adoption of some fixed system of transliterating Eastern languages, based on that originated by ... Sir William Jones.[32] As a result, it was proposed to appoint a Commission of Inquiry to report on the best method of transliteration and the general adoption of a common system.

There is as yet no common standard system in use but the subject of a uniform system of transliteration has been reconsidered from time to time over two centuries and only minor changes are made in Jones's system.

The main significance of Jones's paper on orthography lies in another direction: for the first time it was realized that the ancient Greeks, while writing about India, changed Indian names to suit their own convenience. Jones noted that:

> The ancient Greeks ... who were too vain perhaps, of their own language to learn any other, have ... strangely disguised the proper appellations of countries, cities, and rivers in Asia. ... They had an unwarrantable habit of moulding foreign names to a Grecian form, and giving them a resemblance to some derivative word in their own tongue: thus, they changed the Gogra into Agoranis, or a river of the assembly, Uchah into Oxydrace, or sharpsighted, and Renas into Aernos, or a rock inaccessible to birds.[33]

In this passage lie the seeds of his identification, made almost a decade later, of Chandragupta and Pataliputra with Sandracottus and Palibothra of the Greek texts respectively, a discovery which was to lay the foundations of ancient Indian chronology.

Research in ancient Indian history and chronology seemed to be one of the main tasks of the Society from the very beginning. In fact the very first paper contributed to the Society dealt with history and historical remains. The paper presented by Thomas Law[14] at the third meeting of the Society on 29 January 1784 was 'A short account and drawings of two pillars situated to the north of Patna'. This account is not traceable, nor was it published in the *Researches*. It would however be useful and interesting to indentify the pillars noticed by Law.

The Proceedings of the Society have another significant entry on 19 February 1784 which goes: 'A letter addressed by W. Paterson to Sir William Jones showing the agreement between the Hindu and Greek chronology. . . . Mr Chambers observes that the tables accompanying Mr Paterson's letter were composed by the *munshi* of Dara Shikoh and that he has met with them in Persian authors.'

This letter has also disappeared, nor is the basis for Chambers observation known. This appears to be the first time that an attempt was made to relate the Greek and the Indian chronologies, a method which later yielded significant results for the reconstruction of Indian history. Were the details of this communication to be traced, they might also shed new light on the personality of Dara Shukoh.

The first published article of historical interest was the 'Account of the Sculptures and Ruins at Mavalipuram' by William Chambers. The author had visited the ruins for the first time in 1772, but at that time he neither measured the distances nor the size of the objects, nor committed to writing his observations on them. He would have done so, he tells us, 'had there then existed in India so powerful an incentive to diligent inquiry, and accurate communication, as the establishment of this Society'. No better testimony could there be of the Society' usefulness.

Chambers' article also indicates the prevailing ignorance in India about the country's ancient history. Thus Chambers gives an account of the foundation and the ultimate destruction of the city of Mahabalipuram as he gathered it from the Brahman pundits of the place. According to them, the city was founded by Balee, the grandson of Prahlad, the main figure in the story of Narasimha Avatar, the fourth incarnation of Vishnu.[36]

The destruction of the city was wrought by the god *Indra* when he became jealous of its splendour which rivalled that of his own capital. After giving the pundits' account,[37] Chambers outlined the difficul ties and the arduous task which the early inquirer into ancient Indian history and chronology faced:

> Their poets seem to have been their only historians, as well as divines; and whatever they relate, is wrapped up in this burlesque garb, set off, by way of ornament, with circumstances hugely incredible and absurd, and all this without any date, and in no other order or method, than such as the poet's fancy suggested, and found most convenient. Nevertheless, by comparing names and grand events, recorded by them, with those interspersed in the histories of other nations, and by calling in the assistance of ancient monuments, coins, and inscriptions, as occasion shall offer, some probable conjectures, at least, if not important discoveries, may, it is hoped. be made on these interesting subjects.[38]

In this first published article on Indian antiquities, though the author deals at length with the difficulties facing the European researcher into India's past, there is not a word about the benefits of such studies to the British Empire. Many of these pioneer scholars were thus evidently motivated by scholarship itself and one need not look for deeper motives underlying their labours.

With such valuable contributions, the Society may be said to have begun most successfully. In April, in a letter to Charles Chapman, Jones expressed his satisfaction saying, 'Our meetings are well attended, and the Society may really be said, considering the recent time of its establishment, to flourish.' The Society's well-being, however, was largely due to Jones himself. In his opening address, he had desired that the Society hold 'weekly evening meetings in this hall, for the purpose of hearing original papers read on such subjects as fall within the circle of our inquiries.'[39]

Accordingly we find that between January and June, with the exception of two or three weeks, there were regular weekly meetings of the Society; but during the period July to January when Jones was out of Calcutta, the Society met only twice and nothing of great importance was transacted.

Jones returned to Calcutta in February 1785 and once again we find an almost unbroken record of weekly meetings.

In his second anniversary discourse presented to the Society on 24 February 1785, Jones noted that the Society had passed its state of infancy and was advancing to maturity 'with every mark of a healthy and robust constitution'. He went on to describe various fields of knowledge like medicine, botany, sculpture, painting and history, in which the members' labours could bear valuable fruit. He also had in mind a catalogue of oriental works and exhorted members to do their best towards compiling it.

Max Müller in his opening address to the International Congress of Orientalists held in London in 1874 felt that the study of oriental literature at first was only a matter of curiosity and that William Jones represented most worthily that early phase.[40] Yet, with the broad humanitarian outlook that he possessed, Jones made 'the benefit of mankind, and not the mere acquisition of knowledge, its primary purpose'.[41] Jones himself seemed to refute Max Müller in his second discourse:

> We ought not to condemn the people of Asia, from whose researches into nature, works of art, and inventions of fancy, many valuable hints may be derived for our own improvement and advantage. If that, indeed, were not the principal object of our institution, little else could arise from it, but the mere gratification of curiosity; and I should not receive so much delight from the humble share which you have allowed me to take in promoting it.[42]

His breadth of vision, scholarship, and humanitarianism, as well as his Christian conservatism, were demonstrated in his famous dissertation, 'On the Gods of Greece, Italy and India', read to the Society on 24 March 1785.[43] He remarked:

> When features of resemblance, too strong to have been accidental, are observable in different systems of polytheism, without fancy or prejudice to colour them and improve the likeness, we can scarce help believing that some connection has immemorially subsisted between the several nations who have adopted them.[44]

The dissertation, and particularly this passage, marks the starting-point of the study of Comparative Mythology. Jones himself drew a parallel between a large number of classical gods and goddesses of the west with those of Indian mythology. Thus Janus was found to be similar to Ganesa, Saturn to Manu or Satyavrata, Jupiter to Indra, Hermes to Narada, and Ceres, the daughter of Saturn to Lakshmi, the goddess of abundance. Jones also found a parallel in Indian mythology to the Biblical flood, and felt that this episode 'fixes consequently the time when the genuine Hindu chronology actually begins.' He took care to distinguish the universal deluge connected with the story of the

Matsyavatara from the flood from which Krishna saved Mathura by lifting the mountain Govardhana. At this point, Jones had been in India for less than two years. The fact that his knowledge, though deep, was still imperfect, makes him later in the same dissertation describe Rama as the son of Cush.[45]

The dissertation must have taken the literary world by storm, for Jones had now placed Indian mythology on the same level as that of Greece and Rome, at that time held sacrosanct by the western world.

Jones further declared that each sect must be justified by its own faith and good intentions. Realizing the hostility he would generate in Christian circles, Jones as if to pacify them interspersed his essay with proclamations of the truth of the Christian doctrine as against Hinduism: 'The tenet of our church cannot without profaneness, be compared with that of the Hindus, which has only an apparent resemblance to it, but a very different meaning.' Finally he expressed the view that the only human mode of effecting conversion among Hindus would be to translate into Sanskrit and Persian 'such chapters of the Prophets, particularly Isaiah, as are indisputably evangelical, together with one of the gospels . . . and then quietly to disperse the work among the well-educated natives', adding that even after this, if it failed to make any impact, 'we could only lament more than ever the strength of prejudice and the weakness of unassisted reason.'[46]

Passages such as these must have seemed god-sent to Lord Teignmouth who was 'pathetically anxious to prove Jones his own brand of evangelist'.[47] The leading journal, *The Gentleman's Magazine*, in its review of this dissertation, also laid emphasis only on such passages, adding: 'How much were it to be wished that Sir William Jones would himself undertake the desirable work, [of translating the Scriptures into Sanskrit] as the learned and pious Boyle dispersed Gospels among the Malays in their own language.'[48]

Jones was, however, neither a missionary nor an enthusiast for bringing Christian knowledge to the east. He worked in the opposite direction, that is, carrying knowledge of the east to the west. Thus Arberry calls Lord Teignmouth's attempt to prove Jones an evangelist, 'a patent fraud', and adds, 'Jones was a deeply religious man, but his religion was universal in its theology, personal and practical in its application.'[49] Jones was a pious Christian but a greater scholar, and was trying to reconstruct and give content to the history of Man, rather than to the history of one religion, one community or one nation. The French savant, Jules Mohl, who was Assistant Secretary to the Asiatic

Society of Paris, said of him:

> Formerly oriental studies were confined almost entirely to the languages
> and literature which were used in the interpretation of the Bible . . . Sir
> William Jones was the first to consider Oriental literature as an immense
> whole, which was destined to serve as a foundation for the history of man;
> and of which each part must cooperate in elucidating the others.[50]

The dissertation 'On the Gods' contains another very curious thesis.
After observing that Egypt seemed to be the grand source of knowledge for the western, and India for the eastern part of the globe, Jones
gave several arguments to prove that a group of Egyptian priests had
in some remote age settled down in India. This, in fact, was the main
basis for intellectual intercourse between the two nations. The thesis
was more or less accepted at that time. Jones also mentioned a Father
Marco, a Roman missionary based at Betiya,[51] who told him about a
dictionary of Indian mythological and historical names in which the
word *Tirut*[52] was described as a 'town and province in which the
priests from Egypt settled.' According to Jones, it was for this reason
that the pundits of Tirhut were commonly surnamed *Misra* (from the
word *Misr*, which in Sanskrit means Egypt). He pointed out that the
word 'neel' means blue in Sanskrit, and the river Nile is 'an azure
stream'.

Whatever the truth of this thesis, Jones was certain that a connection had existed between the two nations even before the birth of
Moses.

In 1851, more than fifty years later, John Pickering, the first
President of the American Oriental Society, spoke on the subject in his
maiden address:

> Whether Egypt communicated its knowledge of the arts and sciences to
> India, or the reverse, or whether they interchanged their philosophy and
> the arts with each other, has long been a subject of debate among the
> learned, and which now hardly admits of being satisfactorily settled.
> . . . That there was an intercourse between the two countries in ancient
> times, seems to be beyond dispute.[53]

Thus the matter rested at the same point in 1851 as it did in Jones's
time, and as it does today. With the plethora of new material available
in both Egypt and India, a historian could now explore the subject
further. It is also possible that the Indus Valley script, once deciphered, may shed further light on the subject.

In his address, Jones remarked that his comparisons between the classical and Indian gods 'must needs be very superficial', partly because of his short stay in India, partly for want of leisure, and principally because he had no European books to refresh his memory of old fables. 'A thousand more strokes of resemblance might . . . be collected by any who should with that view peruse Hesiod, Hyginus, Cornutus, and the other mythologies.' This hint was taken up by another Indologist and a great admirer of Jones, Francis Wilford, who engaged a number of pundits to find further parallels between Greek and Roman mythologies, the Old Testament and the Sanskrit texts. These pundits, exploiting the credulity of the too eager European, interpolated into the old Sanskrit texts material cleverly forged so that the Sanskrit texts specifically mentioned Adam, Abraham and other Biblical personages. The forgery was detected by Wilford himself, but only after he had contributed quite a lot of material on the subject in the *Asiatic Researches*—which he sorely regretted later.

Thus, Jones's dissertation 'On the Gods' had positive as well as negative results. Although Max Müller later remarked that Jones's address contained only a superficial comparison of mythology without any specific value,[14] it would be difficult to deny that Jones established beyond dispute the fact of India's connections with both the classical world and Egypt. This was a remarkable achievement considering the times in which such an assertion was made.

If Max Müller expressed doubts about the scientific value of Jones's dissertation, that of another communication is beyond all doubt. This was a 'Description of a Cave near Gaya' by the Society's Secretary, John Herbert Harington, together with 'A Translation of a Sanskrit Inscription',[15] found in the cave by Charles Wilkins, both being presented to the Society on 17 March 1785.

According to Harington, a Mr Hodgekis had already lost his life while on his way to examine the cave. On Sir William Jones's advice, Harington visited the cave he called *Nagarjunee* once again, took its measurements, and engaged a native *munshi* to copy out the two inscriptions on its walls. Harington showed impressions of the inscriptions to a Banaras pundit, who was unable to make anything of them. He then sent the impressions to Wilkins, who could decipher one, but not the other. The longer inscription, according to Wilkins, was in a 'character undoubtedly the most ancient of any that have hitherto come under my inspection. . . . But though the writing be not modern, the language is pure Sanskrit.' The inscription contained no date. Wilkins was convinced that it contained nothing but an invocation to the goddess Durga. The second inscription consisted of a single line in a 'different character', which Wilkins could not decipher.

We now know that the longer inscription was not all that valueless, for it revealed the names of three kings of the Magadhan branch of the Maukhari dynasty: Yajna Varman, Sardula Varman and Ananta Varman. To appreciate the full significance of this inscription, it is important to mention here Wilkins' translations of two other small inscriptions (impressions of which were taken by Wilmot from other caves near Gaya) which were presented to the Society later in the year. The three inscriptions together established beyond doubt the existence of this branch of the Maukhari dynasty which rose on the ruins of the Gupta empire in the sixth century. The Gaya inscription, communicated by Harington, becomes important for another reason. This inscription, together with its translation, was the first of its kind to be presented to the literary world in modern times, and may be taken to mark the beginning of Indian epigraphy. Although Wilkins had translated the Monghyr inscription in 1781, three years before the Society was founded, it was presented to the Society only on 7 July 1785, three months after the Gaya inscription. No matter which of these inscriptions we take to have been presented earlier, it remains beyond dispute that it was Charles Wilkins who was the pioneer in Indian epigraphy.

The Monghyr inscription turned out to be the more important one. The discovery of this inscription together with another on the pillar at Buddal in Dinajpur (a translation of which was communicated just a week after the Monghyr inscription)[56] gave to Indian history the famous Pala dynasty of Bengal. Whereas the Monghyr copperplate inscriptions were discovered by Colonel Watson, the Buddal inscription was discovered, deciphered and translated by Wilkins. His account shows the apathy with which antiquities were regarded in eighteenth-century India, and highlights the zeal of early British scholars to unravel India's past:

Sometime in the month of November, in the year 1780 I discovered, in the vicinity of the town of Buddal, near which the Company have a factory, and which at that time was under my charge, a decapitated monumental column. . . . It stands in a swamp overgrown with weeds. . . . Upon my getting close enough to the monument to examine it, I took its dimensions, and made a drawing of it; and soon after a plate was engraved, from which the accompanying is an impression.[57]

Though both Charles Wilkins and William Jones went wrong in their estimate of the date of the Monghyr and the Buddal inscriptions, believing them to be pre-Christian, their reconstruction of the genealogy of the early rulers of the Pala dynasty was surprisingly accurate. This becomes apparent by comparing Jones's genealogy in his 'Remarks' on Wilkins's communications, with that of D. C. Sirkar in 1975–6:

Jones[58]	Sircar[59]
Gopala	Gopala
Dharmapala	Dharmapala
Devapala	Devapala
Rajyapala	Surapala
Surapala	Vigrahapala
Narayanapala	Narayanapala
	Rajyapala

The Buddal inscription is the only one to also list the ministers of the early Pala kings, a fact which does not seem to have been repeated in any of the Pala inscriptions discovered subsequently.

There is another fact of great significance in the Monghyr inscription which went unnoticed by later scholars. In the inscription, Wilkins came across the word 'Rashtrakuta' which he translated as 'many countries', so that the passage read: 'The prince took the hand of the daughter of Porobol, Raja of many countries, whose name was *Ronnaa Debee*.' Sir William Jones, not satisfied with this rendering, consulted pundits who told him that 'Rashtrakuta' was the name of a certain country.[60] Actually both renderings were wrong: Rashtrakuta, as we know now was the name of a dynasty which was contemporaneous with the Palas and engaged in a struggle of power with them in the eighth and ninth centuries after Christ, which saw a period of warring principalities after the collapse of the powerful Gupta empire.

The last paper presented to the Society in 1785 dealt with the brighter days of the Gupta empire, since it mentions the nine gems of King Vikramaditya's court. This inscription was discovered on a piece of stone by Wilmot, who copied and sent it to Wilkins, who deciphered and translated it. The inscription is an intriguing one and requires closer study by historians.[61] It mentions Amara Deva, one of the nine jewels of King Vikramaditya's court who came to Bodh Gaya. After doing penance, he received a visitation from the gods and commemorated it by building a temple there. In the inscription as

translated by Wilkins, the invocation to Buddha, to whom the temple
was dedicated, goes thus: 'Reverence be unto thee in the form of
Buddha! . . . Reverence be unto thee an incarnation of the Deity and
the Eternal one. . . . Thou art Brahma, Vishnu, and Mahesa!' This
suggests that the temple was dedicated to Buddha and hence was the
famous temple at Bodh Gaya. However, the inscription continues:
'Having thus worshipped the guardian of mankind, he became like
one of the just. He joyfully caused a holy temple to be built, of a
wonderful construction, and therein were set up the divine foot of
Vishnu, forever purifier of the sins of mankind.' This, on the other
hand, would seem to relate to the construction of the temple now
known as 'Vishnupad', or Vishnu's feet. Either way, once the substance of the inscription is further examined, it may shed new light on
one of the two ancient temples in Gaya.

The proceedings contain many other entries which unfortunately
have now been lost, as they were not published in the *Asiatic
Researches*. Why Sir William Jones did not include them in the
Society's publication is now difficult to say: they may not have seemed
of much importance to him, although it can only be regretted that the
communications were not preserved. Some of these communications
were, 'A letter from Harry Stark to George Wroughton containing
some account of the islands of Salsette and Elephanta', presented to
the Society on 3 March 1785; 'Drawings of the caves at Ellora', done at
the request of Colonel Pearse, by Captain Christopher Green, his
aide-de-camp; an account of them by Gilleis, the head surgeon of
Colonel Pearse's detachment, both presented to the Society on 28
April 1785; another account of the caves at Salsette, together with
copies of inscriptions taken by Mallet, presented to the Society on 30
June 1785; and an account of the Nuddea University gathered by
Mackinnon, from a moulvi and a pundit, and read by him at the
Society's meeting on 28 July 1785.

The year 1785 also marked a turning point in Jones's life. Although
he had looked forward to studying the country's history and culture,
he had no intention of adding a new language to his already rich
linguistic acquisitions. Moreover, he thought he could depend upon
Wilkins, who had by then acquired a reputation for his knowledge of
Sanskrit, for guidance in problems which required a knowledge of that
language. Early in 1784 he wrote to Wilkins:

Happy should I be to follow you in the same track; but life is too short and my necessary business too long for me to think at my age of acquiring a new language, when those which I have already learned contain such a mine of curious and agreeable information. All my hopes therefore of being acquainted with the poetry, philosophy, and arts of the Hindus, are grounded on the expectation of living to see the fruits of your learned labours.[62]

Soon Jones realized that he would not be able to do justice to his judicial work if he did not learn the language of the Hindu law books. The pundits employed to translate and interpret for him manipulated the law for monetary or other considerations.[63] This decided him to learn Sankrit. The problem was finding a teacher, as no Brahman was prepared to teach the 'language of the gods' to a foreigner. At last a Pandit Ramlochan who taught Sanskrit at Nadiya agreed to teach him.

Jones himself learnt Sanskrit primarily for professional reasons, but his modesty, love for oriental studies and an awareness of their hidden richness find expression in his *Hymn to Surya*:

> And, if they ask what mortal pours the strain?
> Say for thou seest earth, air, and main,
> Say, 'From the bosom of yon silver isle,
> Where skies more softly smile,
> He came; and lisping our celestial tongue,
> Though not from *Brahma* sprung,
> Draws orient knowledge, from its fountains pure,
> Through caves obstructed long, and paths too long obscure.[64]

The hymn was composed in 1786. By this time he knew enough of Sanskrit to classify it as a 'celestial tongue', and in February he delivered his third annual discourse to the Society, which has now become famous for the following statement:

> The Sanskrit language, whatever be its antiquity, is of a wonderful structure; more perfect than the Greek, more copious than the Latin and more exquisitely refined than either; yet bearing to both of them a stronger affinity, both in the roots of the verbs, and in the forms of grammar, than could possibly have been produced by accident; so strong, indeed, that no philologer could examine them all three, without believing them to have sprung from some common source, which, perhaps, no longer exists.[65]

Several scholars before Jones had spoken about similarities between sounds and words of various languages. In fact, Jones himself was aware of the affinity between several languages long before 1786. On 17 February 1779 we find him writing to Prince Adam Czartoryski:

How so many European words crept into the Persian language, I know not
with certainty. . . . Many learned investigators of antiquity are fully persuaded, that a very old and almost primeval language was in use among
these northern nations, from which not only the Celtic dialects, but even
the Greek and Latin, are derived. . . . We must confess that these researches are very obscure and uncertain.[66]

The first milestone in comparative linguistics, before Jones, was
planted by Leibnitz. In 1710, in a dissertation in *Miscellanea Be-
rolinensia*, Leibnitz tried to construct a comprehensive system of
linguistic genealogy, assuming that the languages of Europe and Asia
as well as of Egypt were descended from the same original language.[67]
Leibnitz's grouping of languages was not based upon any deep
analysis; he could not make out whether the resemblances were due
merely to borrowings or to deeper causes.[68] Jones however spoke not
only of the affinity between Sanskrit, Greek, Latin and even the Celtic
and the Teutonic languages, he also ascribed this affinity to a post-
ulated common source which no longer existed. The French orientalist, Eugène Burnouf, in his *Discourse on the English Language and
Literature*, spoke of the advance made by Jones over Leibnitz and
described Jones's discovery as 'the most remarkable . . . which philology had yielded in our days.'[69]

Franklin Edgerton made what is perhaps the clearest statement
about Jones's contribution:

> That languages often resemble each other is obvious enough. Even the
> specific fact that Sanskrit resembles Greek and Latin had been seen before.
> But no one before Jones had drawn the inference that these resemblances
> must be explained by the assumption of common descent from a hypothe-
> tical earlier language 'which, perhaps, no longer exists'. At this moment
> modern comparative grammar was born.[70]

European scholars, surprised to find a language superior to their
own classical languages and closer to the ancient original one, eagerly
took up the study of Sanskrit. Henceforward, we find an almost
unbroken chain of linguistic studies centring round Sanskrit.[71] Thus, in
1851, the first President of the American Oriental Society in his annual
address felt that no man could claim to be a philologist, 'without some
acquaintance with that extraordinary and most perfect of known
tongues'.[72] More than a century later, in 1955, M.B. Emeneau in his
address to the same Society declared:

It was, as this Society needs no reminding, the linguistics of the India of more than two millennia ago that was the direct germinal origin of the linguistics of the Western world of today.[73]

Even while founding the study of linguistics, Jones was alive to the dangers of making far-fetched deductions based on superficial similarities of sounds in different languages. While the science of linguistics or comparative philology would on the one hand lead us closer to the history of man, and obliterate to an extent the differences between peoples and nations, on the other it would give rise to scholars who would exploit this discovery to the point of absurdity. He warned:

> Etymology has, no doubt, some use in historical researches, but it is a medium of proof so very fallacious, that, where it elucidates one fact, it obscures a thousand, and more frequently borders on the ridiculous, than leads to any solid conclusion . . . when we derive our *hanger*, or short pendent sword, from the Persian, because ignorant travellers thus mis-spell the word *Khanjar*, which, in truth, means a different weapon, or *sandalwood* from the Greek, because we suppose that sandals were sometimes made of it, we gain no ground in proving the affinity of nations, and only weaken arguments which might otherwise be firmly supported.[74]

The importance of this warning is proved by the case of, among others, Edward Pococke, who on the basis of the similarity of words in Greek and Sanskrit, attempted to prove that a group of Rajputs and Brahmans colonized early Greece. The *Friend of India* rightly remarked:

> The mode in which Mr. Pococke has worked out his theory, exaggerates its absurdity. He declares, that the Pelasgi derive their name from Pelasa in Bihar, and Macedonia from the old name of the same province, Magadha. Athens is from Attock, the forts on the Indus, and the Boetians came from Behut on the Jhelum. Larissa was Lahore, and the word Philip instead of a lover of horses, really signified a *Bheel* prince . . . and so on through every possible absurdity of philology run mad.[75]

The year 1786 had little to show except for Jones's discourse. The Society met only four times in the entire year.[76] Lady Jones did not keep good health and Jones spent as much time as he could with her, staying out of Calcutta. Of the twenty-nine letters of Jones available for this year, over twenty were written from outside Calcutta. Clearly, much of the Society's life depended upon the presence of its founder.

With the coming of the new year, 1787, the Society seemed to have revived. In its very first meeting, held on 15 February 1787, Jones read his fourth annual discourse to the Society. This discourse, dealing with Arabia and the Arabian people, was in a way a continuation of the third discourse in which he had outlined his scheme for five discourses:

> The five principal nations who have in different ages divided among themselves, as a kind of inheritance, the vast continent of Asia, with the many islands depending on it, are the Indians, the Chinese, the Tartars, the Arabs and the Persians: who they severally were, whence and when they came, where they now are settled, and what advantage a more perfect knowledge of them all may bring to our European world, will be shown, I trust, in five distinct essays; the last of which will demonstrate the connection or diversity between them, and solve the great problem, whether they had any common origin, and whether that origin was the same which we generally ascribe to them.[77]

Thus by investigating into the languages, philosophies, religions, architectural remains, and written memorials of the sciences and the arts of the five principal Asiatic nations, India, Arabia, Tartary, Persia, and China, Jones hoped to reconstruct human history by going back to the ultimate origins of the world and man. His third discourse, as we have seen, dealt with India and the Hindus. In his fourth discourse Jones enquired into the state of Arabia and the culture of the Arabian people before the coming of Muhammad. He stated that the Arabians were a race distinct from the Hindus, although there might have been intercourse between them. He regretted that the ancient history of Arabia should be as little known before the time of Dhu Yezen, as that of the Hindus before Vikramaditya. With a characteristic broadness of outlook, he proclaimed:

> Men will always differ in their ideas of civilization, each measuring it by the habits and prejudices of his own country; but, if courtesy and urbanity, a love of poetry and eloquence, and the practice of exalted virtues, be a juster measure of perfect society, we have certain proof that the people of Arabia, both on plains and cities, in republican and monarchical states, were eminently civilised for many ages before their conquest of Persia.[78]

In the Society's meeting of 29 March 1787 another communication of historical importance was presented. This was a translation of the inscriptions on six ancient copperplates describing a royal grant of land. The copperplates had been discovered during digging operations for some new works at the fort of Tanna, the capital of Salsette. General John Carnac collected the plates from the Governor of Bombay, who informed him that none of the Brahmans in Gujarat could explain the inscription. General Carnac brought the plates to Calcutta and handed them over to the Asiatic Society. The inscription was then deciphered by Pandit Ramlochan, who had been Jones's Sanskrit teacher. The inscription turned out to be a very valuable one, for it brought to light the existence of the Silahara dynasty of western India. The accuracy of the translation is borne out by the fact that in the comprehensive genealogy of the Silaharas drawn up by Altekar, nearly a hundred and fifty years after Ramlochan's translation, we see many names in common.

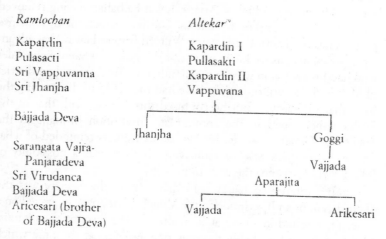

Ramlochan	*Altekar*[a]
Kapardin	Kapardin I
Pulasacti	Pullasakti
Sri Vappuvanna	Kapardin II
Sri Jhanjha	Vappuvana
Bajjada Deva	Jhanjha Goggi
Sarangata Vajra-	
Panjaradeva	Vajjada
Sri Virudanca	Aparajita
Bajjada Deva	
Aricesari (brother	Vajjada Arikesari
of Bajjada Deva)	

Altekar gives eight more generations of rulers, and his datings also are more accurate. What is remarkable, however, is the fact that Ramlochan dates the inscription at A.D. 1018. Since the last king mentioned in the grant seems to be Aricesari, we can presume that the inscription was written during his reign. Now, according to Altekar's genealogy, the period of Arikesarin is c. A.D. 1015 to c. A.D. 1025, the known year being A.D. 1017, almost exactly that derived by Ramlochan.

Another communication of the same year was 'Remarks on the City of Tagara' by Lieutenant Francis Wilford. Surprisingly, little is known of Wilford, who was considered one of the greatest orientalists of the day.[80] He was born in Hanover to a family of rank. He joined the army at an early age and was sent to India in 1781. After the peace of Mangalore (1784), Warren Hastings encouraged him to take up

oriental studies and soon he acquired distinction by his contributions
to the *Asiatic Researches*. By the time he died in 1822, at Banaras,
Wilford had contributed no less than ten articles to the *Researches*.
Unfortunately, Wilford's studies depended on the pundits, who interpolated several passages into the original Sanskrit texts. Wilford fell
an easy prey to their literary machinations because he himself was
given to hasty generalizations. For instance, in his very first communication on the city of Tagara, he tried to find out everything
written about Tagara by Greek authors, but with respect to the
historical part he observed: 'you will find I am not conversant with the
Hindu antiquities: indeed, I have no time to study languages.' So,
apart from stating that 'About the middle of the first century, Tagara
was no longer the capital of Ariaca, Rajah Salbahan having removed
the seat of the empire to Pattan'—a fact which held immense
possibilities of historical discovery, Wilford frittered away that advantage. Salivahana, as we know now, was the powerful Satavahana ruler
who had his capital in what is now Paithan in the Aurangabad district
of Maharashtra. Wilford might have had the credit of discovering the
Satavahana dynasty, [81] but he confused this dynasty with that of the
Silahara mentioned in the copperplate inscription brought to the
Society by General Carnac. In this context, one is reminded of what
Stanley Lane-Poole said of Humayun: 'If there was a possibility of
falling,[82] [he] was not the man to miss it.'

Another interesting paper read that year in the Society was the
'Translation of an Inscription in the Mugg[?] Language engraved on a
silver plate found in a cave at Islamabad'.[83] The inscription is a most
curious one, and probably the only one available at the time which
described the birth, marriage, renunciation and enlightenment of the
Buddha, about whom little was known at that time. The communication, however, like many others, did not receive the scholarly attention
it deserved. It remained like a streak of lightning, which, after casting a
bright light on an obscure fact, plunged all into darkness greater than
before; and hence we find that in spite of this communication, fanciful
theories about the Buddha continued to prevail. To give only two
examples: in 1816 a reader styling himself Mythologus, wrote to the
Editor of the *Asiatic Journal*:

> Buddha I regard as a common name, and as no other than a dialectical
> variation of the English word God. . . . God, Bod, Wod, Godam, Wodim
> Odin, are words of similar signification, and constitute a common, not a
> proper name. Thus, I would say, that Isis and Osiris were the bods o

Buddhas of the Egyptians, and Jupiter and Pallasthe, the bods or buddhas of the Greeks.[84]

The second article, also published in the *Asiatic Journal* in 1823, gave an 'account of the founder of the Buddhist religion' saying:

Fo, or Boudda, was the son of some Indian monarch, who being sent by his father to negotiate a peace with a neighbouring monarch to whom he was tributary, and to whom he had failed to pay tribute, succeeded so well, as not merely to procure a remission of the tribute, but to gain the hand of his daughter in marriage. On his return to the court of his father, he left the affairs of his father's kingdom, and his new wife, and retiring into the desert, was visited by some genii, who suggested to him the laws which he afterwards established for the conduct of his followers.[85]

It was only after the labours of French scholars like Burnouf and Remusat among others, that the history of Buddhism could be adequately constructed, so that, in 1851, Edward Salisbury could say:

It may be taken for granted that Buddhism is of Indian origin. The time has been, when from the want of sufficient materials . . . men of great learning could differ on the question, whether the originator of this religious system was a native of Hindustan, or of Scythia, or a negro. But there is no longer any ground for such disputation.[86]

The year 1787 proved a landmark in the history of the Society for another reason. At its meeting of 6 July, Sir William Jones submitted to the Society a proposal for having the Society's transactions printed by the Superintendent of the Company's press. The proposal was approved and Jones was requested by the Society to conclude the necessary agreement. With this, Jones was able to give a practical foundation to a project he had visualised, in his very first discourse to the Society. He had said:

Let all curious and learned men be invited to send their tracts to our secretary, for which they ought immediately to receive our thanks; and, if towards the end of each year, we should be supplied with a sufficiency of valuable materials to fill a volume, let us present our *Asiatic Miscellany* to the literary world . . .[87]

The plan for publication was however delayed, partly because the papers contributed to the Society in 1784 and 1785 were not so numerous as to make a volume. Meanwhile, Francis Gladwin, a founder-member of the Society, undertook as a private venture the publication of what he called the *Asiatick Miscellany*, the first volume of which was published in Calcutta in 1785 and the second the following year. The *Asiatick Miscellany* carried, among other items, several of Jones's writings, including his hymns to the Hindu deities Kamadeva, Narayana, Saraswati, Ganga, Indra and Surya, four translations of Sanskrit and Arabic verses and the famous poem 'On Parent's Knees'. Primarily because of Jones's numerous contributions, the *Miscellany* was taken to be the Society's official publication, but Jones vehemently denied that the *Asiatick Miscellany* had anything to do with the Society. On 11 September 1787, he wrote to Joseph Cooper Walker: '*The Asiatick Miscellany* . . . is not the publication of our Society, who mean to print no scraps, nor any mere translations. It was the undertaking of a private gentleman.'[88]

Jones found that no Calcutta publisher was ready to undertake publication of the Society's Transactions on his own responsibility. Finally, Manuel Cantopher, Superintendent of the Company's printing office, agreed to take on the job provided each member of the Society purchased at least one copy of the book at Rs 20 per copy.[89] The Government did not give any financial support, and its apathy towards the project is borne out by Jones's letter to the second Earl Spencer: 'Do not raise too high your expectations of entertainment or instruction from the Transactions of our Society, which they print so slowly (the Government constantly using the Press for Orders, Regulations, etc.) that, I left only eight sheets printed, though we have materials for two volumes in quarto.'[90]

The first volume of the Society's Transactions, entitled *Asiatic Researches*, eventually appeared in early 1789. Jones was apprehensive about its success and was not to know that the *Researches* would take Europe almost by storm: that a pirated edition would be brought out in 1798 and that in 1805 it would be published in French.[91] Ironically, Jones even feared it might end in winding up the Society. On 27 February 1789 he wrote to Wilkins: 'The ships of this season will carry home seven hundred copies of our first volume of Transactions; and the second will be ready, I hope, next year: but unless the impression should be sold in London, Harington & Morris (who print the book at their hazard) will be losers, and we must dissolve the Society.'[92]

The Society, however, continued to flourish.

The year 1788 saw valuable contributions from the Society. William Jones's annual discourse, in keeping with his plan of tracing the origins of the five principal Asiatic nations, was devoted to the land of Tartary and the Tartars. Jones admitted that he was not familiar with the Tartar languages and that his observations might not be extremely accurate. The Tartars, according to him, had no proficiency in the arts and the sciences in the early ages. They seemed however to have adopted the traditions and religious beliefs of the Arabs, their own history beginning with their legendary hero and patriarch, Oghuz, whom they placed some four thousand years ago. He concluded by saying that the greater part of Asia from the remotest age had been inhabited by the Hindus, the Arabs and the Tartars, 'all of them so different in form and features, languages, manners and religions, that, if they sprang originally from a common root, they must have been separated for ages.'[93]

Much more important was Jones's paper, 'On the Chronology of the Hindus', presented to the Society on 7 February 1788. This is the first known attempt to draw up a comprehensive chronology of ancient India. Early Indian chronology, even now, is extremely obscure and clouded in myths and legends; to extract some semblance of historical order from the diverse and immense literary material is still not an easy task. To have attempted it in 1788 speaks of Jones's scholarly confidence and initiative.

On the basis of the Hindu scriptures then available (the *Puranas*, the *Manusamhita*, Jayadeva's *Gitagovinda* and other tracts) Jones divided ancient Indian history and chronology into four periods, of which the first three were chiefly mythological, 'founded on the dark enigmas of their astronomers, or on the heroic fictions of their poets.' The fourth age, according to Jones, 'cannot be carried further back than about two thousand years before Christ'. Today, with our greater knowledge, it seems a marvel that Jones achieved such accuracy in his estimate of early Indian history.[94]

The chronological reconstruction of the later period again goes to show the extent of Jones's scholarship, at a time when archaeological remains were still unexplored. He gives a detailed list of the Kings of Magadha starting from Pradyota in 2100 B.C. In 1602 B.C. comes Nanda, about whom Jones says 'This prince, of whom frequent mention is made in the Sanskrit books, is said to have been murdered, after a reign of a hundred years by a very learned and ingenious, but passionate and vindictive Brahman, whose name was Chanakya and who raised to the throne a man of the Maurya race named Chandra-gupta. By the death of Nanda and his sons, the *kshatriya* family of Pradyota became extinct.'⁹⁵

The main outline of events is remarkably correct, except for the dates assigned to Pradyota and Nanda. We must remember that Jones was reconstructing the chronology on the basis of the Puranas which always assigned fabulous periods of reigns to different kings. After narrating the murder of Nanda, Jones gave the genealogy of the Mauryan kings which read thus: Chandragupta 1502 B.C., Varisara, Asocaverdhana, Suyasas, Dasaratha, Saugata, Salisuca, Somasarman, Satadhanwas and Vrihadratha. 'On the death of the tenth Maurya king, his place was assumed by his Commander-in-Chief, Pushpamit-ra, of the Sunga nation or family.' Then followed the genealogy of the Sunga kings: Pushpamitra (1365 B.C.), Agnimitra, Sujyeshtha, Vasu-mitra, Abhadraca, Pulinda, Ghosha, Vajramitra, Bhagavata, and De-vabhuti. Devabhuti was killed by his minister Vasudeva, of the Canna race, who usurped the throne of Magadha. After four Canna kings, Jones came to the Sudra rulers of the Andhra family, which we may safely take to be the Satavahanas, since the first king mentioned by him is Balin whom we may take to be Salivahana. Jones mentioned twenty-one kings of the Andhra dynasty. The last ruler of this dynasty was Chandrabija, after whose death, said Jones, 'we hear no more of Magadha as an independent kingdom—on the whole, we may safely close the most authentic system of Hindu chronology that I have been yet able to procure, with the death of Chandrabija.'⁹⁶

To draw up this chronology, Jones depended not only on the Hindu texts but on his pundits, Radhakanta Sarman and Ramlochan. He also drew upon the works of European scholars like Paterson, Le Gentil and Deguignes, beside consulting the Chinese texts, the *Ain-i-Akbari* of Abul Fazl and the *Dabistan*.

Another important contribution to the Society in 1788 was the translation of the inscriptions on the pillar at Firuz Shah Kotla in Delhi, then known as the 'staff' or the 'lat' of Firuz Shah. Impressions of the inscriptions were procured by Lieutenant Colonel Polier, who presented them to the Society. The inscriptions were deciphered and translated by the famous pundit Radhakanta Sarman. Radhakanta deciphered only five, saying that it would require 'great attention and leisure' to decipher the others.⁹⁷

The others, as we now know, were Asokan inscriptions which, nearly half a century later, were deciphered by Prinsep. The inscriptions which Radhakanta was able to translate were in the *kutila* script, which Wilkins had already made known when he deciphered the Buddal pillar inscription. Since the *kutila* characters resemble the Devanagari, and the language of the inscriptions was Sanskrit, Wilkins and Radhakanta had no great difficulty over them. The five Kotla inscriptions, extolled the virtues of the Sakambhari king Amilla Deva, his son Visala Deva, Prativahamana Tilaca and his prime minister Sri Sallaca.[97a]

The meeting at which Pandit Radhakanta presented the translation of the Firuz Shah Kotla inscriptions, saw another communication of importance. This was an extract of a letter from Alexander Davidson, the Governor of Madras, forwarded to the Society by Samuel Davis. The letter was accompanied by drawings of two Roman coins found at Nellore, about a hundred miles north-west of Madras. While the fact of Indo-Roman trade had already been established, Davidson's communication is nevertheless significant as it marks the first recognition of the importance of numismatics in the study of Indian history. This communication also highlights the tragedy of the loss of valuable sources of Indian history. As Davidson says in his letter, the coins were found in a little pot by a peasant while he was ploughing his field. He sold the coins as gold and many of them were melted down. The nawab of the place, however, was able to procure thirty of these coins which he showed to Davidson, allowing him to choose only two. Davidson found that while many of the coins were as fresh and beautiful as if they had left the mint only the day before, others were defaced and perforated, probably from having been worn as pendants or ornaments for the arms.[98]

A strange entry was recorded for 6 November 1788 in the volume of Manuscript Proceedings stating that the minutes of meetings held between 6 November 1788 and 5 November 1789 were mislaid. We have, however, the record of Jones's sixth discourse, presented to the Society on 19 February 1789. This discourse was devoted to Persia and the Persians, a field of study to which Jones had already devoted many years. Jones's discourse on the Persians was the fourth in his study of the five principal Asiatic nations, and is remarkable for his interesting, though erroneous, generalizations. First, Jones stressed the similarity between the ancient language of Persia, Zend, and Sanskrit, remarking that hundreds of Parsi nouns were pure Sanskrit and that

'*Parsi* was derived from the various Indian dialects.' On this basis he concluded that a powerful Hindu monarchy existed in Iran long before the Assyrian, or Pishdadi government, adding that 'its history has been engrafted on that of the Hindus, who founded the monarchies of Ayodhya and Indraprastha: that the language of the first Persian empire was the mother of the Sanskrit, and consequently of the Zend and Parsi, as well as of Greek, Latin and Gothic.'[99] Jones concluded that it was Persia which was 'the true centre of population, of knowledge, of languages, and of arts', and that the people who were to form the nations of India, Arabia and Tartary migrated from Persia. Thus, Jones took 'a long step toward an hypothesis of common origin'[100] although as we now know his conclusions were not free from error.

The Society's future seemed very uncertain at the time. In October 1789 Jones wrote to Justice Hyde: 'The Society is a puny, rickety child, and must be fed with pap; nor shall it die by my fault; but die it must, for I cannot alone support it.'[101] The number of meetings, as well as attendance at them had dwindled sharply—at times only six members were present.[102] Among those who attended the Society's meetings were some of the most prominent members of the British administration, including the Governor-General, Lord Cornwallis himself. But it must be noted that even during the Society's worst period, the Government of the day gave little evidence of concrete support to the Society, financial or otherwise.

Apart from the sixth discourse by William Jones, there is record of only one other article in 1789. This was a dissertation on the 'Antiquity of the Indian Zodiac', also by William Jones, presented to the Society on 5 November. In this paper, Jones tried to refute the theory of the French mathematician, Montucla, that the Indian zodiac was borrowed from the Greeks and the Arabs. According to Jones, the Brahmans of India were too proud to borrow their science from other nations and the signs of the Indian zodiac differed too much from the Greek to be a mere copy. Here too, Jones was fascinated with the theory of common origin, suggesting that both, the Hindu and the Greeks, received the zodiac from an older nation. He also discounted Newton's theory that the practice of observing the stars began in Egypt, saying instead that it had begun 'with the rudiments of civil society, in the country of those whom we call Chaldeans; from which it was propagated into Egypt, India, Greece, Italy and Scandinavia, before the reign of Sisac or Sacya, who by conquest spread a new system of religion and philosophy from the Nile to the Ganges about a thousand years before Christ.'[103]

The theory of a common origin of the Zodiac led to a violent controversy at the time, but it did lay stress on the fact that intellectual development in ancient India could be compared with that of Greece and Rome. Another significant landmark in 1789 was the publication of the English translation of Kalidasa's *Sakuntala*. Jones tells us in the preface that he had come across references to certain books in north India termed '*natac*', which were said to contain a 'large portion of ancient history, without any mixture of fable'. He had seen this reference in *Lettres Edifantes et curieuses* written by Père Pons,[104] even before he arrived in India. Soon after coming to India, he tried 'to procure access to those books, either by the help of translation, if they had been translated, or by learning the languages in which they were originally composed.' But he was disappointed. The Brahmans told him that the *natacs* were not histories but popular works, full of fables, consisting of conversations in prose and verse, held before ancient kings in their public assemblies. The other Europeans told him that they were merely discourses on dancing, music and poetry. Then one day the learned pundit Radhakant surprised Jones by telling him that the *natacs* corresponded to the English plays which were performed publicly in winter in Calcutta. When Jones asked Radhakant which one he regarded as the best, the latter unhesitatingly mentioned *Sakuntala*. Jones was soon able to find a manuscript copy[105] of the play and with his teacher, Ramlochan's help, began to prepare an interlineary version in Latin, since he wanted to make use of the similarity between the two languages to prepare a faithful European version. 'I then turned it word for word into English,' says Jones, 'and afterwards, without adding or suppressing any material sentence, disengaged it from the stiffness of a foreign idiom, and prepared the faithful translation of the Indian drama. . . . One of the greatest curiosities that the literature of Asia has yet brought to light.'[106]

When the play reached Europe, it aroused more excitement than any previous translation excepting the *Arabian Nights*. The play was widely reviewed and welcomed. It was like the opening up of a new continent in the world of letters, a breath of fresh air from the orient. The *Blackwood's Edinburgh Magazine* wrote in its review of the play:

Will our readers turn from these fierce, wild and turbulent passions, breathed out from the constantly agitated bosom of European life, as exhibited in the English and German drama. . . . One flight of the imagination and we find ourselves almost on another earth. . . . It is delightful to sink away into those old green and noiseless sanctuaries, to look on the Brahmins as they pass their whole lives in silent and reverential adoration,—virgins playing with the antelopes and bright-plumaged birds among those gorgeous woods—and, as the scene shifts, to find ourselves amid the old magnificence of oriental cities, or wafted on the chariot of some deity up to the palaces of the sky.[107]

In spite of such appreciation, the European intelligentsia found it difficult to digest the fact that India, which they felt possessed an inferior civilization, could have produced such literature in remote antiquity. Many of them expressed doubts about the authenticity of the play. Jones did not consider these critics worthy of a serious reply, but voiced his dismay in a letter to Sir Joseph Banks: 'That the poem of Kalidasa entertained you, gives me great pleasure; but it diverts me extremely to hear from others, that the authenticity of the poem is doubted in England.'[108] Moreover, Jones in his Preface had called Kalidasa 'the Shakespeare of India', to which the same *Blackwood's Edinburgh Magazine* which wished to transport its readers from the land of strife to the land of beauty, objected thus:

To call [Kalidasa] the Shakespeare of India—not perhaps a very philo-sophical opinion, for neither the human mind nor human life did ever so exist in India, as to create such kind of faculties as those of Shakespeare, or to furnish field for their inspiration.[109]

The *Quarterly Review* was no less critical:

It is often dangerous to raise high expectations, by appropriating well-known and sacred names to new or foreign candidates for fame, and certainly when Sir W. Jones incautiously, and probably in another sense, designated Kalidasa as the Indian Shakespeare, he created a false impress-ion. . . . Nothing can be more curious than both the similitude and dissimi-litude of the Indian to the different schools of the European drama.[110]

What these critics did not know was that Jones had gone beyond calling Kalidasa the Shakespeare of India. In a letter to Thomas Law, he said: 'I am deep in the second act of a Sanskrit play, near 2000 years old, and so much like Shakespeare, that I should have thought our great dramatic poet had studied Kalidasa.'[111] Such views, were, however, expressed in a private letter, otherwise one can imagine the storm they would have raised among European literati.

In spite of the criticism, the popularity of *Sakuntala* continued to grow. By the end of the nineteenth century it had run into over eighty translations in addition to twenty-one editions of the text and eighteen critical studies. It was translated into English, French, German, Dutch, Swedish, Danish, Italian, Polish, Bohemian, Russian and Spanish besides the Indian languages [112] and had come to be regarded as worthy of a place among the hundred best books of the world.[113] The most effective translation next to Jones's was that of George Forster. It was this translation which caught Herder's attention, who in turn introduced Goethe to *Sakuntala* who immortalized the play in these lines:

> Would'st thou the young year's blossoms
> and the fruits of its decline,
> And all by which the soul is charmed,
> enraptured, feasted, fed?
> Would'st thou the Earth and Heaven
> in one sole name combine?
> I name thee, O Sakoontala! and all
> at once is said'.[114]

Nor was this enthusiasm confined to Europe. Towards the mid-nineteenth century *Sakuntala* dawned on the American horizon. Emerson had the title on his reading list and Thoreau copied several passages from Jones's translation into his private notebook.[115] Indeed, as Mukherjee rightly comments, after Jones's publication of the *Sakuntala* and the *Gita Govinda* no one could deny the merits of Indian literature and even Walpole and Mill had to recognize the beauty of the Hindu drama.[116]

What is perhaps more important is that by bringing to light Kalidasa and his *Sakuntala*, Jones awakened Indians to the beauty of their own literature. The prevailing ignorance about Indian literature amongst Indians in the eighteenth century is indicated by the fact that Jones could procure only a Bengali recension of the play, and the pundit community were ignorant about the content of the play. Jawaharlal Nehru remarked correctly that it is to Jones and to other European scholars that 'India owes a deep debt of gratitude for the rediscovery of her past literature'.[117]

The year 1790 does not seem to have been an important year for the Society. There are records of only six meetings during the entire year. On 25 February, at the second meeting, Jones delivered his seventh anniversary discourse, devoted to the Chinese. Discussing the origins of the Chinese people, Jones noted that there were four opinions in existence, but all of these were 'rather peremptorily asserted than supported by argument and evidence.' He felt that three of the theories—that the Chinese were an original race dwelling from time immemorial in the land they now possessed; that they sprang from the same stock as the Hebrews and the Arabs; and that they were originally Tartars who descended in clans from the steppes of Imaus, could be rejected outright. He found substance in the fourth theory, and set out additional arguments that the Chinese were originally Hindus of the *kshatriya* caste, who, after abandoning their tribe, wandered into the land they now possessed, and there, gradually forgetting the rites and religions of their ancestors, developed the mode of life that was now followed.

This theory came under severe attack, especially from Chinese scholars. T.C. Fan, for instance, charged that Jones, in his eagerness to prove his theory, contradicted some of the important statements made in his article 'On the Second Classical Book of the Chinese'. His meagre knowledge of China was exhibited in the flimsy parallels he drew between Hindu and the Chinese ceremonies and popular superstitions. Jones, however, admitted that he had little time for Chinese linguistic studies, and, as Arthur Waley observed, no one's reputation was hurt by Jones's seventh discourse, not even his own.[118]

The other communication of importance during this period was Jones's 'Supplement to the Essay on Indian Chronology'.[119] This essay was the result of his newly-developed interest in Indian astronomy, which was partly due to the exertions of another great orientalist, Samuel Davis, on the subject. In 1788, Sir Robert Chambers had obtained in Banaras a copy of the ancient Hindu treatise on astronomy, the *Surya Siddhanta*, which he passed on to Samuel Davis for study. Davis found the technical terms used in the treatise very obscure. Soon however, with the assistance of a *teeka* or commentary on the treatise procured through Jonathan Duncan, then at Banaras, Davis was able to study in detail the ancient text on Hindu astronomy. He sent a lengthy essay on this treatise to Jones, who included the essay in the second volume of the *Researches*. In his essay, Davis wrote of the value of astronomical researches in determining the chronology of India.[120] Jones was not only aware of this fact but became perhaps the first person to put it in practice. By the time Jones wrote his *Supplement*, he had studied not only the *Surya Siddhanta*, but other lesser-known tracts such as *Varahasamhita, Panchasiddhantica, Ratnamala* and *Parasari Samhita*. Jones utilized all this knowledge to expound on two of his favourite subjects of enquiry: the theory of the common origin of man and the similarity between the Mosaic and the Indian chronologies. The latter seemed to be a requirement of the times, for, as new lands and people were being increasingly discovered, the European intelligentsia were naturally eager to relate its civilization to that of the newly-discovered ones, if only to prove their own superiority. Jones was, however, above such unscholarly prejudices, and instead of denigrating the alien civilization related it to the European to highlight the brotherhood of man. He wrote:

> We may safely conclude that the Mosaic and Indian chronologies are perfectly consistent, that Manu son of Brahma, was the Adima, or first, created mortal, and consequently our Adam; that Manu, child of the Sun, was preserved with seven others, in a *bahitra* or capacious ark, from an universal deluge, and must therefore be our Noah.[121]

Another subject that interested Jones almost from the time he came to India was the music of Hindustan. In April 1784 he wrote to Charles Wilkins: 'My present pursuit is the Indian system of music, which is comprised, I am told, in a book called *Sengheit Derpan*.'[122]

He was surprised to find how ancient and rich the system of Indian music was and the honour the Indians gave to the art and the science of music. In August 1787 he wrote to his former pupil, now the second Earl Spencer:

> I have many discoveries to make in the music of India. In the reign of Vikramaditya, near 2000 years ago, the art flourished in this country, but, since the Mohammedan conquest, it has declined, and is now almost lost in Bengal . . . The Hindus believe music, as well as poetry, to be celestial arts, practised in heaven from eternity, and revealed to man by different Gods. I am now collating a very ancient Sanskrit book on music in beautiful verse, but very concise; and therefore, obscure. These inquiries go beyond the mere gratification of curiosity: they may suggest improvements in our own musical system.[123]

Jones studied all the Sanskrit and Persian texts on music available at the time, including Damodara's *Sangit-Darpana*, Ahobila's *Sangita Parijata* (in Persian) and Soma's *Ragavibodha* and *Sabhavinod*. He then read to the Society his dissertation 'On the Musical Modes of the Hindus' on 11 November 1790, which was published in the third volume of the *Researches*. With this Jones became the first European to have published a comparative study of Indian music.

For several years, Jones had looked forward to 1790 as marking 'the happy limit of our residence in this unpropitious climate'.[124] But there was now so much to engross his mind that even though he had 'not an hour in the day nor a minute in the hour'[125] at his command, he was thinking of leaving India only by the last year of the eighteenth century.[126] For him, every day and every year seemed to be one of achievement. In 1790, the second volume of the *Researches* was printed[127] and he was already deep in work on the third volume. He had also been able, through Henry Dundas, to bring the first volume of the *Researches* to the attention of King George III, and must have been pleasantly surprised by the royal answer. He wrote to Dundas that he was happy 'that what was intended as a mark of dutiful respect has been received with gracious condescension'.[128] Moreover, by now he almost had a mastery over Sanskrit. 'The good Brahmins', he wrote to Lady Spencer, 'who do not know how much I am assisted by Latin and Greek, are astonished at my progress and make their children copy my Sanskrit verses.'[129] Again to Sir John Macpherson, 'I jabber Sanskrit every day with the *pundits*, and hope, long before I leave India, to understand it as well as I do Latin.'[130] This knowledge of Sanskrit in turn intensified his desire for knowledge of India. Earlier, he had expressed his ambition to know India better than any other European had ever done,[131] but he was now thinking in terms of acquiring a 'complete knowledge of India', which he admitted could only be attained in this country itself.[132]

The most important reason for his not being able to leave India at this time was his preoccupation with the preparation of the Digest of Hindu laws. Jones desired to see that the inhabitants of the land were governed according to their own laws. He was aware of the difficulties of putting this into practice, which was also one of the reasons why, almost as soon as he started learning Sanskrit, he decided that one of his first tasks would be a translation of the Ordinances of Manu.

Translation of an ancient tract on the laws by which the people were governed was important not only because the indigenous advisers were not always to be trusted, but also because English judges, in general, could not be expected to learn the two languages, Sanskrit and Persian, in which the laws of the Hindus and the Mohammadans were framed. A translation of the law books would enable English judges to ensure 'among ten millions of our black subjects, that security of descendable property, a want of which, . . . has prevented the people of Asia from improving their agriculture and mechanical arts'.[133]

For this task of compilation, Jones offered his services free, asking the Company only to defray the cost of employing pundits and *maulvis*. The proposal was readily accepted, and soon Jones was so involved with the project as to 'devote [his] leisure almost entirely to that object'.[134]

One might expect that with the *Digest* occupying so much time and attention, Jones's activities and interest in the Society would have slackened. The year 1791, on the contrary, saw him exerting himself more than ever. He was editing the third volume of *Researches*, in spite of problems he was having with his eyes, and preparing other papers to be read at the Society. At the first meeting of the Society in 1791, he presented a translation of a copper-plate inscription recording a 'Royal Grant of Land in Carnata', which had been forwarded to the Society by Alexander Macleod.[135] This inscription brought to light the existence of the kingdom of Vijayanagar as well as its rulers, especially the famous Krishnadeva Raya. What is more important, the inscription enabled Jones to deduce almost the exact dates of the Vijayanagar empire. In a note to the thirty-first *sloka* or stanza, he says: 'The date of the grant follows the donee. . . . The Sacabda began in Y.C. 78, and the grant was made in Y.C. 1526, the very year in which Babur took possession of Delhi'.[136]

The second meeting of the Society in 1791 saw William Jones present his eighth anniversary discourse. This was devoted to the oriental 'borderers, mountaineers, and islanders', and was a wide-ranging survey covering the Abyssinians, Afghans of Jewish origin, Gypsies of Hindu descent, the Tibetans and the Burmese. In the discourse, he developed the idea of families of languages further, though as we can now see, his conclusions were not free from error. For instance, his argument that the Ethiops were 'the same people with the first Egyptians, and consequently, as it might easily be shown, with the original Hindus'[137] was not tenable.

Another important communication which seems to have gone unnoticed by subsequent writers was an 'account of the Battle of Panipat and of the events leading to it', presented to the Society on 21 April. Written in Persian by one Casi Raja Pundit, this is perhaps the only eye-witness account of the third battle of Panipat and thus an important source article. Casi Raja Pundit, as we are told by the translator, James Browne, was a *muttasadi* in the service of Shuja-ud-Daula. Since he had some Maratha friends who were close to Sadasivarao, Casi Raja played a part in efforts to secure peace between the Marathas and the Rohilla Chief. These efforts were unsuccessful. When the battle was fought at Panipat, Casi Raja Pundit recorded the sequence of events for posterity, giving in detail the strength of both armies, their strategies and the course of the battle. While presenting the English translation of this account to the Society, James Browne made a remark which is significant for the times:

> I cannot avoid believing that the great events of this country will hereafter be sought for with as much diligence, as those of the early part of European history are at present: if I am not mistaken in this, the battle of Panipat will be among those events, which will claim the greatest attention, both as a military action, and as an era, from which the reduction of the Mahratta power may be fixed, who otherwise would probably have long ago reduced the whole Hindostan to their obedience.[138]

The other interesting paper read this year was on the 'Mystical Poetry of the Persians and the Hindus'. As an example of Hindu mystic thought, Jones appended to the essay a translation of *Gita-Govinda*, by the thirteenth-century poet, Jayadeva. He had translated the poem much earlier, in 1789, when learning Sanskrit; but now by publishing it in the *Researches* he was able to make the entire literary world familiar with this greatest of Indian lyric poets. To retain the fidelity of the translation, he first translated it word for word and then polished it into prose which is itself lyrical. Lest the composition itself or its beauty be doubted in the west, Jones assured the readers that 'not a single image or idea has been added by the translator.' [139]

By 1792 Jones seems to have reconciled himself to the fact that he would soon have to send his wife Anna to England in view of her constant ill-health in the Indian climate. The date fixed for her departure was January 1793[140] and he hoped to follow soon. The welfare of the Society, however, lay heavy on his mind. In October 1792 he wrote to Samuel Davis:

> India agrees with me so well, that, if it were not for her [Lady Jones's] sake, I would not leave it even in 1795; but I cannot persuade myself that a dissolution of our Asiatic Society will be the consequence of my departure,

while you are constantly making discoveries in Astronomy; Wilford, in Geography, and others, in different branches of Natural History.[41]

And indeed, the two scholars besides, of course, Jones himself, enriched the Society's proceedings in 1792.

Samuel Davis,[42] born in 1760, came to India as an engineer-officer in the Company's service in Madras. When he was posted to Calcutta, he was sent with Turner to Tibet and being himself an excellent artist, brought back from there a large collection of drawings of the country, its temples and its buildings. On his return to Calcutta, he joined the civil service and was appointed collector of Burdwan, and later was sent as judge to Banaras and the Chief Magistrate. Being a linguist and greatly interested in astronomy, he picked up acquaintance with Brahman pundits and engaged himself in identifying astronomical references in Sanskrit works. He even built an observatory in Banaras. It was there that he met William Jones and the two soon developed a close friendship founded on their common interest in ancient India. During his stay in Banaras, Samuel Davis became a target for Vazir Ali Khan, the disinherited son of the King of Avadh. After killing the Resident, Mr Cherny, Vazir Ali's 200-strong party raided Davis's house. Davis with his wife, two children and a Portuguese nurse took shelter on the terrace which could be approached only by a narrow staircase. Wielding a spear, Davis kept the attackers at bay for over an hour till the English troops arrived. After the incident, Davis was called once more to Calcutta where he developed a friendship with Marquess Wellesley. On his return to England he was asked by a Committee of the House of Commons to make a report on the state of revenues of India, later known as the *Fifth Report*. Eventually, the strain told on his health and he died in 1819, at his house at Croydon, in his fifty-ninth year.

Davis's fame rests mainly on his contribution to the study of Indian astronomy. His communication, 'On the Astronomical Computation of the Hindus' was followed by his translation of the *Surya-Siddhanta*. He became 'the first European who drew a knowledge of Indian Astronomy from the fountain-head.'[43] Another important paper, 'On the Indian Cycle of Sixty Years' was read by Jones himself to the Society in 1792. The communication once again highlighted the level attained in ancient India in astronomy and algebra.

Wilford's essay 'On Egypt and other countries adjacent to the Cali River, or Nile of Ethiopia', was the first of many essays in which, on the basis of ancient Sanskrit texts, he tried to prove far-fetched theories, which at that time were generally accepted. This essay, published in the third volume of the *Researches*, took up three meetings of the Society.[144] The essay was more an exercise in ancient geography in which Wilford tried to identify places on the basis of etymological similarities between the geographical names found in the *Puranas* and those mentioned in Greek texts. The fact that Egypt and India had been closely linked by trade in ancient times had already been established, and Sir William Jones had even argued that in some remote age, a group of Egyptians had set up a colony in what is now known as Tirhut in Bihar. Wilford, on the other hand, pointed out that the movement was the other way round: that it was a group of Indians during the time of Krishna who settled in Egypt. In an observation which is far-fetched but interesting, Wilford remarked: 'Not only the land of Egypt, and the countries bordering the Nile, but even Africa, itself, had formerly the appelation of Aeria, from the numerous settlements, I suppose, of the *Ahirs*, or Shepherds, as they are called in the spoken Indian dialects.'[145]

Although Sir William Jones had warned against drawing fanciful conclusions from superficial similarities, in this case, Jones himself fell a prey to this theory. In his Presidential remarks he supported Wilford's contentions although he added that he 'was not fully satisfied with many parts of Mr. Wilford's Essay, which are founded on so uncertain a basis as conjectural Etymology.'[146]

Jones himself could not follow up his doubts as he was extremely busy with the preparation of the *Digest of Indian Laws*, something which he prized more than recognition of his work from the King himself. Later, Wilford admitted that he had been tricked by his pundit, and regretted that through him, William Jones was also deceived in the matter.

In February 1792 the ninth anniversary discourse by Sir William Jones was delivered before the Society. Here, Jones summed up the results of his inquiry into the common origin of man, made in the previous six discourses, adding that he believed the whole human race to have sprung from three branches, the stem being the human beings preserved after the universal deluge in Persia. From there, according to Jones, they branched out into the Indian, Arabian and the Tartar races. According to one critic,[147] the ninth discourse was Jones's most ingenious one in trying to prove that the human race had originated in Persia.

Reviewing Jones's discourses on the principal Asiatic nations, Wilson later remarked: 'His views were ingenious, and clearly and eloquently expressed, but the dissertations were premature for the materials for such inquiries were defective.'[148]

An article on Hindu astronomy by John Playfair is mentioned as being written in October 1792. (It was received and published much later, in the fourth volume of the *Researches.*) Jones had prefixed the second volume of the *Researches* with an 'Advertisement' inviting learned European societies to 'transmit to the Secretary of the [Asiatic] Society in Bengal a collection of short and precise queries on every branch of Asiatic History,' since he hoped that the Society would gradually be able to provide answers to them which 'may prove in the highest degree beneficial to mankind.'

In response, John Playfair, Professor of Mathematics at Edinburgh, sent to the Society six questions with his own remarks on the development of the mathematical sciences in ancient India. Playfair was convinced that the Indians had in ancient times turned their attention to certain arithmetical investigations of which there was no trace in the writings of even the Greek scientists. He desired the Society to find out if there were books on geometry and arithmetic in ancient India, and also suggested a complete translation of the *Surya Siddhanta*, the drawing up of a catalogue of Sanskrit books on Indian astronomy with a short account of each, and procuring descriptions of astronomical buildings and instruments of ancient India. He recommended that the skies should be studied together with an Indian astronomer to identify stars and constellations for which there were Sanskrit names.

The third volume of the *Asiatick Researches* carrying Wilford's article on the Nile was published in 1793 which was otherwise an uneventful year. At the four meetings held during the entire year,[149] only the tenth anniversary discourse, presented by Jones on 28 February, was of interest. This Discourse on 'Asiatic History, Civil and Natural', is, from our point of view the most important of Jones's discourses, for in it he announced his identification of the 'Palibothra' of the Greeks with Pataliputra, and 'Sandracottus' with Chandragupta.

Attempts had been made earlier to locate the site of Palibothra, capital of the flourishing kingdom Prasii, to which Megasthenes had come as an ambassador of the Greek general, Seleucos Nicator; but

what continued to vex scholars was the identity of the river Erranoboas, at whose confluence with the river Ganga, said the Greek
historian Arrian, Palibothra was situated. Since Arrian had said that
Erranoboas was in magnitude only next to the Ganga and the Indus, it
was natural for one school of scholars, which included the historian
Robertson, to identify Erranoboas with the Jamuna and so fix the
situation of Palibothra at Allahabad.[150] This school also pointed out the
similarity in sound between Prayag, the ancient name of Allahabad,
and Prasii, the ancient apellation of the kingdom of which Palibothra
was the capital.

It must be said to the credit of Major James Rennell that he at one
stage did identify Palibothra with the modern city of Patna. He had
reached this conclusion on the basis of the geographical location of the
city provided by Pliny; but what intrigued Rennell in this identification was again the identity of Erranoboas about which he confessed, 'I
cannot apply the name Erranoboas to any particular river'.[151] It was
this uncertainty that led him to seek an alternative site in Kanauj.
Announcing the important discovery, Jones said:

> I cannot help mentioning a discovery which accident threw in my way,
> though my proofs must be reserved for an essay which I have destined for
> the fourth volume of your Transactions. To fix the situation of that
> Palibothra (for there may have been several of the name) which was visited
> and described by Megasthenes had always appeared a very difficult
> problem; for though it could not have been *Prayaga*, where no ancient
> metropolis ever stood, nor Canyacubja, which has no epithet at all
> resembling the word used by the Greeks; nor Gaur, otherwise called
> Lacshamanavati, which all know to be a town comparatively modern, yet
> we could not confidently decide that it was Pataliputra, though names and
> most circumstances nearly correspond, because that renowned capital
> extended from the confluence of the Sone and the Ganges and Errano-
> boas, which the accurate M. d'Anville had pronounced to be the Yamuna;
> but this only difficulty was removed, when I found in a classical Sanskrit
> book, near 2000 years old, that Hiranyabahu, or golden-armed, which the
> Greeks changed into Erranoboas, or the river with a lovely murmur, was in
> fact another name for the Sone itself; though Megasthenes, from ignorance
> or inattention, has named them separately.[152]

Although one would feel that the controversy about the identification of Palibothra was now settled, it was not so. The first person to
differ with Jones was Francis Wilford, who conjectured that Pali-.
bothra was Rajmahal in the vicinity of the modern town of Bhagalpur.

Picking up Wilford's trail, William Francklin, an officer in the service of the East India Company, published in 1817 an *Inquiry concerning the site of ancient Palibothra*. Francklin identified the river Erranoboas with the river Chandan and travelled along this river right up to its source near Deoghar. He concluded that Palibothra lay somewhere in Bhagalpur district.[153]

When Francklin's book was published, the controversy was once again revived. The contemporary magazine, *Asiatic Journal*, carried an interesting letter dated December 1817 from a William Young who claimed that he had arrived at the same conclusion as Sir William Jones in 1777.[154] According to him, soon after his arrival in Patna in 1775, he became acquainted with a learned Brahman called Suboor Tewary, who informed him that Patna was called Pataliputra in ancient times.

The remarkable similarity between *Pataliputra* and *Palibothra* immediately struck Young, but again the major problem that faced him was the identity of the river Erranoboas. His first conjecture was that this river was the Fulgoo which flowed near Patna, but he rejected the theory on the ground that the Fulgoo was 'not a large stream even in the rainy season.' At this point, the Brahman came to his aid and told him that the Sone had flowed by Patna in ancient times but had gradually changed its course over the years, and now flowed about twenty miles west of the city. According to Young, he had conveyed his discovery to several people like Thomas Law, Sir George Barlow and Lewis Smith long before Sir William arrived in India.

Young's story seems plausible on the whole, except that one fails to understand why he should not have published his discovery through an article in any journal and secondly, the people he said he had written to made no mention of it to Jones although they had been in communication with him.

As with the identification of Palibothra, identification of the 'Sandracottus' mentioned in the Greek texts had also been attempted earlier than Jones. It is said that Maridas Pillai, the chief interpreter to the Supreme Council of Pondicherry, in his translation of the *Bhagavadam* in 1769 listed Chandragupta as Sandragouten; and this in turn led the French scholar Deguignes to identify Chandragupta with Sandracottus, fixing 303 B.C. as the date of the emperor's accession to the throne of Magadh.[155] However, it can hardly be denied that it was Jones's contribution which became part of Indian history. Announcing the discovery to the Society, Jones said:

This discovery led to another of greater moment; for Chandragupta, who, from a military adventurer, became, like Sandracottus, the sovereign of Upper Hindustan, actually fixed the seat of his empire at Pataliputra,. where he received ambassadors from foreign princes; and was no other than that very Sandracottus who concluded a treaty with Seleucus Nicator; so that we have solved another problem, to which we before alluded.[156]

This discovery was also challenged by subsequent scholars. As late as 1920, M.K. Acharya, in a paper presented to the first session of the All India Oriental Conference, called this discovery 'the basic blunder in the reconstruction of Indian chronology', contending that it was actually Chandragupta I of the Gupta dynasty who was the Sandracottus of the Greek texts, the Maurya dynasty coming much earlier than Alexander's invasion. While presenting his thesis, Acharya admitted that his hypothesis resulted in big gaps, especially after the Gupta period, and felt that the task of reconstruction of the chronology of this period would be 'opposed' by western orientalists. Acharya saw a definite vested interest on the part of western Indologists in accepting Jones's discovery. It would, however, be enough to point out that nowhere has Jones, either in his correspondence or in his discourses, provided evidence of any particular motive in announcing this discovery. In fact, he considered 'plain truth as the beauty of historical composition'.[157] Nor can it be denied that this discovery is the 'sheet-anchor of Indian history', for, having once synchronised the history of India with that of Greece, it became possible to make calculations backwards and forwards with some certainty.[158] The discovery provided 'the sole firm ground in the quick-sands of Indian history',[159] and the eminent historian Beveridge likened it to 'the discovery of the identity between Sanskrit and Greek and Latin, which the philosopher Hegel described as resembling Columbus's discovery of the New World.'[160] Besides these two important discoveries, this discourse is important as well as interesting for Jones's views on history. He not only delineated the sources of ancient Indian history (the Puranas, the Itihasas and the dramas), but also laid stress on the importance of primary sources against the secondary ('in history, as in law, we must not follow streams when we may investigate fountains, nor admit any secondary proof where primary evidence is attainable'[161]).

Jones's eleventh discourse on the 'Philosophy of Asiatics' was delivered in 1794, the year of his death. He was only forty-eight then and at the height of his achievement. This discourse, again remarkable for the catholicity of Jones's outlook, contained a discussion on the five divisions of Asiatic philosophy: physiology and medicine, metaphysics and logic, ethics and jurisprudence, and natural philosophy and mathematics. This discourse revealed to the European intelligentsia the treasures of knowledge which lay in India. Jones himself expressed his astonishment at the discovery that an entire *Upanishad* was devoted to the internal parts of the human body 'with an enunciation of the nerves, veins, and arteries; a description of the heart, spleen and liver; and various disquisitions on the formation and growth of the foetus.' He not only showed acquaintance with the six systems of Indian philosophy, including Sankara's commentary on the Vedas, but stated: 'I can venture to affirm, without meaning to pluck a leaf from the never-fading laurels of our immortal Newton, that the whole of his theology, and part of his philosophy, may be found in the Vedas, and even in the works of the Sufis.'[162]

The subject of the discourse, as Jones admitted, was inexhaustible, and at the beginning of the following year, he hoped to 'close these general disquisitions with topics measureless in extent, but less abstruse than that which has this day been discussed.'[163]

Unfortunately Jones did not live to do this. A sudden inflammation of the liver, a disease common in Bengal those days, combined with the pressure of work for the *Digest*,[164] and his wife's absence, led to his early death; although according to Jones himself, 'a man who has nearly closed the forty-seventh year of his age, ... has a right to think of retirement...and ought to think chiefly of preparing himself for another'.[165]

William Jones had not only founded the Asiatic society, but had also been its brightest ornament. He had steered the Society successfully during its difficult periods between continuous economic crises, and gave it a foundation so solid that it survived for two centuries and continues to do so. It is of interest to see how Jones himself looked upon his labours in India. In a letter to the second Earl Spencer, on 23 August 1787, he wrote:

> To what shall I compare my literary pursuits in India? Suppose Greek literature to be known in modern Greece only, and there to be in the hands of priests and philosophers, and suppose them to be still worshippers of Jupiter and Apollo: suppose Greece to have been conquered successively by Goths, Huns, Vandals, Tartars, and lastly by the English, then suppose a court of judicature to be established by the British Parliament, at Athens, and an inquisitive Englishman to be one of the judges: suppose him to

learn Greek there, which none of his countrymen knew, and to read Homer, Pindar, Plato, which no other European had even heard of, such am I in this country, substituting Sanskrit for Greek, the Brahmans, for the priests of Jupiter, and Valmic, Vyasa, Kalidasa, for Homer, Plato, Pindar.[166]

Jones through his indefatigable labours[167] had resuscitated India's ancient culture not only for Europe but for India herself. Now India could boast of a poet as great as Shakespeare, a language that was superior to Greek and Latin, a philosophy that could rival the best of Greek philosophy, and an advanced system of astronomy that was independent of the Greek system. In fact, in one decade, more accurate information on the history and antiquities, on the arts, sciences, and literature of India had been given to the world, than had ever before appeared.[168] Moreover, in the course of his studies, Jones launched a number of new disciplines so that 'scholar after scholar looked back to Jones as the founder of, or the massive contributor to, his own chosen discipline.'[169] What was still more remarkable was the fact that he bore all this learning very lightly. 'No writer', remarks Lord Teignmouth, 'perhaps ever displayed so much learning, with so little affectation of it.' Jones, on the other hand, felt that all men were born with equal talent and capacity for improvement, and that if he had achieved anything remarkable, it was only due to his industry and patient thought. Here, Sir William Jones was certainly wrong.[170] Modesty combined with vast learning and an unbiased outlook towards an alien people and culture endeared Jones to the people of this land. Lord Teignmouth later recalled how a few days after Jones's death, when he met some pundits at a public durbar, they could 'neither restrain their tears for his loss, nor find terms to express their admiration at the wonderful progress which he had made, in the sciences which they professed'.[171] 'When we compare the shortness of his life,' wrote Chalmers in his *Biographical Dictionary*, 'with the extent of his labours, the mind is overpowered.'[172] The *Gentleman's Magazine* felt that 'Sir William Jones was unquestionably one of the most extraordinary men that ever figured on the stage of life.'[173]

In a way, Jones had himself set the criterion by which a man should be judged when he said, ' If I am asked, who is the greatest man? I answer the best: and if I am required to say, who is the best? I reply, he that has deserved most of his fellow-creatures.'[174] Judged by his own criterion, he was certainly the best of men.[175]

At the last meeting of the Society Jones attended, a young man read a paper on 'The Duties of a Faithful Hindu Widow'. This young man was H. T. Colebrooke, who on the death of Sir William wrote to his father, 'You ask how we are to supply his place? Indeed, but ill. Our present and future presidents may preside with dignity and propriety, but who can supply his place in diligent and ingenious researches? Not even the combined efforts of the whole Society and the field is large, and few the cultivators.'[176] Yet it was Colebrooke who carried on Jones's task, and came to be known as the greatest Sanskritist Britain gave to India.

3

H. T. Colebroke and the Sanskrit Renaissance, 1794–1815

'Colebrooke', said Max Müller, was 'the greatest Oriental scholar that England has ever produced', and added that had he lived in Germany, 'we should . . . have seen his statue in his native place, his name written in letters of gold on the walls of academies; we should have heard of Colebrooke jubilees and Colebrooke scholarships. [But] in England . . . we may possibly hear the popular name of Sir William Jones . . . but of the infinitely more important achievements of Colebrooke, not one word.'[1] Unfortunately, in India too, to whose classical languages and literature he contributed so much, he remains an unfamiliar or at best a passing name even to Sanskrit scholars.

Henry Thomas Colebrooke was born in London on 15 June 1765. His father, George Colebrooke, was a member of the House of Commons and was known as one of the chief spokesmen of the East India Company in the House. In 1767 he was elected a director in the company, and in 1769 became its chairman. Also known for his wild speculations, George Colebrooke almost squandered away the vast fortune he had inherited and added to. He was, however, of a scholarly turn of mind and under his guidance and inspiration, his son not only acquired proficiency in the classical languages but also in French and German. He also developed a taste for mathematics, and at seventeen, was said to have gained as much knowledge as could be expected of a university graduate.[2]

Although Henry had a religious bent from his childhood and looked forward to an ecclesiastical career, his father's position and influence in the East India Company pointed in a different direction; and in August 1782 he received a writership in the Bengal service.

Colebrooke arrived in India in April 1783 only to find himself jobless. His father had relied greatly on his friendship with Hastings, 'who promised much out of gratitude for the support he had received from Sir George Colebrooke'', but about this time Hastings had his own share of troubles. Public opinion in England was mounting against his administration in India and he was naturally preoccupied with events in England. Colebrooke thus remained unemployed in Calcutta for nearly ten months, and even after this period had to rest content with a subordinate situation in the Board of Accounts on a meagre salary.

To add to his misery was his distaste for the European society of Calcutta. Gambling and drinking were the common pastimes and having 'a strong head himself, he despised people who lost theirs.'[4] Almost in disgust, he wrote to his father: 'It would alarm you . . . to see the distress depicted on almost every countenance. The truth is, India is no longer a mine; every one is disgusted, and all whose affairs permit, abandon it as rapidly as possible.'[5]

Fortunately, after three years, Colebrooke was appointed Assistant Collector of Revenue in Tirhut in 1786. It was here that he developed his interest in the language and literature of this country. Two factors prompted Colebrooke to take to Indological studies. The first was the presence of a Collector who idled away his time and left the entire work of settlement on Colebrooke's shoulders. This enabled him to collect a mass of data which he utilized for his first publication, *Remarks on the Present State of Husbandry and Commerce in Bengal.* The treatise was not only a masterly survey of the conditions of agriculture in Bengal, but also a forceful plea for the principle of free trade and abolition of the Company's monopoly. The other and more important factor which prompted him to intellectual pursuits was his father, who frequently pressed him to provide information regarding the religion and the literature of the Hindus.

In retrospect, one can see that he attended to his father's demands more from filial duty than because of his admiration of Indian literature which in fact 'repelled him'. He described the *Ain-i-Akbari,* which had been translated by Gladwin as 'a dunghill, in which a pearl or two lie hid'.[6] He was also severely critical of the literary scene in India and thought the small band of scholars who acquired a knowledge of Indian letters to be 'nothing less than pedantic pretenders', whose only motive was to gain fame without much deserving it; and this they accomplished by doing a free translation of 'an ode from Persian, an apologue from the Sanskrit, or a song from some unheard-of dialect of Hinduee . . . [even] without understanding the original.'[7] The only exception, according to Colebrooke, was Charles Wilkins who was 'Sanskrit-mad',[8] and about whose translation of the *Bhagavad-Gita*, he wrote, 'I have never yet seen any book which can be depended on for information concerning the real opinions of the Hindus.'[9]

Knowledge of Sanskrit, at that time, was not easy to acquire. There were no grammars or dictionaries except in Sanskrit itself; and on two occasions, Colebrooke entertained thoughts of abandoning the study. Perseverance was, however, a part of his character and he struggled on. He learnt not only to read the original texts but his interests widened as well. He had started Sanskrit studies as a man of science; in fact, the first original result of his study was his observation on the Hindu divisions of time, about which he wrote to his father in December 1786. Soon, however, the practices and religious rites of the Hindus attracted him and he pored over the Sastras to ascertain their origins. The result was his first publication, 'On the Duties of a Faithful Hindu Widow', which appeared in the fourth volume of the *Researches*. It was presented to the Society at the last meeting that Sir William Jones attended.[10]

Colebrooke's first paper became the most controversial of all his contributions on oriental literature. There is hardly any doubt that Rajendralala Mitra was wrong when he stated that Colebrooke's paper on *sati* showed the departure of present-day Hindu rites from authentic tradition. This was certainly not so, for, not only here but also in his essay 'On the Mimamsa', presented to the Royal Asiatic Society on 4 March 1826, Colebrooke came to the conclusion (in fact he never seemed to doubt it) that the practice of *sati* had been enjoined by the Vedas.

As Max Müller later pointed out, the pundits who protested against the ban on *sati* imposed by Lord William Bentinck, cited Colebrooke's authority in their favour.[11] It was only in 1856 that Wilson in his paper on 'The supposed Vaidic Authority for the Burning of Hindu Widows', showed 'that the text of the *Rig Veda* cited as authority for the burning of widows enjoins the very contrary, and directs them to remain in the world.'[12] A debate then ensued on the source on which Colebrooke had relied for his conclusion. It was now certain that Colebrooke had not consulted the original Vaidic stanza, but had read a later copy, or an adaptation of it. Even Raja Radhakanta Deb, who was a known votary of the Hindu rite and who wrote a long rejoinder to Wilson's paper, admitted as much. Commenting on Wilson's reading of the Vaidic verse, he wrote: 'You may be justified in coming to the conclusion, that the genuine reading of the passage rather discountenances than enjoins *sahamarane*.[13] He then pointed out that Colebrooke had derived his material from the *Suddhitattva* by the famous Bengali pundit Raghunandana.

On the other hand, Max Müller remarked that Colebrooke's essay was a 'literal translation from Gagannatha's *Vivadabhangarnava*'.[14]

With all these different interpretations, the question acquired a new interest and was examined at length by the Sanskrit scholar Fitz-Edward Hall in 1868. He came to the conclusion that Colebrooke could not have taken the passage translated by him either from the *Vivadabhangarnava* of Gagannatha (as supposed by Max Müller) or from the *Suddhitattva* of Raghunandana (as held by Raja Radhakanta Deb). According to him: 'It is not improbable that [Colebrooke] took them, at secondhand, from some of the scores of treatises in which they are adduced. No one can say that he did not assemble them from volumes as numerous as themselves.'[15]

Although Colebrooke committed a grave error in the essay, his reputation hardly suffered. 'Speaking historically', remarked Daniel Ingalls, 'it is less important that Colebrooke made one mistake than that he furnished so many data that were accurate.'[16] What was more significant was Colebrooke's method for studying contemporary Indian society, namely, by seeking the origins of the customs, rites and rituals in the ancient texts, and assessing how far contemporary behaviour conformed to them. It is ironical that a contemporary scholar should try to trace the origins of castes, social customs and feudalism in ancient Indian texts without once referring to Colebrooke, the pioneer of this method of historical study.

The fourth volume of *Asiatic Researches*, which carried Colebrooke's first article, also had another pioneering contribution in Marsden's 'Traces of the Hindu Language and Literature extant amongst the Malays'.

William Marsden was born in 1754. In 1771, at the age of seventeen, he joined the Company's service in Sumatra. Here during his eight-year stay, he acquired such mastery over the vernacular as to compile a dictionary of Malay. When and how he acquired a knowledge of Sanskrit is not known. It is evident, however, that he knew enough of the language to open a new line of inquiry. As he says in his article, the influence of Sanskrit on the languages of Assam, Nepal, Bhutan, Tibet and the southern parts of India had already been established through the studies of the missionaries and other scholars.

But 'the progress it made in early times, amongst the inhabitants of the eastern islands and countries possessed by the *Malays*, has not, I believe, been pointed out by any writer'.[1']

The similarity of the two languages led Marsden to conclude that although the predominant religion in Malaysia was Islam, intercourse between India and Malaysia had existed long before the advent of Islam, and the basis of contact between the two countries was trade and commerce. Marsden was also the first scholar in modern times to establish the influence of the *Ramayana* and the *Mahabharata* on the culture of south-east Asia. Although the discovery that Indian epics are available in the countries of south-east Asia is comparatively recent, culminating in Father Camille Bulcke's study of the origin and the development of the story of Rama, Marsden could be said to have started the process of this discovery when he stated that he met with 'frequent allusions' to the two epics in the writings of the Malays.

Two other articles of interest in the fourth volume of the *Researches* deal with the Qutb Minar and the Elephanta caves. In his article on the *minar*, James Blunt not only described the unique structure in detail but also measured, for the first time, the height of the *minar* on the basis of trigonometrical calculations. When Blunt visited it, the structure lay in a state of total neglect. He 'found the battlements in many parts entirely ruined, and those that were standing, [were] in such a decayed state as to render it a matter of some danger to venture out from the staircase.'[18] Blunt could not read or copy any of the inscriptions because of the height at which they were situated and, there was 'not a bamboo, or wood of any kind produced in that part of the country, calculated to raise a scaffolding with'.[19] Since he could not read any inscription, Blunt surmised, perhaps with some justification, that the *minar* had been built at Qutb-ud-din's expense. However, he added that since Qutb-ud-din reigned only for five years, he could not have completed the building of the *minar*. It was nearly twenty-five years later, in 1820, that Walter Ewer studied and published the inscriptions which ascribed the building of the *minar* to Iltutmish.[20]

The Elephanta caves, unlike the Qutb Minar, were well-known to the west. Garcia da Orta, the first European to record his impressions of the monument, wrote as early as 1534 that the Portuguese had already given currency to the name Elephanta, from the huge sculpture of an elephant that stood at the entrance of the temple, and that its Indian name was Pory (Gharapuri).[21] The monument was also noticed by the French scholar, Anquetil Duperron, and the Danish traveller, Carsten Niebuhr. In 1785, Lieutenant-Colonel Barry observed:

> In several part[s] of the coast about Bombay are found caves of such remote antiquity, that neither tradition nor records can reach their origin; in many of them are inscriptions, written in a language and characters now totally unknown.[22]

J. Goldingham, the author of the article on 'The cave in the Island of Elephanta', was one of the astronomers of the Company, stationed at Fort Saint George. He was 'a person of much ingenuity, and [one] who applies himself to the study of antiquities.'[23]

Goldingham's description of the caves was more detailed and accurate than any previous one, and his ground-plan together with the sketch of the Trimurti was an improvement upon Niebuhr's. Goldingham discounted the theories of the caves being of Egyptian, Jewish or Greek origin and sought to prove that the structure and the figures were entirely Indian. Goldingham's argument however, did not carry weight even with his patron who forwarded the communication to the Society. Thus in his forwarding letter, General J. Carnac wrote:

> Goldingham argues ably in favour of its having been an Hindu temple; yet I cannot assent to his opinion. The immense excavations cut out of the solid rocks at the Elephanta, and other caves of the like nature on the island of Salsette, appear to me operations of too great labour to have been executed by the hands of so feeble and effeminate a race as the aborigines of India have generally been held to be, and still continue.[24]

Goldingham's article on Elephanta was presented to the Society on 20 August 1795. On 3 December the Society heard his paper on the 'Sculptures at Mahabalipoorum; Usually Called the Seven Pagodas.'[25] Mahabalipuram, as we have seen earlier, had been the subject of the first article of historical interest to be published in the *Researches*.[26] Unlike William Chambers (the author of the first article), Goldingham did not speculate on the date or the origin of the structures, but was the first European to have recorded the measurements of the main temple and to reproduce some of its inscriptions.[27] Goldingham, however, was still a long way from establishing the fact that the Mahabalipuram structures were built by the kings of the Pallava dynasty—then an unknown part of Indian history.

At the same meeting, the Society's President, Sir John Shore, laid before it a facsimile of some ancient inscriptions found in the caves of

Ellora. These caves, like the Mahabalipuram structures, had been noticed earlier by the Europeans. Anquetil Duperron had even intended to make a complete iconographic survey of the rock carvings. The task was however completed by Sir Charles Mallet in 1794. With the help of James Manley who prepared the ground plans, and the artists, James Wales and Gungaram, Mallet subjected all the caves and temples to careful scrutiny. 'Each part of a piece of architecture was thoroughly measured, the results being presented in the form of a table . . . so that a complete list of proportions, general design, and the distribution of each element was available to the scholars.' Because of the conflicting accounts provided to Mallet by a Brahman pundit and a Muslim scholar, Mallet could neither determine the age of the monument nor the fact of their Buddhist origin. Their magnificence was, however, most tellingly brought out in Mallet's article. 'Whether we consider the design, or contemplate the execution of these extraordinary works, we are lost in wonder at the idea of forming a vast mountain into almost eternal mansions,' he wrote.[28]

Mallet's article made a deep impact and hereafter, we find an almost continuous chain of studies on the cave temples.

Yet another monument whose importance came to light in 1794 was the *stupa* at Sarnath. The person behind this discovery was Jonathan Duncan, an outstanding officer in the Company's service.

Jonathan Duncan arrived in Calcutta as a minor civil servant in 1772 at the age of sixteen. Lord Cornwallis was impressed by the young man's honesty and diligence and in 1788 appointed him Resident and Superintendent of Banaras. Here he proved himself an able administrator, effectively curbing the corruption prevailing among English officials.

He also played an important role in the abolition of infanticide. Like Colebrooke, Duncan was a man of letters and proficient in the Indian vernacular languages. His love for Sanskrit found shape in the establishment of the Hindu College in 1791 which is today known as the Sanskrit College.

The establishment of this institution together with a chance discovery he made in 1794—the very year he left Banaras—have immortalized Duncan's name. The discovery related to two urns which were found during the digging operations undertaken by the Zamindar Jagat Singh who wanted to save money by collecting stones from the Sarnath ruins for his new building. It was just chance that the two urns fell into Duncan's hands who relayed information about them to the

Asiatic Society. In one of the urns were found some human bones, which were committed to the Ganga, some jewels and a statue of the Buddha with an inscription upon its base, which was then indecipherable. How little was known about the Buddhist faith at that time is evident from the conclusion that Duncan reached about the finds: 'The bones found in these urns', he surmised 'must belong to one of the worshippers of Buddha, a set of Indian heretics, who having no reverence for the Ganges, used to deposit their remains in the earth, instead of committing them to that river.'[29]

Later, when after further digging (which had nothing to do with archaeological excavations) the Sarnath *stupa* emerged, Wilford remarked: 'Similar monuments . . . are often erected by the Hindus, upon the spot where a married woman burned herself with her husband. These monuments are in general called *Sati*; and the enormous one at Sarnath is a sort of *Sati* over the bones of Buddha.'[30]

In fact, it took scholars nearly half a century to establish the value of Sarnath and its place in the history of Buddhism.

Duncan's paper on the urns was presented to the Society at its meeting on 10 September 1795. In the following and last meeting of the year, held on 3 December, the Society heard another paper from Colebrooke. This was on the 'Enumeration of Indian Classes'.

The caste system prevalent in India had been written about earlier, but Colebrooke's paper was the first to examine everyday Indian social life more closely. As in his previous paper on *sati*, Colebrooke tried to trace the origins of the system as outlined in ancient Sanskrit texts. The authorities he consulted for the purpose were the *Jatimala* (Garland of Classes), the *Rudrayamala Tantra* and the *Dharma Purana*. As before, Colebrooke studied how far contemporary social practices conformed to what was enjoined by the Sastras and noted:

> It appears that almost every occupation, though regularly it be the possession of a particular class, is open to most other classes; and that the limitations, far from being rigorous, do, in fact, reserve only one peculiar possession, that of the Brahmana, which consists in teaching the *Veda*, and officiating at religious ceremonies.[31]

The year 1796 found the Society trying to acquire a permanent foundation as an institution. It was over a decade since its establishment and it had earned a reputation among men of letters the world over. In 1795, for instance, the Secretary of the American Academy of Arts and Sciences approached the Asiatic Society for information on

the Jewish diaspora, especially about old Jewish settlements in Malabar. Other learned bodies in the west also directed inquiries about the
east to the Asiatic Society. But the Society had no building of its own,
no funds and no formal rules. It was run according to the one rule that
Sir William Jones had laid down in his preliminary discourse—to have
no rules at all. Although it had four volumes of *Researches* to its credit,
it had no permanent funds, and its occasional expenses were met by
the President, or the Secretary, or both. Its meetings were held in the
court-house, but after Jones's death even this became difficult since
the court-house was not always readily available. Moreover, the
Society had been receiving old books, manuscripts, antiquities and
specimens of various kinds, and there was no place to store these
safely.

Under these circumstances, the Society clearly needed a building of its
own and permanent funding. Accordingly, at the meeting of 19
August 1796 two important resolutions were passed: to apply to His
Majesty for a Charter of Incorporation[32] and to provide the Society
with a building. Further, a Committee was appointed to 'consider the
best mode of carrying into execution the objects of the two foregoing
Resolutions [and] to consider of any Rules and Regulations for
advancing and promoting the objects of the Institution of the Society.'
In the report presented at the Society's meeting of 29 September, the
Committee made some recommendations which were to change the
entire character of the Asiatic Society.

A membership fee was instituted for the first time. The Committee
recommended an admission fee of two gold mohurs, which was to be
paid by the old as well as new members, and provided for a membership fee of four gold mohurs per annum payable quarterly. It was
laid down that if any member failed to pay the subscription within six
months after it became due, he would lose his membership.

Since this membership fee would not cover the cost of a building, it
was decided to open a subscription for voluntary contributions, and
also to request the Government to allot a convenient site to the
Society. The Committee proposed the election of a treasurer to look
after the Society's funds and to keep a record of its expenses. Yet
another of the Committee's recommendations, which had far-reaching
effects, laid down that the Society 'make it publicly known that it is
their intention to establish a Museum and Library, and that donations

of books, manuscripts and curiosities will be thankfully received and acknowledged."³³ In this recommendation lie the seeds of the establishment of museums and the numismatic and anthropological organizations in India.

One of the reasons why the Society was eager to establish a museum was that by this time Englishmen had become aware of the cultural heritage of ancient India and of the importance of preserving and studying its remains. Knowledge of the progress India had made in the physical sciences, especially astronomy, had drawn the attention of many western scientists including Samuel Davis and John Playfair. Another Englishman drawn towards this study was William Hunter,³⁴ who for some time served as the Society's Secretary.

Born at Montrose, Scotland, in 1755, William Hunter had even in his childhood shown a talent for mechanical contrivances. After taking his M.A. degree from the University of Aberdeen in 1777 he arrived in India in 1781. He served the Company with distinction in various capacities during his 30-year stay in India, and was appointed superintendent-surgeon in Java when the Island was wrested from the Dutch in 1811. He died the following year.

During his stay in India, Hunter became interested in the Indian sciences and contributed seven papers to the *Asiatic Researches*. One of these was on the 'Astronomical labours of Jayasinha, Rajah of Ambhere, or Jayanagar',³⁵ which provides the first detailed and scientific account of what are now known as Jantar Mantar, the unique astronomical structures built in the eighteenth century by the astronomer–statesman, Raja Sawai Jaisingh at Delhi, Mathura, Ujjain and Banaras.

By the eighteenth century, as Hunter points out, the Indian astronomical tables were so distorted that they ceased to correspond with the actual appearance of the stars. This led Emperor Mohammad Shah to request Raja Jaisingh, who had studied the ancient Indian sciences and was also aware of the work of western astronomers like Ptolemy, Hipparchus (whom he calls a clown) and Euclid, to draw up a fresh set of astronomical tables. He also undertook the construction of these astronomical structures which provided extremely accurate readings.

While it was generally admitted that the ancient Indians were fairly advanced in scientific, especially astronomical, studies, the question of the Indian sense of time and consequently the chronology of ancient Indian history was a problem for western scholars. Sir William Jones had perhaps rightly guessed that most of what went in the name of history was mere myth and that the recorded history of India did not go beyond two thousand years before the birth of Christ. A more or less similar line of thought was evident in Wilford's article on the 'Chronology of the Hindus', presented at the Society's meeting on 17 November 1796. In this article, Wilford reproduced the genealogical tables given in the *Bhagavat*, the *Vishnu* and some other Puranas, and came to the conclusion that 'as a certain number of years only can be allowed to a generation, it overthrows at once their monstrous system, which I have rejected as absolutely repugnant to the course of nature, and human reason.'[36] In the process of determining early Indian chronology, Wilford tried to reconcile it with Biblical history—and in the process, he himself put forth far-fetched comparisons and theories. He was on firmer ground, as was Jones, when he came to the Magadhan dynasty. Here there was the advantage of contemporary Greek accounts which lent support to Indian dates, events and dynasties. In his article, Wilford challenged Jones's identification of Palibothra with modern Patna and placed the site of the city described by Megasthenes as somewhere near Bhagalpur. It was this conjecture of Wilford[37] which prompted William Francklin to explore the area in detail. He confirmed Wilford's view. Subsequent researches have, however, borne out the correctness of Jones's theory, although, as shown in the previous chapter, there are scholars who still challenge this identification.

Like Jones, Wilford also spoke of Chandragupta and other kings of ancient India as historical figures but could not fathom the mystery behind the Indian concept of time and the astronomical figures associated with the rule of different dynasties. One reason Wilford gave for such exaggeration in historical data was the vanity of Indians. According to him 'there is hardly a Hindu who is not persuaded of, and who will not reason upon the supposed antiquity of his nation.'[38]

Whatever the reason, the fact remains that no satisfactory explanation is yet available of the Pauranic chronologies and time computations. Another Englishman to grapple with the question was John Bentley, who contributed a paper on the 'Principal Eras and Dates of the Ancient Hindus', at the same meeting of the Society at which Wilford read his paper.

Little seems to be known of Bentley's life, although at one time his name was familiar to every Indologist and astronomer. *The Asiatic Journal* in its two-page obituary[39] had only two lines about Bentley's life—the first and the last—and the rest was devoted to his theories and their influence on the literary world. The first sentence of the obituary read: 'This gentleman died at Calcutta on the 4th of March last, aged 67 years.' The last sentence ran as follows: 'In private life, he was universally esteemed as a man of sound judgement, and of the most unblemished integrity.' Many of Bentley's contemporaries would however, have disagreed with the first part of the sentence: Bentley, according to them, did not possess a sound judgment, at least in matters of astronomical scholarship.

The fact that the ancient Hindu books and the Puranas contained exaggerated ideas about the antiquity of Indian civilization, and their chronologies conveyed little factual information about ancient history, had come to be almost universally accepted by scholars by the early nineteenth century. The question, however, remained as to exactly what the astronomical figures regarding *kalpas, mahayugas.* and *yugas* conveyed, and the basis of those calculations. Bentley was one of the first scholars to study this aspect. In the first paragraph of his article he noted:

> The confusion and darkness that pervade and overspread the Hindu chronology . . . proceed from two different causes: the one, owing to the fancy of their *Brahmins* and Poets, in disguising and embellishing their history with allegory and fiction; the other, to the ignorance of the modern Hindus, who, not able to discern the difference between the several eras and modes of dating which were made use of by their ancient historians, Brahmans, and Poets, in recording past events, have blended the whole together, into one mass of absurdity and contradiction.[40]

Bentley then proceeded to distinguish between the poetic, the astronomic and the real eras of different dynasties and kings, placing them in relation to the Biblical figures. He also drew up a chronological table of the solar and lunar lines of ancient Indian kings as well as that of the Magadhan kings beginning from King Pradyota. The article by and large went unnoticed by contemporary as well as later scholars.

In May 1798 Bentley read what was one of the most controversial articles in the history of the Society. This was on the 'Antiquity of the Surya Siddhanta'.[41] *The Surya Siddhanta*, an early work of Indian astronomy, had by this time become widely known among Indologists. According to Indian traditions, it had been composed 21,64,899 years earlier. This of course was unacceptable to any serious western scholar; Sir William Jones himself had reckoned that Varahamihira, the supposed author of the *Surya Siddhanta*, had lived *c.* A.D. 499.

Colebrooke put the time of Varahmihira 1300 years earlier, that is, around 600 B.C. Bentley, on the other hand, after elaborate astronomical calculations stated that the *Surya Siddhanta* was only 731 years old, that is, it was composed *c.* A.D. 1068. Bentley went on to assert:

> Any *Hindu* work in which the name of Varaha or his system is mentioned, must evidently be modern; and this circumstance alone totally destroys the pretended antiquity of many of the *Puranas* and other books, which through the artifices of the *Brahmanical* tribe, have been hitherto deemed the most ancient in existence.[42]

In addition, in his zeal to disprove the antiquity of ancient Indian texts, Bentley pronounced many of them to be modern forgeries.[43]

The first detailed criticism of Bentley's assertions appeared in an article in the first volume of the *Edinburgh Review*. The critic felt that Bentley's discussion on the antiquity of the *Surya Siddhanta* involved 'points of the utmost importance; no less, indeed, than whether the whole of Sanskrit literature shall be considered as the spurious productions of a recent age, or genuine monuments of primeval times.'[44] The critic then proceeded to demolish Bentley's theory systematically.

After the *Edinburgh Review* article appeared, practically every journal and periodical devoted to oriental studies joined the fray. *The Asiatic Annual Register* of 1803 ventured to affirm 'that the data on which Mr. Bentley grounds his calculation, is erroneous, and that all his results, therefore, are widely distant from the truth.'[45]

The following year, at the July 1804 meeting of the Society, Bentley presented his second paper on the subject, in which he attempted to refute the points raised by the *Edinburgh Review*,[46] and gave additional evidence in favour of his contentions. Once again the *Edinburgh Review* sought to pull down Bentley's theories.[47] By this time, the issue had become so public that the *Classical Journal* noted in 1812:

> An unhappy difference in opinion seems to have taken place among the Eastern scholars. It relates to the just, or the false grounds, on which the *Brahmins* build their pretensions to a civilization, so vastly earlier than the European nations of the west.
>
> The writers themselves . . . since the death of Sir William Jones have divided into two parties. The attentive literati of Europe have also marshalled themselves under the same divisions.[48]

The two central figures in the entire controversy were Bentley and Colebrooke who held the two extreme views. The controversy unfortunately extended to personal attacks, with each blaming the other for having fallen a prey to the same kind of fraud of which Wilford had been a victim. Bentley in a later work on Hindu astronomy, published posthumously, asserted that 'Colebrooke's notions are all baseless and unfounded,'[49] and Colebrooke, in the columns of the *Asiatic Journal*, retorted: 'All is confusion worse confounded. Everything which Mr Bentley had before done, all which he had achieved in two laboured essays, goes in the general wreck. Everything has passed away, except his wrath against his opponents.'[50]

But it did not. Bentley's theory remained a dominant factor in Indology and went on to win new adherents. Thus the same *Asiatic Journal* which carried Colebrooke's remarks had the following to say of Bentley and his theory:

> It was Bentley's glory to dispel the illusion, [of the antiquity of Indian civilization] to show that the pretended tables were fictitious; that the observations recorded were inconsistent with the dates assigned to them, and that their errors increased in an exact ratio to their alleged antiquity.[51]

This again, was to say the least, a far-fetched view, and amounted to a condemnation of such scholars as Sir William Jones, Colebrooke, Samuel Davis, Bailly, Le Gentil and others, who had put the issue in the right perspective: Indian civilization was not as old as the ancient texts made it out to be, nor was it as recent as detractors like Bentley claimed.

One of the reasons why the Bentley controversy caught the attention of European intellectuals was that it had originated in the pages of *Asiatic Researches*. By this time the Asiatic Society's reputation was firmly established as the leading institution for the study of the oriental world, especially India. So popular had the journal become that a pirated edition appeared in 1798 which sold rapidly enough for two more editions to be brought out within six years.[52] The French undertook a translation of the first volume of the work and enriched it with 'a series of valuable notes on the philological and historical papers by M. M. Cuvier, Delambre, Lamarck, and Olivier.'[53] Sir William Jones, having at one stage doubted the viability of the publication, would certainly have been surprised at its popularity. Members of the Society were aware more than ever before that the institution could not continue as a loose association of scholars as had been planned by the founder, and so, during 1797-8, they tried to implement some of the proposals put up at the Society's meeting of 29

September 1796 and evolve means of making the Society and its publications permanent.

The first step in this direction was naturally the acquisition of funds. As a result of the 29 September resolution which provided for admission fees, quarterly subscriptions and voluntary contributions, the Society had built up a balance of Rs 4,560 by January 1797, of which it deposited Rs 4,000 in the Government treasury against a twelve per cent interest.[54] By August the amount had increased to Rs 8,832,[55] and by April the following year to over Rs 12,600.[56] This secure financial position, together with the popularity of its *Researches*, prompted the Society's Committee of Papers to put forth a new proposal to the effect that the *Researches* be published at the expense and on account of the Society.[57] Thus seven volumes of the *Researches* (Volumes VI to XII) were published under this arrangement, when the Society once again found the sale proceeds falling very much short of printing costs. Consequently in 1819, it was proposed that the rights be sold to a London publisher.[58]

Unfortunately, when the Society applied to the Governor-General for a convenient plot for the construction of a building, it was informed that 'the Vice-President in Council regrets, that upon enquiry, there is not any spot of ground in the town of Calcutta belonging to the Company which can be spared to the Society for the purpose of erecting a house for the meetings, as well as for the future establishment of a library and museum.'[59]

Some other questions which came up for discussion at the time were: awarding medals for contributions of merit to the *Researches*, purchasing unsold volumes at reduced prices and making them available to public institutions, printing the new rules and regulations of the Society as appendices to the *Researches*, printing in the volumes a list of such subjects as required further investigation and illustration, and expediting their publication.[60]

While these proposals were being framed and considered, there were also signs of trouble. A singular letter on the subject, found in the Society's archives is by a member, A. Burt, who refused to pay his subscription and described the process as 'the metamorphosis of an intellectual institution into a Body Politic'. He felt that the Society 'may in time become monied rather than literary since cash even now secures equal admittance to all persons.'[61]

The years 1797 and 1798 seemed to prove Burt wrong, for, while there was much discussion on giving the Society the shape of a permanent Institution, there were also contributions of lasting value and interest, including articles on the religious ceremonies of the Hindus, the pillar of Firuz Shah in Delhi and the antiquity of the *Surya Siddhanta*, which we have discussed earlier.

The paper on 'The religious ceremonies of the Hindus and of the *Brahmans* especially', was first presented by Colebrooke at the meeting of the Society on 17 August 1797. The paper, like his earlier comprehensive study of the Indian classes, was an outcome of his preoccupation with the preparation of the digest of Hindu law. The plan for the *Digest* had originally been drawn up by Sir William Jones, who had died before he could make much progress. The project had acquired added significance at the time in view of the Cornwallis Code of 1793, which regulated the courts of law within the East India Company's possessions. According to Max Müller, there was 'no man in India, except Colebrooke',[62] who could carry on the work. In the beginning, Colebrooke accepted the task as one to be performed during his leisure hours until some person was found willing to dedicate all his time to it.[63] That, however, did not happen. The work had to be completed by Colebrooke himself, who had at first thought that it would take him about six months, but which actually occupied practically all his time for two years. His brother, who spent some time with him during this period, later told Colebrooke's son how he had 'applied himself so intensely as to alarm his friends for his health. They would sometimes propose sporting excursions, to entice him away from his desk; at other times, they resorted to a more summary method, by breaking in upon his studies, and putting out his midnight lamp.'[64]

The *Digest*, dedicated to the memory of Sir William Jones, was published in four folio volumes in 1798. Colebrooke had refused any remuneration for his labours, but as he had expected, the work did pay rich dividends in other ways. It earned for him the thanks of the Governor-General, and led to his appointment to the Bench of the new Court of Appeal at Calcutta in 1801, where he rose to become President in 1805. Simultaneously Lord Wellesley appointed him Professor of Hindu Law and Sanskrit in the newly-established College of Fort William. More than anything else, the appearance of the *Digest* secured for Colebrooke a lasting reputation as a great Sanskritist.

The reputation was well deserved. The preface, which mentions the various works on which the *Digest* was based, shows Colebrooke's vast learning. These studies would no doubt have helped him in preparing his essay on the religious ceremonies of the Hindus.

The essay was published in three parts, the first in Volume V, and the second and the third in Volume VII of the *Researches*. The first part described in detail the daily ablutions performed by the Brahmans, together with translations of prayers offered on different occasions. In the second and more detailed part, taking Bhavadeva as his guide as well as a commentary on the *mantras* by Guna Vishnu, and the *Achara Chandrica* and other texts, Colebrooke described the sacrament which 'consists in oblations to fire, with prayers addressed to various divinities.' He also provided an extremely detailed description of Hindu funeral rites, from the time a Hindu lay dying, to the last day of mourning followed by the *sraddha* ceremony.

In the notes appended to the article, Colebrooke made certain important observations. Thus, he may well have sounded a heretic to the great number of western intellectuals who saw the Hindu religion as a debased one, when he asserted: 'If the doctrines of the Veda, and even those of the Puranas, be closely examined, the Hindu theology will be found consistent with monotheism, though it contain the seeds of polytheism and idolatry.'⁶⁵ In the note 'Chiefly on the Authority of Verbal Communications', Colebrooke also described in brief the different religious schools of Hinduism as those of Sankara, Vallabhacharya, Madhavacharya, Ramanuja, the *saktas* and others—a theme which was later developed in detail by H. H. Wilson.

In the third essay on the subject, Colebrooke described the marriage ceremonies of the Hindus, citing passages from the *Yajurveda, Samaveda* and Kalidasa's poem *Raghuvamsa*. He also mentioned the fact that in ancient India, a cow was slain for purposes of hospitality, but by the time the *Yajurveda* was composed, the practice had become obsolete.⁶⁶

These essays, running into over a hundred pages were deemed extremely valuable for the light they shed on important and till then obscure aspects of the Indian people and their culture. Thus, according to the *Alexander's East India Magazine*, an important contemporary journal, the essay together with Colebrooke's article on the Sanskrit and Prakrit languages (discussed later) was 'sufficient to place the author in the highest rank of oriental scholars—and which must long continue to form the best textbooks of those who wish to investigate the depths of Indian literature and religion.'⁶⁷

The other important paper on Indian history presented in 1798 (6 December) related to inscriptions on the pillar which at the time was commonly known as the *lat* of Firuz Shah. These inscriptions, as we have seen, had been noticed and copied earlier by Colonel Polier and had even been translated by Jones's pundit, Radhakanta, but it was an imperfect copy which led Sir William Jones to assign one of the inscriptions to A.D. 67 on the basis of misreading the date as 123 of the era of Vikramaditya.

.The inscriptions were now once again copied by Captain James Hoare, a member of the Society, who unfortunately died before his *Book of Drawings and Inscriptions*, containing the ones on the pillar at Firuz Shah Kotla, was presented to the Society. .

Captain Hoare's copy immediately brought to light the errors and deficiencies in Polier's. The date of the inscription was now ascertained as A.D. 1164 corresponding to the year 1220 of Vikramaditya's era.[68] Colebrooke's translation of the inscription also brought out the personality of Vigraha Raja, King of Sakambhari, who, in 1807, was identified as Prithviraj Chauhan. Commenting on this discovery, the *Edinburgh Review* underlined the importance of this inscription in illuminating the history of India just before the Muslim conquest, and wondered why scholars had not so far used their readings of inscriptions found in India to throw light on the history of the country.[69]

The *Review* also pointed out that the existence of the inscription in unknown characters proved that the monument belonged to a much older period than that of Visala Deva. The inscription, as we now know, was the Asokan inscription which, about forty years later, was deciphered by Prinsep.

At the first meeting of 1799, held on 10 January, Sir Robert Chambers, the Society's third President, resigned, the second President to resign within eighteen months. Sir John Shore, the Governor-General, was elected President soon after Sir William Jones's death in 1794 and continued so till October 1797.[70] A scholar of Persian, Sir John showed a deep interest in the Society's affairs not missing a single meeting while he was President. It was during his term that the first steps were taken to establish the Society as a permanent institution. He was also the first biographer of Sir William Jones.

Sir Robert Chambers, who succeeded John Shore as President on 18 January 1798, was already sixty at the time, and, as he confessed in his first discourse to the Society, had 'but a slight and superficial knowledge of any *Asiatic* language.'[71] However, Sir Robert promised: 'If it is now too late, at the age of sixty, greatly to increase my own stock of oriental literature, I will at least endeavour to promote the increase of it in others.' Unfortunately his declining health compelled him to return to England in early 1799, and the Society had to elect a new President. The person elected on 24 January 1799 was Sir John Anstruther, Chief Justice of the Supreme Court in Calcutta, but again a man without any pretensions to oriental studies and knowledge. The consequences were soon evident. Sir Robert Chambers' opening discourse was printed in the sixth volume of the *Researches*[72] with his permission. No such request however was made when Sir John became President, thus marking a departure from the established practice.

The President's lack of interest in oriental studies had its repercussions on other members. In fact, in the meeting of 2 May 1799, neither the President nor any of the Vice-Presidents were present, and the meeting had to be carried on with a senior member of the Committee, Mr Home, in the Chair. Gilchrist proposed that under such circumstances the Society's proceedings should be submitted at the following meeting for sanction, and that 'a proper mode of procedure, in similar circumstances, be then determined'.[73] The following meeting of the Society was held on 4 July 1799 and, while confirming the proceedings of 2 May, it ruled that if the President and the Vice-Presidents were more than fifteen minutes late for a meeting, the senior member of the Society should take the Chair for the evening.

In spite of waning enthusiasm, there were eleven meetings in 1799 and the minimum number of members present at any meeting was seven.[74] In 1800 there was a further decline. Just seven meetings were held, with never more than nine members attending. At the meeting of 4 June 1800, there were only five members present, with the President and the Vice-Presidents being absent. Home proposed therefore that instead of monthly meetings, the Society hold quarterly meetings. At the following meeting of 2 July it was agreed that henceforth the Society's meetings be held on the first Wednesdays of January, April, July and October, with the proviso that intermediate meetings be convened if anything of importance came up.

The first year of the new century seemed to usher in a revival in the Society's activities. Attendance at its meetings improved and papers of importance contributed. Moreover, Colebrooke, who had been in

Nagpur for two years, returned to Calcutta and his arrival was proclaimed by an important paper read in the first meeting of the Society held on 7 January 1801.

The paper, on 'Sanskrit and Prakrit Languages', marked the first attempt to enumerate the works composed for the elucidation of Sanskrit grammar from the earliest period down to modern times. The brief but comprehensive survey of the history of Sanskrit grammar shows a grammarian in the making. In fact, by the time the article was written, Colebrooke in all probability had made up his mind to compose his own Sanskrit grammar.

In the article Colebrooke described the characteristics of other major vernaculars of India like Hindi, Maithil, Oriya, Tamil, Kanarese, Marathi, Punjabi and the Braj Bhasha. He had even prepared a collection of specimens 'of each language, and of the character in which it is written, together with a list of the most common terms in the various dialects of India, compared with words of similar sound and import in the ancient languages of Europe' [75] The list, he felt would 'exceed the limits of a desultory essay', and, moreover it was incomplete at the time. Unfortunately, even this incomplete list which would undoubtedly have been most interesting and instructive, has been lost to us. Nor do we know whether Colebrooke ever completed it. Colebrooke's son, T. E. Colebrooke, who was also his father's biographer and who saw a part of the work, commented: 'The range of his comparison was wide, as it embraced not merely Sanskrit, Greek, and Latin with their derivatives, but the Germanic and Slavonic dialects. In one case (the word brother) it is carried through eighteen variations.' [76]

The extent of Colebrooke's knowledge of the Sanskrit grammarians was made evident in his *Grammar of the Sanskrit Language*, of which only one volume could be published in 1805. The *Grammar* consisted of a systematic arrangement of the intricate and complicated rules enunciated by Panini and commentators on his work. Highly complicated, and lacking illustrations and examples, Colebrooke's *Grammar* was never as popular as Wilkins' more simple *Grammar*, and therefore, remained a work more admired than read. As Max Müller put it: 'Though it [Colebrooke's *Grammar*] was never finished, it will always keep its place, like a classical torso, more admired in its unfinished state than other works which stand by its side, finished, yet less perfect.' [77]

Colebrooke contributed two more papers to the Society in 1801.

The first, read on 1 July, was a continuation of his essay on the religious ceremonies of the Hindus which we have discussed earlier; the other, presented on 7 October, was on 'The origin and peculiar tenets of certain Muhammedan sects'. The article is a study of the Bohras of western India, whose origins had long been a matter of research and study. Colebrooke described how he came across the work *Mejalisulmuminin* composed by a certain Nurullah, who had suffered for his religious opinions in the reign of Jahangir.[78] According to this tract, the Bohras were natives of Gujarat who were converted to Islam about six centuries ago. The article, though brief, 'proves that in the midst of his accurate study of the more secluded literature and monuments of the Hindus—the author was versed also in the learned records of Western Asia.'[79]

A more important contribution perhaps was that of Lewis Ferdinand Smith, presented to the Society at the same meeting. It was published in the *Researches* under the title 'A Chronological Table of the Moghul Emperors, from Umeer Tymoor to Alumgeer II, the father of the present emperor Shah Alum, being from A.H. 736 to 1173 or A.D. 1135 to 1760'.[80] This detailed chronological account not only listed the names and titles of the Moghul emperors but also the names of their parents, the dates and places of their birth, coronation, imprisonment and death.

Another paper dealing with recent history, but far more interesting than Smith's chronology, was the 'Account of the St. Thomé Christians on the Coast of Malabar', presented to the Society on 1 July 1801 by F. Wrede. This was one of the first papers to raise the controversial subject of the Malabar Christians. Daniel Potts cites Pandit Nehru's statement in the Lok Sabha in 1955 when he declared that Christianity was as old in India as the religion itself. 'Nehru', says Potts, 'was referring to the recurring legends and traditions, impossible to test fully by the criteria of modern historical research, which centre around Saint Thomas, the doubting disciple of Christ, honouring him as the first Christian missionary to the East.'[81] According to Wrede, the Malabar Christians were Nestorians 'who fled from the dominions of the Greek emperors after Theodosius II had commenced to persecute the followers of the sect',[82] sometime in the fifth century A.D. According to tradition, the first bishop of these Christians from Syria was Mar Thomé, after whom every ecclesiastical chief or bishop of the sect was named.

The Portuguese, when they landed on the Malabar coast, were at first exhilarated at discovering a colony of Christians in this remote land but were disappointed to find that these were not Catholics but what they considered a heretical sect. In their attempts at conversion, they burned the books of the Nestorians and persecuted and deported their leaders. In the process they successfully superimposed the legend of St. Thomas on that of Mar Thomé. Wrede gives an account of the language, social customs and religious rites of the Malabar Christians, proving that they were not Catholics but Syrians, following the doctrines of Nestorius, who rejected the divine nature of Christ, and who believed that the Virgin Mary was the Mother of Christ, not of God.[83]

The only notable paper contributed to the Society in 1802 was M. Joinville's, on 'The Religion and Manners of the People of Ceylon'. Joinville claimed that his was the first enquiry into the 'religion of Boudhou'.[84] Although it was for him a satisfaction 'to think, that though my information may not be altogether complete, yet it will serve as a clue for future and deeper researches', almost every conclusion of his was eventually either disproved or cast aside. Joinville, who was the Surveyor-General in Ceylon, was no scholar, and hence ignorant of recently-established facts. He stated, for instance, that it was unknown which was the more ancient, the religion of Zoroaster, Brahma or the Buddha and whether 'these three legislators had really existed, or rather if these names are not merely attributes.'[85] Legends and theories of cosmogony and theogony baffled him. Thus, describing the Buddhist idea of heaven where there are 'many living bodies without souls . . . and souls without bodies', he adds, 'As each of us may hope to see this when we transmigrate, I shall not give further detail of it.'[86] In one beautiful passage, however, he gives the Buddhist idea of a *mahakalpa*: Suppose a cubic stone of nine cubits on each side: a goddess of great beauty, dressed in robes of the finest muslin, passes once in every thousand years near this stone, at each time the zephyr gently blowing the muslin on it, till in this way it is worn down to the size of a grain of mustard: the space of time necessary for this is called *antakalpa*; eighty *antakalpas* make one *mahakalpa*.[87]

Much more scholarly than Joinville's paper was one on Hindu religion and mythology by J. D. Paterson[88]—the only paper of significance presented to the Society in 1803.[89]

Paterson took as his starting point Plutarch's statement about the Egyptians—a statement which is perhaps applicable to all ancient religions and folklore.

> The Egyptians had inserted nothing into their worship without a reason, nothing merely fabulous, nothing superstitious (as many suppose); but their institutions have either a reference to morals, or to something useful in life.... The mass of mankind lost sight of morality in the multiplicity of rites; and as it is easier to practise ceremonies than to subdue the passions, ceremonies gradually become substitutes for real religion, and usurp the place of morality and virtue.[90]

Paterson attempted to fathom the scientific basis behind Hindu mythology and traditions. Here, for instance, he tries to explain the attributes of Siva:

> To Shiva they have given three eyes; probably to denote his view of the three divisions of time, the past, the present, and the future. A crescent on his forehead portrays the measure of time by the phases of the moon. A serpent forms a necklace to denote the measure of time by years. A second necklace, formed of human skulls, marks the lapse and revolution of ages, and the extinction and succession of the generations of mankind. He holds a trident in one hand, to show that the three great attributes are in him assembled and united.[91]

The paper was an important study in comparative mythology despite serious gaps in his knowledge. This led, for example, to his attempt to explain the meaning behind the idols in the Jagannath temple at Puri.[92] There is also much which is a result of his insufficient acquaintance with Hindu mythology.

In 1804, the Society entered the third decade of its existence. On 4 July Colebrooke read a paper which opened up a whole new line of inquiry for students of Indology, and which the *Edinburgh Review* considered 'the most important desideratum in Indian literature'.[93] This was his essay on the Vedas, published in full in the eighth volume of the *Researches*.

This essay finally stilled the controversy among western scholars as to whether the Hindus did possess anything like the Vedas and 'if portions of them were still preserved, [and] whether any person, however learned in other respects, might be capable of understanding their obsolete dialect.'[94] Although William Jones and Charles Wilkins were aware of the existence of the Vedic texts, and Jones had even translated some passages of the *Atharva Veda*, the most important Veda, the *Rig Veda*, they hardly knew at all. Later, Colonel Polier obtained the complete text of these scriptures from the Maharaja of Jaipur, to whom he had rendered some medical service, and Sir Robert Chambers collected some fragments at Banaras. But they had never been studied by any western scholar. Colebrooke not only obtained the complete texts, and the commentary of Sayanacharya on the *Rig Veda*, but also made a close study of them. Commenting on the importance of Colebrooke's essay, Wilson wrote:

> It must have been a work of great labour, and could have been executed by no one except himself, as, independently of the knowledge of Sanskrit which it demanded, the possession of the books themselves was not within the reach of any European save one whose position commanded the respect and whose character conciliated the confidence of the Brahmans. This essay is still the only authority available for information respecting the oldest and most important religious writings of the Hindus.[95]

It may be noted here that even after Colebrooke, it was difficult for western scholars, including Wilson, to procure copies of the sacred texts. Max Müller in his autobiography recounted an incident narrated to him by Wilson. Once when Wilson was examining the library of one of the rajas, he saw some manuscripts of the *Rig Veda*. When he started turning the pages over, he observed 'the ominous and threatening looks of some of the Brahmans present, and thought it wiser to beat a retreat.' Max Müller tells of another scholar who got the sacred *mantra* of *Gayatri* printed in Calcutta. The Brahmans were furious at this profanation, and when the gentleman died soon after, they attributed his premature death to the vengeance of the offended gods'.[96]

Colebrooke, on the other hand, wrote as early as February 1797 to his father: 'I cannot conceive how it came to be ever asserted that the Brahmins were ever averse to instruct strangers. . . . They do not even conceal from us the most sacred texts of their *Vedas*.'[97]

Perhaps Colebrooke's studies of the Vedas began at this time, for in January 1801, he wrote: 'I mean to furnish three or four essays to the Asiatic Society this year . . . one on the Vedas, cannot, I fear, be completed until I get back to my library.'[98] The essay which ran into 120 pages, took nearly seven years of intense study and bears ample testimony of it.

Colebrooke examined the authorship and the time of the Vedas, providing the substance of the important hymns, and even made a cursory examination of the Upanishads. Although most of the hymns are given without any comments, in one instance Colebrooke does make an important observation, emphasizing what he had declared earlier in his article on religious ceremonies.

> The deities invoked appear on a cursory inspection of the Veda, to be as various as the authors of the prayers addressed to them: but, according to the most ancient annotations on the Indian scripture, those numerous names of persons and things are all resolvable into different titles of three deities, and ultimately of one god.["]

However Colebrooke also found much in the Vedas with little meaning. He confessed that he had not examined the texts 'more completely, than has yet been practicable.'[100] Since there is much in the Vedas the meaning of which still eludes the greatest scholars, Colebrooke can hardly be blamed for concluding that the contents of the Vedas would hardly reward the labour of the reader, much less of the translator. According to him the ancient texts were worthy of the occasional attention of the oriental scholar, but, their volume and the obscure ancient dialect in which they were composed would probably long prevent the mastery of their contents.[101] 'This prophecy', commented William Whitney, 'was doubtless in some measure the cause of its own fulfilment',[102] for it was only twenty-five years later that another work appeared on the Vedas. This was Friedrich Rosen's *Rig-Vedae Specimen*, published in London in 1830. Rosen had begun to translate the entire Rig-Veda into Latin, and the first volume of the work had been published in 1838. But the death of this promising scholar in 1837, at the age of thirty-two, prevented completion of this grand scheme. The next milestone in Vedic studies was Rudolf von Roth's *Zur Literature und Geschichte des Weda* (On the Literature and History of the Veda) which was published in 1846. 'This little work of his', says Whitney, 'with other similar essays which accompanied or followed it, gave perhaps the most powerful impulse to that movement which has since carried all Sanskritists irresistibly to the study of the Vedas.'[103] The greatest achievement of western scholars in this field was of course Max Müller's edition of the *Rig-Veda* along with Sayanacharya's commentary, published in 1849; this was followed a year later by Wilson's English translation of the first book of the *Rig-Veda*.

In spite of these and other studies of the Vedas such as those of Grassman and Benfey, Colebrooke remained the only scholar to have surveyed these texts as a whole. Writing in 1859, ten years after Max Müller and Wilson's translations, the *Calcutta Review* remarked: 'Colebrooke's masterly analysis of the Vedas is the most valuable contribution to Indian literature that has yet been made. . . . he walked with a firm foot and a clear eye through the quicksands, and has marked out the path most distinctly for those that follow.'[104]

Ever since the study of ancient India was taken up by western scholars, they have fallen broadly into two categories: those who see too much and those who see too little in the ancient Indian texts. Of those who saw too much, one was Francis Wilford. Wilford had gained a good word from Sir William Jones who at one time saw his own mantle fall on him, but from Colebrooke, Wilford received only words of caution. In 1804, Colebrooke wrote to his father:

> Captain Wilford, whose writings in the *Asiatic Researches* are known to you . . . will soon publish his lucubrations . . . on the long expected theme of the British Isles as known to the Hindus. You will find in his treatises on those subjects very curious matter, but very little conviction.[105]

The work which Colebrooke referred to was Wilford's essay on 'The Sacred Isles in the West, with other Essays connected with that work', which was presented first to the Society in a short form in January 1804. Running into over six hundred printed pages, the essay was published in the eighth, ninth, tenth and eleventh volumes of the *Researches*.

The essay was divided into six parts[106]: Essay I was 'On the geographical systems of the Hindus'; Essay II, 'Geographical and historical sketches on Anu-Gangam, or the Gangetic provinces'; Essay III, 'Chronology of the Kings of Magadha, emperors of India'; Essay IV, 'Vicramaditya and Salivahana, with their respective eras'; Essay V, 'The rise, progress, and decline of the Christian religion in India'; and Essay VI, 'The Sacred Isles in the West'.

More than the essays, it is Wilford's introduction which is of interest. Here Wilford tells in detail of the fraud that was practised upon him by the pundit he had employed to help him in his researches. Although this is perhaps the only recorded case of its kind, there is little doubt that similar cases of fraud practised by the pundits on the unsuspecting early western scholars marred many of their achievements.

Although scholars like Sir William Jones and Chezy averred the contrary, Sanskrit is a difficult language to learn and it is almost impossible for any single person to master its vast store of literature even in any one particular field. Wilford wanted to wade through the historical, geographical and mythological literature in Sanskrit and relate the material culled from these to the known history of the west. To help him in this pursuit, he employed a pundit of Banaras and provided him with accommodation and an establishment of assistants and writers.

Although Wilford does not name the pundit, his choice seems to have been a most unfortunate one. He not only embezzled the entire amount given by Wilford but also forged the ancient texts to provide a co-relation between the history and mythology of India and the west. First, he altered one or two keywords in the original Sanskrit manuscripts, substituting them with words like *Swetam* or *Sweta-dwipa,* so that there seemed to be a direct reference to the western world in ancient Sanskrit literature. Secondly, he changed an entire legend to make it correspond to Christian legends; thirdly, he inserted into the abstracts the prepared legends which he remembered having seen in some form or the other in the Puranas. At times he even removed leaves from ancient manuscripts replacing them with leaves that he himself had prepared. These forgeries were soon detected by Wilford.

> I soon perceived [he wrote], that whenever the word *Swetam,* or *Sweta-dwipa,* . . . was introduced, the writing was somewhat different, and that the paper was of a different colour, as if stained. Surprised at this strange appearance, I held the page to the light, and perceived immediately that there was an erasure. . . . I was thunderstruck, but felt some consolation, in knowing that still my manuscript was in my own possession. I recollected my essay on Egypt, and instantly referred to the originals which I had quoted in it. My fears were but too soon realized. The same deception, the same erasures, appeared to have pervaded them. I shall not trouble the Society with a description of what I felt, and of my distress at this discovery. My first step was to inform my friends of it . . . that I might secure, at least, the credit of the first disclosure.[107]

However, the conclusions reached in Wilford's voluminous essay were even more far-fetched than those in his earlier essay on Egypt, and one suspects that Wilford was once again led astray both by his wily pundits, and by his own over-imaginative interpretation of facts. In the following passage, for instance, he tries to prove that the ancient Indians considered Britain and Ireland to be sacred islands:

> *Suvarna dwipa,* or the island of *Su-Varna,* or gold, might be called also, in a

derivative form, *Su-varneya* simply, as *Anglia* or *Engle-lond*. It is called also *Hiranya*, a denomination of the same import, as well as *Canchana-bhumi*, or land of gold. *Hiranya* and *Su-varneya* are obviously the same with *Erin*, and *Juvemica*, or Ireland. Another name for it is *Surya-dwipa*, or the Island of the sun; and it is probably the old garden of *Phœbus* of the western mythologist. . . . We have seen before that *England* is called *Chandracanta*; *Ireland*, *Surya-canta*. *Scotland* is likewise denominated *Ayascanta*.[108]

Although Wilford claimed to have gone through each piece of evidence very carefully, especially after discovering the forgery, he seldom gave particulars of the sources on which he based his fantastic deductions. At best he gave the name of the Purana or the epic, without specifying the chapter or section. For example, he informs us that 'Cassiopea is called Lebana, and the Cepheur Nripa or Nri-rupa, and Persian authors say he is the same with Cai-caous. He is vaguely mentioned in other Hindu books as a great king'![109]

Further, much of the material seems to be presented merely to show off the author's erudition and is unrelated to his argument. It is for these reasons, perhaps, that no attempts were made by scholars to pursue the subject. Wilford's contention that the British Isles were the sacred islands the Sanskrit books referred to remains a solitary statement of a theory.

We have seen how the Society's request for grant of a suitable plot of land for constructing its library and museum was turned down by the Government. In July 1804, Harington once again proposed petitioning the Government for granting 'the ground on which the riding school lately stood', as a site for its library and museum. In May 1805 the Government agreed to the Society's request and granted the land occupied by the Riding House 'with the exception of such part of it as may be required by the Magistrates of Calcutta for the establishment of a Police Tannah and a fire engine — and that the Board of Revenue have been desired to instruct the Collector to grant the Society a *pottah*.'[110]

The Society immediately proceeded to formulate its plans for the building and by July 1805, plans were submitted by a Captain Preston,[111] and Jean-Jaques Pichon, a Frenchman settled as a builder in Calcutta, was chosen to construct the building.

In September 1805, Pichon forwarded to the Society his plan for the Society's building,[112] which was approved in early December 1807, and by January 1808 Pichon reported that the Society's building was 'nearly finished'.[113] On 3 February 1808, the President pointed out that he had 'reason to believe that Pichon has incurred a loss in constructing the house in which the Society are now met', and proposed the appointment of a committee to estimate the amount of compensation Pichon should be paid. The committee found that Pichon had exceeded the sum for which he contracted to complete the work by Rs 4,108, the total cost of construction coming to Rs 28,366 and decided to pay Rs 30,000 to Pichon, who acknowledged the receipt of the amount with 'many thanks' for he felt 'he had no right to expect' this amount.[114]

Although a fair amount of the Society's discussions during 1805 centred around the construction of its building, some valuable papers on Indian history and antiquities were read by its members. Unfortunately, none of these was either published in the *Researches* or maintained in the Society's archives. At its meeting on 2 January, Captain Charles Stewart described a manuscript in Tipu Sultan's library containing a complete history of the reign of Aurangzeb, and the Rev. W. Rotton sent a letter containing an abstract from Abdulla's *History of Akbar*. Another paper presented by J. D. Paterson dealt with 'Krishna, Buddha and Rama', which again was not published. Judging from his earlier papers on the Hindu religion and on the 'Musical Scale of the Hindus',[115] Paterson appears to have been a competent scholar whose work has gone unnoticed.

Yet another valuable paper which has been lost was Dr Anderson's communication containing 'Extracts from a Hindoo treatise on Physiology', presented to the Society at its meeting of 3 July.

One paper which was published in the *Researches* was Major Colin Mackenzie's 'Account of the Jains'.[116] This is perhaps the first study of the sect in modern times. Earlier the Buddhist and the Jain sects were often considered to be the same by many European scholars; from this point of view, Major Mackenzie's paper marks a breakthrough in the study of Jainism. Mackenzie for the first time gave the names of the twenty-four Jain *Tirthankaras* (or incarnations), Jain beliefs and customs and the principal tenets of their religion. Much of the information contained in the essay was gathered by Mackenzie from Charukirti Acharya, the Priest at Sravana Belgola, an important place of Jain pilgrimage.

Mackenzie's paper was followed by two others on the same subject. One consisted of information about the Jains collected by Dr F.

Buchanan from Pandit Acharya Swami, the Jain Guru;[117] and the other was Colebrooke's 'Observations on the sect of Jains'.[118] Buchanan's paper highlights the characteristics of Jain *arahats*, enlightened ones, and touches on their conceptions of heaven and hell. An interesting though improbable statement in the essay is that the Jains at one time were very numerous in Arabia 'but that, about 2500 years ago, a terrible persecution took place, at Mecca, by orders of a King named Parswa Bhattaraca, which forced great numbers to come to this country.'[119]

Colebrooke's article was much more critical and informed. He rightly pointed out that Buddhism and Jainism were later than the Vedic religion,[120] and traced the mention of this religion in the ancient Greek texts. Whereas Mackenzie had merely mentioned the names of the twenty-four Jain *Tirthankaras*, Colebrooke gave the characteristics of each, as gleaned from the important Jain text, the *Kalpa Sutra*. Besides, there is an account, perhaps the first, of the last *Tirthankara*, Mahavira, who occupies a most important place in ancient Indian history. The three communications taken together, thus provide a starting-point for the historiography of Jainism.

> It will perhaps give you pleasure [wrote Colebrooke to his father in a letter dated 9 June 1806] to know that the Asiatic Society has done me the honour of electing me its President. The office imposes on me the duty of endeavouring to promote scientific researches. I shall do so, as far as I am able; and I hope to succeed in stimulating the exertions of those who are best able to forward that object, and in obtaining some requisite aid from Government.[121]

Colebrooke was elected President of the Society on 2 April 1806, following Sir John Anstruther's departure to Europe. His election to the post coincided with certain proposals made at about this time which were designed to broaden the scope of the Society and to make it more effective in the prosecution of oriental studies.

One of these proposals had come to the Society in May 1805 from the Mission at Serampore, which was headed by Carey, Marshman and Ward. All three ardent missionaries were also great scholars. When they approached the Society for financial support for translating and publishing important Sanskrit works, their proposal, did not hint at their real intentions, which was thus described by Marshman:

> It makes us smile . . . when we consider that Satan will probably here be overshot in [by?] his bow. He certainly did not intend when he dictated

those vile and destructive fables, that the publishing of them to the enlightened world, should supply a fund for circulating the oracles of Truth.[122]

The Society, however, had no such motive when it decided to consider the Serampore proposal favourably and constituted a Committee in cooperation with the Council of Fort William College to select the work for translation and publication by the Serampore missionaries.[123]

Another proposal relating to the translation and publication of important Sanskrit and other oriental works was received from Sir James MacIntosh, the President of the Literary Society of Bombay.[124] With Colebrooke as President, the Society's response to the proposal was a predictable one. Accordingly, the Society resolved at its next meeting, to publish, apart from the *Asiatic Researches*, translations of 'short works in the Sanskrit and other Asiatic languages, or extracts and descriptive accounts of Books of greater length in those languages, which may be offered to the Society and appear deserving of publication'. The series, to be entitled *Bibliotheca Asiatica*, was in course of time to extend 'to all works extant in the learned languages of Asia'. However, at the same meeting at which this resolution was passed the Secretary laid before the Society a statement of its funds which showed that it would not be in a position to launch new undertakings.

It was, nevertheless, decided to support the project of the Serampore missionaries, and after taking into account the missionaries' own choice, they were assigned the translation and publication of Valmiki's *Ramayana*. Towards this effort, the Society agreed to make a monthly contribution of Rs 150, on the specific understanding that the work would be completed in three years.

The first volume of the *Ramayana* was published in time, and *The Quarterley Review* commented: 'Whatever may be the result of their [Serampore missionaries] labours in diffusing Christianity in these regions, there can be no question that by their translations they will bring important accessions to our very scanty stock of Asiatic literature.'[125]

After the publication of the first volume of the *Ramayana*, problems cropped up and scarcity of paper made the printing of other volumes difficult. At this stage, Carey proposed that pending the publication of other volumes of the *Ramayana*, the Society subsidise smaller volumes of Sanskrit works, especially those 'which treat of the principles of

Hindoo theology and philosophy.'[126] Carey also suggested that translation and publication of the texts of the *Samkhya* philosophy be 'accompanied with those other treatises upon that branch of Hindu philosophy which are most esteemed, and to follow it at convenient intervals with translations of the *Vedanta*, and other works upon the various branches of Hindu science'.[127]

Again predictably, Colebrooke with his love for Indian philosophy and science approved Carey's proposal, though some members held different opinions. Finally on 7 October 1807 the Society agreed that independently of the *Ramayana* project, it would grant additional support for eighteen months, contributing Rs 150 per month, for translation and publication of the textbooks of the *Samkhya* school of Indian philosophy. Almost a year later, on 2 November 1808, Carey laid before the Society a part of the translated text of the *Samkhya* with the condition that no one else except members of the Society should see it, and that he was willing to release the Society of its obligation for support to the project.[128] There is nothing on record to show the reason for Carey's strange offer, but the society did accept his proposal to relinquish its subscription—and thus ended the *Bibliotheca Asiatica* project.

Lack of funds stood in the way of another useful project. In his letter to his father dated 9 June 1806 Colebrooke wrote: 'A catalogue raisonné of all that is extant in Asiatic literature has long been desired. The utility of such a work would be obvious; and I believe the compilation of it will be now undertaken in good earnest.'[129]

Thus, Colebrooke initiated the scheme for the catalogue which would be taken up along with the *Bibliotheca Asiatica* project. Writing to the Governor-General on behalf of the Society, Colebrooke first outlined the utility of the catalogue. It would guide both researchers and scholars to the books most deserving their attention. The catalogue thus projected was to be an extremely detailed one. It would not only indicate the subject and the scope of each book but also contain extracts from important passages. It would provide details about the author, his life, the name and details of the sovereign under whom he lived and the 'manners and opinions prevalent at the period when he wrote'.

To pay for the work involved in so ambitious a project, and for remuneration to the pundits whose help would be required, Colebrooke asked for an annual sum of five to six thousand rupees so that 'the execution of the scheme might be immediately commenced; and its accomplishment might be expected at a period not very remote.'[130]

The Society's request received immediate support from the Governor-General who forwarded Colebrooke's letter, with his own recommendation, to the Court of Directors. But this was the time when Lord Wellesley was out of favour with the Court over the Fort William College project and it is just possible that the Court did not even go into the merits of the proposal before turning it down.

Although the project of the catalogue did not come through, Captain Wilford managed to prepare indices to the Puranas and the Upa-Puranas which he presented to the Society at its meetings on 2 July 1806 and 1 April 1807 respectively. Both these have now been lost.

Two contributions made during 1806 and 1807 were Colebrooke's essay on the 'Indian and Arabian Divisions of the Zodiac', read on 1 October 1806, and 'Ancient Monuments, containing Sanskrit Inscriptions', presented on 7 January 1807.

The first article attempted to establish correctly the particular stars, 'which give names to the Indian divisions of the Zodiac'. The task was fraught with considerable difficulties which Colebrooke described thus:

> None of the native astronomers, whom I consulted, were able to point out, in the heavens, all the asterisms for which they had names: it became, therefore, necessary to recur to their books, in which the positions of the principal stars are given. Here a fresh difficulty arose from the real or the seeming disagreement of the place of a star, with the division of the Zodiac, to which it was referred: and I was led from the consideration of this and of other apparent contradictions, to compare carefully the places assigned by the Hindus to their *nakshatras* with the positions of the lunar mansions, as determined by the Arabian astronomers.[131]

In the course of comparing the stars in the different *nakshatras* of the Hindus and in the *manzil al-gamar* of the Arabs and then identifying them with those in European catalogues, Colebrooke was led to the investigation of another important question, whether the Indian and Arabian divisions of the Zodiac had a common origin, and whether one borrowed from the other.[132]

Contradicting Sir William Jones's assertion that the Indian and Arab systems had developed independently of each other, Colebrooke wrote:

The coincidence appears to me too exact, in most instances, to be the effect of chance: in others, the differences are only such, as to authorise the remark, that the nation, which borrowed from the other, has not copied with servility — I apprehend that it must have been the Arabs who adopted (with slight variations) a division of the Zodiac familiar to the Hindus. This at least, seems to be more probable than the supposition, that the Indians received their system from the Arabians.[113]

Referring to Colebrooke's qualifications for attempting such a subject, the great Sanskritist, W. H. Mill, later remarked that no one else had greater command over this 'union of Sanskrit learning with competent astronomical science'.[114]

Besides dealing with astronomical subjects, it is of interest that even at that early period Colebrooke gave importance to the social and intellectual, rather than the political history of India: in his introductory remark, Colebrooke commented:

That the dynasties of princes, who have reigned paramount in India, or the line of chieftains, who have ruled over particular tracks, will be verified; or that the events of war or the effects of policy, during a series of ages, will be developed; is an expectation, which I neither entertain, nor wish to excite. . . . But the state of manners, and the prevalence of particular doctrines, at different periods, may be deduced from a diligent perusal of the writings of authors, whose age is ascertained: and the contrast of different results, for various and distant periods, may furnish a distinct outline of the progress of opinions. A brief history of the nation itself, rather than of its government, will be thus sketched.[115]

In Colebrooke's day, ancient literature and inscriptions were the two chief sources for reconstruction of India's ancient history. In his paper 'On ancient monuments', Colebrooke studied nine inscription-finds discovered in different places. Most of the inscriptions brought to light only minor rulers and princes.

Four brass-plates found at Chitradurg by Major Colin Mackenzie related to grants made by the Vijayanagar kings, and revealed the names of several rulers of this dynasty. Most important among these finds was the copper-plate inscription relating to the Pala kings, discovered at Dinajpur. This was the third find relating to this dynasty: the two earlier inscriptions found at Monghyr and at Buddal having been deciphered by Charles Wilkins. As mentioned earlier, Sir William Jones while commenting on Wilkins' paper, supposed these kings to have reigned in the first century B.C. Colebrooke surmised that these rulers existed in the eighth or the ninth century of the Christian era. The inscription moreover revealed names like Lokapala[134] and Mahipala which were not found in the earlier two inscriptions.

By early 1808, the Society had already acquired a rich collection of antiquities and other scientific specimens. These had so far been housed by the Secretary, and moved frequently with the frequent changes of Secretaries. The collection was now shifted to the Society's Museum, and staff consisting of a librarian, a *farash*, a *daftari*, a sweeper and a *durban*, were appointed. Gibbons, a member of the Society, volunteered to look after the establishment and also to take charge of the library if he were permitted to occupy a part of the lower apartments.[136] This was agreed to and thus India's first modern library and museum came formally into existence.

The next step was obviously to enrich them. At the meeting on 3 February 1808, it was resolved that the Secretary would apply to the Council of Fort William College for Tipu Sultan's library, which the English army, after the capture of Seringapatam, had presented to the College. The acquisition was a rare and a valuable one, including several beautifully illuminated manuscripts of the Quran, an old text of the *Gulistan*, said to be the first copy from the author's original, and a codex of the *Padshah namah* bearing an autograph of Shah Jahan.[137]

There were valuable acquisitions from other sources also. In April, the Society of Antiquaries in England presented a facsimile of the 'Greek part of the inscription in three characters imported from Egypt'. Although not specified in the Society's *Proceedings*, this inscription was in all probability the Greek text of the Rosetta stone. That the Society received a copy of the text shows the high esteem it enjoyed in the world of the learned.

India itself, however, was a treasure-house of antiquities and natural specimens. With a view to tapping this source, Dr Hare proposed in June 1808 the appointment of a Committee 'for the purpose of physical investigations, the collection of facts, specimens and correspondence with individuals whose situations in this country may be favourable for such discussions and investigations.' Later Hare modified his proposal and recommended the formation of two committees, one for 'natural history, philosophy, medicine, improvements of the arts, and whatever is comprehended in the general term of physics', and another 'for literature, philology, history, antiquities, and whatever is comprehended under the general term of literature.' Although Dr

Hare's proposal was accepted by the Society, and details regarding the functions of the two Committees were drawn up, there is nothing in the Society's records to show that these Committees were ever active.

Contributions in different fields, however, continued to be made, among others by Sir John Malcolm, 'one of the most distinguished servants of Great Britain in the East',[138] and author of the celebrated *History of Persia*.

Sir John contributed two papers to the Society, both very important. The first, read before the Society on 2 November 1808, consisted of translations of two letters of Nadir Shah which were included in the collection of his letters and original state papers published after his death by his Secretary, Mirza Mehdi. More important for us is the second letter, addressed by Nadir Shah to his son, Reza Kuli Mirza, in which he described his conquest of Delhi after the battle of Karnal in which the Moghul Emperor Mohammad Shah was defeated.

Even more important than the letter, is Malcolm's observation on European historians:

> In describing eastern despots there has often appeared to me a stronger desire to satisfy the public of the author's attachment to freedom and his abhorrence to tyranny . . . than to give a clear and just view of those characters whose history was the immediate object of his labours. . . . [Those] who look to a volume of Asiatic history with no other desire but that of obtaining historical truth . . . will lament the existence of a feeling which was adverse to an impartial consideration of events illustrative of the general history of the human mind.[139]

Malcolm's next paper was a 'Sketch of the Sikhs', presented to the Society on 5 April 1809. In spite of the major role played by the Sikhs during that period, little attention was paid by British Indologists to the study of this community. Even Wilkins' article on the subject, published in the first volume of the *Researches*, consisted of only casual observations. According to Malcolm, though several writers had treated of the subject earlier, their writings 'served more to excite than to gratify curiosity'.[140]

Though entitled only a 'Sketch' Malcolm's article is the first serious study of the history of the Sikhs. He traced the development of the sect from the time of Guru Nanak, and besides giving details of the lives and achievements of the Gurus, also examined the customs and beliefs of the Sikh people.

It is possible that because of the wealth of information about the Sikhs provided by Malcolm, the other paper on the subject was more or less overlooked by the Society — neither preserved in its Archives nor published in the *Researches*. This was 'An account of the Sikhs', by William Ward, presented to the Society at its meeting on 4 April 1810.[141]

The most important paper of 1810 was the essay on the early history of Algebra, read by Edward Strachey on 3 October. Strachey[142] had earlier (4 July 1804) presented his observations on the originality, extent and importance of mathematics among the ancient Hindus and had even provided extracts from the Persian translations of the *Lilavati* and the *Beeja Ganita*. The paper, which traced the origin of the discipline of Algebra to India is a landmark in this branch of study. Colebrooke, in his treatise on Indian algebra (1817), which consisted of translations of the works of Bhaskara and Brahmagupta, preceded by an essay on the state of sciences as known to the Hindus, acknowledged Strachey's contribution in the field.

The first European to point out that the mathematical sciences were highly developed in ancient India was Reuben Burrow, whose paper titled 'A proof that the Hindus had the Binomial Theorem', was published in the second volume of the *Researches*. In this paper, Burrow had shown his awareness of the ancient Hindu works, the *Lilavati* and the *Beeja Ganita*, and stated that he had even translated parts of the latter at a time when no European but himself 'even suspected that the Hindus had any Algebra'. He even tried to prove that although Newton was responsible for the application of the binomial theorem to fractional indices, the 'Hindus understood it in whole numbers to the full as well as Briggs, and much better than Pascal.'[143]

Burrow's views were not taken seriously, primarily because he, like Wilford, was given to exaggerated generalizations. Thus, in the same paper in which he tried to prove that the Hindus of old had a knowledge of algebra, he stated:

> In England, it is obvious, Stonehenge is evidently one of the temples of Boodh; and the arithmetic, the astronomy, astrology, the holidays, games, names of stars, and figures of the constellations; the ancient monuments, laws, and even the languages of the different nations, have the strongest marks of the same original . . . [and further] that the Druids of Britain were *Brahmans* is beyond the least shadow of a doubt.[144]

Although Burrow's views on algebra, lost in his other generalizations, were not widely noticed by scholars they did attract Colebrooke's attention. He started learning Sanskrit primarily to go deeper into the question.[145] Burrow presented his paper in 1804, Colebrooke's work appeared in 1817, and between the two we have Strachey, more reasonable and cautious than Burrow, and leading the way to the more thorough Colebrooke.

Strachey emphasized the fact that Diophantus was the only Greek writer to have spoken of the science of algebra:

> We know of no Greek writer on algebra but Diophantus; neither he, nor any known author, of any age, or of any country, has spoken, directly or indirectly, of any other Greek writer on algebra, in any branch whatever, the Greek language has not even a term to designate the science.[146]

The Diophantus factor later became a major point in the controversy whether algebra owed its origin to India. Strachey held that Diophantus received the knowledge of algebra from 'some Alexandrian merchant, trading to India . . . or might have learned from Indians at Alexandria.'

With the publication of Colebrooke's treatise, the controversy reached its height. The issue essentially was the same as that of Indian astronomy: whether Indian algebra was as old as Colebrooke and others held it to be (about the sixth–seventh century); and whether it originated with the Greeks or the Indians. The main factor in this case was the date of Diophantus. Strachey and Colebrooke held that Diophantus was a later Greek writer who himself borrowed the knowledge from Indian sources, and that the Indians showed a far greater knowledge of the science than Diophantus.

Such controversies about the dating of Indian astronomy and Indian algebra were, however, symptoms of a deeper controversy spelt out in a review of Colebrooke's work which appeared in an issue of the *Edinburgh Review*. 'Party spirit', felt the critic, 'prevails no less in the literary than in the political world; and it is now the fashion to run down everything Indian, particularly Indian science.'[147] In the vanguard of this movement was James Mill, whose book on India appeared the year after Colebrooke's work. Mill criticised Colebrooke for advocating the antiquity of Indian science. So bitter was the controversy that in another review of Mill's work, published in the *Asiatic Journal*, a contributor with the pen-name 'Yavat-Tavat' wrote:

Mr Mill, in his *History of British India*, has given an account of Mr Colebrooke's book on Indian Algebra. . . . From a writer so grossly prejudiced as Mr M. has shown himself to be against the Hindus, it would be vain to expect any impartial discussion. . . . This gentleman labours under another disqualification, namely his utter ignorance of the subject. . . . 'On mathematics', he says, 'I must speak superficially'. Pity it did not occur to him that he had the alternative of not speaking at all![148]

Although Strachey and Colebrooke were proved right by subsequent scholars such as Bhau Daji, it was perhaps unfortunate that it was Mill who continued to cast a major influence on most English historians of India.

There were, however, exceptions. The most important scholar to expose Mill's theories was Horace Hayman Wilson, the central figure in the next phase of the Society's history. Wilson arrived in India in March 1809 and by February 1810 he was elected a member of the Asiatic Society.[149] This was primarily because of Dr John Leyden, who recognized the young man's talents. When Dr Hunter resigned as Secretary because of being posted out of Calcutta, Colebrooke proposed Dr Leyden as Secretary and Wilson became Deputy Secretary. After Leyden's death, Wilson was elected Secretary, on 4 December 1811.

The year 1812 was an inactive one for the Society. Two contributions which might have been of some interest had they survived, were a facsimile of inscriptions that Lieutenant Fell discovered in the fort of Hansi, and facsimiles of two inscriptions found in Kalinjar fort by Colebrooke. Unfortunately, apart from a mere reference to these in the Proceedings, there is no record of the inscriptions or their translations.

A paper presented to the Society by William Price on 3 February 1813 proved to be one of the most valuable contributions to Indian historiography. Price was on duty with his corps in Bundelkhand when he came across a stone 'containing a Sanskrit inscription, lying at the fort of a rocky hill in the vicinity of the town of Mow, about ten miles distant from Chattarpur.'[150]

The inscription contained a genealogy which immediately aroused Price's interest. The stone was being used by the local people to sharpen their knives and swords, which resulted in part of the inscription being erased. Price had the stone removed to save it from further damage and also to read the inscription at leisure. Price received little help in his task. The oldest residents of the town could only offer the information that the stone had been lying there ever since they remembered and that it had been there in their parents' time. Because of neglect and abuse, much of the text, especially the last line, was effaced. Since the last line usually contains the date of the inscription, Price was not able to ascertain the date, nor had he heard of that particular line of princes. There was a reference in the inscription to King Kirtivarman. Price knew of the play *Prabodha Chandrodaya*, and that it was first performed before Kirtivarman. However, Price could not 'determine whether he [Kirtivarman] is the same with the prince of that name mentioned in the inscription: and indeed if they could be identified, the circumstance would lead to no satisfactory conclusion, the age of the play being equally involved in doubt.'[151]

In fact, Price's chance discovery had brought to light the dynasty known as the Chandelas of Bundelkhand. The stone inscription contained the names of the line of princes including that of Dhanga. Dhanga's name was erroneously read as Banga in another inscription of this dynasty, which was discovered in 1838 by Captain T. S. Burt at Kajraha. Price had deciphered it correctly, but his reading was only confirmed in 1860 by Cunningham, who drew up the complete genealogy of the sixteen princes of this dynasty who are now known in Indian history as the Chandelas of Mahoba.[152]

The year 1813 is also important for the publication of Wilson's translation of Kalidasa's poem *Megha Duta*, a copy of which he presented to the Society at its meeting of 13 October. The work immediately established Wilson's name in the ranks of prominent Indologists.

The year 1814, although without any scholarly contribution to compare with Price's, is, however, a landmark in the Society's history. This was on account of Nathaniel Wallich.

Wallich, born in Copenhagen in 1786, was surgeon to the Danish settlement in Serampore when the town fell to the East India Company in 1813. Dr Wallich together with a few other officers were allowed to enter the English service. Wallich seems to have been an avid collector of botanical specimens from the very beginning. After visiting the Asiatic Society, he realized the potential of the institution, and wrote to the Secretary urging the establishment of a public museum in the Society's building.

While the need for a museum was one of the main reasons for the Society constructing a building, no concrete plan for it had emerged, till Wallich took it up. After pointing out the vast richness of this land for yielding specimens and exhibits of all kinds, Wallich added:

The far greater portion of these have hitherto escaped the notice of naturalists, or has been imperfectly, or what is much worse, erroneously described. The deplorable neglect to which the natural history of this country has been exposed is very striking and must principally be attributed to total want in India of . . . a public Museum.[153]

Dr Wallich's letter evoked an enthusiastic response from the Society. The Committee of Papers to which Dr Wallich's letter was referred, commented:

A collection of the substances which are the objects of science, and of those reliques which illustrate ancient times and manners . . . was one of the first objects of the Asiatic Society, and any person engaged in the study of the history and languages of this country or in the investigations of its natural productions must have had frequent cause for regretting that such a purpose should have been hitherto so very incompletely carried into effect. . . . The Asiatic Society is now called upon to adopt active measures for remedying this deficiency, and collecting from the abundant matter, which India offers, a Museum that shall be serviceable to history and science.[154]

The Society then gave a list of subjects on which it invited contributions. These included ancient inscriptions, monuments, coins and manuscripts, instruments of war and music, vessels employed in religious ceremonies, dried or preserved specimens or skeletons of birds and animals, dried plants and fruits, and ores and alloys of metals and minerals of every description. The Society also decided to acknowledge the contributions to its museum and library in the *Researches* and appointed Dr Wallich superintendent of the 'Oriental Museum of the Asiatic Society'.

Secure financially and with a rapidly growing library and museum, 1815 seemed to be a good year for the Society, when the sad news of Colebrooke's return to England arrived. At its first meeting of 1815, Colebrooke presented over seventy-five volumes of books and manuscripts to the library together with his letter of resignation.[155] This was soon followed by Wilson's resignation as the Secretary of the Society.[156]

Wilson soon returned as Secretary, but the loss of Colebrooke was almost irreparable. Through his contributions on Hindu science, their religious ceremonies and, most important of all, the Vedas, Colebrooke had brought immense distinction to the Society, and with it, to Indian studies among European scholars. William Jones paid more attention to the romantic aspect of Sanskrit literature, to its poetry, drama, and music, but Colebrooke brought to light what may be regarded as drier, but more important aspects of Indian literature and culture: its grammar, philosophy and science. It was, in fact, an essential extension of Jones's work.

Colebrooke realized the potentialities of the Society even more than Sir William Jones, and, therefore endeavoured to place the Institution on a sound footing. There is little doubt that the Society still exists because it has got a building of its own and set up its own library and museum. As a loose federation of scholars, as William Jones had desired the Society to be, it might not have survived for even half a century.

Colebrooke's other major organizational achievement was the founding of the Royal Asiatic Society of Great Britain and Ireland, which also survives till today. While there might have been more distinguished Presidents of the Asiatic Society than Colebrooke, none combined the qualities of scholar and administrator to such an extent. Max Müller, speaking about Colebrooke's term as President of the Asiatic Society, felt that the post had never been filled so worthily before or would be after.

4

H. H. Wilson and the Expanding
Frontiers of Historical Scholarship
1815–1832

After Colebrooke's return to England in 1815, it was Horace Hayman Wilson who emerged as the leading orientalist in India. Wilson was born in London in September 1786.[1] Having studied medicine at the St Thomas's Hospital, London, he was appointed Assistant Surgeon in the East India Company's service in 1808. On his way to India he had as fellow-passenger an Indian from whom Wilson received his first lessons in Hindustani.

Soon after his arrival in Calcutta in March 1809,[2] Wilson got an appointment in the local mint, where he was fortunate in being appointed assistant to the famous orientalist Dr John Leyden.[3] He had picked up some knowledge of chemical analysis, properties of metals and the process of assaying[4] in England where he had occasionally accompanied his uncle to his work in the Government mint. Inspired by Leyden and 'excited by the example and biography of Sir William Jones', Wilson took to oriental studies, particularly the Sanskrit language. Arberry describes this transformation thus: 'Wilson had come out to India as a surgeon, but he abandoned the knife for the die, and later exchanged this for the pen and gown.'[5]

Wilson's first achievement was a translation in verse of Kalidasa's the *Megha Dutt*, or the 'Cloud Messenger', which appeared in 1813. The work was an instant success, perhaps because the name of Kalidasa had already been made familiar to English readers by William Jones. It was widely reviewed by the English press. The *Asiatic Journal* called it 'one of the most perfect translations that adorns the literature of the nation',[6] while the *Classical Journal*, on learning that after the *Megha Dutt*, Wilson had taken up the task of compiling a Sanskrit-English Dictionary, wished that he 'had left to others the more laborious, though perhaps more useful, employment of lexicographical compilation, and still continued to transfuse the beauties of eastern poetry into English verse."[7]

The *Megha Dutt* displayed fully Wilson's love of Indian culture.[8] However, his European public, while applauding Wilson's translation, disapproved of this enthusiasm as it had done with Jones over his translation of the *Sakuntala*. For instance, the *Asiatic Journal*, which had been so generous in its praise of the work, also remarked:

> Mr Wilson's taste, though fashioned after the most perfect models, is occasionally a little warped by his enthusiastic estimation of his author, which leads him to admire several prettinesses and fanciful allusions, which, we are convinced, his more sober judgement would teach him to condemn.[9]

Wilson's next project won him universal praise from orientalists. This was the Sanskrit–English Dictionary compiled at the request of the Court of Directors, who had advanced Rs 3,750 to him on 22 June 1816.[10] The work, completed in 1819 consisted of a large quarto volume of over one thousand pages 'comprehending all the radicals of the language, and between 30 and 40,000 derivatives, with their etymological development and characteristic grammatical inflections'. Wilson himself said that 'although the work, . . . [is] necessarily imperfect, it has, I have reason to know, mainly contributed to the extended cultivation of Sanskrit literature on the continent of Europe.'[11]

Once Wilson began work on the *Dictionary*, he had little time for anything else. In spite of this, he managed to function effectively as Secretary of the Society which he was made in June 1816.[12]

Although the year 1816 was, on the whole, uneventful for the Society, there was one paper presented at its first meeting[13] which is a landmark in the study of Greater India. This was on the 'Existence of the Hindu Religion in the Island of Bali', by John Crawford. Crawford was born in 1783 in the island of Islay, and like Wilson, received an appointment in the medical service in India after having studied medicine. After serving for five years in the North-West Provinces, Crawford was transferred to Penang, where he acquired extensive knowledge of the people of Java and Bali. During the English occupation of Java (1811–17), Crawford occupied several important posts but returned to England on the restoration of the territory to the Dutch. He died at the age of 85 and had several works to his credit including the three-volume *History of the Indian Archipelago*. Another two-volumed *Description of India* is preserved in manuscript form in the India Office Library.[14] Being familiar with the languages of the East Indies as well as India, Crawford was in a position to judge the influence of India on the islands of the archipelago. To assess the significance of his paper, it is necessary to examine the progress of studies on Greater India.

The celebrated historian, R. C. Majumdar, was of the opinion that western scholars had overemphasized the isolated character of the Indian civilization, and that the concept of Greater India was one of very recent origin. As proof of this, he pointed out that his matriculation textbook laid emphasis on the fact that shut up by mountains and seas India developed 'a unique civilization, neither influencing nor being influenced by its neighbours'.[15] Elsewhere he said:

> It has *now* been satisfactorily established, on the basis of evidence which has passed even the ordeal of European scepticism, that far from occupying an isolated position apart from the rest, India played almost the same part in the east as Greece and Rome had done in the West.[16] (emphasis added)

Yet articles such as Marsden's and Crawford's on the subject of Indian influence on other countries, including those of south-east Asia, had been published by the Society far earlier. Crawford's article in itself negates Dr Majumdar's views.

Crawford began by observing that the Hindu religion was at one time 'extensively spread throughout the oriental Archipelago',[17] but had since become confined only to the island of Bali. Here, it was the national religion, 'the religion of nine-tenths of the people, of every sovereign on the island, and of every man in power'.[18] He found the social customs of the islanders resembling those of India and observed that there were reflections of the *Ramayana* and *Mahabharata* in local literature. 'The *Indians*', he said, 'have taught the inhabitants of these islands their decimal system. . . . Whatever progress the natives of these islands have made in astronomy, seems in a great measure also borrowed from the same source'.[19]

These facts, together with Crawford's observation that 'many of the English who have visited Java, have had ample opportunity of appreciating the skill and extent with which the Hindus of that island had imitated these Indian arts',[20] goes to show that Indian influence in South-east Asia was taken for granted by European scholars by the early nineteenth century.

Crawford stated furthermore that the first Indian colony was set up in Java in the second century A.D. and that Kalinga was universally considered by the oriental islanders 'as the country from which the civility, laws and religion of India were introduced among them.'

His article also dealt with another aspect of Greater Indian studies discussed recently by Jean Filliozat. In his inaugural address at the 'Greater Indian Studies' Section at the All India Oriental Conference in 1959, Filliozat said that scholars of Greater India laid too great a stress on the Indian elements in the south-eastern civilization, and tended to overlook the non-Indian features and changes that took place in the Indian characteristics of the local civilization.[21] Crawford, on the other hand, described not only the changes that had occurred in Hindu society over the years but also the Muslim and Chinese impact on the society and culture of the people of these islands.

In another article on 'The Ruins of Prambanan in Java',[22] Crawford proved the emigration of Hindus to Java, adding that a large number of settlers came to the island from the kingdom of 'Telinga' in south India. He described the ruins of the temple in Prambanan in detail, showing that at one time Hinduism was the predominant religion on the island.

Other scholars besides Crawford have investigated the phenomenon of Hinduism in south-east Asia. About this time, Colonel Mackenzie explored the ruins of Prambanan and discovered a stone slab with a Devanagari inscription.[23] Dr Tytler, who had accompanied Crawford on one of his visits to Prambanan, collected and presented to the Society 'sundry Hindu statues and vessels discovered on the Island of Java',[24] and also contributed a memoir (of which unfortunately no trace remains) on 'The ruins of Hindu Temples and Images on the Island of Java'. On 6 August 1817, Captain Barker presented a 'Memorandum of Antiquities from Java'. This communication is again lost to us since it was not published in the *Researches*.

Of even greater interest in this connection is that knowledge of the influence of the Indian civilization on south-east Asia was not confined to academic circles; it seems to have been taken for granted by the administration too. Thus in a letter dated 10 January 1817, the Acting Military Secretary wrote to Wilson that the Government had come into possession of a collection of articles formerly belonging to the Emperor of Solo and among them were items which could shed light on the religious customs and manners of the inhabitants of a portion of

India. He offered the collection to the Society, for it to select for the museum, any item worthy of preservation.[25]

As the Government's letter shows, the Society had established itself as a pioneering cultural body in the country. It was also the first institute of oriental study in the world[26] and had come to be recognized as such in the West. Thus, in 1817, the Society entered into correspondence and exchanged publications with such institutions as the Royal Society of Copenhagen, the Literary Society established at the Prince of Wales Island,[27] and the Société d'Agriculture et de Commerce de la Ville de Caen (the Commercial and Agricultural Society of Caen).[28]

We cannot close the review of 1817 without mentioning Francis Ellis's 'Account of a Discovery of a Modern Imitation of the Vedas',[29] presented to the Society on 6 August. The paper dealt with the French publication *Ezour Vedam*, which, as we have seen, was read by Voltaire. Although doubts about the authenticity of the work had been raised earlier, this was the first time that evidence was provided of the work being a forgery. Ellis discovered that the original still existed among the manuscripts in the possession of the Catholic missionaries at Pondicherry. In fact there were forgeries of the other Vedas also, which Ellis discovered were all intended to refute the Hindu doctrines and highlight the absurdity of the *Brahman* ceremonies. On the basis of evidence provided by the local Christians, Ellis guessed, probably correctly, that the *Ezour Vedam* was composed by Robertus de Nobilibus, who had established the Madura mission in 1620.

With the increase in the Society's prestige increased the popularity of oriental studies. At its meeting of 3 June 1818, the Secretary read a letter from Colebrooke, with which he forwarded 'some tracts . . . published by learned foreigners, tending to show the direction of public attention towards oriental literature at universities abroad.'[30]

The Society's library and the museum, especially the latter, continued to grow with donations pouring in from all over the world. Yet its meetings as well as the number of papers presented at them, decreased. The meetings had come to be gatherings where mostly official business was transacted. It was therefore proposed that there should be two meetings held every month at which attention should be confined to 'the promotion of those studies and enquiries which were originally contemplated in the institution of the Asiatic Society'.[31]

There is little evidence, however, for Kopf's statement that 'the primary function of the Society as historical and archaeological repository and headquaters for all of India really began with the Hastings-Wilson reforms of 1818.'[12] The Marquess of Hastings did attend the Society's meetings more regularly than most other Presidents;[13] he also often forwarded papers and articles to the Society, but apart from this there is little to show that there were significant reforms or more frequent meetings.

As for the museum, reforms were carried out in Wilson's absence and also after March 1820. In a letter to Captain A. Lockett, the Acting Secretary of the Society, Dr Wallich, who was earlier the Superintendent of the Museum, wrote, 'There is a notion prevailing of our never having kept the Museum in a proper order nor taken much care to preserve the articles contained in it'.[14] He pointed out that apart from the sweeper, there was no establishment whatsoever attached to the Museum.

The last meeting of 1818 held on 12 December saw an important and an interesting communication by Captain Sydenham of the Madras Establishment. This was 'An Account of Bijapur', which Captain Sydenham had visited in 1811.[15] Although Tavernier and Thevenot had written about the city earlier, Captain Sydenham's account was the first authentic one as it was based on what he called 'an attentive survey'. He described every building giving its accurate measurements. His historical account of the city was based on a close study of earlier works like Ferishta's *History* and Scott's *History of the Dekkan*. He also talked to the local people and recounted legends connected with the rulers of the Adil Shahi Dynasty. Although the entire article makes fascinating reading, there is one observation about Aurangzeb which may be of interest. Describing the plunder of the *Jama Masjid* by Aurangzeb, Sydenham remarks:

He carried off a massy silver chain suspended from the top, to the end of which was fastened a large ruby, which the principal attendant assured me, had a lustre so brilliant as to give light to the mosque at night . . . Every thing that he pilfered was converted into money and distributed to his troops. This account may perhaps be exaggerated; but as this conqueror was not very scrupulous in matters of religion, except in the observance of its outward forms, tho' he once assumed the garb of a *fakir* to cloak his ambitious design; and as he had a numerous army to maintain who were sometimes clamorous for pay, he thought probably as little of robbing a mosque, as some conquerors of the West have done, of plundering churches.[16]

No account of the year 1818 can be complete from the point of view of Indological studies without reference to the publication of James Mill's *magnum opus*, *The History of British India*. Mill is probably the first secular historian who brought to bear a definite ideology on historical writing. To prove a point, or the superiority of the utilitarian school to which he belonged, Mill was prepared to go to any length, including distortion of facts. His enthusiasm for a party, a doctrine or a philosophy led him to criticise practically every achievement of the Asiatic Society. Thus, whereas the Society had been able to prove to the world the fact that India had an ancient and a rich culture, Mill tried to prove that India was a *tabula rasa* on which the chapter on civilization and culture remained to be written through the exercise of judicious laws. This put him in direct opposition to the values cherished by the Society. Thus Wilson, who later edited Mill's work, stated:

> Indignant at the exalted, and it may be granted, sometimes exaggerated descriptions of their advance in civilization, of their learning, their sciences, their talents, their virtues, which emanated from the amiable enthusiasm of Sir William Jones, Mr Mill has entered the lists against him with equal enthusiasm, but a less commendable purpose.... With very imperfect knowledge, with materials exceedingly defective, with an implicit faith in all testimony hostile to Hindu pretensions, he has elaborated a portrait of the Hindus which has no resemblance whatever to the original, and which almost outrages humanity.[17]

In spite of this, Mill's *History* continued to have a profound influence on later historians, probably because many in England wished to see India in the light Mill painted it. On the other hand, several scholars tried to demolish the mistaken facts and ideas which Mill had built up, the most powerful refutation of Mill's ideas about Indian culture coming from H. H. Wilson.

The year 1819 began badly. At the first meeting, on 12 February 1819, J. H. Harington announced his resignation as Vice-President because of his departure for England. Harington was one of the oldest members and earliest office-bearers of the Society. He had served as Secretary during Jones's time, and had been the Society's Vice-President since 1797. He had served in senior positions in the judicial branch of the Government, and was also the most distinguished

Persian scholar of his time, having published translations of the works of the Sufi poet Sadi. We have earlier noticed his paper on the cave inscriptions at Gaya published in the first volume of the *Researches*.[38] He now presented a paper on 'Drawings of two ancient pillars found in Tirhut with copies of the inscription cut upon them in an unknown character'.[39] Harington did not of course know the importance of these inscriptions, and that they would lead to the discovery of Asoka Priyadarsi.

The Society lost another important office-bearer in November, when H. H. Wilson was transferred to Banaras. At its meeting of 13 December, when Wilson presented to the Society a copy of his Sanskrit-English Dictionary, it was announced that in his absence Captain Lockett would officiate as Secretary.[40] The choice was a happy one, for in Captain Lockett, the Society found a very able Secretary who effected a number of improvements which have been attributed to Wilson by Kopf.

The implementation of the plans for improvement carries us into the year 1820. At the first meeting of the year, Captain Lockett, as the officiating Secretary, pointed out the need for repairing the monument of the founder of the Society, Sir William Jones.[41] Lockett also laid before the Society a set of rules formulated by the Committee of Papers to streamline the functioning of the Society's library. [The move had been initiated by Wilson in the earlier meeting of 13 November 1819]. The Library's working hours were regularized and rules laid down for lending and borrowing of books.

Later, steps were initiated to improve the museum also, although these did not bear much fruit. At the second meeting, on 10 March, the Superintendent of the museum, Dr Wallich, pointed out the miserable condition of the museum. The Society was also greatly under-staffed. Dr Wallich suggested that it was essential to have a person in charge of the collection with a writer and one or two servants to assist him. He even suggested the appointment of Ramdhun Sen, the Assistant Librarian, as the officiating Keeper, with a salary of forty to fifty rupees a month. Wallich's proposals were referred to the Committee of Papers, but no action seems to have been taken on them except that at its meeting of 17 June the Society appointed Mr Hutchins superintendent of the museum on a salary not exceeding Rs 150 per month.

In the field of Indian antiquities and history, two important items came up before the Society during 1820. Unfortunately, however, their importance was not recognized, and they have been lost. The first consisted of four large copper-plates full of inscriptions procured by William Moorcroft from a temple near Badrinath.[42] These inscriptions were supposed to contain the 'ancient theological history of the Hindus'. The inscriptions were received by the Society, as was reported in the meeting of 20 December, and Captain Price was requested to examine and report on the plates, but subsequent minutes are silent on the issue. Similarly, no study seems to have been made of a Sanskrit manuscript obtained by Moorcroft from the priests of the temple of Badrinath.[43] The two items must have contained valuable material on Indian history, coming as they did from one of the main centres of Hinduism. A Sanskrit inscription recording the 'genealogy of the King of Guhamandala', presented to the Society by Captain R. Lochlan,[44] had a similar fate.

One communication of importance was however preserved in the *Asiatic Researches*. This was 'An Account of the Cootub Minar, and the inscriptions in its vicinity', by Walter Ewer, presented to the Society at its meeting of 20 December 1820. The Qutb Minar had been first described and measured by Captain Blunt. Blunt however neither copied nor read any of the inscriptions there. Ewer copied and deciphered six inscriptions. The difficulties involved in the task are best expressed in Ewer's own words:

> I have some reason to believe that, with the exception of the first, these have never been read, since the ruinous state of the galleries rendered it dangerous to venture on them: nor could I find that any person in Delhi was in possession of a copy. With the assistance of a telescope of great magnifying power I was enabled to copy them with the utmost facility, and to ascertain the general meaning of the contents of each, although some words remain undeciphered on account of the imperfect state of the letters.[45]

Ewer's communication is important from many points of view. First, it revealed the name of the builder of the monument. Captain Blunt in his article had ascribed the construction of the *minar* to Cuttub Shah; Ewer for the first time read the inscription which stated: 'The Sultan Shems-ul-Hak-wa-ud-Din-Altamesh erected this building'. Further, another inscription stated the fact that the *minar* had been damaged by lightning and repaired in A.D. 1503 during the reign of Sikandar, the son of Bahlol. Ewer also argued that the *minar* was erected within the precincts of a Hindu temple (a fact which explained the presence of Hindu motifs on pillars nearby) and that it had nothing to do with the mosque in the vicinity which was built by Qutb-ud-din Aibak. This article thus established the major historical facts connected with the Qutb Minar.

The year 1821 saw a communication which gave a new dimension to the history of ancient India. This was Wilson's 'Essay on the Hindu History of Cashmir', based on the now famous Kalhana's *Rajatarangini*.[46]

Rajatarangini had no doubt been known earlier to the Mughals and the Europeans. Akbar's court-historian Abul Fazl had included an abstract of the early history of Kashmir in his *Ain-i-Akbari*, citing Kalhana's work as his source.[47] Another Mughal historian, Haidar Malik, wrote an abridged version of the work in Persian during Jahangir's reign.

The first European to show an awareness of the *Rajatarangini* was François Bernier who spoke of 'the histories of the ancient kings of Kachemire made by order of Jehan-Guyre which I am now translating from the Persian.' This translation, evidently based on the work by Haidar Malik, is now lost to us. A century later, the Tyrolean missionary Father Tieffenthaler included in his *Description de l'Inde* a summary of the history of Kashmir, again based on Haidar Malik's work.

Before Father Tieffenthaler's work was printed, Francis Gladwin had published his translation of the *Ain-i-Akbari* in 1776. In this work, he quoted Kalhana's *Chronicle* as the source for his own abstract of Kashmiri history. It was this reference which perhaps prompted Sir William Jones to include among his fields of study the 'history of India from the Sanscrit Cashmir authorities'.[48] It was not until 1805 however that a copy, although an incomplete and defective one, of the *Rajatarangini* was found by Colebrooke. Colebrooke passed on this manuscript to Wilson, who obtained another transcript from Lucknow. Besides these two manuscripts, as Wilson tells us, he found yet another copy by 'accidental purchase', at Calcutta.[49]

Although none of these manuscripts related to the original work (which was seen for the first time only in 1875 by Bühler, and obtained in 1889 by Stein) Wilson gathered enough knowledge about the work to state: 'The only Sanscrit composition yet discovered, to which the title of History can with any propriety be applied, is the *Raja Tarangi-ni*, a history of Cashmir,"[50] a judgement unaltered by any later discovery. Stein agreed with Wilson, and in the Preface to his excellent translation into English, called it 'practically the sole extant product of Sanskrit literature possessing the character of a true Chronicle'.[51] Even R. C. Majumdar, who examined closely the question of 'Ideas of History in Sanskrit Literature', concluded: 'The fact remains that except Kalhana's *Rajatarangini* . . . there is no other historical text in the whole range of Sanskrit literature which makes even a near approach to it, or may be regarded as history in the proper sense of the term."[52] According to A. L. Basham, 'The work *Rajatarangini* is unique as the only attempt at true history in the whole of surviving Sanskrit literature."[53]

This aspect of the *Rajatarangini* was realized even in Wilson's time. The Society's farewell address to Wilson in 1832 noted:

> In the intricate labyrinth of Indian history and chronology, where the erudite labours of Jones, of Hamilton and of Wilford, seemed only to render the darkness visible, and the confusion more hopelessly inextricable, furnishing too just ground for the idea that, in India, mythology and pantheistic mysticism had swallowed up history altogether—you have discovered one point at least, where order could be educed from the chaos of existing materials . . . from which, as way-marks the future investigator might safely proceed in exploring what is elsewhere most doubtful in this vast undiscovered region of Asiatic antiquity . . . This is a correct judgement of your essay on the Hindu history of Cashmir.[54]

Wilson not only gave a critical abstract of the first six cantos of the *Rajatarangini*, but also drew up a chronological table of the reigns of various kings based on Kalhana's work. Through copious footnotes, he scrutinised Kalhana's facts in the light of other works in Sanskrit, Persian and English. Speaking of Wilson's achievement, Stein said:

> The sound judgement and thoroughness displayed in this publication of the distinguished Sanskrit scholar deserve all the more credit, as the three incomplete Devanagari manuscript. at his disposal were so defective that a close translation of them, if desirable, would have been impracticable."[55]

In spite of such defects, Wilson's *Essay* made a great impact on the academic world and made Kalhana a celebrated historian. After its publication, we have an almost unbroken series of studies on Kalhana and his work. Soon after the *Essay* was published, the Society received from Moorcroft, who was in Srinagar at the time, a Devanagari transcript of the *Rajatarangini* which became the basis for the Society's publication in 1835. Five years later, the work was translated by A. Troyer into French for the Société Asiatique at Paris. Troyer found Wilson so helpful in his project that he wrote: 'I have so often and so often repeated your name from the preface down to the end of this work, that you will be persuaded I did not work without you,' and added that Wilson had rendered himself necessary to the Sanskrit world.[57]

At about this time Cunningham was in Kashmir on political duty. His attention drawn to the *Rajatarangini*, he began making local enquiries and then, primarily with the help of numismatic studies, 'correctly ascertained the era employed in Kalhana's chronological reckoning, and thus succeeded in fixing with fair accuracy the dates for almost all the kings from the advent of the Karkota dynasty onwards.'[58] Again, in a paper on 'The ancient coinage of Kashmir, with chronological and historical notes', published in the *Numismatic Chronicle* for 1846, Cunningham proved 'the great value of numismatic evidence for the critical control of Kalhana's records'. Some years later, in the 1860s, Lassen gave an exhaustive analysis of Kalhana's work in his *Indische Alterthumskunde*. All these works, however, were based on the extant defective versions, especially the Calcutta edition of 1835. It was only in 1875 that Bühler, during his visit to Kashmir in search of Sanskrit manuscripts, happened to glance at the *codex archetypus* of the manuscript of *Rajatarangini* in the Sarada letters; and it was not till 1889 that Stein procured the entire manuscript.[59] With Stein's publication of the edited text together with the translation, in 1900, we can say that the work begun by Wilson on the *Rajatarangini* saw fulfilment.[60]

If the *Rajatarangini* brought to light India's past, Wilson's next paper, on 'the Religious Sects of the Hindus', revealed an important aspect of contemporary Indian culture and society. Earlier, some work on these lines had been done by Indians as well as Europeans: Wilson himself mentions the Persian works of Sital Singh and Mathura Nath, who provided a short history of the origin of the various religious sects describing their rituals, and their appearance. Another well-known work, the *Bhakta Mala* of Nabhaji, gave the legendary history of all the celebrated *bhaktas* or devotees of the Vaishnavas. Besides these, William Ward had dealt with some of the religious features of the Hindus in his *History*. Colebrooke too, as we have seen earlier, had given an account of the religious ceremonies of the Hindus. In spite of this, vast areas were still unexplored. Speaking of the difficulties involved in the task as well as of the scope of his own treatise, Wilson wrote:

> To trace the character of those [sects] which have disappeared, or to investigate the remote history of some which still remain and are apparently of ancient date, are tasks for which we are far from being yet prepared; ... so ambitious a project as that of piercing the impenetrable gloom has not instigated the present attempt.... The humbler aim of these researches has been that of ascertaining the actual condition of the popular religion of the inhabitants of some of the provinces subject to the Bengal Government.[61]

The task Wilson set himself was not a simple one. The *Sketch* provided details about the history, rituals, religious beliefs and peculiarities, traditions and religious literature of twenty schools of the Vaishnavas, nine schools of the Saivas, four of the Saktas and ten other miscellaneous sects including seven classes of the Naṇak Shahis.

For this Wilson drew not only on the relevant texts in Sanskrit, Persian and the different dialects of Hindi, but also relied heavily on 'oral report'. One can only marvel at the enormity of the task. The *Sketch* was the most complete work on the subject that had been presented by that time and remains of value even today. Successive writers on the subject have drawn heavily on this treatise, and as the author of *Eminent Orientalists* tells us:

> It is noticeable that Professor Wilson has laid under an immense debt of gratitude the excellent Bengali writer, Babu Akshoy Kumar Datta, who, largely drew upon his work in the preparation of his *Upasaka Sampradaya*—a work upon which his fame as a Bengali writer principally rests.... It is true that Wilson's work contains some errors and inaccuracies, but they were almost inevitable and fairly excusable in a foreigner.[62]

When the *Sketch* appeared, it naturally aroused great interest and curiosity in the Christian world. Bishop Middleton, who was also Vice-President of the Society, remarked that a more valuable paper had never been offered to the Society for publication.[63]

This remark coming from a Bishop may lead one to question Wilson's motives in preparing this paper. Did Wilson draw up his *Sketch* to arm Christian missionaries with the weak points of the Hindu religion? The question, in view of Wilson's later appointment to the Boden Chair is of some interest. The first fact that comes to mind in answer to the question is that nowhere did Wilson himself mention anything about this aspect of his work. Moreover at the beginning of Section II he states:

> Although I have neither the purpose nor the power to enter into any detail of the remote condition of the Hindu faith, yet as its present state is of comparatively very recent origin, it may form a not unnecessary, nor uninteresting preliminary branch of the enquiry, to endeavour to determine its existing modifications, at the period immediately preceding the few centuries, which have sufficed to bestow upon it its actual form.[64]

This would suggest that the research underlying the *Sketch* was a purely academic task for Wilson. He learnt much that was unpalatable or even disgusting to him, especially in the Sakta rituals; but it seems doubtful if he thought that conversion to Christianity was the solution to the problem. He seems to have laid greater stress on education than on conversion, hoping that 'with the diffusion of education, independent enquiry into the merits of the prevailing systems and their professors will become more universal, and be better directed.'[65]

In 1821 Wilford, after a four-year silence presented a long, abstruse article on 'The Ancient Geography of India',[66] which was replete with far-fetched theories and statements without any basis. One example of his etymological juggling will suffice: 'The Sanscrit name of Chunar is Charanadri, or Charana-giri, which is nearly synonymous with Padantica. This last is mentioned in the *Ratna-cosa*, and in some *Puranas*, where it is called *Padapa*'.[67]

Again, without any apparent reason, he equates Yama with Pluto, the river Sarayu with the Sambus of Megasthenes and so on. Though many of his conclusions are drawn without any sound basis and hang in mid-air, one look at Wilford's paper would make obvious the difficulty of judging whether a paper was worth publication in the Society's *Journal* or not. The nine members of the Committee of Papers were all fine scholars but could not be all-knowing. Moreover, the communications received by the Society had grown in number as well as in variety, and it was practically impossible for the Committee to examine them carefully. Wilson therefore proposed a new method for assessing papers in the Society's meeting held on 13 December. It was proposed that the Society should constitute a special committee for each paper, selecting members who were knowledgeable about that particular subject. In this way justice would be done to every communication as well as to the scholars. The Committee of Papers, Wilson suggested, could be reconstituted as the House Committee to 'exercise a superintendence over the affairs and welfare, and maintain the interests and credit of the Society'.[68]

Wilson's proposals though sound did not find favour with the Society. It resolved to continue with the election of members for the Committee of Papers on the old pattern deferring its decision on Wilson's proposals to the next meeting. On 6 February 1822 the Society turned down the entire proposal saying that 'no alteration in the Institution of the Committee appears at present advisable'.

Two new members elected to the Society in 1821 were Rev. W. H. Mill on 14 July, and Antoine de Chezy on 18 October. de Chezy was born at Neuilly in January 1773. His father was an engineer of repute and it was expected that Antoine would follow in his father's footsteps. In 1800, however, he was given a junior position in the department of manuscripts in the Bibliothèque Nationale, the National library of France at Paris, where he developed an interest in Sanskrit literature. In 1803 he began studying Sanskrit, although no grammar or dictionary in French existed. Even without these, he acquired such a mastery over the language in a short time that he could compose verses of great elegance.

Upon the restoration of the Bourbons, the French Government, founded in 1815 two professorships, one in Chinese and the other in Sanskrit, in the Royal Collège of France. de Chezy not only became the first occupant of the first chair of Sanskrit founded on the Continent, but also inspired several scholars, among them Burnouf, to devote themselves to the study of Sanskrit.

de Chezy suffered from ill-health towards the end of his life, but continued to work to the last. He completed the translation of the *Sakuntala* in French only some months before his death in 1832 and planned to publish an analysis of the *Ramayana*—a project which he could not complete.

Although de Chezy did not contribute any paper to the Asiatic Society, the Society in conferring him with honorary membership honoured both him and itself. It was an appropriate choice, for de Chezy, played an important part in the history of western scholarship of the Sanskrit language.

The Member that the Society lost in 1821 was Colonel Colin Mackenzie, whose contribution on the Jains had marked a breakthrough in the study of that sect. Before giving the biographical details of Mackenzie, it is worth quoting a remark with which the Calcutta Government *Gazette* prefaced Mackenzie's obituary notice.

It is a peculiarity in the history of Oriental literature in British India, that its professors seem but little to sympathise with the fate of their associates. They rarely take the pains to communicate to the public, which naturally looks to them for the information, the worth of those labours which are intended to facilitate the study of Oriental letters. . . . The individuals particularised above passed away with little notice, beyond the blank record of their deaths in the common obituary column of the newspapers of Calcutta. . . . The contributors to the Indian press, and it redounds but little to their credit, seem to find it a more grateful occupation to revile the living, than to bewail and do honour to the dead.[69]

Colin Mackenzie was born in about 1753 on the Island of Lewis, Scotland. When he was twenty-eight, he procured a Madras cadetship, landing in India in 1782.[70] The first thirteen years of his life in India, from 1783 to 1796, were as Mackenzie himself tells us, 'of little moment to the objects pursued latterly, in collecting observations and notices of Hindoo manners, of geography and of history.'[71] These years were mostly spent in different campaigns including the capture of Seringapatam and Pondicherry. 'For what is the life of an Indian adventurer but one continued campaign on a more extensive scale?' he mourned in a letter to Johnston. In 1795 Mackenzie was sent as commanding engineer to the Ceylonese campaign.

On his return, he met a learned Brahman, C. V. Boria, with whom he took 'the first step . . . into the portal of Indian knowledge'. And then began the stupendous task of collecting practically everything—manuscripts, coins, inscriptions, etc., that served to illustrate any facet of the country or the people of India. Since his duty was mainly confined to the South, the Mackenzie collection deals mostly with south India. At his death his collection included 1,568 literary manuscripts, of which 681 were in Sanskrit, 274 in Tamil, 176 in Telugu, 208 in Kanarese and the rest in Malayalam, Oriya and Marathi. There were forty-five volumes on Jain literature and 3,000 tracts, comprised in 264 volumes; 8,076 inscriptions copied from stone and copperplates bound in seventy-seven volumes; and translations of local tracts together with the tracts in loose sheets numbered 2,159. There were 2,700 plans and drawings, 6,218 coins, 106 images and 40 antiquities.[72] Wilson, who prepared a catalogue of the collection based on Mackenzie's own copy, described it as one 'which no individual exertions have ever before accumulated, or probably will again assemble.'

Even more remarkable is the fact that the entire collection was Mackenzie's personal one and he himself had to train Indians to collect specimens from throughout south India.

Despite this astounding collection Colin Mackenzie was not a mere collector of antiquities. We have already noticed his contribution in the *Asiatic Researches* on the Jains. Besides this, he wrote an 'Account of the Pagoda at Jerwuttum', and 'Remarks on some Antiquities in the West and South Coasts of Ceylon'. He also contributed a number of articles to the *Asiatic Annual Register* which included: 'A sketch of the life of Hyder Ali Khan'; 'History of the Anagoondy Rajas'; 'History of the Kings of Beejnagar'; 'An Account of the Teachers of the Madhawa Vaishnavas'; and an 'Account of the Bhats, or Indian Bards'.

There is evidence that Mackenzie wanted to achieve much more, including writing a history of the Deccan prior to the Muslim conquest, about which he wrote to his friend Sir Alexander Johnston:

> The Dekhan was, in fact, then a *terra incognita*, of which no authentic evidence existed, excepting in some uncertain notices and mutilated sketches of the marches of Bussy, and in the travels of Tavernier and Thevenot, which convey but little satisfaction to the philosophical accuracy of modern times.[73]

Mackenzie was determined to fill this huge gap, but it remained an unfulfilled desire. He could not even complete a catalogue of his acquisitions, let alone have all his valuable tracts and manuscripts translated into English—a task for which he had even recruited some scholars at his own expense.

In 1801 the Government withdrew its approval of Mackenzie's moderate establishment of three assistants and one naturalist, which he had set up for a comprehensive survey of the south and in 1819 he was moved to Calcutta as the first Surveyor-General of India. Though this was a most honourable appointment, Mackenzie was not happy, as he wrote to Johnston. He described how a transfer to Calcutta would affect his collection and enquiries, but still hoped to complete a 'condensed view of the whole collection, and a catalogue raisonnée of the native manuscripts and books & c., and to give the translated materials such form as may at least facilitate the production of some parts.' This task was accomplished only in 1828 when Wilson published a scholarly catalogue of the Mackenzie collection.

After Mackenzie's death, his entire collection passed to his widow, from whom the Society bought a number of books,[74] the rest being purchased for the Government by the Marquess of Hastings for £10,000 although Mackenzie himself had spent nearly £15,000 on them. These items were shipped to England in three batches in 1823 and 1825, with the exception of manuscripts relating to south India, which were lodged in the library of the Madras College. In 1836 an Indian pundit, Cavelly Venkata Lachmia, wrote to the Governor of Madras, Sir Frederick Adam, seeking financial support for preparing an exhaustive catalogue of the Mackenzie collection at Madras. Cavelly's letter was referred to the Asiatic Society which found Cavelly's qualifications for the job inadequate, since in his letter he had not gone a step further than the scheme proposed by Wilson in his catalogue. At the time another scholar, William Taylor, was working on Mackenzie's Madras collection and had promised 'a paper or series of papers on the subject'. It was proposed by the Asiatic Society that patronage be provided to Taylor instead, and that Cavelly join him at the task.[75]

Though today Colin Mackenzie is more or less a forgotten name and does not find a place even in many histories of south India,[76] his collection contributed greatly to the reconstruction of the history of the Indian peninsula. In fact the knowledge of many dynasties like the Chola, Chera and Pandya, and even that of the Vijayanagar kingdom would be incomplete without a reference to the Mackenzie collection. Mark Wilks gratefully acknowledged the value of the collection for his *History of Mysore*, and it can only be regretted that later historians have failed to utilize the collection.

In a letter to Members of the Convocation resident at Trinity College, Oxford, Wilson, presenting his qualifications as a candidate for the Boden Chair of Sanskrit, wrote:

> During my residence at Benares, and for some time after my return, my attention was directed to a comprehensive view of the dramatic literature of the Hindus, and in the course of 1826–27 I published entire translations of six dramas, with an introductory account of the Hindu dramatic system, and an appendix giving an analytical description of twenty-three other dramatic compositions. In this branch of Sanscrit literature I have left little for my successors.[77]

As noted earlier, it was William Jones who had revealed to the western world the existence of the dramatic literature of ancient India. Although he had highlighted the richness of Hindu dramatic literature, surprisingly little was done in this field after his death. The beautiful translation of *Sakuntala* seemed to have appeared like a blinding light and then as quickly disappeared. It was Wilson who once again gave life to the study of Sanskrit drama. Nor was his publication a mere translation of the Sanskrit plays. As the *Blackwood's Edinburgh Magazine* remarked:

> It is a masterpiece of philosophical criticism, many of his notes are in themselves poems, and his Preface to the Plays are full of the rarest and most interesting historical erudition often throwing great light on the manners and customs of ancient India. . . . Its true praise is that it unfolds before us the whole of the finest part of a national literature, and thereby illustrates a highly interesting national character.[78]

The work which became a landmark in oriental study had a modest beginning at the Society's meeting of 26 December 1822, when Wilson read his 'Remarks on the Hindu Drama illustrated by translated passages'.[79]

In spite of the fact that this communication, together with the publication of *Select Specimens* in 1826–7, opened a whole new vista of Indian dramatic literature to Europeans, the work met with little response in England itself. It was rapidly translated into German and French, but as the *Quarterly Review* remarked, in England many literary men scarcely knew of its existence[80] and *Blackwood's Edinburgh* reviewer had difficulty in getting a copy.[81]

In view of this and two other incidents, the motives of western Indologists in taking up oriental studies deserve examination. The two incidents were the publication of an article by the German scholar, Augustus von Schlegel, in *Indische Bibliotheck*[82], and the farewell address presented by the Society to the Marquess of Hastings on his departure from India.[83]

Schlegel's article is perhaps the first clear expression of the view that the English scholars pursued Indian studies only to enable the British administration to tighten its grip on the Indian empire through greater knowledge of the land and its people. Schlegel wrote:

> In order to perpetuate the duration of an empire more extensive than that of the Mogul, to which they have succeeded, the English have turned their provident attention to the opinions and habits of their subjects. . . . The study of Oriental literature is to the English, rather the means than the end, the instrument of their policy . . . shall then the English be longer suffered to retain a monopoly of Sanskrit literature?[84]

The Society's records, on the other hand, show that it never had any intentions of keeping the fruits of Indological research limited to English scholars. The Society was not only liberal in conferring honorary membership on scholars of other countries (and these included Augustus Schlegel himself),[85] but also in accepting learned contributions from non-British scholars. Scholars like Ventura, Court and above all, Alexander Csoma de Körös contributed more to the Society's transactions than many of its English members. Again, Brian Houghton Hodgson sent many of the valuable Buddhist manuscripts he had collected to the Asiatic Society in Paris. It was these, in fact, which enabled Burnouf to become an authority on Buddhism.

Secondly, while it cannot be denied that the early Englishmen in India learnt the local languages to facilitate their communication with Indians, it must be conceded that the study of Sanskrit and other scholastic subjects were confined to only a few of them who pursued these studies for their own sake and out of personal interest. If indeed, Indological studies were an inalienable part of the empire-building process, one would expect these studies to have expanded with the expansion of the empire. But was it so? Schlegel himself did not think it was, for he remarked: 'Literary or scientific zeal appears to be unknown to the English in India, and the spirit once called into animation by Sir William Jones seems to have now become extinct.' The English journals of the time were no less critical of the apathetic attitude of the Englishmen towards the knowledge of the East. *The Quarterly Review* commented in 1831:

> The indifference of the public opinion of the British public to the religious and political state of the vast empire . . . has been a frequent subject of astonishment and complaint. These regions . . . are supposed to possess no interest except to the holders of the East India stock, or to those who think India an admirable country to provide for younger sons.[86]

Another expression of the motives of English scholars can be found in the Society's farewell address to the Marquess of Hastings on his departure for England. Hastings had become the Society's President after Colebrooke left for England in 1815. Prior to him, only one other Governor-General, Sir John Shore, had agreed to become President of the Society. Warren Hastings, as we have already seen, declined to do so; Lord Cornwallis and Lord Wellesley had often attended the Society's meetings but never as President. Hastings not only agreed to be President, but also participated actively in its deliberations, forwarded to it communications from various officers and presented several articles to the Society's museum.[87] His views on the Society's objectives are therefore important, and equally significant are the views expressed in the address to him which was read at the meeting held on 26 December 1822 by the Vice-President:

> The dissemination of knowledge is in all cultivated societies the worthy occupation of talent and power. Even where that knowledge may not be of generally practical application, its possession may be endowed with specific value, and much that is little essential to the necessities of life, is of high value to intellectual ambition. It may be of trifling import to the welfare of any particular community to discover and adjust the dark tradition of remote antiquity. . . . To the mind that is liberalised by studious enquiry, and elevated by expanded views, these subjects are deeply important and the studies of the scholar and the speculations of the philosopher, cannot be without their effect upon the improvement of the Society, and the happiness of mankind.[88]

In his reply, Hastings, after urging members of the Society not to relax their researches in the 'records of a country heretofore eminently civilized', added:

> I confess that I do not expect anything directly valuable will be found, such traces as remain of the ancient state of India, appear to me as establishing the presumption of progress in mechanical arts rather than in cultivated productions of the mind . . . how far any advancement to science may be hoped, is not here the question. Perhaps nothing.[89]

The question which concerns us is why a Governor-General, who was already burdened with gigantic administrative problems, should still associate himself with studies which apparently were not of much practical use. That Hastings was a man of wide interests and a broad outlook in itself does not provide an adequate answer to the question. A more appropriate answer was perhaps given in the review of Hastings' private journal published in 1858, which went:

> The value of the book must depend on the character of the man. . . . Now the Earl of Moira, afterwards Marquess of Hastings, was not a man of the kind to render his journal valuable. . . . He was vain, exceedingly vain, and resorted to means, both socially and politically to feed that vanity.[90]

What could pander to Hastings' vanity more effectively than associating with some of the greatest scholars in the country and being President of a learned Society that had acquired world-wide recognition? This may also be the reason why important officials including Governor-Generals, maintained a link with the Society, and it is this fact which has probably led subsequent historians to formulate the hypothesis that oriental studies were a part of the empire-building process.

After Hastings, the mantle of Presidentship fell on John Herbert Harington, perhaps the most distinguished Persian scholar of the time. The major event of the year was, however, the establishment of the Asiatic Society of Paris, which had its first meeting on 1 April 1822 with Baron de Sacy making the opening oration. The Secretary of the Society, Abel Remusat, sent a letter to the Society of Bengal in which he proposed that the two groups should enter into correspondence for the advancement of science and oriental literature. The letter also announced the election of Wilson as an honorary secretary-associate of the Institution. The Calcutta Society welcomed the formation of the French Society and presented it with a copy of the *Researches*.

The first meeting of the Society in 1823, held on 8 March, heard an important communication on Orissa by Andrew Stirling, who had been elected a member the previous year.[91] Stirling's account of Orissa[92] is the first comprehensive study of the state: he described its physical features, giving details of the soil, products, rivers and towns, and also dwelt on the population, the castes and customs, political institutions and the land tenure system. Of more interest to us is his account of the history and antiquities of Orissa. While his descriptions of the temples of Bhubaneswar, Puri and Konarak are exact, the history of the region is far from accurate. This is not surprising, since, when he wrote, knowledge of the Maurya dynasty which had a great bearing on the history of Orissa, had not been reconstructed. Stirling's article, therefore, conveys an idea of its past before its ancient history began to be discovered.

In the absence of historical data, Stirling had to draw on myths and legends: the heroes of the *Mahabharata* are the heroes of Stirling's history and we have kings reigning for two, three, five and seven centuries.

Yet, Stirling's account has its own importance. The account of the Moghul period, which was based on recent works such as Ferishta's History and the *Ain-i-Akbari*, was more accurate. Stirling was the first writer after Abul-Fazl to have noticed and described the temple of Konarak, and he pointed out the errors in the latter's account. He was also the first to notice the caves and inscriptions of Khandagiri and Udayagiri, which later revealed to Indian history King Kharavela. Stirling could not decipher the inscriptions in the caves, but he guessed correctly that 'the character has some connection with the ancient Pracrit', and that it resembled the inscriptions on the *lat* of Firuz Shah at Delhi and a portion of the Allahabad pillar. According to the *Centenary Review*, Stirling's remark, though 'based more on conjecture than sound evidence, came really much nearer the truth than he at that time would know.'[93]

With the exception of Stirling's communication, there was little of historical interest in 1823. However, the year is important for the founding of the Royal Asiatic Society of Great Britain and Ireland[94], probably influenced by the foundation of the French Asiatic Society the previous year. There had been widespread criticism in England that the establishment of the Royal Asiatic Society should have taken so long. The *Asiatic Journal* commented:

> That the languages and literary relics of India which till the time of Sir W. Jones, had attracted few British scholars, should long have shared the fate which still, in some measure, attends its history and politics among the generality of English readers, is to be regretted, because our negligence has exposed us to some reproach, as well as to the mortifying rivalry of foreigners, who enjoy few of the advantages heretofore disregarded by us.[95]

The *Oriental Herald* wondered:

> How much might have been accomplished, towards the elucidation of those subjects which it is the peculiar object of the present Society to investigate, had an institution of this description been established in England at a much earlier period; instead of suffering the French, whose interests are so much less connected with the East than our own, to take the lead in the formation of a society for the especial and exclusive cultivation of Oriental research.[96]

The moving spirit behind the foundation of the Asiatic Society in London was H. T. Colebrooke, who had already been in London for nearly eight years. The first step towards establishing the Royal Society was taken only on 9 January 1823 when fifteen people assembled in Colebrooke's house 'to consider the expediency of instituting a Society for the encouragement of science, literature and the arts in connection with India, and other countries eastward of the Cape of Good Hope.'[97] Among those present were Sir Alexander Johnston, Mark Wilks, and Edward Strachey. At the fifth meeting, held on 22 February, the Society assumed the name of the Asiatic Society of Great Britain[98] and recommended the appointment of the Rt. Hon'ble Charles W. W. Wynn as President, and Colebrooke as Director. At the following meeting on 1 March, the Society was informed that the King had agreed to become its Patron.

The year 1824 began sadly, for on 15 February, Captain Edward Fell died at Belaspore. Little is known of Fell's life except that through his perseverance, he became so proficient in Sanskrit that he was 'excelled by few pundits in the command he exercised over the system of Panini.'[99] We catch a glimpse of his personality through a letter he wrote to Wilson: 'You know I have perseverance and inclination to become famed but it requires a superior power to pull one out of the crowd, and to you I look up for this main leading feature.

Don't be offended at what I have stated . . . for become great I must! ! !'[100]

For some time Fell was Superintendent of the Benaras Sanskrit College. On his death, in 1824, the *Gazette* noted that 'the flourishing condition of that institution during the last few years has been his own work'.[101]

Fell had several contributions to his credit. He translated a portion of the *Bhagavad-Gita*, prepared an abstract account of the *Raghuvamsa*, and at the time of his death was engaged upon the translation of the *Mitakshara*, a work on Hindu Law. Fell was also deeply interested in Indian antiquities and was the first European to give an account of the Buddhist monument at Bhilsa. This account was published in the *Calcutta Journal* of 11 July 1819 and so was not considered for publication by the Society. Fell had, however, forwarded a number of inscriptions to the Asiatic Society, which were published together as a tribute to his memory in the fifteenth volume of the *Researches*.

The first of these was the Garha Mandala inscription of A.D. 1667, which gave the names and exploits of some predecessors of King Dalapati and his wife Durgavati. The inscription was remarkable, said Wilson, for here 'the enumeration much exceeds that of any inscription yet discovered.'[102] There was also an account of the battle in which Rani Durgavati gave her life. The inscription listed three more rulers after Durgavati's son confirming the fact that although Akbar defeated Durgavati, he never annexed the kingdom of Gondwana.

Inscription No.II eulogizing the greatness of Prithviraj was discovered at Hansi and had little by way of historical material except for the elusive fact of Prithviraj having slain Hammira, whom the inscription described as 'an arrow to the earth'.

The third section contained the material given in seven copper-plates which were discovered near the 'confluence of the Berna nalla[102a] with the Ganges' in early 1822 by a peasant working in his fields. The first six inscriptions bearing the dates A.D. 1177 and 1179 were formal grants of land by Raja Jai Chandra, while the seventh, bearing the date A.D. 1120, commemorated a land grant by Jai Chandra's grandfather Govinda Chandra. Another land grant of Jai Chandra's was discussed earlier by Colebrooke, who took Vijay Chandra to be the same as Jai Chandra. Fell's inscriptions not only helped remove this error, but also enabled scholars 'to form a tolerably satisfactory idea of the series of princes who reigned at Kanauj and Delhi, in the period between the first Muslim invasion and the final subversion of the native states in the upper parts of Hindustan'.[103] Referring to this achievement, Fell wrote to Wilson:

> I have rectified Mr Colebrooke's mis-statement in a grant by Jaya Chandra. . . . pray give it one of your best introductions to the Society. It is very curious and upsets Mr Colebrooke's statement that Vijaya Chandra was the same with Jayachandra—in this grant it is particularly stated that Jayachandra was the son of Vijayachandra.[104]

Since these inscriptions are dated well before the Battle of Tarain in A.D. 1191 they mention nothing of the enmity between Jai Chandra and Prithviraj, but they did enable Wilson to draw up a more or less accurate genealogy of the Kanauj dynasty, perhaps the last great Hindu dynasty of northern India prior to the Muslim conquest. Wilson's genealogy was as follows:

Ruler	A.D.
Yasovigraha	1024
Mahi Chandra	1048
Chandra-Deva	1072
Madanapala	1096
Govinda Chandra	1120
Vijaya Chandra	1144
Jaya Chandra	1168

Although, as is clear from Wilson's remarks, several points relating to the history of this dynasty still needed clarification, it laid the groundwork for reconstruction of the Kanauj dynasty.

Another discovery of great importance made in 1824 was the collection of forty-three inscriptions on Mount Abu by Captain Speirs, Political Agent at Sirohi.[105] This was a rich find which enabled Wilson, for the first time, to draw up the genealogy of such important dynasties as the Chalukya, Paramara and the Guhila Rajputs. While some work had been done on these dynasties by Abul Fazl, Colonel Wilford, Major Tod and Lieutenant Macmurdo, it was Wilson who drew up a more or less consistent genealogy of the different dynasties based on these inscriptions. Wilson's genealogies were perhaps of especial importance for showing the gaps in our information, and a mountain of research is still needed to reconcile the names and dates of different rulers in India. The genealogies drawn up by Wilson are given in Table 4.1.

Wilson was aware of several inconsistencies in his genealogies, which prevented him from compiling a consistent history of the period. Thus, while it was unusual for the name of Munja to be missing from the genealogy of the Paramaras, King Bhoja being included created other problems. We must, however, remember that most of the rulers of these dynasties asserted their importance during the eleventh and twelfth centuries which constitute one of the most confusing periods in the history of India. The cementing authority of the Guptas had long since faded away, the impact of Muslim rule was yet to be felt, and the two or three centuries in between were marked by the rise of petty dynasties and unimportant rulers who, even if able and brilliant individuals, vanished almost as soon as they had risen. It is even now difficult to construct a consistent history of this period which must be treated as histories of several and comparatively unimportant dynasties like the Chedis, the Chandelas, the Gurjaras, the Paramaras, the Pratiharas, the Gahadavalas and the Sakambharis.

Another important communication presented by Dr Wilson this year was his 'Analytical summary of the contents of the *Vishnu Puran*'.[106] With this essay, began the critical study of the Puranas. Describing the earlier methods of study, Wilson remarked that in order to discover their contents 'with the least possible waste of their own time and labour', western scholars had employed pundits to extract such passages as were most likely to illustrate Hindu mythology, chronology, and history. This process had two major disadvantages: there were times when important passages were missed or overlooked by pundits, and secondly, to please the 'clients' passages were sometimes forged, as in Wilford's case. To avoid these pitfalls, Wilson engaged a number of pundits and asked them to prepare a minute and an exhaustive index of each Purana. In this way, he procured the contents not only of chapters and sections but of almost

Table 4.1 Genealogies of Six Indian Dynasties as given by H.H. Wilson

Royal House of Patten, Nehrwala, or Guzarat	Branch of Anahilla	Pragvata Branch	PARAMARA Rulers of Chandravati	GUHILA House of Meda	VACHHA Sakambari Chauhans
1. Mula Raja			Dhuma	1. Vappaka	1. Sindhuputra
2. Chamunda, 1011 or 1025			Dhundhuka	2. Guhila	2. Lakshmana
3. Vallabha			Dhruva, etc.	3. Bhoja	3. Manikya
4. Durlabha, 1023			1. Ramadeva	4. Kalabhoja	4. Adhiraja
5. Bhima			2. Yasodhavala, 1174–1189	5. Bhartibkata	5. Mahindu
				6. Samahayika	6. Sindhuraja
6. Kaladeva			3. Dharavarsha Prahaladana, 1209	7. Khummana	7. Kulaverdhena
				8. Allata	8. Prabhurasa
		1. Chandapa	4. Soma	9. Naravahana	9. Dundana *Chauban*
7. Siddha Raja, 1094 to 1145			5. Krishna Deva, 1231	10. Saktiverma	10. Samara Sinh
		2. Chandraprasada		11. Suchiverma	11. Udaya Sinh
8. Kumara Pala, 1174				12. Naraverma	12. Manava Sinh
			Visala Deva, 1294	13. Kirttiverma	13. Pratapa Sinh
		3. Soma	*Chauban Princes of Chandravati*	14. Vairi Sinha	
9. Ajaya Pala	1. Ama			15. Vijaya Sinha	
				16. Ari Sinha	
			Teja Sinha, 1331	17. Vikrama Sinha	
			Kahnara Deva	18. Samanta Sinha, 1209	
				19. Kumara Sinha	

Table 4.1 continued

Royal House of Patten, Nehrwala, or Guzarat	Branch of Anahilla	Pragvata Branch	PARAMARA Rulers of Chandravati	GUHILA House of Meda	VACHHA Sakambari Chauhans
10. Mula	2. Lavanaprasada	4. Aswaraja	Samanta Sinha, 1338	20. Mathana Sinha 21. Padma Sinha 22. Jaira Sinha	14. Dasaratha 15. Lavanyakerna Lundha, 1321
11. Bhima, 1209	3. Viradhavala, 1231	5. Luniga, Malla, Teja Pala, Vastu Pala, 1231-37	*Ranas of Chandravati* Kaukala, 1450	23. Teja Sinha 24. Samara Sinha, 1286	
		6. Jaitra Sinha Lavanya Sinha	Kumbhakarna		
Saranga Deva, 1294					

every *sloka* on every page. After this, he employed young Indian scholars to translate the indexes into English. He then went through the indexes and translations and asked for complete translations of passages he found useful.[107]

This exercise enabled Wilson to realize the value of the Puranas as historical sources. Another great Indologist, Vans Kennedy, had said that 'attempting to extract chronology or history from the date of the Puranas must be an operation attended with equal success as the extraction of sunbeams from cucumbers by the sages of Laputa.'[108] Wilson however maintained that 'in the dynasties of kings detailed in the Puranas we have a record, which although it cannot fail to have suffered detriment from age . . . preserves an account not wholly undeserving of confidence, of the establishment and succession of regular monarchies amongst the Hindus, from as early an era, and for as continuous a duration, as any in the credible annals of mankind.'[109]

Wilson's confidence was fully borne out nearly a century later when Pargiter published his *Ancient Historical Tradition*. Walter Eugene Clark in his review of Pargiter's book summed up both, Vans Kennedy and Wilson's viewpoints very ably, thus:

> Western scholars have neglected the Puranas and have been too much inclined to dismiss scornfully and without adequate investigation all their traditions as late fabrications which are false, mythological, and unworthy of being compared in any way with the much earlier and better-preserved Vedic texts. But the Puranas contain traditions which claim to reach far back into India's past. Except for the Veda they are, at present, our only possible means of going back beyond 100 B.C. They deserve to be studied as carefully and as critically as the Vedic texts.[110]

Although the Society's main contributions were in the fields of Indian history and culture, those interested in scientific subjects were by no means inactive. The increasing number of contributions on geology prompted the formation of a separate committee, in March 1824. It was resolved that 'a Geological Committee be instituted, [and] that the Regulations under which the Committee shall act shall be generally those in force for the Physical Committee of which it may be considered a branch [and] that a Secretary be appointed to the Committee.'[111]

Together with learned contributions in different branches of science, the Society's museum also overflowed with curious specimens in natural history and other articles from practically all over the world. In the meeting of 9 March 1825 for instance, as many as sixty-eight items of various descriptions including manuscripts, pictures, utensils and zoological specimens were received from Hodgson at Nepal. As the museum was slowly turning into a godown, Wilson, as the Society's Secretary, recommended the appointment of a person 'to put in order, and keep in condition the objects of Natural History now in the Museum'. Accordingly, Mr Montiers was retained at an allowance of 50 Rupees a month for six months 'after which the question of retaining his services for a further period may be considered.'

Hodgson, like Mackenzie, was not merely a collector of curious specimens. His main aim was to unravel the mysteries of the religion of the Buddha, of which Nepal was one of the principal centres. It was not an easy task, as, on 4 August 1825, he wrote to the Society: 'I have made a large collection of drawings from the Bhoodist images of this valley and am endeavouring to get them explained—in which attempt should I succeed, much information on this dark subject may perhaps be elicited. Were this govt. alive to any of our tastes and pursuits so as not to misconstrue zeal, a rich harvest of Boodism might be reaped here.'[112]

While Hodgson was busy in Nepal, two traveller-scholars were opening up to the western world the mysteries of Tibet. Moorcroft had been drawn to this part of the world through his love of horses but had made important discoveries there. On 7 September 1825 the Society received a letter from him giving a sketch of the 'Language of Tibet illustrated with Drawings of the various alphabets used in that country'. Soon after this, he died at Andekhui under mysterious circumstances.[113]

Before his death, Moorcroft had infected another traveller-scholar with his own enthusiasm for Tibetan studies. This was Alexander Csoma de Körös, one of the most extraordinary personalities in the annals of oriental scholarship. The year that Moorcroft died also saw the association of Csoma with the Society; when on 13 July Wilson read a paper on the 'Literature of Tibet, the date of Buddha, and the progress of the Buddha Religion as derived from information communicated by Mr Csoma de Körös compared with the enquiries of Ancient and Modern writers of Europe on the subject'.[114]

Alexander Csoma de Körös was a Hungarian, born the same year the Asiatic Society was founded. He began his scholarly travels to discover the origin of the Hungarian race, which he believed to lie in the east. He reached Tehran some time in 1820–1 but rumours of Russian forces in central Asia prevented him from journeying through Turkestan. Instead he decided to cross the Khyber, and reach Tibet through Punjab and Kashmir. Realizing the dangers of the venture, Csoma left with his hosts at Tehran a packet containing the only possessions he valued. These were his University diplomas, and he requested that they be returned to his family if he died on the way.

The journey must have been a hard one but Csoma left no record of his wanderings except where they directly concerned his researches. In January 1822 he crossed the Bamian Pass, arrived in Lahore in March, and in June he was in Kashmir. It was here that he met Moorcroft—an event which was to change the course of his life. Moorcroft not only lent Csoma a rough Tibetan dictionary, compiled nearly a century before by a Catholic priest, but also told him about the treasures of knowledge in Tibetan monasteries. As Csoma himself says:

> Though the study of the Tibetan language did not form part of my original plan, but was only suggested after I had been led by providence into Tibet, and had enjoyed an opportunity of learning of what sort and origin the Tibetan literature was, I cheerfully engaged in the study of it, hoping that it might serve me as a vehicle to my immediate purpose, namely, my researches respecting the language and origin of the Hungarians.[115]

And so he came to the remote monastery of Zanskar and set to work on Tibetan manuscripts with the help of the lamas. Here, isolated from the world and buried for months under drifting snow, Csoma delved into the riches of Tibetan literature. Dr Gerard of the Indian Medical Service who visited him in 1827 gives a vivid description of the life Csoma was leading:

> He, the lama (his tutor), and an attendant were circumscribed in an apartment nine feet square for three or four months; they durst not stir out, the ground being covered with snow, and the temperature below the zero of the scale. There he sat, enveloped in a sheep-skin cloak, with his arms folded, and in this situation he read from morning till evening without fire, or light after dusk. . . . The cold was so intense as to make it a task of severity to extricate the hands from their fleecy resort to turn over the pages.[116]

In spite of the great physical discomforts and financial difficulties, Csoma refused every offer of help except for the minimum required for subsistence. Even when he was appointed Librarian of the Asiatic Society, on fifty rupees a month, he drew his salary only for the first two months. Of his manner of living and work, Dr Campbell observed:

> His effects consisted of four boxes of books and papers, the suit of blue clothes which he always wore and in which he died, a few sheets, and one cooking pot. His food was confined to tea, of which he was very fond, and plain boiled rice, of which he ate very little. On a mat on the floor with a box of books on the four sides he sat, ate, slept and studied, never undressed at night, and rarely went out during the day.[117]

Working under these conditons, Csoma revealed a civilization which was barely known of in the west. He was the first European to have acquired a 'systematic, scholarly knowledge of the Tibetan language', and by publishing a *Grammar* and *Dictionary* of Tibetan he enabled scholars to have access to its extensive literature. Although later it was discovered that many of the Buddhist texts in Tibetan were translations of the Sanskrit originals which gradually became available, the Tibetan literature Csoma discovered did throw light on different aspects of Buddhism. Another great service that Csoma de Körös rendered to oriental studies was the influence he cast on a fellow countryman who, a century later, opened up the antiquarian treasures of central Asia. This was Sir Aurel Stein about whom his biographer Jeanette Mirsky says: 'For Csoma de Körös he [Stein] felt something special and, musing on the parallel between Csoma and himself, he saw the hand of fate.'[118]

In 1826 hardly any communication of importance relating to Indian history was made except for brief summaries of the *Kurma Purana* and the *Agni Purana*[119] by Wilson. The Society's scientific activities also slackened. At the meeting of 1 March, the Secretary expressed his feeling 'that the meeting of the Physical Committee occurring but rarely, and being mostly attended by Members usually present at the regular meeting of the Society, it appears unnecessary to hold them distinct in future.' It was therefore resolved 'that the Physical Commmittee be considered as united with the Society.'

Whether because of the slackness of scholarly activities, or to widen its area of interest, or to gain greater patronage from the government, the Society took an important and an unusual step in 1826. Through a letter signed by eleven prominent members including·the President, the Secretary, William Carey, Charles Greg, Andrew Stirling and Nathaniel Wallich, the Society brought to the notice of the Government that extensive tracts of the country, hitherto unexplored, were now being brought to light mainly through official efforts. Officers who visited these areas and gathered valuable information about them filed extensive reports, but these never reached the public. Once the reports became official documents, they were liable 'to become official lumber, and to moulder on the shelves of a department, and perish and be forgotten.'[120]

Under the circumstances, the Society suggested that the *Asiatic Researches* be made the medium of the publication of such reports, which would involve no expense to the Government. Members pointed out that the Society had so far been maintained solely by voluntary contributions which were just sufficient to maintain its small establishment. It had never been able to spend anything for 'the purpose of collecting information or to assist individuals in their enquiries', and that there still remained a vast field to be explored.

The Government agreed to the proposal, permitting the Society's Secretary 'to inspect such papers, maps, and plans in each department . . . as well as to receive copies or extracts of any papers, which it may appear proper to publish in the Transactions of the Asiatic Society', due care being taken to see that passages or papers of a secret nature were withheld from publication. It also decided 'to aid the laudable exertions of the Asiatic Society for the diffusion of useful and scientific knowledge.'[121]

The issue thus, seemed to have been settled to the satisfaction of both the parties concerned; but when in the meeting of 5 July, the Society's communication as well as the Government's reply was read out, a member, C. Smith, moved the following resolution:

> That in addressing to the Governor-General in Council the 8th Paragraph of the letter of the 29th of April last, which points out in general terms the insufficiency of the Society's funds and resources, and solicits permanent pecuniary aid from Government, the Committee of Papers obviously exceeded their powers as defined in the rules of the Society, and improperly and injudiciously though doubtless with the best intentions made an application of a novel nature such as nothing short of the special sanction of a majority of the Society at large could warrant.[122]

The motion was vetoed by twelve votes to four, but it is important to remember that most of the members present were those who had signed the original letter. However, the Government's help and patronage remained a matter of record rather than of practical application.

The financial straits of the Society became evident in the first meeting of 1827, when it found itself unable to vote for a recurring sum for Dr Burline's services in preparing a catalogue for the library. Noting that the Society's funds were wholly inadequate for any permanent expenditure, the Society resolved to make a donation of Rs 500 to Dr Burline for his work.[123]

Towards the end of the year, there was, however, a 'windfall'; when a legacy of £2,000 was bequeathed to the Society by a member, Charles Key Bruce.[124] Little is known of him except that at one stage he was in Calcutta and later settled in New York. The legacy, however, was disputed, and it took some time before the Society obtained the sum.

The year 1828 began with a significant development. Two years earlier the Society had decided to abolish the physical committee, although this had not been approved by some members. Members now felt that the general meetings of the Society were held at long intervals and discussed matters of 'too formal and miscellaneous a nature', and so did not provide appropriate opportunity for discussions on scientific matters. Even the Society's publications, they felt, were of a miscellaneous nature and did not appeal to readers interested in scientific matters.[125]

The Physical Committee then continued its existence, with its own elected officers, and resolved to publish its proceedings and articles separately, but in the same type and form as the *Researches* so that it could conveniently be bound with those volumes.

At about this time. it was discovered that the Society's account had 334 rupees less than the sum required for printing the sixteenth volume of the *Researches*. It is significant that even then, the Society did not request government help, and decided to raise the extra amount needed from its members. While the Society was trying to overcome this financial crisis, came the first hint of trouble about the Bruce legacy.

A letter from J. Cullen, attorney to executors of Bruce's will, was read in the meeting of 3 September. Cullen stated the difficulties in payment of the legacy, suggesting that the Society relinquish its claims to 'any further portion of the property under the will in favour of the brother and sister of Dr Bruce'. The Society decided to write to Cullen recommending that the legacy be deposited in the Bank of Bengal for a year or so after which it would become the Society's property, if there were no further legal proceedings against its claims.[126]

1829 is a landmark in the history of the Asiatic Society for it opened its doors to Indians as full-fledged members. Indians had been associated with the Society from the very beginning, and the very first volume of the *Researches* had carried Indian contributions. Ram Comul Sen had, by now, become an important part of the Society's establishment, yet no Indian had either applied for membership or been admitted as a member—honorary or otherwise. At its meeting held on 7 January 1829, five Indians—Prasanna Kumar Thakur, Dwarkanath Thakur, Sivchundra Das, Rasamaya Dutt and Ram Comul Sen—were proposed as members, and in the subsequent meeting of 4 March, balloted for and elected.

The association of Indians as members of the Society forty-five years after its establishment has naturally given rise to the question why it should have been delayed so long. Was it because of the Society's own reluctance to admit Indians as members or was it that Indians till then had not shown any awareness of the importance of historical and scientific studies and so did not qualify for membership? The impression that the Society was reluctant to admit Indians as members has probably gathered strength due to the fact that in 1833, the Bombay branch of the Royal Asiatic Society voted against the first Indian who sought membership of that Institution.[127] It is easy, therefore, to conclude that the Calcutta Society was also ruled by similar sentiments.

This, however, does not seem to be the case. Sir William Jones himself had not ruled out the election of Indians as members. Since the Society was still in its infancy, he had left the matter open stating, 'whether you will enrol as members any number of learned natives, you will hereafter decide, with many other questions, as they happen to arise'.[128] He added later, 'You will not require, I suppose any other qualification than a love of Knowledge and a zeal for the promotion of it.'

This suggests the reason for the non-association of Indians with the Society as members in the early stages of its foundation. Indians who were men of means and status did not fulfil Jones's qualification, and Indians who were interested in knowledge were mostly pundits who would have felt some inhibition at sitting in the same company as their employers. Although they contributed to the Society's publications they never applied for membership.

Now that the Bengal Society had been admitting Indians as members, it is perhaps the proper place to discuss the character of Indian representation in the Society.

Here it must be mentioned that although the Asiatic Society of Bengal admitted Indians as members only in 1829, the Royal Asiatic Society of Great Britain had, in its first year [1823] conferred honorary membership on two Indians, the Raja of Tanjore and the King of Avadh[129]

It must be admitted, however, that in the early stages, the representation of Indians in the Society was mainly nominal. By the end of the year there were thirteen Indian members, all of whom belonged to the uppermost strata of society, and, with the probable exception of Ram Comul Sen, little interested in intellectual pursuits. Few of the first Indian members attended the Society's meetings, let alone contributed anything substantial to its deliberations. At most, some members presented curiosities or antiquities to the Society's library or the museum. Even Radhakanta Deb had not a single paper to his credit. His only contribution to the Society consisted of a pigeon with two heads[130] and a copy of his publication, the *Sabda Kalpadruma*. Ram Comul Sen contributed only one paper during his long association with the Society. It was only after 1850 and with the coming of Rajendralala Mitra that Indians began to show a genuine interest in the country's history and antiquities. Earlier, Indian members had valued their association with the Society for the social status it gave them, and they utilized membership merely as an ornament. Kali Prosno Singh, for instance, in his book *Savitri Satyavan Natak*, listed the number of Societies he was associated with.

A review rightly called this 'ludicrous vanity' and advised the author to appear simply as 'Kali Prosno Singh', 'without those unmeaning titles'.[131] ·

One Indian, although not a member of the Society, contributed greatly towards a solution of its financial crisis. This was the King of Avadh. In a letter read on 1 July 1829, Calder informed the Society that the King had made a donation of twenty thousand rupees for promoting researches in the literature and natural history of India and that his minister had given another five thousand rupees.[112]

Little else of note took place during the year except that the new Governor-General, Lord William Bentinck, consented to be Patron of the Society. Bentinck, because of his supporting Macaulay's *Minutes*, is generally identified with the anti-orientalist policy of the Raj. Yet there was a time when he had fully supported oriental studies. Before his departure for India, the Royal Asiatic Society in London had sent a deputation to the new Governor-General, conveying the Society's suggestions 'of the means by which his Lordship may promote the interests of the Society in India.' Bentinck, in return, 'expressed his readiness to endeavour to effect the measures proposed to him.'[113] The factors which caused a change in his attitude, therefore, deserve to be studied.

In a review of the seventeenth volume of *Asiatic Researches*, on which work had started around 1830, the *Asiatic Journal* termed the Asiatic Society the parent of all associations established for studying oriental literatures, adding that few literary or scientific bodies had a deeper claim to Europe's obligations than the Asiatic Society of Bengal. It went on to say: 'Until within a very few years past, since continental scholars were attracted to the study of Sanskrit, the *Asiatic Researches* comprehended the sum of our knowledge of the classical literature of India; the European inquirer into that literature began and ended his investigations with this work.'[114] The scene had since changed. The Society was passing through a period of inactivity while European nations were in a state of intellectual ferment as regards Indological studies. Wilson himself was a remarkable scholar but there were few others who made contributions of lasting significance. In Europe, on the other hand, Bopp and Schlegel in Germany, Burnouf, Cherzy and Lassen in France were forging ahead in oriental studies. Under the circumstances, it was natural for the Royal Asiatic Society in London to think of measures for strengthening its position. On 20 May 1826, the Chairman of the Committee of Correspondence, Sir A. Johnston suggested that efforts should be made 'to form a union between the Royal Asiatic Society of Great Britain and Ireland and the several Literary Societies of Calcutta, Madras, Bombay and Ceylon'.[115]

In March 1828 the Society sent a letter to the Governor of Madras, S. R. Lushington, on the subject of amalgamating the Royal Asiatic Society and the Literary Society of Madras. Similarly, Major-General

John Malcolm merged the Bombay Literary Society with the Society of Great Britain.[136]

In a letter dated 24 March 1829 the Acting Secretary of the Royal Asiatic Society, William Huttman, wrote to Wilson proposing the union of the Asiatic Society of Bengal with the London Society. In the terms made between the Royal Asiatic Society and the Bombay Society, provision had been made for the Bombay Society to function independently with regard to administration and control of funds. There were also reciprocal arrangements giving members of each society non-resident membership of the other, which could be converted into resident membership whenever necessary.

While proposing the same terms to the Asiatic Society of Bengal, the Acting Secretary of the Royal Asiatic Society added: 'The Council . . . has not the slightest wish for the Asiatic Society of Bengal to make any alteration in its name or that the separate publication of the *Asiatic Researches* should be discontinued.'[137]

The Asiatic Society of Bengal resolved in January 1830 to combine with that of Britain, but the resolution was never put into effect. The Asiatic Society of Bengal continued to maintain its independent existence and never assumed the subsidiary position that the Bombay and the Madras Societies did. Why this happened remains mysterious. There is no mention of it in the *Proceedings* nor is there any record on the subject in the archives either of the Asiatic Society of Bengal or the Royal Asiatic Society in London.

While the Bengal Society's intellectual activities had declined, its financial situation had somewhat improved especially on account of the donation by the King of Avadh. It was able to liquidate its debts of eight thousand rupees but unfortunately Bruce's legacy ran into further trouble. In November 1829, James Mackillop wrote that lawyers in England were expressing doubts whether the executors of Bruce's Will would be 'justified in paying the legacy, the Society not being a chartered body'. They advised the Society to delegate powers immediately to its representatives in London to claim the amount, so that the Society's claim could be strengthened.[138] Accordingly a power of attorney was sent to the Society's treasurers in England authorising them to apply for the amount of the legacy.[139]

An interesting development in 1830 related to the Society's library. So far the library and the museum had been opened from 10 a.m. to 4 p.m. Now Captain Herbert proposed that they should be opened early in the morning for the convenince of members who could visit them at that hour. The present hours were those when most members were busy with official duties and unable to visit the Society. Captain Herbert objected to the hours of functioning of the Society's library and museum mainly on the grounds of safety: 'during [a] great part of the year few people consider it salutary or even safe to venture to any distance at that time of day.'[140]

So far the Society's interests in London, especially in the matter of purchasing books, for its library, had been looked after by Colebrooke since his return to London in 1815. But after the Royal Asiatic Society was established, he expressed a wish to relinquish the responsibility. In its meeting of 3 November the Society accepted Colebrooke's resignation, requesting him to continue till a replacement was found.[141] Thus the last meeting of 1830 ended Colebrooke's long association with the Asiatic Society in a formal sense.

The meeting, however, opened a new line of enquiry when a letter was read from General Ventura containing a report of his excavations of the *tope* (*stupa*) at Manikyala along with Meyeffred's impressions of three coins found during the digging operations. This communication opened up a whole vista in the history of ancient India, especially that of Buddhism and of the Indo-Scythian kings, who were till then more or less an unknown factor in Indian history.

The year 1831 was as devoid of any important contribution to Indian hisorical research as the previous ones. The only communication of some importance was Wilson's 'Remarks on the portion of the Dionysiacs of Nonnus Relating to the Indians' presented at the Society's meeting of 9 March.

Nonnus, as Wilson tells us, was a native of Panopolis in Egypt who lived at the end of the fourth or the beginning of the fifth century. His poem, *The Dionysiacs*, composed in Greek ran into as many as forty books. Several of these described the conquest of India by the hero of the poem, Bacchus or Dionysos. An Egyptian work containing references to India was a natural attraction for early orientalists who were eager to discover the links between Egypt and India in ancient times. Sir William Jones, who had tried to establish the identity between Greek and Indian gods, found Nonnus an extension of his field of enquiry. Jones later acknowledged that he had never read more than half this poem, on which basis he drew a parallel between the *Dionysiacs* and the *Ramayana*, concluding that 'an accurate comparison of the two poems would establish the identity of Dionysos as the elder Rama.'[142] This conclusion must be placed in the context of Jones's initial enthusiasm to relate the unknown of Indian culture to the known of the western or other ancient cultures like the Egyptian. It was certainly a hasty judgement, for as Wilson pointed out, there was no resemblance between the heroes of the two works in name attribute, or in the course of events.

Francis Wilford, who was given to fanciful theories, went a step further than Jones. According to him, a certain Dionysiacs 'wrote also a history of the *Mahabharata* in Greek, which is lost; but from the few fragments remaining, it appears, that it was nearly the same with that of Nonnus, and he entitled his work *Bassarica*.'[143] According to him, the *Dionysiacs* of Nonnus even filled in some gaps regarding emigrations which took place as a result of the *Mahabharata* war.

Wilson examined all the forty books of the *Dionysiacs* and came to the conclusion that Nonnus knew little about India except what he had gathered from Arrian, Strabo and other classical writers, and that his work had, in spite of some resemblances in names of persons and places, nothing in common with the Indian epics. It cast no additional light on ancient Indian history nor did it confirm the Grecian fables regarding the conquests or the origin of Bacchus.

In 1831 the Society added to its list of honorary members some distinguished oriental scholars from Germany and France including Bopp, Burnouf and Lassen.[144] A disturbing feature, on the other hand, was that during 1830–1, seven members withdrew from the Society.[145] Since their reasons for doing so are not on record, it is difficult to draw any conclusion: but since in earlier cases reasons for member's resignations were always mentioned, one can presume that all was not well with the Society.

> We do most heartily exhort the Asiatic Society to continue in the course which they have thus so nobly begun; to rouse themselves from the deadly apathy which seems so long to have beset them, and to stand forward as they ought to do, the patrons of talent and industry wherever they be found-
> . . . . They may be assured that in so doing they will best fulfil the intentions of their illustrious founder. We trust, our contemporaries too, will aid us in reminding them of this duty in future; for ourselves, we promise them that, if they again go to sleep—*Inshallah* we will slap them.[146]

Thus did the important newspaper of the day, the *Bengal Hurkarrah* exhort the Asiatic Society at the beginning of 1832. Little did the paper realize that a glorious period of achievement lay ahead, for 1832-3 marked the beginning of the golden period of the Society under James Prinsep.

The *Hurkarrah* comment was made along with news of the presentation of a collection of specimens of natural history to the Society by John Royle.

John Forbes Royle, b. 1799, came to India as an assistant surgeon. Here he amassed a huge collection of specimens of natural history and wrote valuable papers on the antiquity of Hindu medicine and other apects of botanical science. He exhibited his collection of over 30,000 specimens containing about 4,000 species of plants, 233 specimens of birds, a number of cabinets of insects, geological and mineralogical specimens from all over the country and over 400 drawings of rare plants, at the Society in March 1832. Seeing the collection, a member exclaimed: 'This, Sir, must be the work of ten gentlemen's lives; no one can do so much '.

At the same meeting, permission was granted to James Prinsep, who had taken over editorship of the journal *Gleanings in Science* from J. D. Herbert, to continue the publication with the title *The Journal of the Asiatic Society of Bengal*.

The first volume of the *Journal* was published in 1832; the same year saw the publication of the seventeenth volume of the *Researches*. Thereafter, the *Journal* took precedence over the *Researches* in publishing articles of importance on Indian history and culture. There was, however, one, article in the seventeenth volume of the *Researches* which set a trend which was more fully developed in the *Journal*. This article, entitled 'Description of Select Coins, from Originals or Drawings in the possession of the Asiatic Society', by Wilson, may be said to mark the beginning of numismatic studies in India. As Wilson stated the study of Indian numismatics had received little attention for various reasons. One was that the collection of coins had been primarily the work of individuals. In a collector's lifetime, only his friends were able to see the collection and after his death, the collection was either dispersed and lost or sent to England where again it was lost through neglect. The Asiatic Society, however, provided a secure place for finds of ancient coins. Although initially regarded as curios, the Society's collection became an important source for the reconstruction of India's past.

The first person to have taken a scholarly interest in ancient Indian coins was James Tod, who deputed some Indians to collect ancient coins for him. His article on ancient coins in the first volume of the *Transactions* of the Royal Asiatic Society evoked wide interest. The discovery of a large number of Roman and Bactrian coins in India made it obvious that a study of coins found in India would also contribute to the study of the history of ancient Europe. It was this fact which prompted Wilson to a study of the coins in the Asiatic Society collection. Wilson examined and described about 120 coins in his article. Although he did not go deep enough to draw conclusions important for the reconstruction of Indian history, the article proved an inspiration for James Prinsep who later reconstructed the history of such important dynasties as the Indo-Scythian, Indo-Bactrian, the western Kshatrapas, the Gupta, and several others through Indian coins.

Another paper of importance presented during 1832 was E. C. Ravenshaw's translation of some inscriptions of Vijayanagar. These inscriptions were presented to Ravenshaw by the Guru of the royal family, whose duty was to maintain the *Book of Chronicles*. The same priest furnished Ravenshaw with a genealogy of the Vijayanagar kings which was traced back to mythical origins.

On the basis of this genealogy and other material available on the subject, Wilson tried to reconstruct a comprehensive genealogy of the Vijayanagar dynasty. This article, published in the twentieth volume of the *Researches*, has great significance for scholars of Vijayanagar history because it marks the first attempt at a clear delineation of the political history of this Empire through sources available till that time.

Another important event of this year was the realization of a part of Dr Bruce's legacy. Soon after the Society received an application from the executors of Bruce's will requesting the Society to forgo its claim to any further share in favour of Dr Bruce's brother and sister. The Society deferred its decision on the matter till the exact amount of the legacy was known.

The amount received was meanwhile invested in Government securities. The unrealized amount of the legacy, arrears in subscription and the expected expenditure on its publications prompted Babu Ram Comul Sen to propose a revised plan for the Society's expenditure which was expected to result in a monthly saving of Rs 73, a sizeable sum in those days. He even proposed to forgo his own salary of Rs 50 per month. The Society accepted the proposal and showed its appreciation by electing him Secretary.[147]

The last regular meeting of 1832 was held on 12 December. A week later (on 19 December) an extraordinary meeting was held, at which it was decided to present an address to Wilson on his departure for England to assume the Boden Chair of Sanskrit.[148] The address would dwell on Wilson's merits as a scholar and would request him to agree to having his bust sculpted by 'Chantrey or by one of the most distinguished sculptors in England—that it may be placed in this room as a durable monument.'[149]

Accordingly on 31 December 1832, the President accompanied by most members of the Society met Wilson at his residence. Sir Edward Ryan read out the address which stated that none had with greater assiduity or more splendid success, contributed to the advancement of the Society's objectives than Wilson.[150] Referring to his work on the Puranas, the Society hoped that the far more difficult monuments of Hindu antiquity, the Vedas, would also receive his attention—a hope which was amply fulfilled. Wilson not only translated the *Rig Veda* but was also the inspiration for Max Müller's edition—the first modern one. He obtained for Max Müller not only the patronage of the Court of Directors and the Secretary of State—without which the task of publishing the work would have been impossibly expensive—but also many of the valuable manuscripts on which Max Müller's edition was based. None could be in a better position than Max Müller to pay tribute to Wilson:

> Wilson had lived through almost the whole history of Sanskrit scholarship, and had taken part in nearly every important work that marked an epoch in the study of Indian literature, history, and religion. Every one of his own works represents a new conquest. He never followed, he was always the first . . . others followed in the paths which he had opened and smoothed.[151]

Wilson undoubtedly opened up many fields of enquiry for Indian scholarship; but it must be admitted that during his tenure, the Society passed through a period of comparative inactivity. One reason for this may have been the fact that Wilson was associated with a number of literary bodies—he was for many years Secretary to the Committee of Public Instruction, and as such is said to be 'the first person who introduced the study of European science and English literature into the education of the native population, whose knowledge of English had hitherto been confined to qualification for the situation of an office clerk.'[152] He was also Visitor of the Anglo-Indian College and Vice-President of the Managing Committee of Hindu College. Besides, he was greatly interested in music and the theatre, and it is said that the Chowringhee Theatre owed its success mainly to Wilson's management and histrionic talents. His proficiency in music made him a familiar figure at concerts.

Official duties combined with the responsibility of managing of several institutions, his artistic interests and his own oriental studies, would have left Wilson little time to attend fully to the Society's more mundane activities. Again this may explain why his contributions to Indian studies increased after he left India. His articles in the *Journal of the Royal Asiatic Society* and his publications in England, including the translation of the *Rig-Veda* and the monumental *Ariana Antiqa* were perhaps more valuable than contributions made during his stay in India. But then as Max Müller said, Wilson had prepared the ground, and, also, inspired another scholar to take to Indian studies. This was James Princep—who ushered in what may be called the golden period of the Asiatic Society.

5

James Prinsep and the Period
of Great Discoveries, 1832–1838

In early 1830, Victor Jacquemont, the celebrated French traveller, happened to visit Banaras and commented in his diary:

> Attended two dinner parties where even the champagne that was drunk in abundance could not melt the ice of etiquette which prevails at those reunions; every one the next day complained of the dullness of the preceding evening. There is one man however who compensates for the antisocial disposition of his fellow countrymen—James Prinsep; he devotes his mornings to architectural plans and drawings, his days to assaying at the mint, and his evenings to musical concerts.[1]

Indeed, architecture, official duties at the mint, and music, together with painting, had been the three major preoccupations of James Prinsep before he took up the post of Secretary of the Asiatic Society in 1832.

The seventh son of John Prinsep, who had made a considerable fortune and won a seat in Parliament from Queensborough, James Prinsep was born in August 1799. From his early childhood he displayed an unusual skill with his hands. His elder brother, Henry Toby Prinsep, another member of the Prinsep family to have distinguished himself in the East India service, recalled how James in his childhood had fashioned a model of a carriage not exceeding six inches in length, complete with springs, doors and windows which opened and shut, and lamps, and steps which could be let down at will.[2]

Prinsep's skill in designing pointed to architecture as a career, but he had to give up his architectural studies because of an injury to his eyes caused by close and constant application to mechanical drawings. Although his eyesight was completely restored later, Prinsep had to give up his aspirations to becoming an architect. His father then arranged for him to attend chemical lectures at Guy's Hospital, after which he was apprenticed to the assay-master of the royal mint in London. After receiving a certificate of proficiency from there, he was appointed assistant to the assay-master of the Calcutta mint.

James arrived in India in September 1819. The assay-master at Calcutta at this time was none else than H. H. Wilson, who aroused young Prinsep's interest in oriental studies. Soon after Prinsep joined the Calcutta mint, Dr Wilson was sent to Banaras on a special mission to remodel the mint there. Wilson returned to Calcutta a year later, and Prinsep was nominated assay-master at the Banaras mint.

Shortly after his arrival at Banaras, Prinsep gave evidence of his architectural skill. Construction had started on the mint building although there was a defect in its design. Prinsep immediately submitted revised plans and completed the building at the estimated cost of the original design. His talent flowered in other areas too. He was responsible for laying an underground drainage tunnel in the city which passed under seven-storied houses in the most populous parts of the city and opened into the Ganga. He drew up the first map of the city. He also conducted the city's first census which was later published by the Asiatic Society.[3] He found time for studies in chemistry and physics, devised a new method for measurement of heat, which was published in the *Transactions* of the Royal Society in London; and prepared for purposes of assay, a balance which could measure a three-thousandth part of a grain.

In 1830 the mint at Banaras was abolished and Prinsep was recalled to Calcutta as deputy assay-master in the Bengal mint under Wilson. Wilson, recognizing young Prinsep's talent, tried to interest him in Indological studies and introduced him to the Asiatic Society. At the meeting of 5 May 1830, Wilson himself proposed Prinsep s name for membership, and he was duly elected on 7 July.

It seems that the first important task which Prinsep performed for the Society was one which drew upon his architectural skill. At its meeting of 4 January 1832 it was reported that the lower storey of the Society's building needed to have its floor relaid, and Prinsep was requested to report on the best mode of doing it.

Prinsep was responsible for another major development in the Society's history. In 1829, Major J. D. Herbert, a scientific officer in the Company's army, had started a periodical called *Gleanings in Science*. His object was to make known in India the latest discoveries and developments in the arts and sciences of Europe, and also to provide a forum for those interested in the sciences in India to communicate their own discoveries and ideas. In 1831 Major Herbert was appointed Astronomer to the King of Avadh, upon which he transferred responsibility for the publication to James Prinsep. In Prinsep's hands the journal took a new shape and direction. Its circulation and content improved rapidly so that 'it was brought at last to such a condition as to rival publications of the same character in Europe.'⁴

In March 1832 Prinsep asked the Society for permission to continue the publication under the new name *The Journal of the Asiatic Society.* The Society agreed 'as long as the publication is under the charge of one or both the Secretaries of the Society.'⁵ The *Journal* did not supersede the *Researches,* as the latter continued to be published till 1839, although it was the *Journal* which came to be widely regarded as the organ of the Society as it also carried the Society's Proceedings.

1832 was, as we have already seen, the year in which Wilson left India to take up the Boden Chair of Sanskrit at the University of Oxford. Prinsep was his natural successor to Secretaryship of the Society. The year also marked a new phase in Prinsep's scholarly activities. Till then he had distinguished himself in the field of science through his contributions in architecture, chemistry, and statistics; now he turned to history. His scientific bent of mind enabled him to turn the search for India's past into a scientific quest. So far, Indologists had mainly depended upon literature to understand its past, and articles on numismatics and archaeology were few and not considered very significant. Prinsep's coming changed all that. Now it was coins, epigraphs and archaeological sites which caught the antiquarian's attention and he approached their study in a scientific spirit.

Cunningham described this change as one from the era of what he called 'closet or scholastic archaeologists' to that of 'field archaeologists', or 'travelling antiquarians'.⁶ The results were remarkable. Within six years, between 1833 and 1838, many of the ruling dynasties of ancient India came to light, and more of its ancient history reconstructed than ever before or since in the same span of time.

His official duties at the mint led to Prinsep's first contribution in the field of numismatics. On 4 July, when he became acting Secretary, Prinsep read a paper on the 'Ancient Roman coins in the Cabinet of the Asiatic Society'. He regretted that several individuals who had developed a taste for collecting antiquities and coins had carried their treasures back to Europe where they were dispersed and lost in private and public cabinets, and emphasized that had they been left in India, they would have been more useful in promoting valuable research.[7]

When Prinsep presented the article to the Society, there were only fifty or sixty Roman coins in the Society's collection. Within three months, however, the Society acquired 250 Roman coins purchased from an Armenian, and fourteen coins from a Mr Avdall who had procured them in Persia.

Prinsep's first year in office as Secretary to the Society (1833) had an unfortunate start. The Society lost its entire cash balance of Rs 11,397.12.6, on account of its agent going bankrupt. In addition it had on its hands a debt of Rs 5,554.13.1.[8] The financial disaster was, however, compensated by the richness of its academic contributions. In January, Prinsep continued his study of coins in the Society's collection by examining the Greek and the Persian coins. Although there were not many of these, Prinsep gave drawings and descriptions of them 'to furnish tolerable guides for the assistance of the student in discriminating the coins of these countries at different periods of their history.'[9] The person who contributed most in this direction during the year was Alexander Burnes. Burnes had first visited the Punjab as an emissary of the British Government, being in charge of English horses presented to Ranjit Singh. The journey had whetted his appetite for seeing more of the country. The circumstances too were favourable at the time, for the British Government wanted 'some intelligent officer [to] be sent to acquire information in the countries bordering on the Oxus and the Caspian'.[10] And so, donning an Asiatic robe, and shedding European habits and manners, Burnes set out on the journey accompanied by a young assistant surgeon, Dr Gerard and two Indians—Mahomed Ali, in the capacity of surveyor, and Mohun Lall, who acted as his *munshi*. Although the trip was a political one, Burnes found time to collect a large number of coins which went a long way in adding a new chapter—that of the Indo-Bactrian kings—to the history of India.

Earlier, little had been known about Bactrian India except that, after Alexander's death, Bactria had become an independent principality ruled by Greek sovereigns. The classical writers gave the names of one or two of the kings, and on the basis of these writers and some Chinese authorities, it was known that Bactrian rule was overthrown by the Scythians—but this was practically all. The interval between the Macedonian invasion and the Scythian conquest was clouded by hazy details.[11]

The process of clarifying these events may be said to have started with Colonel Tod who collected about 20,000 coins from mainly around Mathura. But Tod remarked about the collection 'There may be not above one hundred calculated to excite interest, and perhaps not above one-third of that number to be considered of value: but among them there is an Apollodotus and a Menander, besides some rare medals of a Parthian dynasty, probably yet unknown to history.'[12]

Tod returned to England soon after, but he had aroused the interest of antiquarians in old coins of India. The most prominent of these was Dr Swiney, who made a large collection of coins gathered in the vicinity of Karnal. These coins were studied by Prinsep and in August 1833, he published descriptions and engravings of eighteen of them, 'amongst which were now made known, for the first time, some of the drachmae no doubt spoken of by Arrian, those of Menander and Apollodotus.'[13]

While the names of these two Bactrian monarchs were thus discovered and confirmed, Burnes's collection not only shed light on the Bactrian line of kings but also contained a large number of Indo-Scythian coins. On one coin the name of Euthydemus was quite distinct. About another coin in the Burnes collection Prinsep wrote:

> This coin is of very great value, from the circumstances of its being the only one out of many discovered in the same neighbourhood, upon which the characters are sufficiently legible to afford a clue to the Prince's name. . . . Should my conjecture prove correct, the discovery of this coin will be hailed as of the greatest value by all who are engaged in the newly developed study of Bactrian antiquity. I supposed it to be a coin of KANISHKA, a Tartar or Scythic conqueror of Bactria.[14]

This indeed was the first time that a Kanishka coin was discovered, providing valuable numismatic evidence for many disputed facts earlier. It confirmed the overthrow of the Bactrian rulers by a line of Scytho-Parthian princes and also helped in fixing the date of the Buddha.

Burnes's antiquarian discoveries aroused great public interest, although the Government was primarily concerned with the political results of his journeys. A correspondent wrote in 1835:

> The journey of Messrs Burnes and Gerard into Bactria and Transoxiana was not undertaken a day too soon. Another year, and even the minor glory of participation in the discoveries made by foreigners in these regions would, to our eternal shame, have been snatched from our hands. . . . It surprises me much that the English power never consider of such valuable

discoveries respecting the old Grecian provinces, which history tells us existed in these very tracts, while the gentlemen of foreign countries wear the crown of knowledge and fame, by disclosing the treasures of antiquity.[15]

The most important communication of the year, however, was presented only in the last meeting on 26 December. This related to the Allahabad pillar which played such an important role in the reconstruction of the two most important dynasties of ancient India—the Maurya and the Gupta. As the major part of the discussions and discoveries arising from the study of this column took place only in 1834, the paper on the subject communicated by T. S. Burt will be treated later.

In the midst of all these achievements, financial constraints continued to plague the Society. James Mill, now an important official in the India Office, was beginning to influence policy on India. In his reply to a despatch containing a proposal to improve the Hindu College at Banaras and the Mohammedan College in Calcutta, Mill severely remarked: 'In professing to establish seminaries for the purpose of teaching mere Mohammedan literature, the Government bound itself to teach a great deal of what was frivolous, not a little of what was purely mischievous, and a small remainder indeed in which utility was in any way concerned. The great end of Government should be, not to teach Hindu or Mahomedan learning, but useful learning.'[16] Further, Macaulay's opinion that oriental literature had little or nothing to contribute to an enlightened mind was also gaining ground. Lord William Bentinck was deeply influenced by Mill and Macaulay, and in spite of the influence of such men as H. H. Wilson, Indology seemed to be fighting a losing battle.

The Asiatic Society felt the impact of the Government's thinking in 1833. On 2 December, it received a letter from G. A. Bushby, the officiating Secretary to Government that the Governor-General had decided to discontinue, after six months' time, the exemption of postage for the Society's publications, including the *Journal*.[17] The blow came at a most inopportune time. The Society had enjoyed the privilege of free postage since 1829. As Prinsep explained in the Preface to the second volume of the *Journal*, he had never intended to make any profit either from the *Gleanings* or from the present work, but even then it left the Editor 'out of pocket upwards of Rs 2,000 as the reward of his labour for two years.'

The position of the Society's own publication, the *Researches*, was no better. On 27 March 1833, Ram Comul Sen submitted a memorandum stating that the sale of the *Researches* had been very limited and hence it was not a financially sound proposition. Since the losses had amounted to Rs 72,800 on thirteen volumes, Sen proposed that 'in future, the matter for publication should be transmitted to Europe, where a printer may be found to print it on his own account.'[18]

Sen's proposal, in fact, amounted to giving up publication of the *Researches*, for it was not to be expected that a European publisher would take on such a risk. The Society then appointed a Committee of four members 'to consider the best mode of publishing . . . the *Researches*'. In its report the Committee noted:

> The reputation of the Society, its character, nay indeed its very existence depends upon the publication of its *Researches*. Neither can we coincide with the Baboo in recommending, that the Transactions, if printed at all, should be printed in England. . . . The moment we transfer the printing of our Researches to England, we commit an act of *felo de se*, and merge at once into the subordinate character of a branch of the London Asiatic Society, as has been the fate of the Literary Societies, of the two sister presidencies.[19]

The Committee suggested certain measures such as keeping aside 100 rupees every month of the Society's earnings for publication of the *Researches*, substituting the octavo form for the quarto, calling upon the Medical Society to contribute to the Society's funds by paying rent for the area occupied by them, and suggesting that fifty rupees or thirty-two gold mohurs, which would be equivalent to seven years' subscription, inclusive of the admission fee, 'be adopted as the amount of composition of new Members; with a proportionate scale of rates for those who are already Members.'

In 1834, the Society completed fifty years of its existence and despite setbacks it had two substantial achievements to its credit: it had successfully delved into India's past, and made the world aware of its rich cultural inheritance. It had also inspired the foundation of many similar Societies in India and abroad. Referring to this, Prinsep said:

> The tree which was auspiciously planted by the great Sir William Jones . . . has spread its roots in distant lands, where the arts of cultivation [cultivation of art(?)] are better understood, and the value of its produce can be more skilfully developed; but we must not forget that we here assemble under the shade of the original tree, and that however decayed

the parent stock may have been, while its more vigorous branches are taking root in France, Germany, and England,—still it is to the Asiatic Society of Bengal that belongs with propriety the motto assumed by one of its illustrious scions, '*Quot rami tot arbores*'.[20]

1834 also witnessed the greatest number of important historical contributions to the Society since it was founded. It is of interest that these contributions were made at a time when the Government attitude to such studies was apathetic, if not hostile.

A beginning was made with the Allahabad pillar inscription, studied by T. S. Burt which cleared the mystery of the Gupta dynasty, earlier taken to be the same as the Maurya. Burt, who happened to be in Allahabad, was asked by Prinsep to send facsimiles of all the inscriptions on the ancient stone pillar then lying neglected in the Allahabad fort. Burt was interested in antiquarian studies, and complied with this request assiduously. He not only sent drawings of the pillar together with facsimiles of all the inscriptions, but also a detailed account of his own efforts at deciphering them. The paper with facsimiles of the inscriptions and an accurate drawing of the pillar showing the exact position of the different inscriptions on it, was published in the third volume of the *Journal* together with Prinsep's observations.

Burt's account together with Prinsep's remarks throw light on a number of issues, including the state of apathy prevailing in India towards the country's monuments. The pillar itself lay on the ground without its capital. Rain water collected in the cavities of the letters, and then soaked into the stone. Moisture alternating with heat caused the outer surface of the stone to split and peel off in many places, thus effacing several portions of the inscriptions. Describing the importance of such monuments to the opening up of Indian history, as well as the general apathy towards their preservation, Prinsep wrote:

> Aware indeed that the only accurate data we possessed for adjusting the chronology of Indian princes were those derived from ancient monuments of stone; inscriptions on rocks and caves . . . discovered accidentally in various parts of the country;—I could not see the highly curious column lying at Allahabad, falling to rapid decay, without wishing to preserve a complete copy of its several inscriptions. . . . It is greatly to be regretted that the task was not accomplished twenty or thirty years ago; for the ravages of time, or climate, have probably in that short period committed greater injuries on its surface, than during an equal number of centuries antecedent.[21]

An effort to preserve the Allahabad column had been made earlier in 1826, when Major Irvine prepared an estimate of Rs 1,800 for erecting and preserving it. The Governor-General, Lord Amherst, however objected to the proposals, on account of its being useless expenditure, and later, General Kyd, aptly named the 'vandal engineer' by Cunningham, pulled down the pillar because he found that it stood 'in the way of his new line of rampart near the gateway'.[22]

The local population's apathy equalled the government's. Burt states that Indian legends described the pillar as the *gada* of Bhimsen, one of the five Pandava brothers. It was said that the staff was used by Bhimsen to grind his *bhang* (an intoxicant) and that the vessel in which the *bhang* was ground was thrown into the Yamuna when the English conquered the fort. In any event, the pillar remained unnoticed and uncared for for centuries.

The inscriptions on the pillar, Burt and Prinsep stated, were of three distinct types, besides 'detached names and dates in modern Nagari, Bhaka, Marhatta, & c. . . . not worth the trouble of transcribing'.[23] Of these, one giving the genealogy of the Mughal emperors was easily decipherable. Unfortunately, this inscription was right in the middle of the pillar obliterating a portion of the older inscription.

The other type of inscription, which Prinsep rightly guessed to be the more ancient, was, as we know now, the famous Asokan inscription, deciphered by Prinsep some years later.

The third type of inscription, characterized by Burt as No. 2, resembled the Devanagari one. On going through the volumes of *Asiatic Researches*, Burt found the inscriptions to be the same as those discovered at Gaya which were deciphered by Charles Wilkins and published in the first volume of the *Researches*. He felt that although the first type of inscription, that is the Asokan, might take some time to decipher, that of the second category could be read by a Sanskrit scholar. Facsimiles of this were given to Captain A. Troyer, a great Sanskrit scholar and Secretary of the Sanskrit College. Troyer with the help of the college librarian, Pandit Madhava Ray, was able to read many portions of it. The inscription yielded the name of Samudragupta 'whose fame caused by the conquest of the whole earth . . . was equalling Tridasapat (Indra).'[24] This king, whose exploits were extolled so greatly, was unknown. However, to Troyer's delight, he found one name he was familiar with. This was Chandragupta, and it was repeated twice—as that of the great-grand-father, and also the father of Samudragupta.[25]

Having identified this name, it was natural for Troyer to connect it immediately with Chandragupta of the Maurya dynasty whose identity had already been established by Sir William Jones. But Troyer also harboured serious doubts about this identification. He felt that it would be 'adventurous to assert that Chandragupta of line 25th, was the founder of the Maurya dynasty: all that appears in the inscription is, that a Raja Samudragupta (the sea-protected) was a descendant in the fourth generation of a Chandragupta.'[26]

This posed a problem. There was little doubt that the reading of the name was correct. Prinsep himself had 'extracted the name and titles of Chandragupta, and placed them in the plate under the alphabetical key, to show that it has been faithfully rendered by the *pundit*'; but there was strong reasons for doubting that this Chandragupta was the one of whom the Greek historian Arrian spoke. One of the factors was the location of the monument—Allahabad—which was inconsistent with the capital of Chandragupta Maurya identified by Sir William Jones to be the modern Pataliputra or Patna. Secondly, Prinsep could not find the name of Samudragupta as a fourth descendant of Chandragupta in the catalogues of the Maurya dynasty.

Prinsep, for the time being, left the problem at that, probably because he found the other inscription more challenging, and felt instinctively that its decipherment would lead to the opening up of a new chapter in the process of the rediscovery of India's past.

The study of the Samudragupta inscription was taken up two months later by W. H. Mill. Mill had come to India in the ecclesiastical service of the East India Company, and was for a long time Principal of Bishop's College at Sibpur in Howrah. While in India, he acquired such deep knowledge of Sanskrit as to be a serious contender for the Boden chair.

Mill re-translated the entire portion of the inscription starting from the premise that the Chandragupta of the Allahabad inscription was the same as the Chandragupta identified by Sir William Jones, but soon discovered that there were too many discrepancies between the two. One was the fact that the Chandragupta of the inscription distinctly belonged to the solar race of the *kshatriya* kings, whereas the founder of the Maurya dynasty belonged to the lunar race.[27] Moreover, the names of the kings of the two dynasties were already at variance, as was the doubt expressed about the capitals of their kingdoms.

Having once accepted the fact that this line of kings belonged to a dynasty other than the Maurya, the problem of establishing its identity remained. In the process of re-translating the inscription, Mill corrected the names of two kings mentioned in line 25 which had been rendered by Captain Troyer as Chandragupta (great-grandfather of Samudragupta) and Yagnakacha (the grandfather). Mill re-read these names as 'the great King Gupta' (in place of Chandragupta) and 'Ghatotkacha' (in place of Yagnakacha). Fortunately, at about this time, Prinsep and Mill also read the legends on the ancient Hindu coins discovered by Colonel Tod and Wilson, and they found that not only were the legends in the same kind of letter as the inscription on the Allahabad pillar, but that they carried the same names, Ghatotkacha, Chandragupta, and Samudragupta. On the basis of the evidence available, Mill, for the first time in modern Indian historiography, drew up this genealogy of the Gupta kings:[28]

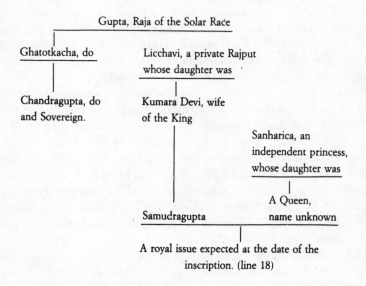

This achievement was a remarkable one, for except for the missing links, it corresponds very closely to Gupta genealogy as we know it today.

With these names at hand, Mill scanned ancient Sanskrit texts like the *Bhagavat*, the *Hari-Vamsa* and the *Vamsa-lata*, as well as the other Puranas, down to the early Rajput dynasties like the Chauhan, but he was still unable to identify the dynasty.

The inscription in the other character (Burt's No.1), posed a greater problem, for they were still indecipherable. All that Prinsep could say about them was that this type of inscription was the principal and the original one, antedating the other, which resembled Sanskrit characters. Giving his reasons for this, he wrote:

> This may, I think, be proved first, by the position it occupies on the Allahabad column, as well as on that of Delhi, called *Feroz's lath*; ... secondly, the simplicity of this character and the limited number of radicals, denote its priority to the more complicated and refined system afterwards adopted; while thirdly, the very great rarity of its occurrence on ancient monuments, and the perfect ignorance which prevails regarding its origin in the earliest Persian historians, who mention the *lath* of Feroz Shah, confirm its belonging to an epoch beyond the reach of native research.[29]

Prinsep also identified the character of these inscriptions with those on the Khandagiri rocks in Orissa, which had been copied and published by Andrew Stirling. He disagreed, however, and rightly so, with Stirling's contention that many of the letters of the inscription resembled Greek characters, holding that this similarity was purely accidental and that the alphabet was related to the Sanskrit family.[30]

Prinsep carefully classified each letter of the inscription together with the inflections of each radical letter; but he did not as yet have a key to its decipherment. Burt and his brother also made several unsuccessful attempts to have the inscription deciphered with the help of pundits from Banaras and Kanpur. It took another three years for the inscription to be read. One of the early breakthroughs in this direction came from Brian Houghton Hodgson, then residing at Nepal. On reading Princep's article, Hodgson wrote to the Society that eight to ten years earlier, he had written about three other such pillars in Bihar. One of these was situated at Lauriya Nandangarh, and Hodgson had sent a description of it as well as a copy of the inscription on the pillar. Hodgson felt that in view of the wide diffusion of this kind of inscription all over India, there was hardly any doubt about their being derived from the Devanagari.[31]

The Nandangarh pillar proved to be an important find on account of the capital being almost intact.[32] Hodgson sent to the Asiatic Society another copy of the inscription on the pillar which Prinsep compared with the inscriptions on the one known as the *lat* of Firuz Shah, and the Allahabad column. Of the results of his efforts, Prinsep wrote:

> I was led to a most important discovery: namely, that all three inscriptions are identically the same. Thus, the whole of the Bettiah inscription is

contained verbatim in that of Feroz *Lath* . . . and all that remains of the
Allahabad inscription can with equal facility be traced in the same plates,
with exception of the five short lines at the bottom, which appear to bear a
local import."

Prinsep, was however, no wiser about the contents of the inscriptions, or the importance of the pillars bearing them.

The Society's efforts at deciphering the Asokan inscriptions yielded
one important result which seems to have been overlooked by subsequent historians. This was the communication on the 'Restoration and
Translation of some Inscriptions at the Caves of Carli' by J. Stevenson,
which was read at the Society's meeting on 5 November. Stevenson
had been trying for almost a year to find a key to the inscriptions in the
caves at Karle near Pune in Maharashtra. The local pundits he tells us,
sent him to the Marathas and to the Kanarese, and they in turn to the
Tamilians, and so on, without any result in endless succession. He
then collected specimens of all the scripts used in western India and by
comparing these to the Karle inscriptions, tried to decipher them. At
this stage, he was sent the March issue of the Society's *Journal*, which
carried facsimiles of the inscriptions on the Allahabad pillar.
Stevenson compared the two and wrote to the Society, 'I have been
able to decipher some of our inscriptions; and hope that if you have
not found the key to the character of Inscription No. 1, my alphabet
may carry you several steps towards its attainment, and so repay the
debt I owe for the assistance derived from your Journal.'[14]

Stevenson then proceeded to read a portion of the Allahabad
inscription, which also occurred several times on the Delhi pillar, and
felt that it contained an address, probably to the sun—in pure
Sanskrit. This portion of the inscription he deciphered as (*Dvedharam
piye piya dwamobharjamegavam*) द्वेधारं पिये पिय इमोभाजंमेगवं and translated it as 'In the two ways (of wisdom and works?) with all speed do I
approach the resplendent receptacle of the ever-moving luminous
radiance'.

Although Stevenson was way off the mark as far as the meaning of
the inscription was concerned, he was very close to the actual value of
the letters in the first part of the inscription. *Dvedharam piye piya
dwamobharjamegavam*, is extremely close to the actual text *Devanampiya piyadassi*. If Stevenson's line of enquiry had been pursued, there is
hardly any doubt that the Asokan inscriptions would have been
deciphered much earlier. Unfortunately, Stevenson's paper was not

given the attention it was due, and Asoka remained more or less an unknown identity to the historian.

The year 1834 is also the high-water mark of studies in Indian numismatics, especially as regards their importance in reconstructing the history of the Indo-Greek and the Indo-Scythian line of kings in Bactria. The labours of several scholars like Charles Masson, General Ventura, Dr Gerard and Alexander Court contributed to the process. Their excavations, especially of structures known as *topes*, and their discoveries in Afghanistan and the Punjab had aroused the interest of scholars throughout the world and had 'stimulated persons less favourably circumstanced . . . to look around them for such remains of past times as India might afford.'³⁵ One of these was Captain P. T. Cautley, the superintendent of the Doab Canal, who, while clearing out the bed of a canal discovered near Behat the site of an ancient town situated nearly seventeen feet below the surface. Captain Cautley enthusiastically described the site as an Oriental Herculaneum. Among other specimens, Cautley collected 170 coins, sometimes by giving new rupees for old ones, and he sent almost the entire collection to the Asiatic Society. From their appearance and the fact that he found the positions of other nearby towns and villages 'invariably fixed either on the highest spots or on the slope of the valleys', Cautley guessed that the town was of great antiquity. Not being an antiquarian himself, Cautley referred the entire question to Prinsep,³⁶ who while communicating Cautley's paper to the Society, added his own note on the coins found, after engraving the more important of these.

The site was indeed an ancient one, for some of the coins were of the Indo-Scythic type. Others bore legends of the No. 2 type found on the Allahabad pillar which closely resembled Devanagari. On one of the coins Prinsep deciphered the words *Sri madghavakacho*. This, Mill remarked, after a slight alteration became 'Ghatat-kacho', the name of the father of Chandragupta of the Allahabad pillar inscription. Here then was further proof of the accuracy of the Gupta genealogy Mill drew up.³⁶ᵃ

The publication of Cautley's communication drew others' attention towards the importance of ancient coins. In May 1834, the Society received several coins from A. Conolly at Kanauj and in September, the coins obtained at Chittore by Major Stacy. All these were studied, described and drawn by Prinsep, who discovered that some of these bore legends in the character of the No. 1 inscription of the Allahabad pillar, which could not be deciphered at the time.

Another major acquisition of coins during this period was through Shaikh Karamat Ali, the agent of the Supreme Government of India, and a companion of Conolly's on his journey from Persia to India. When Karamat Ali left Calcutta in 1832, he took plates of all the ancient coins which had been printed till that time, and searched for new coins wherever he went. Acknowledging his contribution of 383 coins, the Society noted:

> Bringing none of the knowledge of the subject possessed by his European competitors, his comparatively undirected efforts have been wonderfully successful: the collection transmitted comprises numerous coins of Apollodotus, Menander, Hermaeus, Eucratides, Kanerkos, Kadphises, and indeed almost all of those enumerated by Mr. Masson's Memoir besides some very curious Parthian and many gold and silver Hindu coins.[17]

Masson's *Memoir* which has been referred to earlier, was presented to the Society at its meeting of 30 April 1834 and published in that month's issue of the *Journal*.

Charles Masson,[38] almost a forgotten name now, was one of the most romantic figures of the period. At one time he was taken for a Russian spy, even considered a key figure in the rebellion of Khelat in 1841, and was detained. The *Bombay Times* said he was a native of Kentucky in the United States; but he turned out to be an Englishman and 'a member of a good family, not of that name, however, for like many others who have left their friends and joined the army in a moment of desperation, he assumed a name not his own'. Shortly after joining the army, he deserted after the siege of Bharatpur. He seems to have been a compulsive traveller, and if we are to believe the *Bombay Times* (much of its information was contradicted later on), he travelled to France and Russia. . . . Journeying to Sind, he was robbed and had to continue his travels disguised as a *faqir*. From Sind, he proceeded to Peshawar, and journeyed extensively in Baluchistan, Afghanistan and the Punjab during the years 1826 to 1838. An account of these journeys was published in four volumes. Having heard stories of innumerable ancient coins and other relics being freely available in Beghram village, Masson made his way there.[39] Over a period of six months (till November 1833) he collected 1,865 copper coins, fourteen gold and silver ones, and in the next four years amassed more than thirty thousand coins of different kinds.[40]

Staggering as this figure is, the still greater number that must have been lost was computed by Masson himself:

> I suppose that no less a number than thirty thousand coins, probably a much larger number, are found annually on the *dusht* or plain of Beghram, independently of rings, seals, and other trinkets. Gold and silver coins occur but rarely. If we allow a period of five hundred years, since the final extinction of this city, and if we allow, as I presume is reasonable, that the same or not a less number of coins has been annually extracted from its site, we have a total of fifteen million, a startling amount, and which will not fail to excite curiosity as to this second Babylon.[41]

Masson divided his collection of Beghram coins into five categories: Greek, Indo-Scythic, Parthian, and Guebre, Brahmanical, and Muhammadan. In his communication, however, he dealt only with the Greek and the Indo-Scythian finds, and it is the former class that makes his discoveries remarkable and important for our knowledge of the Bactrian line of kings.

Earlier to Masson's discoveries, the names of only nine of the Indo-Greek kings were known to history. On the basis of scattered references in classical literature and the collection of coins found till that time, Professor Schlegel had drawn up a list which was published in *Journal Asiatique* in 1828.[42] This list was:

255 B.C.	Theodotus I	
243	Theodotus II	Fixed historically by Strabo
220	Euthydemus of Magnesia	
195	Apollodotus Soter Menander Nikator	Alluded to by Plutarch Trogus and Arrian, their coins prevalent in Baroach, A.D. 200
	Heliocles Dikaios	On the authority of Visconti and Mionnet, from a single medal
	Demetrius	Son of Euthydemus, doubtful if he reigned in Bactria
181	Eucratides I	Artemidorus calls him the "Great King"
146	Eucratides II	Murdered his father and was himself slain
125	Destruction of the Empire by the Tartars and the Scythians or Sacae	

Masson's discoveries not only confirmed the existence of at least three of these kings, Menander, Apollodotus and Eucratides, but added the names of Antialkides, Agathocles, Pantaleon, Hermaeus I, Hermaeus II and Hermaeus III,[42a] Sotermegas, and Unadpherros to the list of Bactrian rulers, thus extending the era of Bactrian history. Of the Indo-Scythian kings, Masson discovered sixty-eight coins of King Kanerkos (identified by Prinsep as Kanishka), and as many as 291 belonging to King Kadphises.

The greatest breakthrough in research on the history of the Indo-Scythian kings was made by General Chevalier Ventura, another colourful personality.[43] After having participated in Napolean's Russian campaign under the command of General Beauharnais, Ventura came to India and joined the service of Ranjit Singh, as commander of a regular infantry corps. On one occasion, referring to Ventura's complaint against misgovernment in Kashmir, the Maharaja said 'Truly, this worthy gentleman is lavish of his imputations against others — he wishes, I suppose, to make us believe that he is himself a paragon of excellence and purity'. He then accused Ventura of embezzling two lakhs of rupees.

From this, one would hardly expect General Ventura to show interest in antiquarian researches, but it is to his efforts that we owe much of our knowledge of the Kushana kings. The main site to have attracted Ventura's attention was the *stupa* at Manikyala.

Manikyala is a village near Kabul in Afghanistan, lying on the route between Attock and Lahore. The great structure in the village, known as the *tope*, was first visited and described by Mountstuart Elphinstone in his *Account of the Kingdom of Cabul*. On his way back from his mission at Kabul in 1808–9, Elphinstone thus described his discovery of the *tope*:[44]

The most remarkable sight we met with in this part, and perhaps in the whole of our journey, was an edifice about fifteen miles from Banda, our second march from Rawalpindi. The heaviness of the rain prevented our marching from that place on the day after we reached it; and as we were near the place which Major Wilford supposes to have been the site of Taxila, a party determined to set out in quest of the ruins of that city. . . . We met with no ruins of such antiquity. . . . We, however, at length discovered a remarkable building, which seemed at first to be a cupola, but when approached, was found to be a solid structure, on a low artificial mound. There was nothing at all Hindu in the appearance of this building; most of the party thought it decidedly Grecian. . . . The natives called it the *Tope* of Maunicyaula, and said it was built by the gods.[45]

After such a description, it is surprising that Elphinstone did not investigate the structure further. While the local Muslim belief was that the *stupa* contained the remains of all the Muslim soldiers who died in the battle which took place at that site between the Afghans and Raja Man;[46] the Hindus believed, as Elphinstone pointed out, that the structure was a creation of the gods, where they offered the first cuttings of the hair of their male children.

With General Ventura began the process of studying these structures from an antiquarian point of view. General Ventura was not a scholar himself, and so although his main discoveries on the opening of the biggest *stupa* at Manikyala had been made by June 1830, it was not till four years later that the finds were studied critically, and his achievements were made known through the *Journal*.

In June 1833, Captain C. M. Wade, the Political Agent at Ludhiana, met General Ventura and had a long discussion about the Manikyala antiquities. He referred to Prinsep's remarks, published in the Society's *Journal*, that they hoped Ventura would 'no longer think us [the Society] unworthy of being made the medium of their introduction to the knowledge of the world.' Ventura then most generously offered to deliver, absolutely free and without conditions, all the coins and other remains discovered by him in the *stupa*.

This offer elicited from Prinsep an equally generous reply: 'I could not but disclaim all permanent interest in the relics, and request M. Ventura to consider them still at his disposal, although I should be proud, whilst they were deposited in my care, to do my utmost in making them more fully known to the world.' 'This contest of liberality', remarked Wilson, '. . . ended in Mr Prinsep's consenting to retain one or two specimens of such of the coins as were in any number.'[47]

General Ventura's gift to the Society resulted in three articles by Prinsep, published in the *Journal* for July, September and November 1834. The first of these communications, presented to the Society at its meeting of 20 March, gave a detailed account of General Ventura's operations, together with drawings of the various finds, while the second communication dealt with the coin-finds.

In this communication, Prinsep, on the basis of the discovery of Sassanian coins among the remains, contradicted his earlier and correct conclusion that Kanerkou was none other than the King

Kanishka mentioned in the annals of Kashmir. The discovery of another gold coin of King Yasovarman of Kanauj led him to place the construction of the *stupa* at a much more recent date. Both these conclusions were, as we now know, wrong, and subsequently the reading of the inscription on the stone slab Ventura dug out resulted in one of the most significant discoveries in Kushana history: that the *stupa* had been built by King Kanishka in the eighteenth year of his reign. It was also later concluded correctly that King Yasovarman had made extensive repairs to the *stupa* in about the eighth century A.D.

General Ventura's project was the first to yield archaeological evidence of the Kushana dynasty, especially of Kanishka, although the fact was not sufficiently clear at the time primarily because the inscription on the stone slab of the relic chamber could not be fully deciphered. Still Ventura's operations inspired several others to take to archaeological pursuits. Among these was A. Court, another officer in the Sikh army of Ranjit Singh. Court opened up no less than fifteen *stupas* in the vicinity of the great *stupa*, and uncovered valuable data on Kushana history. Among Court's coin-finds were those of Vima Kadphises and Kujula Kadphises; and it is on the basis of these that historians treat the two as Kanishka's predecessors rather than his successors.[48] On the other hand, the discovery of several Roman and Sassanian coins among the remains led Prinsep to place the construction of the structure in about the fourth century A.D. or even later. This marked the beginning of the great debate on the period of Kanishka's reign, although the period assigned by Prinsep is no longer taken account of. In fact, it was contradicted forcefully the same year in an article entitled 'Correction of a mistake regarding some of the Roman coins found in the *tope* at Manikyala opened by M. Court', published in the December issue of the *Journal*. Beside stating that 'the *tope* must have been constructed about the commencement of the Christian era', a conclusion more correct than Prinsep's, the article is important as the first written by Alexander Cunningham, who became one of the greatest Indologists of the modern period. Prinsep, as Editor of the *Journal*, prefaced the article with the note: 'We compliment our young friend upon the success with which he has commenced his numismatic studies, and shall always be happy to profit by his criticisms.' Prinsep did not agree with Cunningham's conclusion; nor has it been unanimously accepted even now. The date of the construction of the *stupa*, and consequently the date of Kanishka and the year in which he began his reign, remain one of the most debated points in oriental history.[49]

With Cunningham's appearance on the scene of Indian studies, James Prinsep at the height of his powers, and valuable contributions from other scholars, the Asiatic Society had in its fifty years indeed come a long way from its humble beginnings. Wilson, comparing the Asiatic Society of Bengal to other Societies in England in a letter to Ram Comul Sen remarked:

> As far as I have yet had an opportunity of comparing it with Societies here [England], it need not shrink from a comparison, containing as much talent and energy as any, and conducting its proceedings with quite as much method and spirit. . . . What I did not expect here is great idleness—great waste of time. . . . Even in Oxford there is little study—not above four hours a day . . . what can be effected in these few hours?[50]

Besides the important contributions mentioned above, the Society in 1834 had the distinction of seeing the completion of the Tibetan dictionary by Alexander Csoma de Körös, which was printed at the government's expense under the auspices of the Society. The *Dictionary* marked a milestone in the history of the Society. Not only was it a pioneering effort at making this abstruse language known to the world, but it gained for the Society fame such as few events had.[51]

An unfortunate loss to the Society was the death of Dr William Carey, on 9 June 1834 in his seventy-third year. Dr Carey had been a member of the Society for twenty-eight years and a member of the Committee of Papers since 1807. Although he contributed only two papers to the Society, one on the agriculture of Dinajpur (printed in the tenth volume of the *Researches*) and the other on the funeral ceremonies of a Burman priest (printed in the twelfth), he made major contributions to the development of the Bengali language and the history of Indian botany. His role in the translation of the *Ramayana* into English is known of, but what is little known is that Carey had prepared, after years of great labour, a polyglot in thirteen Indian languages, part of which was destroyed in the fire which burnt down the Serampore Press. He had also prepared a massive Sanskrit dictionary (the manuscript of which is still available in the Serampore Library)[52] and rendered great assistance (as the author acknowledged) towards the Anglo-Bengali Dictionary prepared by Ram Comul Sen.

James Prinsep, writing the Preface to the volume of the *Journal of the Asiatic Society* for 1835, must have done so with a sense of great satisfaction:

> The *Journal* has now survived its fourth year of existence, or including the *Gleanings in Science*, its seventh; yet so far from feeling its vigour abated, or finding its contributors grown languid, or its supporters falling off, the past year has produced a volume overflowing with original matter. . . . The demand for the work in England increases daily, and much of the new matter it contains is greedily transferred to the pages of European literary and scientific periodicals of wide established circulation."

This sense of satisfaction was justified for the Asiatic Society's achievement had come about despite the almost hostile official attitude of the Government, which seemed set against the very purposes for which the Society was founded.

While much has been written on the subject of the introduction of English as a medium of education in India and its far-reaching effects, the role of the Asiatic Society in the entire affair remains more or less unknown.

One of the results of the Macaulay–Bentinck insistence on anglicizing Indian education was the latter's decision to stop releasing funds for the printing of oriental works. It was at this stage that the controversy, so far confined to the General Committee of Public Instruction, entered the precincts of the Asiatic Society. Members of the General Committee of Public Instruction who took active part in the language controversy included several members of the Asiatic Society who held opposing views on the subject and yet the controversy, fierce as it was, had till then been kept out of the Society.

The proclamation against printing all oriental works then in press⁵⁴ went sharply against the Society's interests. Prinsep described the Government's decision as one 'not far outdone by the destruction of the Alexandrine library itself', and felt that the Society should exert its influence in every way not only to save Indian literature from a catastrophe, 'but also to rescue our national character from the stigma of so unjust, unpopular, and impolitic an act.' He then proposed the setting up of a special committee for completing the books on which work had been stopped by Bentinck's proclamation. He also suggested that the 'Oriental Publication Committee' should send an urgent Memorial to the Government requesting it to continue its patronage to oriental publications.⁵⁵

The Government's reply was predictable, and signed by G. A. Bushby, Secretary to Government and an Anglicist to the core, who was also an important member of the Committee of Public Instruction. A copy of the Governor-General's proclamation was attached to his letter as the final word on the issue. Bushby added that a great portion of the limited Education Fund had already been spent on publication of editions of Oriental works which had led to 'little purpose but to accumulate stores of waste paper'. He agreed however to hand over the sheets already printed to the Asiatic or any other Society which would volunteer to complete them at their own expense.

If the Society acted in a restrained manner, the Press made up for it. Bushby's observation was widely noticed and vehemently criticised. *The Friend of India* felt that refusal of financial assistance to the Asiatic Society was not unexpected in view of the Burmese war, but it was 'scarcely prepared for the sweeping condemnation of treasures of Oriental lore, expressed in the phrase that they were but an accumulation of waste paper.' It called the step nothing short of Gothic barbarism, and suggested that the Dharma Sabha pass a vote of censure on the whole Council.[56]

The *India Review*, which had started publication in 1837, took up this question in its first volume and commented:

When the Consul Mummius sacked the Grecian city, he designated in his ignorance of their value the most precious specimens of painting and sculpture, as mere waste lumber. The cases are to our judgement nearly parallel . . . a more unhappy measure never emanated from the resolutions of this Governement.[57]

The *Asiatic Journal* wrote that the Government's action was comparable to the doom effected in China by one of its sovereigns who burned all the books in the country to give the nation a new and a better form of civilization than that advocated by Confucius.[58] The *Alexander's East India Magazine* felt that in view of the hostility of the Government, the Asiatic Society should approach the Court of Directors, adding that 'The printing of correct editions of Sanskrit classics is an object of national importance to which the Government of India cannot be indifferent'.[59]

It was a heroic decision to take on the printing of the oriental works at a time when the Society's finances were not too happy. Just over three thousand rupees were in hand in January 1835[60] and the *Journal* had shown an overall loss of Rs 516.11.4. James Prinsep, howevei wrote with a sense of just pride and satisfaction in the preface to the Journal of 1835:

> If it be asked, what has been the most prominent object of interest discussed in the present volume, the answer must naturally point to the Proceedings of the Asiatic Society, in regard to the publication of the Oriental Works which had been suspended by an order of the Supreme Government. . . . It may be allowable in this place to prophesy, that the conduct of the Asiatic Society, in stepping forward to rescue the half-printed volumes of Sanskrit, Arabic, and Persian, will be approved and applauded by every learned Society and every scholar in Europe.[61]

Seldom have the world of scholarship and the dictates of government been so clearly opposed. Yet there is little doubt that the majority of the Society's members were in favour of spreading English education in India, while they also clearly saw that it was only through a study of its own literature and an understanding of its heritage that renascent India would be able to find its feet.

In 1835 the Society conferred Honorary Membership on several distinguished scholars including Professors Heeren, Klaproth and Rosen, the Hungarian scholar Alexander Csoma de Körös, and the soldier-archaeologists General Ventura and A. Court. Another scholar to be honoured likewise was the Honourable George Turnour, whose name was proposed by Mill and seconded by Prinsep. Turnour at the time was posted in Ceylon and was endeavouring to open up the treasures of historical knowledge hidden in the Pali canons. In his letter acknowledging the honour, Turnour spoke of the importance of and difficulties inherent in translation of the important Pali work *Mahavamso*, which provided a chronologically connected Buddhist history of India, from 590 to 307 B.C.:

> After the disappointments which have hitherto attended the labour of orientalists in their search for historical annals, comprehensive in date and consistent in their chronology, a translation alone of a Pali History of such extensive pretentions, would be justly received with repulsing scepticism, as to its authenticity, by the literary world. I have therefore decided on publishing the text also in Roman characters . . . As the publication however is undertaken entirely at my own expense, official demands on my time may prevent the early completion of the whole work. The reception the first volume may meet with, and other circumstances over which I can exercise no control, will hereafter decide whether I proceed beyond that volume.[62]

We shall see later the role Turnour's translation played in solving one of the greatest riddles of Asokan history. Meanwhile, Prinsep was trying his utmost to have the Asokan inscriptions deciphered. He had by now facsimiles of several inscriptions like those on the Allahabad, Delhi, and the Lauriya Nandangarh pillars. With this material in hand, he was constantly collating, comparing and preparing more and more correct facsimiles. In 1835 he published the entire inscription on the Radhiah pillar, comparing each letter with that of the Delhi inscription, indicating the minutest difference between the two.[63] Prinsep also inspired others from Britain to collect whatever material came to their notice, particularly ancient inscriptions. His efforts bore results. Major Colvin of the Engineers communicated to the Society notices of two more pillars: one at Hissar and the other at Fatihabad,[64] and Lieutenant Kittoe once again studied the Allahabad pillar and made the startling discovery that the Asokan inscription, designated as Inscription No. 1 by Burt, was interlined with a more modern alphabet. At Kittoe's request, Walter Ewer re-examined the pillar and wrote back: 'True enough, the unknown character is interlined with Sanskrit which is the least distinct, and appears to be the older of the two.' To this Prinsep added the hopeful comment that it was possible for the two writings to be contemporaneous, in which case 'there will be an end of the mystery which has hitherto hung over this writing.'[65]

Another significant discovery in this field was that of the 'ruins and site of an ancient city near Bakhra, 13 cos (about 25 miles) north of Patna and six from Singhea', by J. Stephenson.[66] Stephenson discovered yet another pillar and found that the local residents as usual had named it Bhimsen's *gada* (mace) and had woven a fantastic story round it.

More important and interesting than the discovery of the pillar was what Stephenson found with a Hindu *faqir* who made clay images. Stephenson recounted his discovery in these words:

> One of these images, coloured black, attracted my notice from its singular grotesque appearance: on closer inspection, I discovered that the lower part was of stone, finely sculptured, and altogether different from the upper which I found to be made of clay. . . . On the lowest part of the fragment is an inscription in Sanskrit, which the *pundits* of this part of the country cannot as yet decipher.[67]

At the time when Prinsep received the facsimile of the Tirhut inscription from Stephenson, Captain Thoresby, Secretary of the

Sanskrit College at Banaras, together with Lieutenant Grant and Alexander Cunningham, was busy excavating the Buddhist *stupa* at Sarnath. During the digging operations Cunningham came upon an inscription on a stone slab—a facsimile of which he forwarded to Prinsep. Prinsep noticed that the two inscriptions (the Sarnath inscription and the one at the base of the statue sent by Stephenson) were similar, although he was not yet able to decipher them. He showed both inscriptions to Wilson's pundit, Govind Ram Sastri, who discovered that this inscription was similar to that found at Gaya and deciphered by Wilkins. The two inscriptions were then submitted to Mill who deciphered the whole, the Tirhut inscription reading thus:

ये धर्मा हेतुप्रभवास्तेषां हेतुं तथागत उवाच तेषां
च यो निरोध एवं वादी महाश्रमण: ।

Prinsep, after comparing the two inscriptions concluded that although they were not copies, they were so similar in content that they must contain some very common text from the Buddhist scriptures. With this in mind, he approached Alexander Csoma de Körös who was then working on the Tibetan books on Buddhism.

Csoma at first did not recognize the text, but soon afterwards realized that the Sarnath inscription agreed word for word with the text given in the Kahgyur collection, but the inscription was only a portion of the text. He gave the full version in the roman character as:

Ye dharma hetu prabhava, hetun
teshan Tathagato hyavadat
Teshan cha yo nirodha, evam vadi Maha Shramanas
Sarva papasyakarani (?am)
kushalasyopasapradam,
Sva chittam paridamanum, etad
Buddhanushasanam.

This was translated as:

Whatever moral (or human) actions
arise from some cause,
The cause of them has been declared by
TATHAGATA:
What is the check to these actions,

Is thus set forth by the great SRAMANNAS
No vice is to be committed:
Every virtue must be perfectly practised:
The mind must be brought under
entire subjugation;
This is the commandment of BUDDHA.[68]

Mill broadly concurred with Csoma, and the whole text received further confirmation from a Ratna Pala, 'a Christian convert from Buddhism', who informed them that the verse was quite common among the Buddha's disciples.

The finishing touch to the entire episode was provided by Brian H. Hodgson who sent a letter on the subject which was read out at the Society's meeting of 6 May. The letter said:

> I have just got the 39th Number of the Journal and hasten to tell you that your enigma requires no Oedipus for its solution at Kathmandu, where almost every man, woman, and child, of the Buddha faith, can repeat the *confessio fidei* (for such it may be called), inscribed on the Sarnath stone.[69]

If the year 1835 marked a great advance in the deciphering of important inscriptions and, as shown above, in the discovery of a basic tenet of Buddhism, it marked no less progress in the study of numismatics. The main figure in the process was certainly James Prinsep, but he would have been able to achieve little had not a number of persons showed interest in the collection of ancient coins in different places. No one was more aware of this than Prinsep himself. Thus he wrote about Colonel Stacy:

> Here he would be seen putting up with every inconvenience, enduring the burning heats of May, or the cold of December, under trees or in common *sarais* in Central India, digging in deserted ruins, or poring over the old stores of village moneychangers . . . sparing neither money nor time to gain his end, and after a hard search and fatigue, sitting down, while his impressions were still warm and vivid, to communicate the results of his day's campaign.[70]

While Stacy was thus engaged in Chittor and Udaipur, Lieutenant Conolly was searching the plains and hills of Jaipur, Captain Wade was active at Ludhiana, Captain Cautley at Saharanpur, Colonel Smith at Patna, Tregear at Jaunpur and, above all, Alexander Cunningham (then a Lieutenant) at Sarnath and Banaras. Working in Punjab and Afghanistan were General Ventura, A. Court, Dr Gerard, Charles

Masson, Shaikh Karamat Ali and Mohan Lall. Beside these, Prinsep received coins from Hamilton, Spiers, Edgework, Gubbins and Captain Jenkins, who collected coins in different districts. With this rich and varied collection for Prinsep's genius to work on, valuable results emerged to give ancient Indian history and chronology a sound foundation.

Although only three papers were read on numismatics during the year 1835, an immense wealth of material came to light. The first paper, 'Further Notes and Drawings of Bactrian and Indo-Scythic Coins',[71] by James Prinsep, appeared in the June issue of the *Journal* and by itself marks an important stage in numismatic studies. The coins of Menander and Apollodotus which had been discovered upto this time, had carried Greek inscriptions on one face and on the other, a legend in unknown characters. By presuming that the legend in the undeciphered character bore the same import as the Greek legend, and by collating and comparing, Prinsep had at last the clue to the unknown alphabet (Kharosthi).[72]

In an effort to reconstruct a continuous chain of events making up the history of India, Prinsep first wanted to establish a connection between the Indo-Scythian coins and the Hindu coins discovered at Behat, Kanauj, Saurashtra and other places. His two memoirs, 'On the connection of various ancient Hindu coins with the Grecian or Indo-Scythic series',[73] and 'Notices of Ancient Hindu Coins',[74] were both published in the Society's *Journal* of 1835. In these two communications, we find the first ray of light cast on many new kings and dynasties which later assumed great importance in Indian history.

Perhaps the most interesting, and the one which later acquired great importance, was the coin of Samudragupta (now so famous as to be reproduced in textbooks) in which he is shown playing a harp. Although the legend on the coin was incomplete and only the portion reading *Maha rajadhi Raja Sri ... dra Gupta* could be deciphered, Prinsep had no difficulty in connecting it with the name Samudragupta. Other coins yielded the names of Kumaragupta, Chandragupta, Vikramaditya and Sasigupta. Prinsep at that time could not have imagined the prominence these kings or the Gupta dynasty would come to acquire in Indian history.

It is now known that the period between the downfall of the Gupta empire and the early Muslim invasions of India was a period of political instability with little principalities warring against each other. Petty adventurers and kings rose like meteors and appropriated titles proclaiming themselves conquerors of the world and the universe, and then as suddenly disappeared. Every such king minted a new coin which floated for a time and then lay buried as useless metal. This state of affairs is amply reflected in Prinsep's efforts to co-relate the coin-finds so as to yield a systematic history of the period down to Muslim rule. The continuation of his communication on 'Notices of ancient Hindu coins' bears all the marks of the difficulties and deficiencies of a pioneer: names of kings keep cropping up without any evidence which could place them in a chronological framework, and wild conjectures and guesswork had to be resorted to. It would be a near impossible task to examine each hypothesis or conjecture about each coin, inscription, or the name of a king or dynasty, and one can only highlight certain important aspects of the communication.

In the first section of the paper called 'Hindu coins of mid age', based on the collections of Smith, Swiney, Cunningham, Karamat Ali and above all Stacy, one of Prinsep's important theories was that although the Palas originally belonged to Bengal, they had, nevertheless, at one time acquired paramount sovereignty over India with their capital at Kanauj. From the fact that coins found as far apart as Gujarat and Chittor bore names and titles of kings terminating in the term Pala-deva, Prinsep came to the conclusion that 'it marks the spread and paramount sovereignty of the Gaur family across the whole continent of India.'

In the section called 'Rajput Coins', Prinsep concentrated on the coins found largely in Stacy's collection. He divided these coins into three categories: those bearing genuine Hindu names, those bearing Muslim names, either alone or conjointly with those of the Hindu princes inscribed in the *nagari* character, and those bearing purely Arabic inscriptions.

Prinsep described the coins falling into each category and compared the names yielded by them with those of the Rajput princes then known of, mostly in Tod's *Annals*. From the study of this class of coins, Prinsep drew up a chronological list of the sovereigns who 'nearly fill up the first century of the Patan monarchs of Dihli'. His reconstruction of this period of India's history reads thus:

Sri Muhammad Same is, I presume, Muhammad bin Sam-ul-Ghori, the first of the dynasty, commonly known by his cognomen Shahab-ud-din, who possessed himself of the throne of Dihli,   A.H 588   A.D. 1192.

Shams-ud-din, in Nagari and Arabic, is Altamsh	A.H. 607	A.D. 1210
Mu'az-ud-din, must be Bairam Shah, his son Kai Kubad	" 637	" 1239
'Ala-ud-din, may be Masaud, the son of Firoz	" 640	" 1242
Nasir-ud-din, denotes Mahmud, son of Altamsh	" 643	" 1245
Ghias-ud-din, Balban	" 664	" 1265
'Ala-ud-din, Muhammad Shah, bears its own date	" 695	" 1295
Ghias-ud-din, Tughlak Shah, cannot be mistaken	" 721	" 1321[75]

This marks the first attempt by a modern historian to reconstruct the dynastic history of the period of the Delhi Sultanate and, although much came to light later on, especially the name of Razia Sultan, one can see how close Prinsep was to the actual genealogy.

The third section of this article dealt with 'Saurashtrian Coins', again, the first attempt to study this series of coins. Although Prinsep could not deduce any historical information from them, it was only a matter of time before these coins began to yield information not only about the Gupta dynasty, but about several others like the Naga and the Mitra, who would perhaps otherwise have remained unknown to us.

Coincidentally, the communication which first brought to light an important dynasty of Saurashtra was also presented this year. The September issue of the *Journal* carried the 'Account of the inscriptions upon two sets of copper plates, found in the western part of Gujerat', by the Persian Secretary to the Bombay Government, W. H. Wathen. Wathen was inspired to take up Indological studies by Mountstuart Elphinstone, who gave him several inscriptions requesting him to translate them at leisure and send the results to the Literary Society. 'My own curiosity was so much excited by the perusal of their contents', wrote Wathen, 'that I made every exertion, and spared no expense to procure as many more as possible. I was so fortunate as to obtain, in the course of some years, as many as fourteen, consisting partly of copper inscribed plates, and partly of inscriptions copied from pillars and ruins of ancient buildings, temples, & c.'[76]

Unfortunately for the Asiatic Society of Bengal, Wathen communicated translations of only two copperplate inscriptions to the Society, while the same year, translations of no less than ten inscriptions were sent to the Royal Asiatic Society of Great Britain. These inscriptions, some of which were reproduced in the journals of that Society, yielded much more valuable information on little known dynasties like the Silahara, the Rashtrakuta and the Chalukya.[77] Wathen's communication to the Bengal Society brought to light the important dynasty of the Valabhis. The existence of this dynasty was known in a vague way to Tod, who had stated in the *Annals* on the authority of Jain records, that the Gehlot Rajputs either founded, or became masters of the city of Valabhipur (which was, according to him, the Byzantine of Ptolemy), some time after the second century A.D. Tod was aware of only three rulers of this line, Kaneksen, whom he took to be founder of the dynasty, Vijaya, and Siladitya, the last of the line, in whose reign Valabhipur was besieged and captured by the barbarians.[78]

Wathen's communication marks a milestone in the discovery and historiography of this dynasty. The two copperplates on which Wathen's communication was based were discovered by some labourers while digging the foundations of a house at Danduca and another one at Bhavnagar. The incriptions found on them enabled Wathen to draw up a genealogy of the Valabhi Kings in the following manner:

A.D. 144 or 190	1. Senapati Bhatarca
	2.　　　　　　 Dhara Sena
	3. Maharaja Drona Sinha
	4.　　　　　　 Dhruva Sena I
	5.　　　　　　 Dharapattah
	6.　　　　　　 Griha Sena
A.D. 300	7.　　　　　　 Sridhara Sena I[79]
	8. Maharaja Siladitya I
	9.　　　　　　 Charagriha I
	10.　　　　　 Sridhara Sena II
	11.　　　　　 Dhruva Sena II
	12.　　　　　 Sridhara Sena II[80]
	13.　　　　　 Siladitya II.

At this point the writing is obliterated so that the names of two or three princes cannot be made out. Then follow:

	16.	Maharaja Charagriha II
A.D. 524	17.	Siladitya III
	18.	Siladitya Musalli IV

Subsequent to this, several other inscriptions and Valabhi coins were discovered and outstanding scholars including Princep, E. Thomas, Bühler, Rajendralala Mitra, Bhau Daji and R. G. Bhandarkar, made valuable contributions to the study of this dynasty. In spite of this, the dynasty probably has not been given its due importance in Indian history. General histories of India convey the impression that it was but a minor one among the plethora of ruling lines which ruled different parts of the country in the period between the decline of the Gupta empire and the Muslim invasions. This was probably not so. The Valabhi dynasty was one of the two most important ones to follow the Gupta empire, the other one being the dynasty of Thaneswar which saw the rise of Harsha. More important is the fact that the Valabhi dynasty was the only one which survived nearly three hundred years and spanned the gap between the fall of the Guptas and the rise of Muslim power. A dynasty which stayed in power for so long when conditions in the country were all but stable could by no means have been a minor one, but further research is required to give it its proper importance in Indian history. Another dynasty to be discovered at about this time was the Chahamana of Sakambhari. The July issue of the *Journal* carried a 'Notice of the Temple called Seo Byjnauth (Siva Vaidyanath) discovered by Sergeant E. Dean on 3 December 1834 on the Hill of Unchapahar in the Shekawati Territory'.[81] While exploring the temple, Sergeant Dean came across 'a large slab of black stone, about 3½ inches thick, and 3 feet square, in which was cut an inscription in a fine clear character, in good preservation.' Dean made a facsimile of the inscription[82] and forwarded it to the Society where it was deciphered and read by Mill together with Dean's communication.[83] Later known as the Harsha (Haras) inscription, it was one of the two (the other being the Bijolia inscription), which provided the main basis for reconstruction of the history of the Chahamanas of Sakambhari.

This inscription yielded names of six kings of this dynasty.[84] Mill gave their genealogy thus:

Guvaka   Became king probably about
                                    800

Chandra Raja	830
Guvaka	860
Chandana	890
Vakpati (conqueror of Tantrapala)	920
Sinha Raja	950
And his successor (not by natural descent) Vigraha Raja certainly about	968

Although we now have a list of as many as sixteen kings of this house[85] the genealogy provided here corresponds with that given in the Bijolia inscription, the other princes coming prior to Guvaka.[86]

The year 1836 seemed to usher in an auspicious era for the Society. The dark clouds, in the shape of the victory of the Anglicists over the Orientalists, which had threatened the Society's fortunes the previous year now seemed to disperse. Two developments took place at about this time which brought about the change in the atmosphere.

One was Lord Auckland's appointment as Governor-General. In March he took over the reins of government, and in May accepted the office of Patron of the Society, promising that he would be glad 'if, at any time, I should find it in my power to promote the objects of so excellent and so interesting an Institution.'[87] Coupled with this was the important fact that H. T. Princep, an ardent Orientalist, replaced G. A. Bushby, a die-hard Anglicist, in the office of Secretary to Government. With these two men at the helm, the Society had some unfavourable decisions reversed, and even launched new schemes conducive to orientalist studies. However, the help rendered by Government was always very modest. Thus, even while valuable contributions to Indology poured out from the Society, its financial situation remained precarious. It had started the year 1836 with a comfortable balance of Rs 3,000, and made Rs 3,367.2.7 from the sale of its publications.[88] The finances however, were depleted steadily so that by the beginning of 1837 it had on its hands a deficit of Rs 193.11.4.[89]

One of the main reasons for such heavy expenses was the Society's effort to complete the printing of those works whose publication had been stopped the previous year by Government. The new Government of Lord Auckland not only partially subsidized the works already in hand but also extended its help to new publications like the *Cochin-Chinese Dictionary*[90] and the *Alif-Leila*.[91]

The Society's publication of oriental works brought it great appreciation from the European intelligentsia. F. Mohl, the Secretary of the Asiatic Society of Paris wrote to the Bengal Society that five copies of the *Mahabharata* had been sold in a single day and that there might be a demand for 100 copies more.⁺² He went to the extent of saying that the Paris Society was prepared to share the expenses of completing the printing of works stopped by the former government.⁹³

As for researches and communications, the year 1836 seemed to be dominated by Charles Masson. He contributed four memoirs on Afghan antiquities and coins, providing a wealth of information about Indo-Bactrian kings. The researches carried on in Bactriana, together with the large number of coin-finds, had caught the fancy of scholars all over Europe, for here was the place where west met east through Alexander's campaigns and the different cities he had founded. A great exercise had therefore begun not only to identify the route taken by Alexander but also to locate the different cities he had founded, or the ones he passed through. One city, to identify which great efforts were made, was naturally Alexandria ad Caucasum. Classical authors like Arrian, Curtius, Diodorus and Strabo had all mentioned the city: but their descriptions were vague and sometimes contradictory.

Now Masson, in his first communication to the Society in the year, entitled 'Second Memoir on the Ancient Coins found at Beghram, in the Kohistan of Kabul', put forward arguments identifying Beghram as the site of ancient Alexandria.⁹⁴

Masson's third memoir on the subject,⁹⁵ together with the communication by James Prinsep on 'New Varieties of Bactrian Coins engraved from Mr Masson's drawings and other sources',⁹⁶ sum up, though not without error, the knowledge of this part of the globe gleaned through numismatic studies and other antiquarian sources.

Like Masson, who was busy in Afghanistan collecting material on the Indo-Bactrian and Indo-Scythian kings, Brian Houghton Hodgson was collecting material on Buddhism in Nepal. Hodgson stands out as one of the most active members of the Society in its entire history. Though not a resident of Calcutta, he kept in constant touch with the Society. His contributions numbering more than 125 papers on subjects including antiquities, anthropology, botany and zoology, were communicated to the Society and published in its *Researches* and the *Journal*.

Nothing sums up Hodgson's varied life so well as the opening paragraphs of his biography by W. W. Hunter.

Brian Hodgson died in 1894, in his ninety-fifth year. Had he died seventy years previously, he would have been mourned as the most brilliant young scholar whom the Indian Civil Service has produced. Had he died in middle life, he would have been remembered as the masterly diplomatist who held quiet the Kingdom of Nepal and the warlike Himalayan races throughout the disasters of the Afghan war. Had he died at three-score years of age, he would have been honoured as the munificent Englishman who enriched the museums of Europe with his collections, enlarged the old boundaries of more than one science, and opened up a new field of original research.

He outlived his contemporaries. In 1883 the learned Italian, Count Angelo di Gubernatis, when introduced to him, exclaimed: 'Surely not the venerable Hodgson, the founder of our Buddhist studies!'[97]

Hodgson's interest in Buddhist studies began when he was appointed assistant to the Resident in Nepal in 1824. He found that his efforts at collecting manuscripts and inquiring about the religion was resented 'out of the jealousy of the people in regard to any profanation of their sacred things by an European.'[98] However, with the aid of the Chief Minister of the mountain kingdom, he was soon able to collect a large number of valuable manuscripts on Buddhism. His ardour at collecting manuscripts was rivalled by his generosity in donating them. His donations, from 1824 onwards, amounted to ninety-four Sanskrit Buddhist manuscripts to the Asiatic Society;[99] sixty-six to the College of Fort William; seventy-nine to the Royal Asiatic Society in London; thirty to the India Office Library and seven to the Bodleian Library at Oxford. Besides, he transmitted no less than 147 manuscripts to the French savant, Eugène Burnouf, to be deposited in the Société Asiatique de Paris. 'He collected', remarked Burnouf 'a larger body of original documents on Buddhism than had up to that time been ever gathered together either in Asia or in Europe.' Nor was Hodgson a mere collector. He talked to the pundits in Nepal tallying what they said with the texts of the original manuscripts and studying the texts himself with their aid.

He also contributed valuable articles to different journals including that of the Asiatic Society of Bengal. The results of his study, 'amounted to a new revelation to the western world of scholarship, and earned for Hodgson the title given to him by Eugène Burnouf as "The Founder of the true study of Buddhism on the basis of the texts and original remains".'

Hodgson's real contribution to the study of Buddhism can be fully appreciated only in the context of the general ignorance about the religion at that time. Even the birthplace of the Buddha was in doubt. some scholars holding that he was born in Ethiopia, some that he was born in Abyssinia. Sir William Jones thought Buddha to be a native of Egypt who took refuge in India after persecution in his native land for his heretical views. The fact that in most statues Buddha was depicted with curled hair, lent credence to the belief that he was a native of Africa. Buddha's doctrines were also not clear since most of them were contained in books which European scholars could not read. In India its study had died after the decline of Buddhism and in those countries where it was prevalent, it was practised rather than studied for its philosophy.

Scholars of Buddhism who followed Hodgson and sometimes devoted a lifetime to the study, looked upon him as their source of inspiration. One of the greatest of them, Burnouf, admitted that his great work on Buddhism was based on the manuscripts presented by Hodgson to the Asiatic Society of Paris.[100] Mountstuart Elphinstone noted in his *History of India* that even his general 'account of the Bauddha tenets is chiefly derived from the complete and distinct view of that religion given by Mr Hodgson'. Alexander Cunningham wrote to Hodgson, 'I found in your work the only clear and intelligible account of Buddhism'; and the Royal Asiatic Society in London in its obituary of Hodgson summed up his achievements thus: 'To him the world still owes the materials for a knowledge of the great proselytising faith which was the one civilizing influence in Central Asia.'[101]

Through his articles in the Society's *Journal*, Hodgson became the first European scholar to expound such doctrines of Buddhism as the *Swabhavika Doctrine*, the *Aiswarika System*, the *Karmika System*, the *Yatnika System*, the *Adi Prajna* or *Dharma*, and the *Adi Sangha* by quoting from original Buddhist texts like the *Ashta Sahasrika*, the *Divya Avadan*, the *Buddha Charitra*, the *Kalpalata*, the *Swayambhu Purana*, the *Lalita Vistara*, and others.[102]

Meanwhile, Csoma de Körös was unlocking the treasures hidden in the Tibetan Buddhist texts. The *Researches* published this year carried two lengthy articles by him entitled 'Analysis of the Dulva, a portion of the Tibetan work entitled the Kah-gyur',[103] and 'Notices of the Life of Sakya extracted from the Tibetan Authorities'.[104]

More important for us is the second article in which the life of Buddha is divided under twelve heads, which in themselves are very interesting: I. He descended from among the gods. II. He entered into the womb. III. He was born. IV. He displayed all sorts of arts. V. He was married, or enjoyed the pleasures of the conjugal state. VI. He left his house and took the religious character. VII. He performed penances. VIII. He overcame the devil, or god of pleasures (Kama Deva). IX. He arrived at supreme perfection, or became *Buddha*. X. He turned the wheel of law or published his doctrine. XI. He was delivered from pain, or died. XII. His relics were deposited.

In this article, even amidst legendary and miraculous embellishments, one is clearly able to trace the main events of Buddha's life as we know them today. The article thus marked a great advance in the historiography of Buddhism.

To return to the *Journal* of the year 1836, we find another communication throwing valuable light on ancient Indian history. This was the 'Translation of a *Tamba Patra*, which was found in a field of the village of Pipalinagar in the Shujalpur Pargana, by a Kisan engaged in ploughing, and presented to Mr L. Wilkinson, the Political Agent at Bhopal, by the Jagirdar.'[105]

Wilkinson, though he transmitted the communication to the Society, did not think it of much importance. But Wilkinson's discovery added four names after Ajayavarma to what we now know as the Paramara dynasty of Malwa,[106] and provided a genealogy of the kings following the famous king Bhoja.

The Kings mentioned in succession were: Raja Bhoja; Udayaditya; Raja Naravarma; Yashovarma; Ajayavarma; Vindhyavarma; Amushyayana; Subhatavarma, and Arjuna Raja.

Wilkinson's genealogy corresponds closely to the Paramara genealogy as we find it brought up to date in the Bharatiya Vidya Bhavan (BVB) series, with two exceptions.[107] The BVB series has the name of Jayasimha who is said to have ruled after Raja Bhoja. This name, as we can see, is missing in the Pipalinagar inscription. Secondly, Wilkinson's article refers to Amushyayana as the son and successor of Vindhyavarma. He is omitted in the BVB series, according to which Subhatavarma succeeded Vindhyavarma directly.

Another communication which shed light on ancient Indian history was that of the French scholar Eugène Jacquet. Jacquet had come across references to the Valabhi dynasty in a Chinese chronicle by a Buddhist traveller who had described Valabhi as a flourishing city at the time of his journey in A.D. 632.[108] Now, according to Tod, the Valabhi dynasty had seen its last days nearly a century earlier to this.[109] References to this dynasty in the seventh century discovered by Jaquet not only helped clarify the chronology of the Valabhi dynasty, but also opened up a new source for Indian history: the accounts of the Chinese travellers.

The contributions of Jacquet, Burnouf, and other foreign scholars to the Society's *Journal*, indicated the popularity and importance not only of the Society but also of Indological studies. Communications, articles, facsimiles and translations of ancient inscriptions were constantly received by the Society, and it was feared that some might be misplaced, lost, or neglected and some remain unread for want of time. Keeping these factors in view, Prinsep started an important and useful practice: publishing in the *Journal* facsimiles of ancient inscriptions, together with whatever information that was available about them at the time.

The usefulness of this step was evident from the fact that in the very volume in which Prinsep published these inscriptions, there were some whose full importance could be realized only later on. One of these was an inscription which D. M. McLeod, assistant to the Commissioner of the Narbada district, received from a local *zamindar*. The *zamindar*, says McLeod, had five copperplate inscriptions recording land grants in his possession, of which only one was given to McLeod. The writing was completely illegible as far as the local pundits were concerned, and so McLeod forwarded a copy of the inscription to the Society. Prinsep transcribed, lithographed and translated the inscription but could make little of its importance. He recorded in the *Journal*:

> Concerning the purport of the inscription little need be said. It is an ordinary grant by one Raja Pravara Sena, of a piece of ground in a conquered district to his officiating priest, in perpetuity:—but neither the country nor the boundary [of] villages [is] mentioned, nor any of the said Raja's family can be recognized.[110]

This dynasty, however, was the Vakataka, 'the most important power that held sway over parts of the Deccan (sometimes with portions of Central India) after the fall of the Satavahanas and before the rise of the Chalukyas about the middle of the sixth century.'[111] It was only later when other inscriptions, together with the mention of this dynasty in the Puranas were traced, that the Vakatakas got their due place in Indian history.

Yet another unknown dynasty that came to light through an inscription published in the *Journal* was that of the Kadambas of

North Kanara or Banavasi, one of the many dynasties which gained prominence after the Gupta power weakened in the sixth century A.D. The inscription was first discovered at Asirgarh by Swiney and had been in Mellish's possession from 1805. It was now translated by Mill and for the first time brought the names of the Kadamba rulers to light.[112] The genealogy on the basis of this inscription would be as follows:

Hari-Varman m. Anka Devi
|
Aditya-Varman m. Arikari (eldest daughter of the Gupta race)
|
Isvara-Varman m. Arikari (eldest daughter of the Gupta race)[113]
|
Maharajadhiraja Varman Sinha – m. Bhara Kamahari
|
Maharajadhiraja Kharva-Varman.

This inscription suggests that the Kadambas were not as minor a dynasty as is generally held. A dynasty which lasted for five generations, entered into matrimonial alliance with the powerful Gupta kings, and had rulers who assumed titles like *Maharajadhiraja* could not have played a minor role in Indian history. Moreover, the inscription begins with Hari-Varman, whereas according to R. C. Majumdar, Hari-Varman was practically the last important ruler of the line.[114] More research is therefore needed to give this dynasty its proper historical significance.

Prinsep also published facsimiles of several other inscriptions including those found at Ajanta, Bodh Gaya and other places, although none of them was as important as the ones mentioned above.

The one exception was an inscription found at Chunar, which supplied the names of three rajas ruling in Banaras during the thirteenth century, of whom nothing else is known.

More important than the historical aspect of the inscription is the scholar who discovered it. This was Alexander Cunningham, about whom Prinsep said that he had brought so many facts and antiquities to light as to 'make me blush for my own inactive residence there.'

Lieutenant Alexander Cunningham, later Major-General Sir Alexander Cunningham, K.C.I.E., C.S.I., C.I.E., R.E., was yet another scholar who was inspired by James Prinsep to taking up Indology. Although he had communicated a paper to the Society in 1834,

Cunningham became associated with the Society as Member only in 1836, his name being proposed by Prinsep himself.[115]

It was a fortunate chance that brought Alexander Cunningham to India. One day when he was fourteen years of age, and his elder brother John, sixteen, their father Allan was having breakfast with Sir Walter Scott, a family friend. Sir Walter asked Allan: 'What are you going to make of these boys?' 'I ask that question often at my own heart, and I cannot answer it', replied Allan, adding that although the eldest wanted to be a soldier, he, as a father, would prefer him to go to India where 'the pay is a maintenance.' Sir Walter approached Lord Melville, then President of the Board of Control, and extracted from him a promise of a cadetship for one son. Five days later, he met John Loch, another influential member and extracted from him a similar promise. Thus Alexander too managed to land in India, obtaining his first commission as second Lieutenant in the Bengal Engineers in June 1831. Recalling his association with Prinsep, Cunningham wrote in 1871:

> During a great part of the years 1836 and 1837, the most active period of his career, I was in almost daily intercourse with Prinsep. With our mutual tastes and pursuits this soon ripened into the most intimate friendship. I thus had the privilege of sharing in all his discoveries during their progress. . . . When I recollect that I was then only a young lad of twenty-three years of age, I feel as much wonder as pride that James Prinsep should have thought me worthy of being made the confidant of all his great discoveries.[116]

Prinsep had unerringly chosen a worthy pupil. His numerous books and articles, and his services to the Archaeological Survey of India, of which he was the founder-Superintendent and Director-General, made Alexander Cunningham perhaps the most outstanding Indologist in the post-Prinsep period in the nineteenth century. He seemed to possess an instinct for historical sites and went on discovering, opening, excavating one important site after another. His reports to the Archaeological Survey provide a mine of information to the student of ancient history of India and reveal the debt we owe him for reconstruction of our ancient past.

It was a great tragedy that the vessel *Indus* in which Cunningham shipped to England his large store of books, papers, notebooks and photographic negatives, was wrecked off Ceylon in 1885. The collection entirely perished, 'the loss to science we shall never know'.

During the year 1836 Alexander Cunningham communicated notices of two of his discoveries to the Asiatic Society—both of monumental importance. Of these, one was the site of Sarnath, one of the most important landmarks in the history of Buddhism. Cunningham had begun his excavations at the site in 1834, little realizing its importance. As he wrote later:

When I began the work I was not aware that many of the most hallowed of the Buddhist monuments were memorial *stupas*, raised over spots rendered famous by various acts of Buddha. Such as we know from Hwen Thsang's account was the great tower near Benares, which was erected by Asoka near the spot where Buddha had begun to 'turn the wheel of the law', that is, to preach his new doctrine.[117]

Cunningham was not, however, the first person to excavate the site. It had been dug up as early as 1793–4 by Jagat Singh, the Diwan of the Raja of Banaras, but for an entirely different reason. Jagat Singh had dug up the site to collect building materials for his palaces and the bazar (*ganj*) which still bears his name. The havoc he wrought upon the site is evident from what Cunningham later wrote:

I may mention also, on the authority of the work-people, that the dilapidated state of the lower part of the Dhamek Tower [the main structure at Saranath] is due entirely to the meanness of Jagat Singh, who, to save a few rupees in the purchase of new stones, deliberately destroyed the beautiful facing of this ancient tower. Each stone was slowly detached from the monument by cutting out all the iron cramps by which it was secured to its neighbours. The actual saving to the Babu could have been but little; but the defacement to the tower was very great, and, as the stones were removed at once, the damage done to the tower is quite irreparable.[118]

During the excavations, Cunningham collected the stone-figures and bas-reliefs with inscriptions on them and sent them to the Society 'in the hope that the inscriptions . . . may be translated, and help to throw some light upon the Buddhist religion, as well as upon Sarnath.'[119]

The other paper Cunningham presented to the Society in 1836 was a facsimile of the inscription on the Bhitari *lath* near Ghazipur together with a drawing of the pillar.[120] The pillar on its eastern face contained an inscription of nineteen lines of well-shaped characters of the Gupta period. In the meanwhile, the Society received a letter from Vincent Tregear[121] stating that the pillar stood 'isolated, half-buried in the ground, and in no way regarded by the people' and offered to transport it to the Society's museum where it would be permanently accessible to the antiquarian.

It was decided that 'if the removal could be effected at a moderate cost, Mr Tregear's obliging offer should be accepted',[122] and also 'that a respectful representation should be made to the Government of India, on the expediency of taking measures to preserve the monument at Allahabad from further decay, by setting it up, with a pedestal and railing, in such position within the fort or elsewhere as may appear most appropriate.'[123] Accordingly, in a letter dated 10 September 1836, Prinsep asked for the Government's help in restoring and preserving the column.[124] This letter is important for it marks the Society's first attempt to involve the Government in the task of preservation of Indian antiquities.

The inscription of the Bhitari pillar was read by Dr Mill and the text forwarded to the Society. Prinsep immediately recognized its importance and reserved the full text of Mill's article for the next volume of the *Journal*. But he couldn't help expressing his joy at the important find. In the Preface to the *Journal* published in 1836 he noted:

> We may be allowed a moment's exultation at the highly envious train of discovery, connected with this monument. . . . Not only has a dynasty before wholly unknown to the Indian historian, been traced by coins and inscriptions through seven generations in its own line, but two collateral alliances with other reigning princes have been brought to light: while extracts from ancient Chinese authors, independently scrutinised in Europe, have helped to determine their exact chronological epoch.[125]

The dynasty hitherto 'wholly unknown to the Indian historian', was the Gupta dynasty, one of the most important of ancient India.

As Prinsep had mentioned in the Preface to the sixth volume of the *Journal*, the 1837 *Journal* opened with a communication on the 'Restoration and Translation of the Inscription on the Bhitari *Lat*, with critical and historical remarks', by the Rev. Dr W. H. Mill.[126] The inscription helped clear up many points regarding the Gupta dynasty although at that time Mill felt that 'except [for] the bare point of succession, and some adventures rather alluded to than related in the verses of a somewhat obscure style of composition, the information of a directly historical nature extends little beyond what is obtained from the numismatic researches so ably and indefatigably conducted by our Secretary.'[127]

The Bhitari inscription added three more important names to the

Gupta dynasty. These were Chandragupta II, Kumaragupta, and Skandagupta, with indirect references to his successor, who was a minor at the date of the inscription. The genealogy of the Gupta dynasty now fixed by Mill on the basis of the inscriptions on the Allahabad and the Bhitari pillars was:[128]

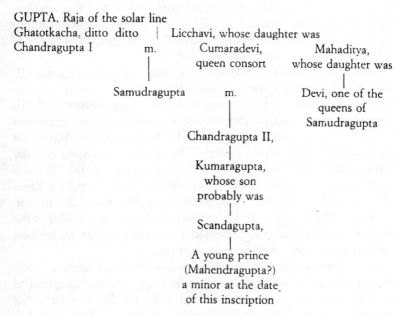

GUPTA, Raja of the solar line
Ghatotkacha, ditto ditto | Licchavi, whose daughter was
Chandragupta I   m.   Cumaradevi,   Mahaditya,
       | queen consort   whose daughter was
       | |
     Samudragupta   m.   Devi, one of the
                      | queens of
                      | Samudragupta
              Chandragupta II,
                     |
              Kumaragupta,
                whose son
            probably was
                     |
              Scandagupta,
                     |
           A young prince
          (Mahendragupta?)
          a minor at the date
          of this inscription

We can see how closely this genealogy corresponds to the genealogy we have today but for the later Guptas.

Secondly, this inscription was final proof that the dynasty was not the same as the Maurya dynasty. 'It is needless to pursue the discrepancy of the genealogies further', wrote Mill, 'the *Vaishnava* Kumaragupta and the *Saiva* and *Sakta* worshipper, Skandagupta, have nothing in common with the Buddhist descendants and successors of Dharmasoka.'[129]

The fact that the Gupta dynasty was totally distinct from the Maurya also meant that it existed in a different period. Mill initially placed the dynasty 'between the 1st and 9th centuries of our era',[130] and then, on the basis of the information available in the *Vishnu-Purana*, came much nearer the actual date: 'It is scarcely possible', he wrote, 'to fix the subjects of our present inquiry, the Guptas, higher than the age of Charlemagne in Europe.'[130a]

The mention of the Gupta dynasty in the *Vishnu-Purana* also gave an idea of the extent of the early Gupta empire, since it mentioned, besides Magadha, four other cities of the Doab (Padmavati, Kantipuri, Mathura, and Prayaga) as being under Gupta rule.[131]

From such uncertain origins did reconstruction of the Gupta dynasty begin. It would certainly have surprised Mill or Prinsep were they ever to learn that the dynasty so discovered would eventually figure as a 'Universal Empire', in Toynbee's scheme of *A Study of History*.

Another significant contribution was made to uncovering the history of the Guptas when Captain Edward Smith forwarded to the Society facsimiles of inscriptions from the *stupa* at Sanchi.[132] His communication, together with Prinsep's observations, was presented to the Society at its meeting of 7 June 1835—an extremely significant date in the history of the Society. The inscription termed no.1 by Captain Smith was taken from the front of the eastern gate. It was a small inscription and was deciphered by the Society's pundit Rama Govinda and translated by Prinsep. The inscription stated that the son of one Amuka (Amrakardava?), through the bounty and favour of the great King Chandragupta, presented a piece of ground, five temples and twenty-five dinars to five *sramanas* (ascetics).

The *sramanas* referred to were obviously Buddhist ascetics, while the era of the inscription placed it in the reign of Chandragupta II of the Gupta dynasty. It was natural therefore for scholars to assume that Chandragupta was a Buddhist.[133] Only much later was it realized that Chandragupta's grant to Buddhist ascetics did not indicate his personal religion but the catholicity of outlook of the Gupta Emperor.

By far the most important aspect of the Sanchi monument was the other class of twenty-three inscriptions (nos. 3–25 of Captain Smith's catalogue) which provided Prinsep with the key to the Asokan inscriptions. If Prinsep had done nothing else but decipher the Asokan inscriptions, he would be entitled 'to rank with the men who unlocked the mysteries of the hieroglyphic and cuneiform writings and so revealed the long-lost histories of Egypt and Babylonia'.[134] The discovery has yet to be equalled in the annals of Indian historiography, since it gave to India's past its most glorious chapter 'the era of Asoka and Buddhism.'

To return to the process of discovery. As Vincent Smith says: 'Prinsep, being absolutely devoid of the jealousy which too often is a blot on the scholarly temperament, made no mystery of his researches, and never hesitated in his ingenious papers to let the world see into his workshop and watch discoveries in the making.'[135] Let us then look at this important discovery in Prinsep's own words:

> In laying open a discovery of this nature some little explanation is generally expected of the means by which it has been attained. Like most other inventions, when once found it appears extremely simple; and, as in most others, accident, rather than study, has had the merit of solving the enigma which has so long baffled the learned.
>
> While arranging and lithographing the numerous scraps of facsimiles, I was struck at their all terminating with the same two letters, 𝟓 ꞷ. Coupling this circumstance with their extreme brevity and insulated position, which proved that they could not be fragments of a continuous text, it immediately occurred that they must record either obituary notices, or more probably the offerings and presents of votaries, as is known to be the present custom in the Buddhist temples of *Ava*; where numerous *dwajas* or flag-staffs, images and small *chaityas* are crowded within the enclosure, surrounding the chief cupola, each bearing the name of the donor. The next point noted was the frequent occurrence of the letter ⋏, already set down uncontestably as *s*, before the final word:—now this I had learnt from the *Saurashtra* coins, deciphered only a day or two before, to be one sign of the genitive case singular, being the *sea* of the Pali, or *sya* of the Sanskrit. 'Of so and so the gift', must then be the form of each brief sentence; and the vowel *a* and *anuswara* led to the speedy recognition of the word *danam*, (gift) teaching me the very two letters, *d* and *n*, most different from known forms, and which had foiled me most in my former attempts.
>
> Since 1834 also my acquaintance with ancient alphabets had become so familiar that most of the remaining letters in the present examples could be named at once on re-inspection. In the course of a few minutes I thus became possessed of the whole alphabet, which I tested by applying it to the inscription on the Delhi column.[136]

Prinsep first applied his discovery to decipher the legends on different coins, especially those discovered by Conolly and Stacy: these however revealed names of only minor kings, some of whom remain unidentified till today.

When he came to the Delhi pillar inscription, Prinsep discovered that the opening sentence of the inscription was a common one, being repeated in the Girnar inscription sent by Wathen, the Dhauli inscription transmitted by Kittoe and the pillars found in northern India. Having compared all these inscriptions and taking into account all the variations, Prinsep determined the sentence to be:

Devanampiya piyadasi laja hevam aha

This sentence again showed errors of grammar and construction. These were, however, removed by studying the Girnar inscription more thoroughly. The sentence as rendered here was:

Devanampiya Piyadasi raja evam aha

What did the sentence signify? Prinsep wrote:

Collecting together the above evidence, I think it will be admitted that the initial sentence is satisfactorily determined, and that it has every appearance of being the declaratory formula of some royal edict, or some profession of faith. The simplicity of the form reminds us of the common expression in our own scriptures—'Thus spake the prophet' or in the proclamation of the Persian monarch—'Thus saith Cyrus, King of Persia.'[137]

The question now was, who was this person, *Devanampiya Piyadasi*? At one stage Prinsep toyed with the idea that it could be the Buddha himself, for, as far as scholars then knew, no single Indian monarch had ruled over such a vast territory as was covered by these pillar and rock inscriptions. This explanation, however, had soon to be given up because the inscriptions frequently referred to 'such and such year of my reign'. Since Buddha was by no means a monarch or a king, the question remained, 'Who could this potentate have been, to spread his edicts all over India and even beyond'? Prinsep wrote:

In all the Hindu genealogical tables with which I am acquainted, no prince can be discovered possessing this very remarkable name. If there ever reigned such a monarch in India, his memory must have been swept away with every other record of the Buddhist dynasties we know to have ruled in India unrecorded by fame.[138]

The difficulty of identifying *Devanampiya* was multiplied further by a passage in *An Epitome of the History of Ceylon*, by George Turnour. According to this, a Ceylonese king, Devenipeatissa, soon after he ascended the throne, 'induced Dharmasoka, a sovereign of the many kingdoms into which *Dambadiva* [*Jambudwipa*, or India] was divided, and whose capital was Pattilpatta [Patna], to depute his son Mihindu and his daughter Sangamitta, with several other principal priests, to Anuradhapura for the purpose of introducing the religion of Buddha.'

From the similarity between Devanampiya and Devenipeatissa, Prinsep concluded that they were the same persons, and that *Devanampiya* was a Ceylonese king who was responsible not only for the introduction of Buddhism on the island but also for the several rock and pillar inscriptions. In support of this thesis he wrote:

> [The age of Devenipeatissa] was also the most flourishing period of the Ceylonese sovereignty then enriched by a commerce which has in subsequent ages gradually passed into other channels. The monuments and rock excavations attributed to the ancient sovereigns of Ceylon abound with inscriptions in a character not essentially differing from these four on the continent of India. We have thus a strong *prima facie* argument in favour of the hypothesis that Devanampiyatissa, the royal convert, caused, in his zeal, the dogmas of his newly adopted faith to be promulgated far and wide at his expense.[139]

This colossal error was unexpectedly removed, and the riddle of Devanampiya's identity was solved by the very person whose work had occasioned Prinsep's error, George Turnour.

Turnour was born in Ceylon in 1799. After being educated in England, he joined the Ceylon Civil Service in 1818, and distinguished himself by his interest in the native languages and vernaculars. Gradually his attention was drawn to Pali, which is the basis of Sinhalese, much as Sanskrit is the basis of most Indian vernaculars. But the difficulty in learning the language seemed to be insurmountable since 'no dictionaries then existed to assist in defining the meaning of Pali terms and no teacher could be found capable of rendering them into English.'[140]

In spite of the difficulties, Turnour persevered. Soon a great discovery came his way. The chief priest of a *vihara* at Saffragam gave Turnour a Buddhist work, the *Mahavamso*,[141] which contained details about the early history of the Island. Turnour then began to translate it and apprised the Asiatic Society of his work.

The importance of Turnour's discovery was immediately recognized by the scholarly world. Mill, while examining the work on behalf of the Asiatic Society so that the Government might be persuaded to subsidize the project commented:

> The literary benefit is very far from being confined to the single subject of Ceylon: it extends to the whole of India; and yields in importance to nothing that has yet been produced on that most perplexed and generally unproductive subject, the history of India prior to the thousandth year of our era.[142]

Although Turnour had decided to publish the *Mahavamso* with an English translation at his own expense, the Government of India, on the recommendation of the Society, gave a modest subsidy to the work by sanctioning a subscription of thirty copies.[143]

The *Mahavamso* did throw a flood of light not only on the history of Ceylon, but also on that of Buddhism. But it created difficulties about the personality of King Asoka. The record, however, was set right again by Turnour.

At about this time (August 1837), while going through a large collection of works on Pali Buddhist literature brought to Ceylon from Siam by George Nadoris, who was once a Buddhist priest, Turnour came across another major work on Buddhism, the *Dipowanso*. 'In running over the book cursorily', Turnour's eyes suddenly lighted on one passage, which when rendered into English read:

> Two hundred and eighteen years after the beatitude of Buddha, was the inauguration of Piyadassi. . . . who, the grandson of Chandragupta, and own son of Bindusara, was at that time Viceroy at Ujjayani.[144]

Here, then, in clear terms was revealed the identity of Piyadassi, who was none else but King Asoka himself. Turnour immediately communicated his discovery to the Asiatic Society: Prinsep, while publishing it, spoke of his own error and freely acknowledged Turnour's contribution:

> I had ascribed the foundation of these pillar monuments to a King of *Ceylon*,[145] because his was the nearest or the only approach to the name recorded in the inscription. I did so before I had read it through, or I should perhaps have felt the difficulties of such a supposition. . . . It was but the utter absence of any such name in our Indian lists that drove me to a neighbouring state. . . . Mr Turnour has [thus] most satisfactorily cleared up a difficulty that might long have proved a stumbling block to the learned.[146]

Some months later, Turnour received additional proof of this identification as well as of the fact that the Ceylonese King Devanampiyatissa, although known to, and an ally of Asoka, was altogether a different king.

> On my return to Kandy, and on production of the *Dipawanso* to the Buddhist priests, who are my coadjutors in these researches, they reminded me that there was a Pali work on my own shelves, which also gave to Dhammasoko, the appellation of Piyadaso.[147]

After this, there was little doubt that King Piyadassi of the inscriptions and King Asoka were one and the same person. Indeed, the discovery proved a 'turning point of Indian historical research'.[148]

In the process of deciphering the Asokan inscriptions, Prinsep had received a clue from the legends on the Saurashtra coins which he had deciphered only a day or two earlier. Though this achievement did not yield results as valuable as the Asokan inscriptions, it nevertheless marks an important phase in the rediscovery of Indian history, and testifies to Prinsep's remarkable skill and ingenuity in deciphering ancient inscriptions.

In early May 1837 Prinsep received the engravings of twenty-eight coins from Saurashtra, sent by J. R. Steuart. The coins bore very legible inscriptions in characters which closely resembled the Greek alphabet. Immediately, he applied himself to the task of deciphering them. His enthusiasm and eagerness are all vividly brought out in his letter to Cunningham on 11 May 1837 in which he exclaimed 'Oh! but we must decipher them! I'll warrant they have not touched them at home yet. Here to amuse you try your hand on this', and with this Princep forwarded to Cunningham a copy of three of the coin legends.

Cunningham, however, did not need to apply himself to the task. The very next morning he received another letter in which the master-scholar triumphantly wrote: 'You may save yourself any further trouble. I have made them all out this very moment on first inspection. . . . every one of them gives the name of his father ... and we have a train of some eight or ten names to rival the Guptas!! Hurra! I hope the chaps at home won't seize the prize first.'[149]

In fact the speed with which Prinsep could decipher the most difficult of inscriptions led Vincent Smith to remark that Prinsep was gifted with lightning intuition.[150]

The reading of the Saurashtrian coins revealed the existence of the western *Kshatrapas.* Prinsep called this line of Kings the Sah dynasty, from the epithet which formed the second part of the names of many of these kings, and they were known as such for some time. It was only later that scholars discovered that 'Sah' was a wrong reading for either Simha or Sena. Prinsep, however, had set in motion the study of a dynasty which was later worked on through coins and inscriptions by such eminent Indologists as Bhau Daji, Bhagwanlal Indraji, Bühler, Kielhorn, Sir George Jacob, Fleet and others, and which contributed an important chapter to India's ancient history.

Yet another important dynasty was made known by Prinsep when he deciphered the Hathigumpha inscription which Stirling had communicated to the Society. Prinsep divined that the inscription was of importance and he requested his colleague Lieutenant Kittoe, who was then in Cuttack, to take the first opportunity of copying the inscription and send it to him. The task was not an easy one, and Kittoe gives a vivid description of his labours:

> Having no means of erecting a scaffolding, added to the limited leave granted me, I was obliged to defer the agreeable task of copying the great inscription till a future opportunity, which unfortunate circumstances prevented till the latter end of November, when having previously sent on people to make preparations I followed by *dawk*. After a whole day's hard work, I transcribed the most part of the great inscription and re-compared all the minor ones; I worked for upwards of an hour by torchlight and returned to cantonments, having travelled 38 miles out and home again.[151]

Once Prinsep received the copy of the Hathigumpha and the Udayagiri cave inscriptions, he set to decipher them, and once again he lets us peer over his shoulders while he works:

> In my search for some of the catchwords which had proved of such avail in explaining the purport of the inscriptions at Bhilsa and Sainhadri, I would neither meet with the *danam* of the former, nor the *dayadhamma* of the latter,—but in their stead I remarked a very common if not constant termination in a word of two syllables ⨝⨾ *lonam*, or ⨼⨝⨾ *lenam* preceded in most instances by the genitival affix ௺ *sa*; and in the only case, as of exception, by an equally regular genitive ௺᠆ᛁᴣ *sirino* from the noun *siri* (Sanskrit root सीर gen. सीरिणः): a worshipper of the sun. It was not until after many futile attempts with the *pundit* to find a better, that we were led to the supposition that the words *lonam* or *lenam*, must be the Pali equivalent for the Sanskrit participal noun लूनं *lunam*, 'cut or excavated', in this the vowel is changed from *u* to *o* and the *n* from the dental to the Prakrit cerebral: but in sound it must be confessed that there is little difference; while in sense, the term satisfied precisely the circumstances of the *Udayagiri* caves, which are generally small holes cut with the chisel from the solid rock—a stone of loose consistency easily worked with the rudest tools. The catch-word once attained, the reading of this new string of inscriptions was an easy matter.[152]

In the article carrying the decipherment of the inscription, Prinsep regretted the lack of time which did not allow him to do the inscription full justice. Thus, although he deciphered the name Kharavela correctly, Prinsep could not gather details about the personality or the rule of the prince which later historians like K. P. Jayaswal, R. D. Banerjee and others did. Prinsep, however, realised the value of the discovery, and called the inscription 'the most curious that has yet been disclosed to us'.[153] Despite the hasty and incomplete work,

Prinsep started a process which brought to light one of the most important and fascinating characters of Indian history—King Kharavela of Kalinga.

As Dr K. Sitaramaiya points out, Kharavela's greatest act, more than his conquests was this inscription. It brought to light, not only the golden age of Kalinga, but also facts about the contemporary political situation—some of which have been examined in Sitaramaiya's paper. The most important of these perhaps was the name of King Satakarani of the Satavahanas.[154]

Another important inscription to be re-studied was the Maukhari inscription in the Nagarjuni cave at Gaya, brought to the Society's notice earlier by John Harington and translated by Wilkins for the first volume of the *Researches*. While conveying information about his discovery to the Society, Harington had mentioned that there were several other caves in the adjoining hills with inscriptions. He hoped that these would be studied and a date relating to the Nagarjuni inscription discovered.[155]

This hope was now fulfilled. Hathorne, whom Prinsep asked for copies of all inscriptions in the Gaya caves, sent accurate impressions of these. These were twenty-three in number including the Nagarjuni cave inscription of Harington. Prinsep got this inscription re-translated by a bright student of the Sanskrit College, Sarodaprasad Chakravarti, who had also assisted Captain Troyer in translating many of the Sanskrit textbooks.

The Nagarjuni inscription had earlier revealed three names: Yajna Varman, Sardula Varman and Ananta Varman; now another inscription from the arch of the main door of the *haftkhaneh* or the seven-chamber cavern, yielded the name of Krishna, whom Prinsep supposed to be either the son of Ananta Varman or a powerful general 'in the army of the existing monarch of the day, whom we may now venture confidently to assume, from the alphabetical conformity, to have been one of the Gupta dynasty.'[156] The problem, however, remains unresolved till now. Another new piece of information yielded by this inscription was the name of Sardula Varman's queen, Maukhari, after whom the dynasty was named.[156a]

The Gaya caves brought to light yet another inscription of great value. This was in the Asokan character, and carried the name of Dasaratha, the beloved of the gods. The name Dasaratha immediately brought to Prinsep's mind the father of Rama, but almost as quickly he realized that the inscription could not have referred to the Dasaratha of the *Ramayana* as he 'belongs rather to the mythological period than to the limits of sober history.'[157] Prinsep then referred to the *Bhagavata Purana*, in which a commentary on one of the *slokas* revealed the fact that Dasaratha was the fifth ruler in the Maurya line which started with Chandragupta. This was an important discovery and Prinsep happily noted:

> We must consequently hail his [Dasaratha's] restoration as another impor-
> tant point fixed in the obscure history of that interesting period — another
> proof of the great utility of studying these indelible and undeniable records
> of antiquity.[158]

Still another inscription which was re-studied was the Allahabad pillar inscription. Captain Edward Smith, supposing that the pillar inscription might reveal more facts if copied more accurately, got down to making facsimiles once again. This time, through immense labour, Smith was able to give the facsimiles 'as perfectly as any inspection of the stone itself.' In fact, 'more distinctly . . . for the relief of the coloured ink brings cut the characters with a precision not perceptible on the pillars.'[159]

When copies of the inscription arrived in Calcutta, Prinsep immediately got down to re-examining them and found that there were 'many discrepancies' in Burt's copy of the No 1 inscription.

One of the new discoveries made while examining the inscriptions afresh was the fact that 'the Buddhist monarch [Asoka] enjoyed a plurality of wives after his conversion, and that they shared in his religious zeal.'[160]

Of much greater significance was the inscription which related to Samudragupta. On re-examination, it revealed a wealth of material not only regarding Samudragupta but also about the contemporary political situation. The inscription carried the names of the ten kings whom the Gupta emperor subdued, and gave the important fact that Samudragupta carried his arms even to the *Dakshinapatha*, and to territories and peoples 'extending beyond the boundries of India proper into the regions of the "great king" of Persia and the hordes of the Huns and the Scythians'. In fact, this inscription is the primary basis on which the extent of Samudragupta's empire is determined and his greatness established.

Prinsep began the communication on the Allahabad pillar by regretting that he could not make over this task to Mill who would, through his critical acumen, have tested 'the numerous alterations suggested or necessitated in the former version by the infallible text

now pla~ed in our hands.' This was because Mill had now left for
England. In the meeting on 6 Septenber 1837 the President, Sir
Edward Ryan, suggested that the Society express formally to Dr Mill
the loss the Society would sustain through his departure. Seconding
Sir Edward's proposal, W. H. MacNaghten remarked that in no
member 'had greater erudition ever been witnessed, nor had any
converted profound learning to uses calculated more to benefit the
country and to dignify the study of oriental learning'. The significant
part of the episode was that when Prinsep asked one of the greatest
pundits of the day, Kamalakanta, about his opinion of Dr Mill, he
answered: 'Where among all the English who have studied our
language, was there yet one who could compose a poem in the style
and language of our most classical ages? Verily he is Kalidasa come
again among us.'[161]

It is of interest that Mill had endeared himself to the pundits in spite
of the fact that he himself was a missionary. It is more than obvious
that the cementing factor of scholarship was stronger than the anti-
pathy generated by religious differences.

The formal address to Mill was presented at the meeting on 4
October 1837. Mill replied:

It never appeared to me either wise or worthy to ask at every turn what
special usefulness, or bearing on present concerns, may appear in each part
or section of the study before us . . . Nothing that gives us clear knowledge
of the history of man and the progress of mind ought to be deemed
unimportant by us.[162]

Here was a missionary anticipating the thoughts of critics who feel
that cultivation of all learning by missionaries was conversion-
oriented.

The year which saw Mill's departure fron India also witnessed the
loss of H. T. Colebrooke. Just before his death on 10 March 1837, his
essays had been compiled into two volumes by his son, T. E. Colebrooke, a copy of which was presented to the Society. At its meeting
of 2 August, the Society observed that it could not place Colebrooke's
last donation on its shelves 'without recording a tribute of affection for
his memory, of admiration for his great talents, and regret for the loss
sustained by oriental literature through his lamented death.'

The Society's financial condition was worsening again at this period.
At the meeting of 5 April 1837, when estimates were submitted for
repairs to the premises as well as to Sir William Jones's monument, it
was resolved to postpone these for at least a year. The department

which stood to suffer most was the museum. The previous year, provision had been made for a paid curator and it was expected that the Society would make occasional purchases to enrich its collection, there were now no funds available for these projects. When it was suggested that money for this purpose could be drawn from Bruce's legacy, which had been vested in government securities, there was immediate protest from some members.

Under the circumstances, J. T. Pearson, the Society's curator for two years, suggested that Government be approached for financial aid for upkeep of the museum, and a memorandum was sent to the Government suggesting that maintenance of the museum should be viewed as a national objective and requested a yearly grant of Rs 10,000.

In its letter, the Society also pointed out that it had already spent three lakhs of rupees for the prosecution and publication of researches, and that there was 'no branch of useful knowledge connected with this country that has not received illustration through the judicious employment of its funds.' It made the significant point that although on one or two occasions the Society had been the recipient of handsome donations from individuals, 'it has never yet solicited or received public aid from the Government.'[163] Despite the fact that it was the first time the Society had approached the Government for a grant, and its members included several eminent men of the British community, and that it would provide the Government an excellent opportunity to associate itself with a museum perhaps unparalleled in the entire world, the Government rejected the Society's request.

The Governor-General, while applauding the Society's achievements, replied that the Court of Directors was already incurring a considerable expenditure towards maintaining the India House Library and Museum in London, and that he could not sanction the amount without making a reference to the Court of Directors.

The Government's answer must have deeply disappointed the Society. But the upkeep of the museum was not a small matter. The members discussed the Government's reply, and then decided that pending the reference to the Court of Directors, the Society should again approach the Government but with a much more modest request. It asked now for Rs 200 which would be just enough to maintain the museum, and another sum of Rs 800 for acquiring objects of scientific interest and value.[164]

On 26 July 1837, the Society was informed that pending the

decision of the Court of Directors, the Governor-General had sanctioned Rs 200 for upkeep of the museum but felt compelled to decline
the request for Rs 800, adding that the Society could approach the
Government for funds for purchasing specific objects for its museum
whenever such an occasion arose.

It is said that a flame burns brightest just before it is extinguished. The
truth of this adage is perhaps borne out in the Society's activities
during 1838. The year was the highpoint of the Society's activities,
although it also witnessed an irreparable loss in Prinsep's departure
for England. The truth of this adage is again borne out by Prinsep's
life. His activities during 1837–8 marked the peak of his achievements
after which ill-health affected his abilities and enthusiasm. His departure to England in 1838 and his death two years later marked the end
of an important phase in Indological studies. In 1837–8 he was at the
height of his achievements. The deciphering of the Asokan script and
its application to one inscription after another revealed a wealth of
material on Asoka, a name that made a western scholar remark that
this one name was enough to put to shame the entire western
civilization.

The first inscription to catch Prinsep's attention in 1838 was the
rock inscription at Girnar in Gujarat. Facsimiles of these inscriptions
had been taken by the Rev. Dr Wilson, the President of the Bombay
Literary Society who forwarded them to Prinsep through Wathen. At
about the same time, Kittoe had forwarded to the Society facsimiles of
inscriptions at Dhauli near Cuttack. Prinsep compared the Girnar and
Dhauli inscriptions and to his 'surprise and joy' discovered that 'the
greater part of these [Dhauli] inscriptions (all indeed save the first and
last paragraphs which were enclosed in distinguishing frames), was
identical with the inscription at Girnar.' A still greater surprise,
however, was in store: this was the recurrence of the name Antiochus,
the *Yona raja* in both the inscriptions. After the identification of
Sandracottus with Chandragupta Maurya, this was the second time
that Greek and Indian history seemed to meet. So excited was Prinsep
at the discovery that he wrote:

> I have now to bring to the notice of the Society another link of the same
> chain of discovery, which will, if I do not deceive myself, create a yet
> stronger degree of general interest in the labours, and of confidence in the
> deductions of our antiquarian members than any that has preceded it. I feel

it so impossible to keep this highly singular discovery to myself that I risk the imputation of bringing it forward in a very immature shape.[165]

The Girnar inscription not only revealed the existence of connec- tions between Asoka and the Greek kings, it also helped to ascertain the boundaries of Asoka's empire and, more important, portray him as one of the most humane kings in all history. The second tablet of Girnar spoke of medical aid given both men and animals, and Prinsep rightly observed that even at such a remote age, a medical service 'seems to have been instituted and supported at the expense of the state, with depots of herbs and drugs.'[166]

After producing these valuable results for the scholarly world, Prinsep's intuition suggested that the Girnar and the Dhauli edict had much more to reveal. Prinsep requested Wilson to send him another facsimile of the Girnar rock inscription. While it was on its way, Prinsep continued to pore over the two inscriptions, re-reading, collating and interpreting them. Then, about a month after his last communication,[167] he came across another startling fact, described best in his own words:

> There is another passage in this Gujarat edict more calculated to rivet our attention than all that I have briefly alluded to above. . . . Asoka's acquaint- ance with geography was not limited to Asia, and that his expansive benevolence towards living creatures extended, at least in intention, to another quarter of the globe;—that his religious ambition sought to apostolize Egypt;—and that we must hereafter look for traces of the introduction of Buddhism into the fertile regions of the Nile, so prolific of metaphysical discussions from the earliest ages![168]

The discovery which occasioned Prinsep's remark was contained in the fifth line from the foot of the Girnar rock edict. Being in a corner, it had first gone unnoticed by Prinsep. On re-reading, it revealed the names of three Egyptian kings: Ptolemy, Gongakenos and Magas, who were obviously contemporaries of Asoka. Although Prinsep could not fathom the identity of the second king, the fact remained that India and Egypt at that time had a thriving exchange, not only of commerce, but also of philosophical ideas.

The Girnar and Dhauli inscriptions, besides bringing to light Asoka's links with Egyptian and Syrian rulers, contained the names of contemporary Indian kingdoms also, providing valuable material for the reconstruction of the political history of the Asokan age.

While studying the rock inscriptions, Prinsep found that the Dhauli inscriptions contained two edicts which were not there in the Girnar inscriptions. He studied these two separately and found a reference to a 'young prince of Ujjein', who was exhorted to 'enforce with devotional fervour the self-same conduct'. Prinsep was almost immediately able to identify this prince with Mahindo (Mahendra), 'son of Dharmasoka who entered the priesthood at an early age, and who was deputed along with his sister Sangamitta to spread Buddhism in the Island of Ceylon in the year 306 B.C.'[169] One of the factors which helped Prinsep to make this identification was Turnour's work on the *Mahavamso*. While Prinsep was busy reconstructing the history of Asoka through pillar and rock edicts and inscriptions, Turnour in Ceylon was poring over the *Mahavamso* and other Pali texts to understand the history of Buddhism. The work of the two scholars complemented each other so greatly, that Prinsep once remarked that he was growing too fond of quotations from his constant textbook, the *Mahavamso*.[170]

The same year, Turnour brought to a conclusion his 'examination of the Pali Buddhistical Annals', begun the previous year. Here we are provided with a near-complete picture of Buddha's life and the legends surrounding him. We also find here Buddha's discourses and his fascinating dialogues with his disciple Ananda, the legends of the courtesan Amrapali, and the republican tribe of the Lichchavis. In his account, Turnour also covered the Buddhist Councils and the spread of Buddhism under Asoka.

In 1838 W. Taylor presented the first fruits of his examination of the Mackenzie manuscripts containing texts in different languages and on different topics. In four communications, Taylor laid before the scholarly world the contents of different items of the collection. As Colonel Mackenzie had amassed this collection at random with no fixed aim or plan, there was much in the collection that was of little use. There was, however, some material of value which helped to shed light on different dynasties in India. Thus Taylor's analysis showed that the collection could considerably enrich historical literature on the Jains, the Cholas, the Vijayanagar kingdom, some aspects of Maratha and Moghul history, and contained manuscripts depicting the life of Sankaracharya and Timur.[171] It is a fair guess that much of the Mackenzie collection, in Madras as well as in England, still remains unscrutinized by scholars.

The revelation of a wealth of material on Asoka through a study of his rock and pillar edicts, on Buddhism through examination of the

Pali Buddhist texts of Ceylon, and on numerous dynasties of ancient and medieval India contained in the Mackenzie collection, would by themselves have made 1838 a memorable year for the historiography of ancient India. There were, however, other achievements. In the 'Facsimiles of Ancient Inscriptions', published in the January number of the *Journal*, Prinsep published the translation of a 'mutilated fragment of the inscription on the column at Bhagalpur'. The inscription showed another Gupta king, Skanda Gupta, in all his glory, by calling him 'the chief of a hundred kings'. This name had figured in the *Bhitari* inscription as well as on the coins collected at Kanauj, but that he was such a powerful ruler had not been known earlier. Prinsep remarked that Skanda Gupta's as well as his predecessor Kumara Gupta's names on the coins discovered as far away as in Saurashtra, 'went to prove that the epithet was no empty boast and that Skanda Gupta's sway was nearly as potent as the expression "lord of a hundred kings"'.[172]

The same communication which revealed Skanda Gupta's name mentioned yet another important dynasty: the Senas of Bengal. Although this line of kings had been mentioned in the *Ain-i-Akbari*, this was the first copperplate inscription to be discovered relating to the dynasty. Interestingly, this copperplate had been discovered while digging a piece of land lying in the *zamindari* of Coloylal Tagore. Tagore kept the inscription for some months before Prinsep could persuade him to part with it. Once it was brought to light, three pundits got together to work on the inscription: Govinda Rama, the Society's pundit who was entrusted with the transcription of the contents; his work being revised by Kamalakanta; and the English version prepared by young Sarodaprasada.

The copperplate inscription, while eulogising the bounty and might of Kesava Sena, also described the magnanimity of his predecessors, Vijay Sena, Ballala Sena and Lakshmana Sena.

Yet another copperplate discovered at about this time shed additional light on the Valabhi dynasty which had been discovered three years earlier, in 1835. Its genealogy had been reconstructed on the basis of the copperplate inscriptions found by Wathen in Gujarat. The inscription discovered now by Burns furnished additional information on the Valabhis. Although it added no new name to the genealogy given in Wathen's communication, it helped to resolve some misconceptions about the Valabhi era which Wathen presumed to correspond to the era of Vikramaditya.[173]

These major discoveries, described above, mainly centre around inscriptions on copperplates, rocks and pillars. Significant discoveries flowing from numismatic studies had already made the Asiatic Society a celebrated institution in this branch of science. Now the Society was honoured with gift of the enire coin collection of Masson, Alexander Burnes, and Lord for carrying out further studies. Besides these, another collection of coins, that of MacLeod, the Inspector-General of hospitals to His Majesty's forces in India, numbering some thousands, had arrived in Calcutta. Such a treasure could lead to a mine of information on Indian hisory, but it needed great skill, perseverance, knowledge and even intuition. Perhaps the only person gifted with all these qualities was Prinsep and he would no doubt have taken up the task with pleasure. But even while these materials were on their way, Prinsep had submitted his letter of resignation, dated 1 November 1838, saying that he was compelled to leave the shores of India on account of ill-health. He, however, looked forward to coming back after 'two, or perhaps three years'.

In view of his hopes of return, the Society made an unprecedented gesture when it unanimously resolved that 'the resignation of Mr James Prinsep be not accepted; but the Society hopes that he will return to resume the situation of Secretary, which he had filled so much to the credit of the Society for a period of five years.'[174]

That unfortunately was not to be. Prinsep's robust constitution had at last sunk under 'the incessant labour and close attention given to these favourite studies at the very moment when the richest collection of inscriptions, coins and relics, that had ever been got together in India were actually on their way to Calcutta as materials for maturing the results he had achieved.'[175] His condition worsened on arrival in England. After suffering for nearly a year, he breathed his last on 22 April 1840. He was then only forty years old. His death was lamented by the entire world of letters, and was the greatest blow to Indological studies since Jones's death. In an obituary published in the *Colonial Magazine*, Dr Falconer pointed out that Prinsep had left enough proof behind him to 'establish that he was one of the most talented and useful men that England has yet given to India.'[176] Speaking about his ability to enthuse and inspire others, Dr Falconer continued:

> Himself the soul of enthusiasm, he transferred a portion of his spirit into every inquirer in India; he seduced men to observe and to write; they felt as if he observed and watched over them; and the mere pleasure of participating in his sympathies and communicating with him, was in itself a sufficient

reward for the task of a laborious and painful investigation. Had he done nothing else, he would have reserved an immortal remembrance in India.[177]

With Prinsep ended the finest phase not only of Indological studies but also of the Asiatic Society. As the President of the Society, Sir Edward Ryan, pointed out, Prinsep had raised the Society to a state 'surpassing even that it had attained in the days of Sir William Jones or Mr Wilson', adding that it had never stood so high 'as at present, which was to be ascribed entirely to Mr Prinsep's great exertions.'[178] Two years after Prinsep's death the *India Review* commented:

> There is much in this excellent institution which needs reform. In the first place its meetings are far from interesting or instructive. . . . The object of the Asiatic Society was to have meetings for the exclusive purpose of hearing original papers read and according to its illustrious founder these papers were to illustrate whatever is rare on the stupendous fabric of nature. . . . Many of these great subjects have been discussed as will be seen by reference to the early transactions of the Society, but latterly we regret to say there has been a great falling off.[179]

Coming from Frederick Corbyn, one of the most enlightened Englishmen in India at the time and a prominent member of the Society, the criticism carries weight.

6

Conclusions

In an essay called 'The Enlightenment and the History of Ideas', the historian Frank Manual expresses the view that even if Newton had died at birth, the development of western science in all probability would have been the same.[1] This — the concept of historical inevitability — is a controversial issue among historians and philosophers of history. This study, however, suggests that without the Asiatic Society and the work of scholars like William Jones, Charles Wilkins, H. T. Colebrooke, H. H. Wilson, W. H. Mill, George Turnour, James Prinsep and others, knowledge about India and her rich past would not be what it is today.

By the eighteenth century, India had lapsed into a sort of amnesia about its ancient past, and in the process become apathetic to its historical remains. Manuscripts were destroyed, coins melted and turned into amulets and ornaments, new structures were constructed on historic sites, and ancient buildings raided by marauders in search of hidden treasures, or pulled down by *zamindars* for 'nothing more than collecting bricks for their new houses'.

From the way ancient coins, manuscripts, inscriptions and other relics were being destroyed — there is little doubt that over the period of a century, or even fifty years, much historical data would have been lost for ever. What could a Jones, Colebrooke or even a Prinsep do if there were no historical materials available for study? We learn from Colin Mackenzie's account, for example, that there was an impressive *stupa* at Amravati — of which nothing remains now — and all historical data it must have hidden within itself has been lost forever.[2] The Asiatic Society, for the first time, took up in an organized manner the task of retrieving, restoring, preserving and studying the ancient remains of the country, and so revealing the country's past. The Society's library and museum were the first to be established in India, and provided the model for numerous institutions including the Numismatic Society, the Indian Museum, the Anthropological Society, and others.

Despite all this, few in India, even in scholarly circles, seem to be aware of the full range of the contribution of the Asiatic Society and the early British Indologists. One of the reasons is the paucity of studies on the subject. Thus, barring a few exceptions, C. H. Philips' statement remains true still: 'Historians who have devoted themselves to the study of the peoples of the sub-continent' have shown little self-awareness, and little tendency to evaluate the work of their predecessors so that the student seeks in vain for even a single published article in which the character of their work is examined.'[3] Even today,[4] this literature is very meagre. Of the prominent members of the Society, only Sir William Jones seems to have found favour .... scholars,[5] and biographies of Colebrooke and Brian Houghton Hodgson were written in the last century.[6] Apart from these, there is practically nothing. Francis Wilford, Samuel Davis, H. H. Wilson, James Prinsep, W. H. Mill, Edward Fell, and even Alexander Cunningham, to mention only a few, seem at this distance of time merely shadows with little said or written about them.

Since individuals have thus suffered by neglect, it is only natural that the Society with which they were associated should suffer the same fate. So it is, that although we have allusions to the role of the Asiatic Society of Bengal in the discovery of India's past in the writings and addresses of Indian historians, the real impact of the Society on the cultural history of India has not been fully assessed. It is therefore difficult to understand the validity of certain statements made about the development of knowledge of India's ancient history. To cite a typical example, according to R. S. Sharma, 'The first serious attempt at the study of India's past, on the part of both the western as well as the Indian scholars began after the revolt of 1857–59.'[7] Even if we overlook for the moment the contributions of the several Asiatic and Oriental Societies established in India and abroad, we find that the Asiatic Society of Bengal alone had been able to lay the firm foundation of the study of India's past well before 1857. Between the years 1784 and 1838 (the period covered by the present study), India's forgotten and buried past emerged and took the shape of coherent history. The first major contribution in this direction was made by the Society's founder and first President, Sir William Jones, when he identified, on a firm basis, Chandragupta Maurya and his capital Pataliputra with the Sandracottus and Palibothra of the Greek texts. This provided a point of synchronization between Greek and Indian history; and since the history of Greece was well-known, it now became possible to fix dates in Indian history with some certainty. Jones also resuscitated the ancient Indian dramatic literature by translating *Sakuntala*. And Jones was the first European to write on Indian classical music. Charles Wilkins laid the foundation of epigraphy in India, and in the process brought to light the existence of the Pala and Maukhari dynasties. William Chambers wrote about the Mahabalipuram ruins and John Harington discovered the inscriptions in the Nagarjuni caves of Gaya. General John Carnac acquired the copperplate inscriptions which revealed the existence of the Silahara dynasty,and provided its genealogy, which is by and large accepted even today. This was also the period when systematic studies were undertaken in ancient Indian astronomy by William Jones, Samuel Davis and John Playfair; and Reuben Burrow surmised that the ancient Indians were so advanced in the knowledge of algebra as to be aware of the binomial theorem.

Besides these achievements during the first decade of the Society's existence, we find Sir William Jones evolving a system of orthography of Indian alphabets in Roman letters—a system which, in its basic principles, is still followed; and laying the foundations of the disciplines of Comparative Mythology and Comparative Philology, or the science of Linguistics.

H. T. Colebrooke, the next important scholar-President of the Asiatic Society, made, for the first time, a critical study of the Vedas, and also started the process of examining contemporary social customs and rituals in the light of the what was ordained in and sanctioned by the sacred books of the past—an important aspect of ancient Indian historiography. He revealed the antiquity of Hindu astronomy and mathematics, making it possible for later historians to reconstruct the history of the sciences in ancient India. Through his studies of the ancient Sanskrit texts, Colebrooke virtually revived this rich language. Between 1794 and 1815, James Blunt wrote about the Qutb Minar, Goldingham about the Elephanta caves and Mallet on the Buddhists caves of Ellora. Jonathan Duncan drew the attention of Indologists to Sarnath, about which little was then known, and William Hunter highlighted the importance of the astronomical structures known as the Jantar Mantar. J. D. Paterson tried to fathom the deeper meaning of the stories of Indian mythology, Colin Mackenzie made a breakthrough in the study of Jainism, and John Malcolm made one of the earliest studies of the history of the Sikhs and their religion. Captain James Hoare's study of the inscriptions on the *lat* of Firuz Shah brought to light the personality of Prithviraj Chauhan, and William Price discovered for Indian history the Chandela dynasty of Bundelkhand.

Horace Hayman Wilson was never President of the Society, but during his tenure as Secretary (1815–32), he discovered and studied the main historical text of ancient India, the *Rajatarangini*, and started the process of examining the Puranas for historical material. His sketch of the religious sects of the Hindus marked the beginning of the study of the social history of India, and his study of the inscriptions discovered by Captain Speirs helped in drawing up the genealogies of the Chalukyas, the Paramaras and the Guhila Rajputs. During this period, Captain Sydenham measured and wrote about the important historical monuments of Bijapur, and Walter Ewer, for the first time, deciphered the name of the builder—Iltutmish—of the Qutb Minar. Andrew Stirling wrote the first detailed essay on Orissa in which he drew the attention of scholars to the cave inscriptions of Udayagiri and Khandagiri; Captain Edward Fell shed valuable light on the Chauhans—the last important Hindu dynasty prior to the Muslim conquest of India, and John Crawford, through his study of the people and culture of Java and Bali added another concept—that of Greater India—to the study of Indian history.

During James Prinsep's tenure as Secretary (1832–8), the Society experienced a period of great discoveries. Himself a genius, Prinsep had the rare gift of enthusing others with his love of learning, so that they bore all kinds of hardships, undertook difficult journeys and spent their own money for the purpose. During this period, the very character of Indological studies changed, with greater emphasis being laid on visiting archaeological sites, collecting specimens and coins and deciphering the ancient scripts of India. The scene changed from a room stocked with manuscripts where a Jones, a Colebrooke, or a Wilson worked, surrounded by Indian pundits, to the field where the Indologist sweated in the sun uncovering buried sites, collecting and copying whatever seemed important and then trying to study his acquisitions in his camp at night. Prinsep thus provided a sound footing for the study of archaeology and numismatics, and discovered several important kings and dynasties of ancient India. His greatest achievement was undoubtedly the decipherment of the Ashokan inscriptions, without which who knows for how long Asoka would have remained unknown to Indian history. It was Prinsep again, who, on the basis of the coin collection of Alexander Burnes, brought to light King Kanishka, and later, other kings of the Indo-Scythian dynasty. The western *kshatrapas* were also revealed to history through Prinsep's discoveries. During this period, Alexander Csoma de Körös discovered the ancient Buddhist texts of Tibet, and Hodgson became the founder of Buddhist studies by revealing the wealth of material available on the subject in Nepal. Through his collection of ancient coins, Charles Masson made possible the reconstruction of the Indo-Bactrian and Indo-Scythic dynasties. Mill and Troyer deciphered the Allahabad pillar inscription and brought to our knowledge the kings of the Gupta dynasty, including Samudragupta. General Ventura's excavation of the *stupa* at Manikyala showed the way to gathering more historical material on Buddhism; and George Turnour, through his study and translation of the Buddhist texts of Ceylon enriched not only the history of Buddhism but also that of the Maurya dynasty.

In view of such achievements between 1784 and 1838, we may question a statement which ascribes all serious study in Indian history to the post-1857 period. By linking studies in history to a political event (mutiny or the first war of independence of 1857), Sharma highlights another aspect of Indian historiography: suspicion of the motives of British Indologists.

In a recent publication, Edward Said voices the opinion of this school of scholars with vehemence:

> Taking the late eighteenth century as a very roughly defined starting-point Orientalism can be discussed and analysed as the corporate institution for dealing with the Orient—dealing with it by making statements about it, authorising views of it, describing it, by teaching it, settling it, ruling over it: in short, Orientalism as a Western style for dominating, restructuring, and having authority over the Orient.[8]

Said goes on to say:

> I doubt that it is controversial, for example, to say that an Englishman in India or Egypt in the later nineteenth century took an interest in those countries that was never far from their status in his mind as British colonies. To say this may seem quite different from saying that all academic knowledge about India and Egypt is somehow tinged and impressed with, violated by, the gross political fact—and yet that is what I am saying in this study of Orientalism.[9]

In this view, Said has no dearth of support from Indian historians. One has only to go through the Presidential addresses delivered from the platform of the Indian History Congress to be convinced that the history of India needs to be re-written in view of the distortions imposed upon it by imperialist historians who wrote mainly for two reasons: to strengthen the British hold on its colonial empire and secondly, to pave the way for a more effective process of conversion of the pagan Hindu to Christianity. What is surprising is that this is not a post-independence phenomenon. For instance, according to Indubhusan Banerjee, the President of the Modern Indian Section at the eighth Indian History Congress held at Annamalainagar in 1945:

> European writers on Indo-British history have often failed to rise above . . . the political exigencies of the situation, and that is why it has been said that British Indian history has been the 'worst patch in current scholarship'. Historians . . . appear as pitiful apologists for British rule in India.[10]

One could cite a number of similar passages from the proceedings of different Congresses. We find the same theme recurring in books. For instance in the introduction to his book on Sir William Jones, S. N. Mukherjee says:

> It is often forgotten that all Oriental studies in the eighteenth century had a political slant, and all political pamphleteers writing on East Indian affairs based their theories of Indian politics on Oriental researches. . . . For a better understanding of the British response to Indian civilization we should study it within the context of the British and European economic system, social structure and intellectual movements and with reference to the problems of the British administration in India. Early Orientalists were not an isolated group. They were involved in the political conflicts of the time and their 'theories' about Indian history and culture were influenced by their respective political positions and intellectual convictions.[11]

This theme of British scholars on India being motivated by ulterior reasons is not 'often forgotten' but only too often and too well remembered. So often has the theme been repeated that side by side with the belief that British historians, through their motivated writings, created 'stereotypes of Indian History', it seems that Indian historians have created their own stereotype about British historians and scholars.

This work hopes to establish, maybe to a limited extent, that the world of scholarship and the world of administration during this period were worlds apart and not necessarily complementary to each other. Although most of the scholars were in the civil service, they were rarely extended patronage by the administration. Nor is there much evidence that the administration directed in any manner their scholarly efforts.[12] Thus each scholar pursued the subject of his interest. Jones was fascinated by ancient Indian literature, especially poetry and drama; Colebrooke, Davis, Burrow, Edward Strachey and others took up the ancient Indian sciences; Wilson, Paterson, Mackenzie, Hodgson, Csoma and Turnour, the ancient religious and historical texts; and Prinsep, Masson, Mill, Cautley, Conolly, Cunningham, Burt and many others ancient inscriptions, archaeology and numismatics. Each of these, and many other scholars worked independently of the administration and with whatever time and energy their official work left them at the end of the day.

As for the Society, we have seen that for all its contribution, its financial state was seldom satisfactory. Till 1836 the Society neither asked for nor received any substantial help from the government. The plot of land it received was only after its request was initially turned down and the Government provided no aid for construction of its building.

Furthermore, under Bentinck the administration stopped all help and encouragement to Indian studies. The Society's efforts to carry on regardless of the hostility shown by the Administration constitutes one of the brightest phases in its history.[13]

The apathy of Government towards an institute of oriental learning was not exclusively directed towards the Bengal Society. We find that the Royal Asiatic Society in England shared the same fate. Its repeated requests for suitable accommodation were ignored, and there is no evidence that the institution received financial help from the administration. Indological studies were not seen, either by the British government or the scholars themselves, as being complementary to, or assisting in, the strengthening of the British hold on India. The motives for the study of India's past were, in fact, as diverse as the number and associations of scholars themselves. For instance, commenting on the third report of the proceedings of the Committee of the London Society, the *Alexander's East India Magazine* noted:

> The surest way of inducing the natives of India to improve their understanding and to make themselves thoroughly acquainted with the history and the real interests of their country, is for public bodies in England and in India to encourage natives of all classes to communicate to them such literary and other information as they can collect, and to hold up their literary exertions and talents to the public applause in such a manner as may not only flatter their feelings, but prove their capacity for filling the highest situations in the Government of their country.[14]

Daniel Ingalls was probably right in commenting that 'All dogmatic statements concerning choice of approach and motive in the study of the past are foolish. They are worse than foolish; they are pernicious.'[15]

Bernard Lewis in his *History—Remembered, Recovered, Invented* reiterates this point:

> The accusation is often made that Orientalists were the servants of imperialism and that their researches and writings were designed to serve imperial needs. There is some color in this accusation, in that empire and still more trade provided the opportunity and the means for European scholars to study oriental texts, documents, and archives. As an assessment, however, of either the attitude or the achievement of the great European orientalists the accusation is grotesquely false. Few of them were in any way servants or employees of imperial or commercial interests; many were actively critical of imperial rule and showed greater sympathy with their subjects than with their compatriots.[16]

On the other hand to deny altogether the imperialist approach or that a biased attitude was adopted by many British historians writing about India would be equally unrealistic. As Ingalls points out,

> The motives for studying the past [are] as various as the motives of humans for any other endeavour. Colebrooke's were certainly different from Müller's and if one were to speak of other historians one would add as many motives as biographies.[17]

This leads us to examine the second powerful motive ascribed to British Indologists—the religious. On this, R. S. Sharma writes:

> A perusal of some introductions to *Sacred Books of the East* reveals the motive underlying this great venture. . . . According to Max Müller, to the missionary an accurate knowledge of the sacred books was as indispensable as the knowledge of the enemy's country to a general.[18]

This quotation calls for examination. In the first place, Max Müller's quotation does not form part of the introduction to the *Sacred Books* but belongs to the piece called 'Programme of a Translation of The Sacred Books of the East',[19] in which he says, 'I here subjoin the program in which I first put forward the idea of a translation of the Sacred Books of the East, and through which I invited the cooperation of Oriental scholars in this undertaking.' The following paragraph sets the context for Sharma's quotation:

> Apart from the interest which the Sacred Books of all religions possess in the eyes of the theologian, and, more particularly, of the missionary, to whom an accurate knowledge of them is as indispensable as a knowledge of the enemy's country is to a general, these works have of late assumed a new

importance, as viewed in the character of ancient historical documents. In every country where sacred books have been preserved, whether by oral tradition or by writing, they are the oldest records, and mark the beginning of what may be called documentary, in opposition to purely traditional, history.[20]

Viewed in this perspective, it is clear that Max Müller's emphasis is not on the purpose the *Sacred Books* would serve for the missionaries, but the importance they assumed as historical documents.

In the actual 'Preface' to the *Sacred Books*, Max Müller stated:

> To the patient reader these same books will, in spite of many drawbacks, open a new view of the history of the human race, of that one race to which we all belong, with all the fibres of our flesh, with all the fears and hopes of our soul. We cannot separate ourselves from those who believed in these sacred books. There is no specific difference between ourselves and the Brahmans, the Buddhists, the Zoroastrians, or the Taosze. . . . If some of those who read and mark these translations learn to discover some such precious grains in the sacred books of other nations, though hidden under heaps of rubbish, our labour will not have been in vain, for there is no lesson which at the present time seems more important than to learn that in every religion there are such precious grains.[21]

Thus, far from being a spokesman for Christian missionaries for whom the Bible was the only sacred text, Max Müller, like William Jones before him, was considered to discredit Christianity.[22] Since Max Müller's views go against Said's argument, he has only this significant remark to make:

> Any work that seeks to provide an understanding of academic Orientalism and pays little attention to scholars like Steinthall, Müller, Becker, Goldziher, Brockelmann, N'oldeka—to mention only a handful—needs to be reproached, and I freely reproach myself.[23]

Let us also examine here the motive for establishing the Boden Chair of Sanskrit in Oxford in 1832. Joseph Boden, the founder of the Chair, though not a Sanskrit scholar himself, held that 'a more general and critical knowledge of the language [Sanskrit] will be the means of enabling my countrymen to proceed in the conversion of the natives of India in the Christian religion, by disseminating a knowledge of the sacred scriptures among them, more effectual than by all other means whatever.'[24]

This sums up the religious motives commonly attributed to British Indologists; and it is natural that Indian historians should use it to prove the bias of British scholars in studying Indian history an culture.[25]

What is overlooked, however, is that in spite of the emphasis laid o the 'missionary' character of the Chair by its founder, the Selectio Board seemed to put more value on scholarship than on religious zea Among the first candidates, there were at least two missionaries– Thomas Proctor and W. H. Mill. The latter was not only an eminer Sanskritist but also the author of *Christa Sanghita.* Another Sanskr scholar and candidate for the Chair was G. C. Haughton, the compile of the *Manava Dherma Sastra.* Haughton, in his letter to the Selectio Board, had even highlighted his achievements in propagating th Gospel in the East.

The candidate finally selected was Wilson. His letter to the Selec tion Board did not contain a single reference to the religious aspect c his scholarship, and at one stage his selection was even threatene because he did not combine learning with religious zeal. On th subject of election to the Boden Chair, a resident Fellow of Jesu College, Oxford, wrote:

> The contest is between Wilson and Dr Mill. . . . In spite of the false an injurious reports to which some of the letters allude Wilson is considere to have a majority of resident votes—but we are afraid of his bein overwhelmed by the London & county clergy, to whom Mill's name familiar from his connection with different religious societies; wherea Wilson is chiefly known to the literati, like Bentham.[26]

These 'false and injurious reports' were, in fact, reports in whicl doubts were expressed if Wilson was a true Christian. Here we find repetition of the charge that had been levelled at Sir William Jones Although Jones's friend and biographer, Lord Teignmouth, went ou of his way to defend Jones by recalling every small detail to prove tha he believed in everything Christian, this did not prevent others fron expressing doubts about Jones's beliefs. Thus as late as 1846 (over fift years after Jones's death), a critic wrote in the *Calcutta Review:*

> It is to us a matter of deep regret, that he does not seem to have derive from Christianity any very large measure of that solid joy which it is fitte to impart . . . that while his amazing learning is everywhere and alway apparent, his religion requires to be searched for. Well it is that it can b found on searching; but better for that no search were required.[27]

Such critics overlook the fact that if British Indologists valuec Indian culture, it was a natural result of the interaction between tw cultures. Thus, Hunter in his biography of Brian Hodgson notes that 'the assumption of exclusive salvation sometimes put forward by British Christians made him indignant.' Hunter recalls an incident when a Dean, ridiculing the Buddhist faith, asked Hodgson if there was anything worthwhile in the pagan faith, Hodgson replied:

> Sir, Buddhism is simply the creed most widely spread over the face of the earth . . . and older than our own. It has a vast and learned literature. Perhaps you might find it not unworthy of the attention of an educated man or even of a dignitary of the Church.[28]

William Jones wrote to Lord Althorp in a similar vein:

> I am no Hindu, but I hold the doctrine of the Hindus concerning a future state to be incomparably more rational, more pious and more likely to deter men from vice, than the horrid opinions inculcated by Christians on punishments without end.[29]

Such pronouncements, together with their deep study of an alien culture, made them subject to criticism from both extremes: fellow Christians looked upon them as heretics and Indians considered them such blind Christians as to study Hinduism only to facilitate the conversion of Hindus to the Christian faith. Both groups of critics were wrong since they overlooked the fact that a catholic outlook is the inevitable result of deep study, whether of religions or cultures.

This urge for discovering and understanding Indian culture soon caught the attention of Europe. According to Wilson: 'At the period when [the Asiatic Society of Bengal] was formed . . . of India little was known, and that little was superficial and inaccurate. . . . The literature and languages of India . . . were not within the pale of European acquirement.'[30]

What proved a major inspiration to the west was discovery of the richness of the Sanskrit language, and its likeness to Greek and Latin. Within a span of about half a century, the Asiatic Society made Sanskrit almost a world language, which had such an impact on western consciousness that Macdonell in his *History of Sanskrit Literature* remarked:

> Since the Renaissance there has been no event of such world-wide significance in the history of culture as the discovery of Sanskrit Literature in the latter part of the eighteenth century.[31]

The scholars of the Asiatic Society not only brought to light the richness of Sanskrit literature, but also the fact that this language hid in its bosom the secrets of bonds which had existed between Europe and this part of the world in the remote past. This awareness gave a great impetus to western scholars to study the language and with it, the history and culture of India. As a result, Societies similar to the Asiatic Society of Bengal began to be established all over the western world[32] — and all these Societies turned to the parent Society and, particularly, to its founder, for their ideals and inspiration. With Jones, therefore, it may be said, began a new phase of European enlightenment with its centre in the east. So much had this movement gained within a century that in 1882 Max Müller could proclaim:

> If I were asked under what sky the human mind has most fully developed some of its choicest gifts, has most deeply pondered on the greatest problems of life, and has found solutions of some of them which well deserve the attention of those who have studied Plato and Kant—I should point to India. And if I were to ask myself from what literature we, here in Europe, we, who have been nurtured almost exclusively on the thoughts of Greeks and Romans, and of one Semitic race, the Jewish, may draw that corrective which is most wanted in order to make our inner life more perfect, more comprehensive, more universal, in fact more truly human, a life, not for this life only, but a transfigured and eternal life—again I should point to India.[33]

This passage marks the peak of Europe's awareness of Indian culture and discovery of India's past and reveals the transition in Indology from Jones's work, as a pioneer—to Max Müller's, who symbolised its fulfilment.

More than the impact the Society had on Europe was its influence on the stream of Indian thought and life. Not only did it give back to India its forgotten past, but what is more, by 1840, the Society was able to establish the fact that India at one time had possessed a very rich culture and had progressed no less than Europe in the arts, sciences and literature. This in turn had two long-term effects. First, the discovery of the country's past and consequently the evolution of historical consciousness in its people helped in heralding the Indian renaissance. 'The great ages of renaissance in history', remarked Rabindranath Tagore,[34] 'were those when men suddenly discovered the seeds of thought in the granary of the past.' Considered from this point of view, the period 1784 to 1838 was certainly a 'great age', and if there is one institution to which the beginnings of the Indian renaissance can be traced, it is the Asiatic Society of Bengal.

The second effect was that the discovery of a rich past fostered a sense of nationalism and patriotism among Indians. 'It was one of the long-term ironies of history', says A. L. Rowse, 'that it was British rule that led to the renaissance of India, consciousness of her identity and her past, the ultimate emergence of Indian nationalism.'[35]

After all this, it seems a tragedy that British historians and scholars of India were either forgotten or viewed as generally prejudiced and imperialist. Moreover, this was done, as has been shown, without a detailed study of their lives and work. The writer of an unpublished thesis on James Mill has put the point succintly: 'With all our eagerness to hang the British historians, no serious study had been undertaken to analyse their works, their "crimes" if we may so call them. . . . We have just given them a bad name.'[36]

One reason for this seems to be that the work of the British Indologists was followed by a strong wave of nationalism. In fact, the very sense of nationalism which was fostered by their work, became a reason for them to be rejected. Indian historians were more than eager to accept the glory of India's past as revealed by British historians, but the historians themselves were rejected as biased and motivated.

The present study of the Asiatic Society and of the early members who discovered India's history will, we hope, help in highlighting the fact that many of them were scholars in the true sense of the term; and it may lead to further studies on the lives and works of British historians. Such studies, when undertaken, will in all likelihood bring out the soundness of the advice:

> Let knowledge grow from more to more,
> But more of reverence in us dwell.[37]

Abbreviations

AAR	*Asiatic Annual Register*
AEICM	*Alexander's East India and Colonial Magazine*
AIOC	*All India Oriental Conference (Proceedings)*
ASIR	*Archaeological Survey of India Reports*
As. Jr.	*Asiatic Journal*
As. Res.	*Asiatic Researches*
ASAM	*Asiatic Society Archival Material*
Blackwoods	*Blackwoods Edinburgh Magazine*
BSOAS	*Bulletin of the School of Oriental and African Studies*
Cal. Rev.	*Calcutta Review*
Cent. Rev.	*Centenary Review of the Asiatic Society*
Cl. Jr.	*Classical Journal*
DHNI	*Dynastic History of Northern India*
DNB	*Dictionary of National Biography*
Ed. Rev.	*Edinburgh Review*
Gent. Mag.	*Gentleman's Magazine*
Ind. Cul.	*Indian Culture*
IHC	Indian History Congress
IOL	India Office Library
JAIH	*Journal of Ancient Indian History*
JAOS	*Journal of the American Oriental Society*
JAS	*Journal of Asiatic Studies*
JIH	*Journal of Indian History*
JORAS	*Journal of the Royal Asiatic Society of Great Britain and Ireland*
NAI	National Archives of India
Or. Herald	*Oriental Herald*
PASOB	*Proceedings of the Meetings of the Asiatic Society of Bengal*
PIHC	*Proceedings of the Indian History Congress*

PRASOGBI	*Proceedings of the Meetings of the Royal Asiatic Society of Great Britain and Ireland*
Quart. Rev.	*Quarterly Review*
SIH	*Studies in History*

Notes

Chapter 1. THE BACKGROUND

1. Quoted by K. K. Datta, in Presidential Address, 21st session, IHC, at Trivandrum, *PIHC,* 1958, XXI, p. 17.
2. Macaulay, quoted in N. K. Sinha, *The History of Bengal,* Calcutta University, 1967, p. 5.
3. Bahadur Shah (1707–12) died a natural death; Jahandar Shah (1712–13) murdered; Farrukhsiyar (1713–19) murdered; Rafi-ud-Darajat (Feb. 1719–Jun. 1719) deposed; Rafi-ud-Daula (Jun. 1719–Sept. 1719) died of diarrhoea; Mohammad Shah (1719–48) died a natural death; Mohammad Ibrahim (Oct. 1748–Nov. 1748) deposed; Ahmed Shah (1748–54) deposed; and Azizuddin (1754–9) murdered.
4. H. N. Sinha, 'The Main Currents of the Eighteenth Century', *JIH,* vol. IX, 1930.
5. Datta, Presidential Address, *PIHC,* XXI, p. 16.
6. See Rajat Datta, 'Aspects of the Agrarian System of Bengal during the Second Half of the Eighteenth Century', M.Phil. thesis, JNU, 1980; and Shaukat Ullah Khan's 'Superior Zamindars in the Mughal Subah of Gujarat during the First Half of the Eighteenth Century', M.Phil. thesis, JNU, 1977. I am grateful to Professor Harbans Mukhia of JNU for drawing my attention to them. Dr M. Alam, also at JNU, is working on the same lines on Avadh. See also Phil Colkin's 'The Formation of a Regionally Oriented Ruling Group in Bengal, 1700–1740', *JAS,* vol. XXIX, no. 4, 1970.
7. According to Bearce, the utilitarians portrayed India as being in a state of decline in the eighteenth century so that they could advocate a scheme of thorough change from their own point of view; the missionaries did it to justify their missionary activities in this part of the world; and modern Indian historians were 'strongly inspired by the movement for national independence and unity', and perpetuated the general impression because they had to explain why India lost its independence in the eighteenth century. George Bearce, 'The Culture of Eighteenth Century India: A Reappraisal', *PIHC,* 24th session, Delhi, 1961, pp. 287–96.
8. See A. Jan Qaisar, 'Level of Technology in India on the Eve of the Eighteenth Century: The Case of Glass', *SIH,* vol. II, no. 1 (Jan.–Jun.) 1980, pp. 81–93.
9. H. Goetz, *The Crisis of Indian Civilization in the Eighteenth and Early Nineteenth Centuries,* Calcutta University, 1938, pp. 6–7.
10. This survey is largely based on *The History of Mankind,* vol. IV, Pt. II,

UNESCO; and *The History and Culture of the Indian People*, vol. VIII, Bharatiya Vidya Bhavan.

11. FitzEdward Hall, 'The Source of Colebrooke's Essay, "On the Duties of a Faithful Widow"', *JORAS*, vol. III (n. s.), 1868, p. 190.

12. D. C. Sen, *History of Bengali Language and Literature*, Calcutta University, 1954, p. 520.

13. See G. C. Pande, *Itihas: Swaroop evam Siddhanta* (Hindi), Rajasthan Hindi Granth Academy, Jaipur, 1973, p. 46.

14. Ibid., p. 47.

15. Amaury de Riencourt, *The Soul of India*, Jonathan Cape, London, 1961, pp. 15–16, 26.

16. Ibid., p. 107.

17. P. V. Kane, Presidential Address at 16th session of IHC, Waltair, *PIHC*, XVI, 1953, pp. 1–2.

18. See V. S. Pathak, *Ancient Historians of India*, Asia, Bombay, 1966; A. K. Warder, *An Introduction to Indian Historiography*, Popular Prakashan, Bombay, 1972; R. C. Majumdar, 'Ideas of History in Sanskrit Literature', in C. H. Philips (ed.), *Historians of India, Pakistan and Ceylon*, O.U.P., London, 1961, pp. 15–20; R. C. Majumdar, 'Sources of Indian History', in *History and Culture of the Indian People*, vol. I, *The Vedic Age*, Bharatiya Vidya Bhavan, Allen & Unwin, London, 1951, pp. 47–51.

19. Majumdar, *The Vedic Age*, p. 47.

20. Charles Masson, 'Memoir on the ancient coins found at Beghram, in the Kohistan of Kabul', *JASOB*, vol. III, p. 153.

21. Alexander Allanson, 'To Sarnath', *The Bengal Annual*, 1836, p. 195.

22. Ranjana Mukherjee, 'The History of the Andhra Region, c. A.D. 75–350', Ph.D. thesis, SOAS, 1965, p. 425 fn.

23. *Bengal Past and Present*, vol. 39, 1930 (Jan.–Jun.) p. 68.

24. Of course, fantastic accounts of India continue to appear till this day. This is perhaps because of man's love for the mysterious and the fantastic.

25. The writings of some missionaries like the Abbé Raynal and Baldaeus also fall into this category, and hence have been treated here.

26. J. B. Harrison, 'Five Portuguese Historians', in C. H. Philips (ed.), *Historians of India*, O.U.P., London, 1967, p. 160.

27. E. M. Pope, *India in Portuguese Literature*, Tipographia Rauge, Bastora, 1932, p. 116.

28. *Eclectic Review*, vol. 14, 1820 (Dec.), p. 559.

29. Pope, *India in Portuguese Literature*, pp. 40–1.

30. Ibid., p. 33.

31. K. W. Goonewardena, 'Dutch Historical Writings on South India', in Philips (ed.), *Historians of India*, p. 171.

32. S. P. Sen, 'French Historical Writing on European Activities in India', in Philips (ed.), *Historians of India*, p. 186.

33. *Gent. Mag.*, vol. 73, Pt. I, 1803, p. 518.

34. The title page of the book does not carry the author's name. This is obtained from a pencilled note about him on the copy in the Asutosh

Collection, National Library, Calcutta, under the number 954.03/3.
35. F. Wilhelm and H. G. Rawlinson, 'India and the Modern West', in A. L. Basham (ed.), *A Cultural History of India*, O.U.P., London, 1975, p. 470.
36. A German translation of the book was published at Nuremberg in 1663. The Dutch original was published in 1915 at The Hague.
37. *Cal. Rev.*, vol. 29, 1857, p. 241.
38. Alfred Master, 'The Influence of Sir William Jones on Sanskrit Literature', *BSOAS*, vol. XI, pp. 789–806.
39. These were published in Latin.
40. The entire work was published by Colebrooke in 1808 from the Serampore Press.
41. D. F. Lach, *Asia in the Making of Europe*, University of Chicago Press, 1965, p. 6.
42. Ibid.
43. J. Burgess, *Hindu Astronomy: History of our Knowledge of It*, p. 97. (Preserved as a Tract in the Asutosh Collection, National Library, Calcutta).
44. Anquetil Duperron's work has not been included in the survey as his translation of the *Zendavesta* was published in 1796 and his translation of the *Upanishads* (*Oupnekhat*) in 1801, both after the foundation of the Asiatic Society. More information on Anquetil is available in Arthur Waley's excellent article, 'Anquetil du Perron and Sir William Jones', *History Today*, vol. II, Jan. 1952, pp. 23–33.
45. Quoted in P. J. Marshall, *The British Discovery of Hinduism in the Eighteenth Century*, Cambridge University Press, 1970, p. 47.
46. Ibid., pp. 49–50.
47. J. S. Grewal, *Muslim Rule in India: Assessment of British Historians*, O.U.P., Calcutta, 1970, p. 47.
48. A. Dow, *History of Hindostan*, vol. I, London, 1770, p. xx.
49. Quoted in Marshall, *British Discovery*, p. 12.
50. Shafaat Ahmad Khan, *The History and Historians of British India*, Srimant Sayaji Rao Lectures, Baroda, 1938.
51. A copy of the poem is in the Carey Library, Serampore, No. BRT.1.
52. D. Kopf, *British Orientalism and the Bengal Renaissance*, Firma K. L. Mukhopadhyay, Calcutta, 1969, p. 21.
53. *JORAS*, vol. XVII, 1860, p. 245.
54. From *Proceedings of the Committee of Circuit at Kasimbazar*, 15 August 1772, quoted in Bharatiya Vidya Bhavan, *History and Culture of the Indian People*, vol. VIII, p. 361.
55. S. N. Mukherjee, *Sir William Jones, A Study in Eighteenth Century British Attitudes to India*, Cambridge University Press, 1968, p. 79.
56. F. Wilhelm and H. G. Rawlinson, 'India and the Modern West', in Basham, *A Cultural History of India*, p. 473.
57. The full text of the letter can be found in Marshall, *British Discovery*, pp. 184–91. (This passage occurs on p. 189).
58. Marshall, *British Discovery*, p. 13.
59. This is based on Will Durant and Ariel Durant, *The Age of Voltaire*,

Simon and Schuster, New York, 1965, pp. 498–9.
60. Ibid.
61. The Batavian Society of Arts and Sciences, founded on 24 April 1778 by Jacob Cornelius Mattheus Radermacher, preceded the Asiatic Society of Bengal, but as will be obvious from its Regulations (IOL, MSS. Eur. E. 118, Mackenzie Papers) it was purely utilitarian in nature, unlike the Bengal Society.
62. J. Bronowski and Bruce Mazlish, *The Western Intellectual Tradition*, Penguin, 1960, pp. 282–3.
63. Carl Becker, *The Heavenly City of Eighteenth Century Philosophers*, New Haven, 1964, p. 20.
64. J. W. Thompson, *A History of Historical Writing*, vol. II, Macmillan, New York, 1942, pp. 134–5.
65. Later, Herder was to exclaim: 'Behold the East — the cradle of the human race, of human emotions, of all religion!' But this was only after he came across *Sakuntala* which was made known to the west by Jones.
66. William Jones, 'A Discourse on the Institution of a Society for Enquiring into the History, Civil and Natural, the Antiquities, Arts, Sciences, and Literature of Asia', *As. Res.*, vol. I, pp. ix–x.
67. William Jones not only predated Oswald Spengler who for the first time spoke of the 'Copernican form of historical process' (Oswald Spengler, *The Decline of the West*, Allen and Unwin, London, 1971, p. 25) but also seems to be better qualified for being termed the 'Copernicus of history', since Spengler ultimately returned to the western civilization in spite of his broad outlook.

Chapter 2. THE FOUNDER'S DECADE, 1784–1794

1. Lord Teignmouth, *Memoirs of the Life, Writings, and Correspondence of Sir William Jones*, London, 1804, p. 228. Jones was highly systematic in his thinking. Early in life, he had prepared an andrometer, defined as 'a scale of human attainments and enjoyment'. Assuming the span of human life to be seventy years, he allotted a particular study, occupation or attainment to each year. (Teignmouth, *Memoirs*, pp. 137–8). In another memorandum drawn up in 1780, he planned his studies thus: 'Resolved to learn no more rudiments of any kind, but to perfect myself in, first, 12 languages, as the means of acquiring accurate knowledge of the

I. History of
1. Man   2. Nature

II. Arts
1. Rhetoric   2. Poetry
3. Painting   4. Music

III. Sciences
1. Law   2. Mathematics
3. Dialectic

The 12 languages are—
Greek
Latin
Italian, French, Spanish, Portuguese,
Hebrew, Arabic
Persian
Turkish
German, English. (Ibid., p. 192)

2. Ibid., p. 34.
3. It is ironical that Mukherjee should remark: 'Born in an age of child prodigies, he [Jones] was no exception.' S. N. Mukherjee, *Sir William Jones, A Study in Eighteenth Century British Attitudes to India,* Cambridge University Press, 1968, pp. 18–19.
4. Teignmouth, *Memoirs*, vol. I, p. 42.
5. Jones kept up a regular correspondence with Lord Althorp to the end of his life. Theirs was the ideal student-teacher relationship.
6. Jones's *Grammar* remained a standard work on the subject and went into several editions. Among those whom this book inspired to take up the study of Persian was Edward Fitzgerald, who translated the *Rubaiyat of Omar Khaiyyam.*
7. Jones to Edward Gibbon, 30 Jun. 1781, in Cannon, *Letters of Sir William Jones* (2 vols.), O.U.P., 1970, vol. II, p. 481.
8. Jones left behind a memorandum in which he enumerated the languages he had studied: 'Eight languages studied critically: English, Latin, French, Italian, Greek, Arabic, Persian, Sanskrit.
'Eight studied less perfectly, but all intelligible with a dictionary: Spanish, Portuguese, German, Runick, Hebrew, Bengali, Hindi, Turkish.
'Twelve studied least perfectly, but all attainable: Tibetan, Pali, Pehlavi, Deri, Russian, Syriac, Ethiopic, Coptic, Welsh, Swedish, Dutch, Chinese' (Teignmouth, *Memoirs*, p. 376).
9. Quoted in A. J. Arberry, *Oriental Essays,* Allen and Unwin, London, 1960, p. 79.
10. Quoted in Ibid., p. 76.
11. Jones to Viscount Althorp, 1 Mar. 1782, in Cannon, *Letters*, vol. II, pp. 515–17.
12. Jones married Anna, daughter of Jonathan Shipley, the Bishop of Asaph. Jones had known Anna for nearly sixteen years, and been engaged to her for a long time, but had decided to marry only when he was a man of means and high reputation.
13. *Centenary Review of the Asiatic Society of Bengal from 1784 to 1883,* Asiatic Society, Calcutta, pt. II, p. 82.
14. A. J. Arberry, *British Orientalists,* Collins, London, 1943, p. 28.
15. Mukherjee, *Sir William Jones,* p. 46.
16. G. Cannon, 'Sir William Jones's Indian Studies', *JOAS*, vol. 91, p. 419.
17. William Jones, 'A Discourse on the Institution of a Society", *As. Res.,* vol. I, p. x.
18. Jones delivered his first charge to the the Grand Jury in December 1783.
19. This letter seems to have been lost.

20. G. Cannon, *Oriental Jones*, Asia, Bombay, 1964, pp. 117–18.
21. J. Collegins, 'Literary Characteristics of the Most Distinguished Members of the Asiatic Society', *AAR*, 1802, p. 108.
22. William Jones, 'A Discourse on the Institution of a Society', *As. Res.*, vol. I, pp. x–xi.
23. A. J. Arberry, *Asiatic Jones*, Longmans, Green, London, 1946, pp. 22–3.
24. 'Life of Sir William Jones', *As. Jr.*, vol. II, 1830, p. 128.
25. NAI, Home Miscellaneous. O.C. 20 Feb. 1784, No. 90. The founder-members of the Society included all the judges of the Supreme Court. By requesting Council Members to become 'Patrons', it was expected that the prevailing tensions between the Court and Council would be somewhat reduced.
26. *As. Res.*, vol. I, pp. vii–viii.
27. Ibid., p. xvi.
28. Ibid., vol. I, p. 3.
29. Jones used the letters of the Bengali alphabet which he mistakenly called Devanagari. However, since the letters resembled each other, the mistake is of little consequence.
30. *As. Res.*, vol. I, p. 13.
31. *Cent. Rev., Proceedings of the Special Centenary Meeting of the Society.*
32. M. Monier-Williams, 'Two Addresses delivered before the International Congress of Orientalists at Berlin on 14 September 1881'. See tracts in the Asutosh Collection, the National Library, No. A.C. 915. 4 TB, vol. 16, p. 9.
33. *As. Res.*, vol. I, p. 2.
34. Little is known of Thomas Law. He came to India to serve the Company in 1773 and rose to be a member of the Board of Trade. He seems to have been deeply interested in oriental studies as this article and his correspondence with Jones bear out.
35. *PASOB*, 17 Jun. 1784. William Chambers, the younger brother of Sir Robert Chambers, preceded him to India. Charles Grant wrote of him to his brother in 1776: 'I have met with one such character, a man whom religion animates and directs. He is the happiest in his temper, the purest and most dignified in his mind... Besides acquiring in this country the Greek and Latin... he has studied no less than six or seven eastern languages and speaks Persian with the same ease and fluency as he does English.' See IOL, Eur. MSS D. 491, which contains two packets of his letters.
36. Prahlad's father, according to the legend, had been granted a boon whereby he could not be killed by man or beast, by day or night. Having become all-powerful, he became a tyrant and began torturing even his son, who was a devotee of Vishnu. To save his devotee, Vishnu assumed a half-lion, half-man form and slew Hiranyakashipu (Prahlad's father) at dusk (neither day nor night).
37. Among the Orme manuscripts (IOL, Orme MSS. India. XVIII, pp. 5186–7) we find another 'fabulous account of the pagodas at Mavaly-varan'. According to what Orme learnt, the Mahabalipuram structures were built by one Mavaly, who to satisfy his ambitions, began

to have his 'own image set up in diverse parts of this country and entirely drew the people from the worship of the High God, which so angered him that Hiree himself came upon the earth and after chaining him kicked him into hell, of which by this time he may be Havildar.'

38. William Chambers, 'Account of the Sculptures and Ruins at Mahavali-puram', *As. Res.*, vol. I, pp. 157–8.
39. *As. Res.*, vol. I, p. xv.
40. F. M. Max Müller, *Chips from a German Workshop*, Longmans, Green. London, 1867, p. 338.
41. A. J. Arberry, 'The Jones Tradition', *Indian Art and Letters*, vol. xx, no. 1, p. 3.
42. *As. Res.*, vol. I, p. 407.
43. Though Jones presented the paper in 1785, the first draft was ready in 1784. Max Müller, without much justification, remarked that Jones gave his address an earlier date in order to be one of the first orientalists to have studied the sacred literature of the Brahmans (*Chips from a German Workshop*, p. 99). This criticism seems all the odder since we find Jones unhesitatingly praising, on several occasions, Halhed and Wilkins' earlier studies of Sanskrit.
44. William Jones, 'On the Gods of Greece, Italy and India', *As. Res.*, vol. I, p. 221.
45. Ibid., p. 258.
46. Ibid., p. 275.
47. Arberry, *Oriental Essays*, p. 83.
48. 'Analysis of the first volume of Asiatic Miscellanies', *Gent. Mag.*, vol. LX, pt. 1, p. 220.
49. Arberry, *Oriental Essays*, p. 83.
50. Jules Mohl, 'Extracts from the report made to the Paris Asiatic Society on 30 May 1842', *JAOS*, vol. I, p. 68.
51. A small town in Bihar now called Bettiah.
52. A part of northern Bihar now spelt Tirhut.
53. *JAOS*, vol. I, p. 6.
54. G. Cannon, *William Jones, An Annotated Bibliography*, University of Hawaii Press, Honolulu, 1952, p. 54.
55. *As. Res.*, vol. I, pp. 276–87.
56. *PASOB*, 14 Jul. 1785.
57. Charles Wilkins, 'Inscription on a Pillar near Buddal Translated from the Sanskrit', *As. Res.*, vol. I, p. 131.
58. Ibid., pp. 142–3. Jones's estimates were far removed from the generally accepted dates. Jones assigned 23 B.C. as the date for Devapala and A.D. 67 for that of Narayanapala, whereas Professor Sircar gives A.D. 812–50 for Devapala, and A.D. 860–917 for Narayanapala. Sircar gives a list of twenty rulers against Jones's six. For other studies in the chronology of the Pala dynasty, see editorial comments in S. K. Mitra, *East Indian Bronzes*, Calcutta University, 1979, pp. 148–50.
59. *JAIH*, vol. IX, pp. 200–10.
60. *As. Res.*, vol. I, p. 142.
61. *PASOB*, 29 Dec. 1785.

62. Cannon, *Letters,* vol. II, p. 646.
63. In a letter dated 24 Oct. 1786, Jones wrote to Boughton Rouse, Secretary to the Board of Control for India: 'Never imagine, that I have an unreasonable prejudice against the natives, but I must declare what I know to be true . . . God knows I have no object on this occasion but the public good. Pure integrity is hardly to be found among the pundits and the *maulvis,* few of whom give opinions without culpable bias, if the parties can have access to them.' Cannon, *Letters,* vol. II, pp. 720–1.
64. Teignmouth, *Memoirs,* p. 266.
65. *As. Res.,* vol. I, pp. 422–3. Jones was so fascinated by the affinity of Sanskrit to Greek and Latin that he referred to it time and again in his letters. See, for instance Cannon, *Letters,* vol. II, pp. 711, 727, 747 and 777.
66. Teignmouth, *Memoirs,* p. 168.
67. Holger Pederson, *The Discovery of Language,* Indiana University Press, Bloomington, 1962, p. 9.
68. Ibid.
69. See the English translation of this discourse in *Biblical Repository,* vol. III, nos. ix–xii, pp. 707–21.
70. Franklin Edgerton, 'Sir William Jones', *JAOS,* vol. 76, p. 186. (Edgerton in this article also refuted the contention that Father Cœurdoux anticipated Jones in Comparative Philology. See his Additional Note No. 44 to this article.) See also Alfred Master, 'Jones and Panini', *JAOS,* vol. 76, p. 186.
71. Obviously, Jones's outlook would have been repudiated by many European intellectuals imbued with the idea of European superiority. Professor Dugald Stewart, for instance, used the basis of the similarity between Greek and Sanskrit to argue that Sanskrit was fabricated by the Brahmans within two generations after Alexander's invasion of India. To this H. H. Wilson gave a detailed reply which was published in *As. Jr.,* vol. XXVI, 1828, pp. 17–25.
72. *JAOS,* vol. I, p. 42.
73. M. B. Emeneau, 'India and Linguistics', *JAOS,* vol 75, p. 145.
74. *As. Res.,* vol. I, p.416.
75. *Friend of India,* vol. IX, 1853, pp. 22–3.
76. These meetings were held on 19 Jan., 2 Feb., 2 Nov. and 7 Dec. 1786.
77. William Jones, 'The Third Anniversary Discourse', *As. Res.,* vol. I, pp. 417–18.
78. William Jones, 'The Fourth Anniversary Discourse', *As. Res.,* vol. II, p. 3.
79. A. S. Altekar, 'The Silaharas of Western India', *Ind. Cul.,* vol. II (Jul. 1935–Apr. 1936), pp. 393–434.
80. For further information about Wilford see *The Annual Biography and Obituary,* vol. VIII, p. 471; and 'India and Comparative Philology', in *Cal. Rev.,* vol. 29, 1857, pp. 263–4. See also J. Collegins, 'Literary Characteristics of the Most Distinguished Members of the Asiatic Society', *AAR,* 1801, p. 114.
81. Wilford had identified this place correctly as Aurangabad.

82. The term 'failing' would be more apt for Wilford.
83. The *Proceedings* of the Society mention that the paper was communicated on 22 Nov. 1787 to the President by Henry Chickley Plowden. An article with this title appears in the second volume of the *Researches*, but this states that the paper was communicated by John Shore. However, I have presumed it is the same paper. If not, the first by Plowden must be considered as lost.
84. *As. Jr.*, vol. I, 1816, pp. 114–16, 222–5, 315–17.
85. 'Account of the Founder of the Buddhist Religion', *As. Jr.*, vol. XVI, 1823.
86. Edward Salisbury, 'Memoir on the History of Buddhism', *JAOS*, vol. I, 1851, p. 82.
87. *As. Res.*, vol. I, p. XV.
88. Cannon, *Letters*, vol. II, p. 770. See also Jones's letter to Sir Joseph Banks, ibid., p. 814.
89. *Cent. Rev.*, pt. I, p. 47.
90. Cannon, *Letters*, vol. II, p. 746. Mukherjee in his book on Sir William Jones (p. 85) stresses that the Society always received official support, adding that 'the Company also lent its press for publication of *Asiatic Researches* in 1788.' As we see, the press showed little enthusiasm over the publication while the printing of the *Researches* was taken up by Manuel Cantopher as a private venture.
91. *Cent. Rev.*, pt. I, pp. 47–8.
92. Cannon, *Letters*, vol. II, p. 828. Harington, Morris and Arthur Mair took over as Superintendents of the Company's Press in 1787, but how and why Manuel Cantopher transferred his interests in the *Researches* to Harington and Morris is not clear.
93. William Jones, 'The Fifth Anniversary Discourse', *As. Res.*, vol. II, p. 40.
94. If we do not take into account the period of the Indus Valley Civilization (which came to light nearly 150 years after Jones), Jones's estimate of India's historical age as beginning with the Vedic civilization is remarkably close to the date generally agreed upon by contemporary historians, i.e. between 2000–1500 B.C.
95. William Jones, 'On the Chronology of the Hindus', *As. Res.*, vol. II, p. 139.
96. Ibid., pp. 142–3.
97. Radhacanta Sarman, 'Inscriptions on the Staff of Firuz Shah', *As. Res.*, vol. I, p. 315.
97a. Surprisingly, none of these names are to be found in the genealogies of the Sakhambaris as given in standard publications on ancient India, e.g., R. C. Majumdar (ed.), *The History and Culture of the Indian People*, Bharatiya Vidya Bhavan, Bombay, 1980; vol. IV, *The Age of Imperial Kanauj*, 1964, pp. 525–6; and vol. V, *Struggle for Empire*, p. 856.
98. 'Extract of a letter from Alexander Davidson', *As. Res.*, vol. II, p. 332.
99. William Jones, 'The Sixth Discourse on the Persians', *As. Res.*, vol. II, pp. 51, 64.
100. Cannon, *Oriental Jones*, p. 159.
101. Teignmouth, *Memoirs*, p. 332.

102. For instance, see records of meetings held on 19 Jan. 1786 and 7 Feb. 1788.
103. William Jones, 'On the Antiquity of the Indian Zodiac', *As. Res.*, vol. II, pp. 289–306.
104. This letter, dated 23 Nov. 1740, was written by Père Pons to Père du Halde, and dealt seriatim with Sanskrit grammar, the dictionaries, treatises on versification and poetry, history, the Vedas, mathematics and philosophy of the ancient Indians. The *natacs* were mentioned as part of the historical literature of India. Durgaprasanna Roychaudhuri, *Sir William Jones and his Translation of Kalidasa's Sakuntala*, Calcutta, 1928, p. 71.
105. According to Garland Cannon, this was a Bengali recension, although in the preface Jones mentions that the manuscript copy was in Sanskrit. At the time, says Cannon, it was the only copy available and Jones had no idea that it was a diffuse, padded version. Cannon, *Oriental Jones*, p. 164.
106. 'Sacontala: or The Fatal Ring; an Indian Drama by Calidas, Translated from the Original Sanskrit and Pracrit', *Gent. Mag.*, vol. LX, p. 1014.
107. *Blackwood's*, vol. VI, 1820 (Oct. 1819–Mar. 1820), p. 417.
108. Cannon, *Letters*, vol. II, p. 894.
109. *Blackwood's*, vol. VI, p. 417.
110. *Quart. Rev.*, vol. XLV, 1831, p. 39.
111. Cannon, *Letters*, vol. II, p. 806.
112. This data is taken from the compilation made by Montgomery Schuyler Jr. See *JAOS*, vol. XXII, 1901 (Jul.–Dec.), pp. 237–48.
113. M. Monier-Williams, 'Preface to the Eighth Edition of Sakuntala', London, 1898.
114. Ibid., pp. xx–xxi.
115. G. Cannon, 'Sir William Jones and the Sakuntala', *JAOS*, vol. 73, 1953, p. 201.
116. Mukherjee, *Sir William Jones*, p. 121.
117. Jawaharlal Nehru, *The Discovery of India*, p. 317. In 1946, the Asiatic Society commemorated Jones's bicentenary by launching a scheme for a variorum edition of the play based on the recensions available in Bengali, Kashmiri, Devanagari, and the South Indian scripts. The plan, however, never materialised. Kshetreschandra Chattopadhyay, 'The Sakuntala Problem', *Sir William Jones Commemoration Volume*, Royal Asiatic Society of Bengal, Calcutta, 1948, p. 167.
118. Cannon, *William Jones, an Annotated Bibliography*, p. 47.
119. *PASOB*, 17 Jun. 1790.
120. *As. Res.*, vol. II, pp. 225–87.
121. Ibid., p. 401.
122. Cannon, *Letters*, vol. II, p. 646.
123. Ibid., pp. 759–60.
124. Ibid., Jones to Elizabeth Shipley, 7 Sept. 1786, p. 703.
125. Ibid., Jones to Walter Pollard, 14 Sept. 1789, p. 840.
126. Ibid., Jones to Wardley-Wilmot, 20 Sept. 1789, p. 848.
127. Reviewing the second volume of the *Researches*, the leading English

journal of the day, the *British Critic*, noted: 'Some copies of this second volume . . . arrived in England a considerable time ago; but as it is a work so peculiarly circumstanced in point of publication, so high in price, so little accessible to the generality of readers, and yet so very interesting in its contents that we venture, in this single instance, which cannot become a precedent, to deviate from our general determination, not to notice books that appeared before the present year and to gratify our friends with an account of its contents.' *The British Critic*, Jun. 1793, p. 117.

128. Jones to Henry Dundas, 23 Jan. 1791, in Cannon, *Letters*, vol. II, p. 880.
129. Ibid., Jones to Lady Spencer, 8 Oct. 1787, p. 784.
130. Ibid., Jones to Sir John Macpherson, 15 Oct. 1790, p. 875.
131. Ibid., Jones to the second Earl Spencer, 18 Aug. 1787, p. 751.
132. Ibid., Jones to John Eardley Wilmot, 20 Sept. 1789, p. 848.
133. Ibid., Jones to William Shipley, 5 Oct. 1782, p. 714.
134. Ibid., Jones to William Shipley, 27 Sept. 1788, p. 820.
135. *As. Res.*, vol. III, pp. 38–53. The dateline on Macleod's forwarding letter is Conjevaram, 7 Apr. 1791. This is probably an error, for Jones had presented the translation of the inscription at the Society's meeting on 13 Feb. 1791. Macleod's letter must, therefore, have been written in April 1790.
136. This date seems to be correct, for the period of Krishnadeva Raya's rule was 1509–29.
137. *As. Res.*, vol. III, p. 4.
138. Ibid., pp. 88–9.
139. Ibid., p. 183.
140. Jones to Lady Spencer, 24 Oct. 1791, Cannon, *Letters*, pp. 900–1.
141. Ibid., Jones to Samuel Davis, 20 Oct. 1792, p. 911.
142. The facts about Samuel Davis's life have been taken mainly from the article, 'Samuel Davis and the Domestic Thermopylae at Benares', in W. F. B. Laurie, *Sketches of Some Distinguished Anglo-Indians*, Allen, London, 1807–8.
143. Jones to Samuel Davis, 12 Feb. 1792, Cannon, *Letters*, vol. II, p. 907.
144. *PASOB*, 5 Jul., 16 Aug. and 8 Nov. 1792.
145. *As. Res.*, vol. III, p. 329.
146. Ibid., p. 467.
147. 'Account of Books', *AAR*, 1799, pp. 214 ff.
148. IOL., MSS. Eur.D.304 (Wilson Collection), folio 6.
149. These meetings were held on 28 Feb., 21 Mar., 11 Jul. and 11 Dec. 1793.
150. W. Robertson, *Historical Disquisition Concerning Ancient India*, Astraham & T. Condell, London, 1791, p. 196.
151. James Rennell, *Memoir of a Map of Hindostan*, Reprint, Calcutta, 1976, p. 49.
152. *As. Res.*, vol. IV, pp. 10–11.
153. William Francklin, *Inquiry Concerning the Site of Ancient Palibothra*, Black, London, 1815–20.
154. *As. Jr.*, vol. V, pp. 103–5. The numerous articles on the site of Pali-

bothra published in the *Asiatic Journal* in 1817 and 1818 show how alive the question was at the time.

155. Mukherjee, *Sir William Jones*, pp. 105–6.
156. *As. Res.*, vol. IV, p. 11.
157. Ibid., p. 7.
158. *Cent. Rev.*, pt. II, p. 86.
159. S. Roy, *The Story of Indian Archaeology*, Delhi, 1961, p. 14.
160. J. Beveridge, 'On the Study of Indian History', *Cal. Rev.*, vol. 87, 1888, p. 43.
161. *As. Res.*, vol. IV, p. 5.
162. Ibid., p. 169.
163. Ibid., p. 173.
164. The *Digest* unfortunately remained unpublished and was completed by Colebrooke in 1797.
165. Jones to the second Earl Spencer, 25 Sept. 1793–24 Nov. 1793, Cannon, *Letters*, vol. II, p. 921.
166. Ibid., Jones to the second Earl Spencer, 23 Aug. 1787, pp. 755–6.
167. 'This then is my rule', wrote Jones to the second Earl Spencer on 24 Aug. 1787, 'I hold every day lost, in which I acquire no new knowledge of man or nature.' Cannon, *Letters*, vol. II, p. 756.
168. Teignmouth, *Memoirs*, p. 336. (Teignmouth, however, mentions two decades).
169. Arberry, *Oriental Essays*, p. 76. Edward Said (*Orientalism*, Routledge & Kegan Paul, London, 1978, p. 77) seems less than fair when he remarks: 'Whereas Anquetil opened large vistas, Jones closed them down, codifying, tabulating, comparing.' This entire chapter amounts to a refutation of Said's contention, which is a part of his general critical view of western orientalists.
170. Jones's friend, Thomas Law, composed a poem on this to which Jones also replied in verse. The two poems are given below:

Sir William, you attempt, in vain,
By depth of reason to maintain,
That all men's talents are the same,
And they, not Nature, are to blame.
Whatever you say, whatever you write,
Proves your opponents in the right.
Lest genius should be ill-defined,
I term it *your superior mind*,
Hence to your friends 'tis plainly shewn,
You're ignorant of yourself alone.

Jones's Answer

Ah! but too well, dear friend, I know
My fancy weak, my reason slow,
My memory by art improv'd,
My mind by baseless trifles mov'd.
Give me (thus high my pride) I raise

The ploughman's or the gardener's praise,
With patient and unceasing toil,
To meliorate a stubborn soil.
And say (no higher need I ask)
With zeal hast thou perform'd thy task.
Praise, of which virtuous minds may boast,
They best confer, who merit most.

Teignmouth, Memoirs, pp. 384, 396.

171. Ibid., *Memoirs*, p. 400.
172. A. Chalmers, *The General Biographical Dictionary*, London, 1812–17, p. 128.
173. *Gent. Mag.*, vol. 71, pt. II, p. 64.
174. Teignmouth, *Memoirs*, vol. I, p. 207.
175. The briefest and perhaps the most apt tribute was paid by Jones's friend, Dr Samuel Parr, who said, 'It is happy for us that this man was born.' Teignmouth, *Memoirs*, p. 401.
176. T. E. Colebrooke, *Miscellaneous Essays of H. T. Colebrooke with the Life of the Author* (3 vols.) Trubner, London, 1873, p. 82. (The first volume deals with the life of H. T. Colebrooke.)

Chapter 3. H. T. COLEBROOKE AND THE SANSKRIT RENAISSANCE, 1794–1815

1. F. M. Max Müller, 'Biographical Essays', in *Collected Works*, vol. VI, Longmans, Green, London, 1910, p. 230.
2. L. Namier and J. Brodbe, *The History of Parliament: The House of Commons, 1754–90*, London, 1964, pp. 235–7; A. Natesan, *Eminent Orientalists*, Natesan & Co., Madras, 1922, p. 48.
3. T. E. Colebrooke, *The Life of H. T. Colebrooke*, Trubner, London, 1873, p. 21.
4. *DNB*, Article on H. T. Colebrooke.
5. 'Memoir of the Late Henry Thomas Colebrooke', *Friend of India*, vol. V, no. 223, 28 Mar. 1839.
6. Colebrooke, *Life*, pp. 27–8.
7. Ibid.
8. This was by no means a derogatory remark as has been suggested by David Kopf. (*British Orientalism and the Bengal Renaissance*, Firma KLM, Calcutta, 1969, p. 28).
9. Colebrooke, *Life*, pp. 27–8.
10. *PASOB*, 3 Apr. 1794.
11. Max Müller, *Chips from a German Workshop*, pp. 34–5.
12. H. H. Wilson, 'On the supposed Vaidic authority for the burning of Hindu Widows, and on the funeral of the Hindus', *JORAS*, vol. XVI, 1856, p. 201.
13. 'Remarks by Raja Radhakanta Deb on Article XI, *JORAS*, vol. XVI,

p. 201, with observations by Professor H. H. Wilson', *JORAS*, vol. XVII, pp. 209–20.

14. FitzEdward Hall, 'The source of Colebrooke's Essay "On the Duties of a faithful Widow"', *JORAS*, vol. III (n.s.), 1868, pp. 183–92; 196–8.
15. This quotation is from the supplement to the main Essay. An offprint of the essay and the supplement are bound in a volume of treatises in the Asutosh Collection, National Library, Calcutta. At the end of the essay, Sir Asutosh has written in his own hand the following, which must be regarded as a unique piece of information revealing why FitzEdward Hall found it necessary to add a supplement:

    Mr. FitzEdward Hall [writes Sir Asutosh] in giving me the copy of the paper published in the Jour. As. Soc. Vol. stated that whilst it was in the printers' hands, a proof was submitted to Prof. Max Müller, who prepared an answer to it wh. was to have appeared in the same No. of the Journal. Mr. Hall having heard of this, went to the printer and got a proof of Müller's paper, to wh. he wrote the reply contained in the "Supplement" and sent it to the Secy. As. Socy. stating how and why he had penned it. On this, he stated, Max Müller withdrew his answer altogether and the two notes of Dr Hall appeared in these [. . . words cut during binding of the volume].

16. Daniel Ingalls, 'On the study of the Past', *JAOS*, vol. 80, 1960, p. 193.
17. William Marsden, 'On the Traces of the Hindu Language and Literature extant amongst the Malays', *As. Res.*, vol. IV, p. 221.
18. James T. Blunt, 'A Description of the Cuttub Minar', *As. Res.*, vol. IV, p. 314.
19. Ibid.
20. See below, pp. 126–7.
21. Partha Mitter, *Much Maligned Monsters*, O.U.P., London, 1977, p. 35.
22. Lt. Col. Barry, 'Some short account of the Caves on the Elephanta Island near Bombay', *Gent. Mag.*, vol. LV, pt. 1, 1785, p. 414.
23. See the letter of J. Carnac to Sir John Shore, the Governor-General and President of the Society, forwarding Goldingham's article. *As. Res.*, vol. IV, p. 407.
24. Ibid.
25. J. Goldingham, 'Sculptures at Mahabalipoorum', *As. Res.*, vol. V, pp. 69–80.
26. See above, pp. 38–9.
27. Although Goldingham reproduced the inscriptions, it was a long time before they could be deciphered, and it be established that the sculptures belonged to the Pallava dynasty.
28. Charles Mallet, 'Description of the caves or Excavations, on the mountain, about a mile to the eastward of the town of Ellore, . . . or, as called on the spot, Verrool, though therein appears inaccuracy, as the foundation of the town is attributed to Yelloo, or Elloo rajah, whose capital is said to have been Ellichpore.' *As. Res.*, vol. VI, p. 386.
29. Jonathan Duncan, 'An Account of the Discovery of the two urns in the vicinity of Benaras', *As. Res.*, vol. IV, p. 132.
30. Francis Wilford, 'Essay VI of the two Tri-Cutadri, or the Mountain with

three Peaks', *As. Res.*, vol. X, p. 130.
31. H. T. Colebrooke, 'Enumeration of Indian Classes', *As. Res.*, vol. V, p. 64.
32. This request was not granted.
33. *PASOB*, 29 Sept. 1796.
34. These details about Hunter's life are based on the article in the *DNB*.
35. William Hunter, 'Some account of the astronomical labours of Jayasinha, Rajah of Ambhere, or Jayanagar', *As. Res.*, vol. V, pp. 177–211.
36. Francis Wilford, 'Chronology of the Hindus', *As. Res.*, vol. V, p. 241.
37. Ibid., pp. 262–83.
38. Ibid., p. 243.
39. 'Obituary of the late Mr. Bentley', *As. Jr.*, vol. XVIII, 1824, pp. 393–4.
40. John Bentley, 'Remarks on the Principal Eras and Dates of the Ancient Hindus', *As. Res.*, vol. V, p. 315.
41. *PASOB*, 31 May 1798.
42. J. Bentley, 'On the Antiquity of the *Surya Siddhanta*', *As. Res.*, vol. VI, p. 574.
43. Ibid., pp. 575–6.
44. 'Review of Asiatic Researches, vol. VI', *Ed. Rev.*, vol. I, 1814, p. 42.
45. J. Bentley, 'On the antiquity of the *Surya Siddhanta*', *The Annual Register for the year 1803*, London, 1804, 'Account of Books', p. 33.
46. *PASOB*, 4 Jul. 1804.
47. 'The Hindu system of Astronomy . . . in ancient and modern times. By J. Bentley, Esq', *Ed. Rev.*, vol. XII (Apr. 1808–Jul. 1808), pp. 41–3.
48. 'A Critique on the VIth and VIIth volumes of the Asiatic Researches', *Cl. Jr.*, vol. V, 1812, p. 239.
49. 'Hindu Astronomy. Mr. Colebrooke's reply to the attack of Mr. Bentley', *As. Jr.*, vol. XXI, 1826, p. 362.
50. Ibid.
51. 'Obituary of the late Mr. Bentley', *As. Jr.*, vol. XVIII, 1824, p. 393.
52. *Cent. Rev.*, pt. I, pp. 47–8.
53. Ibid.
54. *ASAM*, sl. no. 2, dt. 4 Jan. 1797.
55. Ibid., sl. no. 10, dt. 17 Aug. 1797.
56. *PASOB*, 3 May 1798.
57. Ibid.
58. *Cent. Rev.*, pt. I, p. 49. The proposal however did not take effect.
59. *ASAM*, sl. no. 110, dt. 20 Feb. 1798. It is interesting to note that later, the efforts of the Royal Asiatic Society of Great Britain and Ireland to get suitable accommodation alloted by the Government also bore no fruit. (See *PRASOGBI*, 28 Jun. 1828 and 26 Jul. 1828).
60. *PASOB*, 6 Dec. 1798.
61. *ASAM*, sl. no. 29, dt. 20 Jun. 1798.
62. Max Müller, 'Biographical Essays', *Collected Works*, vol. VI, p. 244.
63. Colebrooke, *Life*, p. 76.
64. Ibid., p. 86.
65. H. T. Colebrooke, 'On the Religious Ceremonies of the Hindus, and of

the Bramens especially', Essay II, *As. Res.*, vol. VII, p. 279.
66. Ibid., Essay III, p. 293.
67. '. . . Tribute to the memory of H. T. Colebrooke', *AEIM*, vol. 15, 1838, p. 377.
68. H. T. Colebrooke, 'Translation of one of the Inscriptions on the pillar at Dehlee, called the Lat of Feroz Shah, with Introductory Remarks by Mr. Harington', *As. Res.*, vol. VII, p. 175.
69. 'Review of Asiatic Researches, Vol. VII', *Ed. Rev.*, vol. IX, 1807, p. 284.
70. Shore's letter of resignation was presented at the Society's meeting of 2 Nov. 1797.
71. Robert Chambers, 'A Discourse delivered at a meeting of the Asiatic Society on the 18th of January 1798', *As. Res.*, vol. VI, p. 5.
72. *PASOB*, 18 Jan. 1798.
73. Ibid., 2 May 1799.
74. Ibid., 4 Jul. 1799.
75. H. T. Colebrooke, 'On the Sanskrit and Prakrit Languages', *As. Res.*, vol. VII, p. 231.
76. Colebrooke, *Life*, pp. 92–3.
77. Max Müller, 'Biographical Essays', in *Collected Works*, vol. VI, p. 244.
78. H. T. Colebrooke, 'On the Origin and Peculiar Tenets of certain Muhammadan Sects', *As. Res.*, vol. VII, p. 336.
79. Tribute to H. T. Colebrooke, *AEIM*, vol. 15, p. 377.
80. The article does not bear a page number and is found between pp. 444 and 445 of *As. Res.*, vol. VII.
81. Daniel Potts, *British Baptist Missionaries in India, 1793–1837*, Cambridge University Press, 1967.
82. F. Wrede, 'Account of the St. Thomé Christians on the coast of Malabar', *As. Res.*, vol. VII, p. 366.
83. Ibid., p. 368.
84. M. Joinville, 'On the Religion and Manners of the People of Ceylon', *As. Res.*, vol. VII, p. 397.
85. Ibid.
86. Ibid., p. 411.
87. Ibid., pp. 402–3.
88. Not much is known of Paterson's scholarly activities except for the two papers he presented to the Society. He was a servant of the East India Company whose name figures in one of the most controversial episodes in the impeachment of Warren Hastings. Paterson was asked by the Supreme Council to inquire into the causes of unrest in Rungpur and he reported that they had been provoked by extortionate demands on the peasantry, enforced by the use of torture. For his report, Burke praised Paterson as one who 'never tottered in his principles, nor swerved to the right or to the left from the noble cause of justice and humanity in which he had been engaged.' Paterson, however, regretted that his report had been misused against Hastings, for Hastings was never on the scene and had little to do with the causes of the unrest. See *The Correspondence of Edmund Burke*, ed. Holden Furber and P. J. Marshall, Cambridge University Press, 1965, pp. 372, 381, 386.

89. *PASOB*, 6 Apr. 1803. This paper was later published as 'Of the Origin of the Hindu Religion' in *As. Res.*, vol. VIII, pp. 44–87.
90. Ibid., p. 46.
91. Ibid., p. 56.
92. Ibid., pp. 61–2.
93. 'Review of Asiatic Researches, Vol. III', *Ed. Rev,*, vol. XII (Apr. 1808–Jul. 1808), p. 36.
94. H. T. Colebrooke, 'On the Vedas, or sacred writings of the Hindus', *As. Res.*, vol. VIII, p. 377.
95. See article on Colebrooke in *DNB*.
96. F. M. Max Müller, *My Autobiography*, Longmans, Green, London, 1901, p. 186.
97. Colebrooke, *Life*, p. 87.
98. Ibid., p. 139.
99. *As. Res.*, vol. VIII, p. 395.
100. Ibid., p. 378.
101. Ibid., p. 497.
102. W. Whitney, 'On the main results of the later Vedic Researches in Germany', *JAOS*, vol. III, 1853, p. 292.
103. Ibid.
104. 'Vedic India', *Cal. Rev.*, vol. 32, 1859, p. 401.
105. Colebrooke, *Life*, p. 217.
106. F. Wilford, 'An Essay on the sacred Isles in the West, with other Essays connected with that work', *As. Res.*, vol. VIII, p. 266.
107. Ibid., p. 248.
108. *As. Res.*, vol. XI, pp. 21–2.
109. Ibid., vol. VIII, p. 258.
110. *PASOB*, 15 May 1805.
111. Ibid., 3 Jul. 1805. It is not clear on what basis Rajendralala Mitra said that the plan was drawn up by Captain Lock of the Bengal Engineers (*Cent. Rev.*, pt. I, p. 21).
112. *ASAM*, Sl. No. 125, dt. 20 Sept. 1805. Pichon's letter may well be of interest to architects since it describes the plan, the building material and the estimates for construction on the basis of prices prevailing at the time.
113. Ibid., Sl. No. 128, dt. 26 Jan. 1808.
114. Ibid., Sl. No. 129, dt. 13 Apr. 1808.
115. *PASOB*, 2 Apr. 1806; *As. Res.*, vol. IX, pp. 454–69.
116. *As. Res.*, vol. IX, pp. 244–78.
117. F. Buchanan, 'Particulars of the Jains', *As. Res.*, vol. IX, pp. 279–86.
118. *As. Res.*, vol. IX, pp. 287–322.
119. Ibid., p. 284.
120. Ibid., p. 293.
121. Colebrooke, *Life*, p. 226.
122. Joshua Marshman's MSS Journal(fragment), 26 Jun. 1805, quoted in Mary Drewery, *William Carey*, London, 1978, p. 158.
123. *PASOB*, 3 Jul. 1805.
124. Ibid., 2 Apr. 1806.

125. 'The Ramayana of Valmeeki, translated from the Original Sungskrit, with explanatory notes. By William Carey and Joshua Marshman, *Quart. Rev.*, vol. III, no. 6, May 1810, p. 388.
126. *PASOB*, 7 Oct. 1807.
127. Ibid.
128. *PASOB*, 2 Nov. 1808.
129. Colebrooke, *Life*, p. 226.
130. *PASOB*, 1 Jul. 1807.
131. H. T. Colebrooke, 'On the Indian and Arabian Divisions of the Zodiac', *As. Res.*, vol. IX, p. 323.
132. Ibid.
133. Ibid., p. 324.
134. Colebrooke, *Life*, p. 233.
135. H. T. Colebrooke, 'On Ancient Monuments, containing Sanskrit Inscriptions', *As. Res.*, vol. IX, p. 398.
135a The name of Lokapala is not found in any of the known Pala inscriptions. This is most likely a misreading of the name.
136. *PASOB*, 6 Apr. 1808.
137. *Cent. Rev.*, pt. 1, p. 24.
138. See article on John Malcolm in *DNB*.
139. John Malcolm, 'Translations of two letters of Nadir Shah, with introductory observations in a letter to the President', *As. Res.*, vol. X, pp. 526–47.
140. John Malcolm, 'Sketch of the Sikhs', *As. Res.*, vol. XI, pp. 197–292, see p. 197.
141. The Society archives contain a document which shows that Ward's paper on the Sikhs was referred to the Committee of Papers for their opinion on whether it should be published in the *Researches*, which it was not. *ASAM*, Sl. No. 231, dt. 28 Jun. 1810.
142. Edward Strachey, who had come to India as a writer in 1793, rose to be a judge and was also employed in the diplomatic service. Mountstuart Elphinstone, a close friend of Strachey's, said that in his early years he was much influenced by Strachey's example. On his return to England in 1811, Strachey became an examiner at the India House and here he developed a lasting friendship with Thomas Carlyle. Strachey had mastered Persian and in 1813 translated the *Bija Ganita* into English from a Persian version of this work.
143. Reuben Burrow, 'A Proof that the Hindoos had the Binomial Theorem', *As. Res.*, vol. II, p. 494.
144. Ibid., pp. 488–9.
145. Colebrooke, *Life*, p. 53.
146. Edward Strachey, 'On the early history of Algebra', *As. Res.*, vol. XII, p. 164.
147. 'Letters to the Editor', *As. Jr.*, vol. VI, 1818, p. 239.
148. Ibid., p. 590.
149. *PASOB*, 7 Feb. 1810.
150. W. Price, 'Translation of a Sanskrit Inscription on a stone found in Bundelkhand', *As. Res.*, vol. XII, p. 360.

151. Ibid., p. 361.
152. *Cent. Rev.*, pt. II, pp. 124–5.
153. *PASOB*, 2 Feb. 1814.
154. Ibid.
155. *PASOB*, 1 Feb. 1815.
156. Ibid., 7 Jun. 1815.
157. Max Müller, *Biographical Essays*, p. 256.

Chapter 4. H. H. WILSON AND THE EXPANDING FRONTIERS OF HISTORICAL SCHOLARSHIP 1815–1832

1. The *Cent. Rev.* mistakenly gives Wilson's year of birth as 1784 (pt. I, p. 78).
2. The voyage took about six months, as there was an accident on the way.
3. John Leyden was one of the greatest Orientalists and linguists of the day. William Erskine, who completed the *Commentaries of Babar* started by Leyden, felt that in eight years, Leyden had done as much for Asia as the combined scholarship of centuries had done for Europe. His work on the Indo-Persian, Indo-Chinese and Deccani languages seemed to justify Leyden's own remark that he could excel Sir William Jones in his own particular sphere. *DNB*, article on John Leyden.
4. Natesan, *Eminent Orientalists* pp. 65–6.
5. Arberry, *British Orientalists*, pp. 65–6.
6. 'Review of the Megha Dutt or Cloud Messenger', *As. Jr.*, vol. I, 1816, p. 257.
7. *Cl. Jr.*, vol. XII, 1815, p. 436.
8. One of Wilson's characteristic footnotes reads: 'I may perhaps come under the denunciation of those who according to the illiberal and arrogant criticism of such a writer as a Mr. Pinkerton prove, "That the climate of India, while it inflames the imagination, impairs the judgement." Standing in very little awe of such a poetical censor, I advance an opinion, that we have few specimens either in classical or modern poetry, of more genuine tenderness or delicate feeling.' (Wilson, *Megha Dutt or Cloud Messenger*, College of Fort William, Calcutta, 1813, p. 86 fn).
9. *As. Jr.*, vol. I, 1816, p. 260.
10. Kopf, *British Orientalism*, p. 168.
11. See Wilson's letter to the selection board of the Boden Chair of Sanskrit, in which Wilson put forward his qualifications for the post (*As. Jr.*, vol. VII, 1832, pp. 24–45). There seems to be absolutely no grounds for the allegation that Wilson based his work on Colebrooke's *Dictionary* (Gerald and Natalie Sirkin, 'Of Raising Myths for Fun and Profit', *Columbia Forum*, vol. II, no. 3, 1968). Wilson's work was of a totally different nature. While Colebrooke's work was for accomplished scholars, Wilson's was directed towards those who wished to learn Sanskrit, one reason why his work was patronised by the Court of Directors.

12. *PASOB*, 7 Jun. 1816.
13. Ibid., 9 Feb. 1816.
14. IOL, MSS. Eur. D. 457/B.
15. R. C. Majumdar, 'Greater India', in K. S. Ramachandran and S. P. Gupta (ed.), *India and South East Asia*, B. R., Delhi, 1979, pp. 1–2.
16. R. C. Majumdar, *Ancient Indian Colonization in South East Asia*, The Maharaja Sayajirao Gaekwad Honorarium Lecture, 1953–54, Baroda Oriental Institute, 1955.
17. J. Crawfurd, 'On the Existence of the Hindu Religion in the Island of Bali', *As. Res.*, vol. XIII, p. 128.
18. Ibid.
19. Ibid., p. 148.
20. Ibid., p. 151.
21. Jean Filliozat, 'Greater Indian Studies', *AIOC*, vol. XX, 1959, p. 238.
22. *As. Res.*, vol. XVIII, pp. 337–68. This paper was presented to the Society on 12 Apr. 1817.
23. Ibid., p. 347.
24. *PASOB*, 11 Oct. 1816.
25. Ibid., 5 Feb. 1817.
26. Although the Batavian Society of Arts and Sciences was founded earlier (24 Apr. 1778), it was very short-lived and contributed little towards knowledge of the history and culture of the region.
27. *PASOB*, 12 Apr. 1817.
28. Ibid., 3 Dec. 1817.
29. *As. Res.*, vol. XIV, p. 1.
30. *PASOB*, 3 Jun. 1818.
31. Ibid., 1 Apr. 1818.
32. Kopf, *British Orientalism*, p. 171.
33. Hastings' seriousness towards the Society's meetings is reflected in a letter of 20 June 1822 which he addressed to Wilson, saying: 'I know not how to apologise sufficiently for my forgetfulness. In utter oblivion that this was the night for the Asiatic Society, I had invited company to a great dinner; and it is but this instant that General Hardwicke has made me sensible of my mistake.' (IOL, MSS Eur.301/E, vol. I, Wilson's Correspondence, folio 89).
34. *PASOB*, 10 Mar. 1820.
35. *As. Res.*, vol. XIII, pp. 433–55.
36. Ibid., p. 441.
37. J. Mill, *The History of British India*, ed. H. H. Wilson, James Madden, London, 1840–6, Preface of the Editor, pp. vii–viii.
38. See above, pp. 43–4.
39. *PASOB*, 12 Feb. 1819.
40. Ibid., 13 Dec. 1819.
41. Ibid., 17 Jun. 1820.
42. Ibid., 8 Jan. 1820.
43. Ibid., 17 Jun. 1820.
44. The Society's Proceedings mention that the inscription was read and translated into English by Captain Price, but again, neither the transla-

Notes

257

tion nor the original inscription was preserved.

45. *As. Res.*, vol. XIV, pp. 480–1.
46. *PASOB*, 14 Jul. 1821; *As. Res.*, vol. XIV, pp. 1–119. Kalhana's work remains the most important single source for the early history of Kashmir and all subsequent writers have depended heavily on it. In 1957 when Sunil Chandra Ray published his *Early History and Culture of Kashmir*, the reviewer Stanley Wolpert remarked, 'The author relies so heavily, in fact, on the classic twelfth century chronicle . . . that the greater portion of this book is virtually a commentary on the earlier chronicle.' *JAOS*, vol. 80, 1960, p. 264.
47. *Rajatarangini*, tr. R. S. Pandit, Sahitya Akademi, New Delhi, 1968, p. xiii.
48. M. A. Stein, *Kalhana's Rajatarangini*, vol. I, Constable, London, 1900, reprint Motilal Banarasidass, Delhi, 1979, p. viii.
49. *As. Res.*, vol. XV, pp. 2–5.
50. Ibid., p. 1.
51. Stein, *Kalhana's Rajatarangini*, pp. vii–viii.
52. R. C. Majumdar, 'Ideas of History in Sanskrit Literature', in Philips (ed.), *Historians of India*, p. 25.
53. A. L. Basham, 'The Kashmir Chronicle', in Philips (ed.), *Historians of India*, p. 58.
54. *PASOB*, 19 Dec. 1832.
55. Stein, *Kalhana's Rajatarangini*, vol. I, p. viii.
56. *PASOB*, 12 Nov. 1823.
57. Troyer to Wilson, letter dt. 10 Sept. 1840.(IOL, Wilson Correspondence, vol. V, folios 140–1).
58. Stein, *Kalhana's Rajatarangini*, vol. I, p. xi.
59. The entire episode of how Stein was able to procure the *codex archetypus* of the *Rajatarangini*, which was copied by Ratnakanta sometime in the seventeenth century makes fascinating reading. The manuscript was in the possession of a Pandit Kesavaram, who allowed Stein to have no more than a glimpse of the manuscript and absolutely refused to part with it. When Kesavaram died, his three heirs divided the *codex archetypus* among themselves. They too were as reluctant as Kesavaram to part with the manuscript and yielded only after the intervention of Pandit Suraj Kaul, Member of the Kashmir State Council. On receiving all the three portions, Stein collated them and prepared the complete text. (See 'Prospectus of a new edition of Kalhana's Rajatarangini' by M. A. Stein. The Prospectus is preserved as a tract in the Asutosh Collection of the National Library, Calcutta).
60. At about this time another edition of the *Rajatarangini* was published in Bombay by Pandit Durga Prasad. Sir Aurel Stein referred to this work in the 'introduction' to his own translation saying: 'The Pandit's edition contains a considerable number of useful new emendations. . . To the scholarly merits of his work I may hence be allowed to render here a well-deserved tribute.' See R. S. Pandit (trans.), *Rajatarangini*, Sahitya Akademi, Delhi, 1968, pp. xix–xx.
61. H. H. Wilson, 'A Sketch of the Religious Sects of the Hindus', in *Essays*

and *Lectures on the Religions of the Hindus*, ed. Reinhold Rost, London, 1862, vol. I, pp. 7–8.

62. Natesan, *Eminent Orientalists*, p. 76.

63. 'The Boden Professorship of Sanskrit at Oxford', *As. Jr.*, vol. VII, 1832, p. 242.

64. Wilson, 'The Religious Sects of the Hindus', p. 13.

65. Ibid., p. 369.

66. *PASOB*, 13 Apr. 1821; *As. Res.*, vol. XIV, pp. 373–470.

67. *As. Res.*, vol. XIV, p. 459.

68. *PASOB*, 13 Dec. 1821.

69. 'Biographical Memoir of Colonel Mackenzie, C. B., Late Surveyor General of India', *As. Jr.*, vol. XII, 1821, p. 537.

70. *DNB*, article on Colin Mackenzie.

71. Mackenzie's letter to Sir Alexander Johnstone, dated 1 Feb. 1817, repr. *As. Jr.*, vol. XIII, 1822, p. 242.

72. 'The Mackenzie Collection', *As. Jr.*, vol. XXVII, 1829, p. 130; 'Literary and Antiquarian Collections of the Late Colonel Mackenzie', in *John Bull*, repr. *As. Jr.*, vol. XVI, 1823, pp. 137–8.

73. Mackenzie's letter to Johnstone, *As. Jr.*, vol. XXVII, 1829, p. 242.

74. *PASOB*, 14 Jul. 1821; 19 Oct. 1821.

75. Ibid., 7 Sept. 1836; NAI, Home Pub., 21 Sept. 1836, Nos. 6 and 8.

76. Nilakanta Sastri, well-known historian of South India, makes a curious remark in his book, *A History of South India* (O.U.P., Madras, 1976, p. 21) while surveying the sources of the history of the region. 'The semi-historical works', he says, 'produced at the beginning of the nineteenth century to the orders of Col. Colin Mackenzie do not concern us as they deal with recent events outside the scope of this book.' Mackenzie never ordered any work to be produced. He employed people mainly for the task of collecting antiquities and manuscripts, and later for translation. It is also difficult to say what Sastri means by 'semi-historical works'.

Secondly, it is still stranger that Sastri referred to Mackenzie's work as dealing with 'recent events'. It was the Mackenzie collection which first yielded the names of several dynasties of ancient India including the Rastrakutas, the Cheras, the Pandyas. Cunningham pays a rich tribute to Mackenzie for having collected material which went a long way in the reconstruction of ancient Indian history (*ASIR*, vol. I, Introduction).

77. *As. Jr.*, vol. VII (n.s.), 1832, p. 242.

78. *Blackwood's Edinburgh Magazine*, vol. XXXIV, Nov. 1833, pp. 715–38.

79. *PASOB*, 26 Dec. 1822. Surprisingly, this paper was not published in *Asiatic Researches*.

80. 'Sanskrit Poetry and Hindu Drama', *Quart. Rev.*, vol. XLV, 1831, p. 39.

81. *Blackwood's*, vol. XXXIV, p. 716.

82. The English version of the article together with Wilson's comments were presented at the Society's meeting of 19 October 1821. The communication was, however, neither reproduced in the records of Proceedings nor published in the *Researches*. It was published in *As. Jr.*, vol. XIV, 1822, pp. 37–40.

83. *PASOB*, 26 Dec. 1822.

84. *As. Jr.*, vol. XIV, 1822, pp. 37–40.
85. In its meeting of 20 June 1822 the Society conferred honorary membership on Professors Ramussen and Oersted of Copenhagen and at its meeting of 12 April on Professor Augustus von Schlegel himself.
86. *Quart. Rev.*, vol. XLV, 1831, pp. 1–2.
87. For example, in the Society's meeting of 7 August 1816, the Marquess of Hastings communicated Fraser's journal of a tour to the sources of the Yamuna, the Sutlej and the Ganga; on 7 December 1816 he presented specimens of mineralogy and botany of the Himalaya; on 12 April 1817, an account of the ruins of Prambanan with illustrative drawings, and on 10 August 1818 he communicated Captain Hodgson's report of the Survey to the heads of the rivers Ganga and the Yamuna. Hastings' interest in the Society's proceedings is again evident from the fact that at the meeting of 12 February 1819 he himself recommended W. B. Bayley and Colonel Hardwicke for the office of Vice-President.
88. *PASOB*, 26 Dec. 1822.
89. Ibid.
90. 'Review of the private journal of the Marquess of Hastings . . . edited by his daughter, the Marchioness of Bute', *Cal. Rev.*, vol. 31, 1858, p. xxxvii.
91. *PASOB*, 6 Feb. 1822.
92. A. Stirling, 'An account, geographical, statistical and historical, of Orissa proper or Cuttack', *As. Res.*, vol. XV, p. 257.
93. *Cent. Rev.*, pt. II, p. 66.
94. The Society was granted a Charter of Incorporation from George IV in August 1824.
95. 'Review of the *Transactions of the Royal Asiatic Society of Great Britain and Ireland*, vol. I, pt. I, London, 1824', *As. Jr.*, vol. XIX, 1825, p. 40.
96. 'The Royal Asiatic Society of London', *Or. Herald*, vol. IV, 1825 (Jan.–Mar.), p. 179.
97. *PRASOGBI*, 9 Jan. 1823.
98. The words 'and Ireland' were added at the meeting of 8 March.
99. 'Obituary of Captain Fell', *As. Jr.*, vol. 18, 1824, p. 265.
100. E. Fell to Wilson, letter dt. 3 May 1823. IOL, Wilson Correspondence, vol. I, 1812–31, folios 110–11).
101. 'Obituary of Captain Fell', *As. Jr.*
102. 'Sanskrit Inscriptions by (the late) Captain E. Fell, with observations by H. H. Wilson', *As. Res.*, vol. XX, p. 436.
103. Ibid., p. 460. Possibly the river Varuna which meets the Ganga at Rajghat in Banaras.
104. IOL, Wilson Correspondence, vol. I, folios 95–6.
105. *PASOB*, 5 May 1824.
106. Ibid., 6 Sept. 1824.
107. H. H. Wilson, 'Essays on the Puranas', *JORAS*, vol. V, 1839, pp. 62–4.
108. 'Review of the Vishnu Purana', *Cal. Rev.*, vol. III, 1845, p. lxi.
109. *JORAS*, vol. V, pp. 62–4.
110. 'Review of Ancient Historical Tradition by F. E. Pargiter', *JAOS*, vol. 43, 1923, p. 132

111. *PASOB*, 7 Sept. 1825.
112. *ASAM*, sl. no. 543, dt. 4 Aug. 1825.
113. Moorcroft was on his way back from Bukhara in August when he separated from his party to visit Maimama. On the way, he was waylaid by robbers and died soon after, according to some, of fever, while others suspect he was poisoned. His body was brought by camel to Balkh and he was buried outside the city's walls.
114. The paper was unfortunately neither preserved nor published in the Society's *Journal*.
115. H. G. Rawlinson, 'A Forgotten Hero. Some notes on the life and work of Csoma de Körös, traveller and scholar (1784–1842)', *AIOC*, vol. V, 1928, p. 319.
116. Ibid., p. 321.
117. *ASAM*, sl. no. 150. (The description on the file cover is incorrect. The letter dated Subathoo, 21 January 1829 is from Dr Gerard to Fraser.)
118. J. Mirsky, *Aurel Stein*, Chicago, 1977, p. 21.
119. *PASOB*, 4 Jan. 1826; and 1 Mar. 1826.
120. Ibid., 5 Jul. 1826. The letter is dated 29 April 1826.
121. Ibid. The letter is dated 11 May 1826.
122. Ibid.
123. Ibid., 3 Jan. 1827.
124. See the note preceding the Society's *Proceedings*, 4 Jul. 1827.
125. *PASOB*, 2 Jan. 1828.
126. Ibid., 3 Sept. 1828.
127. Sarat Chandra Mitra, 'Biographical sketches of Indian Antiquarians: Bhau Daji', *Cal. Rev.*, vol. 94, 1892, pp. 10–11.
128. W. Jones, 'A Discourse on the Institution of a Society', *As. Res.*, vol. I, p. xv.
129. *PRASOGBI*, 26 Apr. 1823; 13 Feb. 1824; 27 Feb. 1824; 9 Apr. 1824; 21 Jan. 1826.
130. *PASOB*, 7 Mar. 1832.
131. 'Review of Savitri Satyawan Natak, a comedy', by Kali Prosono Singh, Member of the Asiatic and Agricultural and Horticultural Societies of India, and of the British Indian Association, and President of the Bedoyth Sahivi Sabha of Calcutta, etc. etc. *Cal. Rev.*, vol. 32, 1859 (Jan.–June), p. xix.
132. *PASOB*, 1 Jul. 1829.
133. *PRASOGBI*, 4 Oct. 1827; 12 Nov. 1827.
134. *As. Jr.*, vol. XII (n.s.), 1833 (Sept.–Dec.), p. 1.
135. *PRASOGBI*, 20 May 1826.
136. Ibid., 25 Oct. 1828.
137. *PASOB*, 6 Jan. 1830.
138. Ibid., 5 May 1830.
139. Ibid.
140. Ibid., 7 Jul. 1830.
141. Ibid., 3 Nov. 1830.
142. H. H. Wilson, 'Remarks on the portion of the Dionysiacs of Nonnus relating to the Indians', *As. Res.*, vol. XVII, p. 607.

143. F. Wilford, 'An Essay on the Sacred Isles of the West', *As. Res.*, vol. IX, pp. 93–4.
144. *PASOB*, 7 Sept. 1831.
145. Ibid., 7 Jul. and 3 Nov. 1830; 9 Mar. and 6 Jul. 1831.
146. Quoted in *AEIM*, vol. IV, 1832, p. 280.
147. *PASOB*, 12 Dec. 1832.
148. Surprisingly, not much is known about Joseph Boden, the founder of the eponymous Chair at the University of Oxford, which became the most prestigious Chair of Sanskrit in the world. Boden started his career in India as a lieutenant in the Bombay native infantry and held successively the offices of Judge-advocate, aide-de-camp to the Governor, quartermaster-general, and member of the military board at Bombay. He died in 1811, and on the death of his 19-year old daughter in 1827, his residuary property, valued at about £ 25,000, passed on to the University of Oxford. According to his will, the money was 'towards the erection and endorsement of a professorship in the Sanskrit language.' There seems to be no evidence that Boden himself was an author or a scholar of Sanskrit. His offer was accepted by the University in 1827 and the first election to the Boden Chair took place in 1832.
149. *PASOB*, 19 Dec. 1832.
150. This address follows the Proceedings of 19 December 1832.
151. F. M. Max Müller, *On Ancient Hindu Astronomy and Chronology*, Oxford, 1862, p. 73.
152. *JORAS*, vol. 18, 1861, p. v.

Chapter 5. JAMES PRINSEP AND THE PERIOD OF GREAT DISCOVERIES 1832–1838

1. 'Review of Jacquemont's Travels in India', *Cal. Rev.*, vol. IV, 1845 (Jul.–Dec.), p. lxix.
2. H. T. Prinsep, 'Memoirs of the Author', in *Essays on Indian Antiquities*, ed. James Prinsep, John Murray, London, 1858, p. ii.
3. *As. Res.*, vol. xvii, pp. 470–98.
4. Prinsep, *Memoirs*, p. xvii.
5. *PASOB*, 7 Mar. 1832.
6. A. Cunningham, *ASIR*, vol. I, pp. xviii–xix.
7. *JASOB*, vol. I, p. 392.
8. *PASOB*, 9 Jan. 1833. The amount is given in terms of rupees, annas and paise, now replaced by rupees and paise. In the earlier system, 4 paise made one anna and 16 annas, one rupee.
9. James Prinsep, 'On the Greek coins in the cabinet of the Asiatic Society', *JASOB*, vol. I, p. 27.
10. J. W. Kaye, *Lives of Indian Officers*, Vol. II, J. J. Keliher, London, 1904, p. 20.
11. *Cent. Rev.*, pt. II, p. 92.
12. *JASOB*, vol. II, p. 29.

13. H. H. Wilson, *Ariana Antiqua*, Reprint, Oriental Publishers, Delhi 1971, p. 10.
14. James Prinsep, 'On the Greek Coins', *JASOB*, vol. I, p. 27.
15. *As. Jr.*, vol. XVII (n.s.), 1835, p. 9.
16. J. C. Marshman, *The History of India* (3 vols.), Longmans, Green London, 1867, vol. III, p. 64.
17. *PASOB*, 2 Dec. 1833.
18. Ibid., 27 Mar. 1833.
19. Ibid., 26 Jun. 1833.
20. Ibid., 30 Jan. 1834.
21. J. Prinsep, 'Note on Inscription No. 1 of the Allahabad Column' *JASOB*, vol. III, 1834, p. 114.
22. A. Cunningham, *ASIR*, vol. I, p. 300.
23. J. Prinsep, 'Note on . . .the Allahabad Column', *JASOB*, vol. III, p. 115
24. A. Troyer, 'Remarks upon the second inscription of the Allahabad Pillar', *JASOB*, vol. III, pp. 119–20.
25. Ibid.
26. Ibid.
27. W. H. Mill, 'Restoration of the Inscription No. 2 on the Allahabad Column', *JASOB*, vol. III, p. 267. The ascription of these dynasties to solar or lunar lines is not tenable now.
28. W. H. Mill, 'Supplement to the Historical Remarks on the Allahabad Inscription, No. 2', *JASOB*, vol. III, p. 344.
29. J. Prinsep, 'Note on Inscription No. 1 of the Allahabad Column', *JASOB*, vol. III, p. 116.
30. Ibid., p. 117.
31. B. H. Hodgson, 'Notice of some ancient Inscriptions in the characters of the Allahabad Column', *JASOB*, vol. III, pp. 481–2.
32. For a detailed description of the pillar, see *Corpus Inscriptionum Indicarum*, Indological Book House, Varanasi, 1961, vol. I, pp. 41–2.
33. J. Prinsep, 'Note on the Mathiah Lat Inscription', *JASOB*, vol. III, p. 484.
34. J. Stevenson, 'Restoration and Translation of some inscriptions at the caves of Carli', *JASOB*, vol. III, p. 495.
35. Wilson, *Ariana Antiqua*, p. 16.
36. P. T. Cautley, 'Further account of the remains of an ancient town discovered at Behat, near Saharanpur', *JASOB*, vol. III, pp. 223–4.
36a The gold coin of Ghatotkacha attributed to the second king of the Gupta dynasty actually is an issue of a son of Kumaragupta I.
37. *PASOB*, 28 May 1833.
38. The account of Masson's life is based on the material given in *As. Jr.*, vol. XXXIV, 1841 (Jan.–Apr.), pp. 23–4.
39. C. Masson, *Narrative of Various Journeys* (3 vols.), reprint, O.U.P., Karachi, 1975, vol. III, pp. 141–2.
40. Wilson, *Ariana Antiqua*, p. 1.
41. C. Masson, 'Memoir on the ancient coins found at Beghram, in the Kohistan of Kabul', *JASOB*, vol. III, p. 153.
42. Reproduced in *JASOB*, vol. II, p. 315.

42a Actually there was only one king of this name.
43. The sketch of General Ventura's life is based on material given in *As. Jr.*, vol. XI (n.s.), 1833 (May–Aug.), pp. 212–13; vol. XIII (n.s.), 1834 (May–Aug.), p. 82; vol. XIV (n.s.), 1834 (May–Aug.), p. 169.
44. Cunningham's remark on the use of the word *tope* is relevant: '*Stupa* is the Sanskrit term for a mound or barrow, either of masonry or of earth. The Pali form is *Thupi*, and also *Thupa*, and even *Thuva* in the early inscriptions from the Punjab. The term now used, i.e. *Thup* is applied to a much ruined barrow. It is, therefore, much to be regretted that we should have adopted the word *Tope*, which preserves neither the spelling nor the pronounciation of the true name.' (A. Cunningham, *ASIR*, vol. II, p. 159.
45. M. Elphinstone, *An Account of the Kingdom of Cabul*, Richard Bentley, London, 1839, pp. 78–80.
46. A. Court, 'Further information on the *Topes* of Manikyala', *JASOB*, vol. III, p. 558
47. Wilson, *Ariana Antiqua*, p. 13.
48. F. R. Allchin, 'The Taxila Evidence', in *Papers on the Date of Kanishka*, ed. A. L. Basham, London, p. 26.
49. Walton Dobbins, in 1971 ('The Stupa and Vihara of Kanishka') felt that the issue of Kanishka's reign had finally been settled through radiocarbon dating of a piece of charcoal from a house supposed to have been burnt down during Kanishka's reign, conducted by Prof. Dani of Pakistan. According to these tests, the year A.D. 78 marked the beginning of Kanishka's reign. But Dobbins seems to have overlooked Prof. Basham's note when Dr Dani's communication was presented at the conference on Kanishka's dates. 'This evidence is not absolutely conclusive', remarked Prof. Basham, 'since the dates refer to the cutting of the trees from which the charred wood was sown, and not to the actual burning of the timber.' A. L. Basham, *Papers*, at the *Conference on the date of Kanishka*, p. 436.
50. P. C. Mitra, *Life of Dewan Ram Comul Sen*, I. C. Bose, Calcutta, 1880, p. 16.
51. The Archives of the Asiatic Society possess many letters from eminent persons and institutions of different countries praising Csoma's achievement.
52. Both works remain unpublished.
53. J. Prinsep, 'Preface', *JASOB*, vol. IV, p. v.
54. *PASOB*, 6 May 1835. There were nine manuscripts in press at various stages of printing. Five of these were in Sanskrit: the *Mahabharata*, the *Rajatarangini*, the *Naishada*, the *Susruta*, and the *Sarira Vidya*. Four were Arabic works: the *Khaznat al Ilm*, the *Inaya*, a treatise on algebra by Dr Mill and the *Fatwa e Alamgiri*, the sole exception on which work was allowed to progress.
55. *PASOB*, 1 Jul. 1835.
56. *Friend of India*, 9 Jul. 1835.
57. *Ind. Rev.*, vol. I, 1837, p. 33.
58. *As. Jr.*, vol. XVIII (n.s.), 1835, p. 239.

59. *AEIM*, vol. XI, 1836, p. 78.
60. See the balance sheet given in *PASOB*, 14 Jan. 1835, reproduced in *JASOB*, vol. IV, p. 407.
61. J. Prinsep, 'Preface', *JASOB*, vol. IV, p. vii.
62. *PASOB*, 11 Mar. 1835.
63. *JASOB*, vol. IV, pp. 124-5.
64. J. Prinsep, 'Further Particulars of the Sarun and Tirhut Laths', *JASOB*, vol. IV, p. 128.
65. Ibid.
66. Stephenson's paper was presented to the Society on 14 Jan. 1835 (*PASOB*) and published in *JASOB*, vol. IV, pp. 128-38.
67. *JASOB*, vol. IV, p. 132.
68. Ibid., pp. 135-6.
69. B. H. Hodgson, 'Further note on the Inscription from Sarnath', *JASOB*, vol. IV, p. 211.
70. J. Prinsep, 'On the Connection of various Hindu coins with the Grecian or Indo-Scythic Series', *JASOB*, vol. IV, p. 622.
71. *PASOB*, vol. IV, pp. 327-48.
72. Ibid., pp. 328-9.
73. Ibid., pp. 621-43.
74. Ibid., pp. 668-90.
75. *JASOB*, vol. IV.
76. *JORAS*, vol. II, pp. 378-9.
77. Ibid., vols. II, III, IV and V (see relevant articles).
78. *Cent. Rev.*, pt. II, p. 114.
79. These seven names were based on the first inscription, the following on the second one (Wathen's note).
80. This name is a repetition and probably an error. If so, the genealogy would consist of seventeen names, and not sixteen, as mentioned by the author of the *Cent. Rev.*, pt. II, p. 111.
81. *JASOB*, vol. IV, pp. 361-6.
82. A facsimile of the same inscription had been forwarded earlier to the Society by G. E. Rankin. This copy, however, was so mutilated in transit that it became completely illegible (*PASOB*, 11 Mar. 1835).
83. *PASOB*, 5 Aug. 1835.
84. According to Dr Mill: 'None of its six names are to be found elsewhere, in any published monument within my knowledge' (*JASOB*, vol. IV, p. 390).
85. R. C. Majumdar (ed.), *History and Culture of the Indian People: The Age of Imperial Kanauj*, Bharatiya Vidya Bhavan, Bombay, pp. 525-6.
86. H. C. Ray, *DHNI*, pp. 1060-93.
87. *PASOB*, 4 May 1836.
88. Ibid., 4 Jan. 1837.
89. Ibid.; also *JASOB*, vol. V, pp. 833-4.
90. NAI. Home Pub., 20 Jul. 1836, No. 15.
91. *PASOB*, 3 Aug. 1836.
92. Ibid., 7 Sept. 1836.
93. Ibid., 7 Dec. 1836.

94. Wilson in *Ariana Antiqua* gives the grounds on which this theory was not tenable.
95. *JASOB*, vol. V, pp. 537–47.
96. Ibid., pp. 548–54, 720–4.
97. W. W. Hunter, *Life of Brian Houghton Hodgson*, John Murray, London, 1896, p. 1.
98. Letter to Nathaniel Wallich, quoted in Hodgson's *Literature and Religion of the Buddhists*, pp. 49–50.
99. The Asiatic Society of Bengal received the oldest manuscript of the lot. This was the *Prajna Paraamita Ashtasahasrika*, dating to A.D. 1071. The entry against no. A15 in Rajendralala Mitra's catalogue assigning the date A.D. 1231 to this work is obviously an error. Hunter, *Life of Brian Houghton Hodgson*, p. 266.
100. Ibid., p. 267.
101. For other tributes, see Hunter's *Life*, pp. 276–8.
102. B. H. Hodgson, 'Quotations from original Sanskrit authorities in proof and illustration of Mr. Hodgson's sketch of Buddhism', *JASOB*, vol. V, pp. 71–96.
103. *As. Res.*, vol. XX, pp. 41–93. The Kahgyur, as Körös tells us, was 'the great compilation of the Tibetan sacred books in one hundred volumes'.
104. *As. Res.*, vol. XX, pp. 285–317.
105. *JASOB*, vol. V, pp. 377–82.
106. Ibid. See Prinsep's note on *JASOB*, vol. V, p. 377.
107. R. C. Majumdar (ed.), *The History and Culture of the Indian People*, vol. III, *The Classical Age*, 1970, pp. 66–72, p. 853.
108. *JASOB*, vol. V, pp. 685–8.
109. For a detailed discussion of this issue, see Wilson's *Ariana Antiqua*, pp. 408–9.
110. *JASOB*, vol. V, p. 727.
111. R. C. Majumdar (ed.) *The History and Culture of the Indian People*, Vol. II, *Age of Imperial Unity*, 1980, p. 217.
112. *JASOB*, vol. V, pp. 482–4.
113. This is obviously an error. As Mill says in his footnote to the articles: 'The recurrence of the same name and description is singular. It is impossible that they should be the same person, such incest being unknown even to the heroic age of India.'
114. R. C. Majumdar, *Ancient India*, pp. 428–9.
115. *PASOB*, 3 Feb. 1836; 2 Mar. 1836.
116. A. Cunningham, *ASIR*, vol. I, Introduction, pp. vii–x, p. 112.
117. Ibid.
118. Ibid., p. 119.
119. *PASOB*, 5 Oct. 1836.
120. Ibid., 1 Jun. 1836.
121. Tregear's name was proposed for honorary membership by Alexander Cunningham on 7 Sept. 1836 and on 5 Oct. he was unanimously elected.
122. *PASOB*, 7 Sept. 1836.
123. Ibid.
124. NAI. Home Pub. 14 Sept. 1836, No. 20.

125. J. Prinsep, 'Preface', *JASOB*, pp. ix–x.
126. *JASOB*, vol. VI, pt. 1, pp. 1–17.
127. Ibid., p. 1.
128. Ibid., p. 8.
129. Ibid., p. 16. Contrary to what Mill has said, Scandagupta was also probably a Vaishnava.
130. Ibid., p. 9.
130a The basis of this observation is not clear since the Vishnu Purana verse, as given in R. C. Majumdar and A. S. Altekar, *The Vakatakagupta Age* (Motilal Banarasidass, Delhi, 1986) mentions none of these places. The verse is as follows:
        'Anu-Ganga Prayagam he Saketam Magadhamas tatha
        Etan janapadam Sarvan bhoksyante Gupta-Vamsjah.'
131. Ibid., p. 12.
132. J. Prinsep, 'Note on the facsimiles of Inscriptions from Sanchi near Bhilsa', *JASOB*, vol. VI, pt. I, pp. 451–77.
133. A. Cunningham, *The Bhilsa Topes*, Smith Elder, London, 1854, pp. 152–62.
134. V. Smith, 'James Prinsep', *East and West*, vol. V, 1906 (July), p. 636.
135. Ibid., pp. 637–8.
136. J. Prinsep, 'Note on . . . . Inscriptions from Sanchi', *JASOB*, vol. VI, pt. 1, pp. 460–1. Though Prinsep announced the discovery on 7 June, he had the main clue a few days earlier. This is evident from his letter to Cunningham, dated 23 May 1837.
137. Ibid., p. 470.
138. Ibid., p. 472.
139. Ibid.
140. James Emerson Tennent, *Ceylon: An Account of the Island*, Longman, Green, Layman and Roberts, London, 1860, vol. I, pp. 312–13 (fn).
141. G. Turnour, *An Epitome of the History of Ceylon*, Ceylon, 1836, pp. ii–iii.
142. *PASOB*, 4 Jan. 1837.
143. NAI, Home Pub., 25 Jan. 1837, No. 35.
144. *JASOB*, vol. VI, pt. 2, p. 791.
145. So confident was Prinsep of the veracity of the theory that he wrote: 'I trust that this point has been set at rest, and that it has been satisfactorily proved that the several pillars at Delhi, Allahabad, Matthia, and Radhia were erected under the orders of King Devanampiya Piyadassi of Ceylon about three hundred years before the Christian era.' J. Prinsep, 'Interpretation of the most ancient of the inscriptions on the pillar . . . near Delhi', *JASOB*, vol. VI, pt. 2, pp. 560–610.
146. Ibid., pp. 790–1.
147. G. Turnour, 'Further note on the Inscriptions on the columns at Delhi, Allahabad, Bettiah & c.', *JASOB*, vol. VI, pp. 1055–6.
148. *DNB*. Article on George Turnour.
149. Cunningham, *ASIR*, vol. I, p. ix.
150. Smith, 'James Prinsep', p. 636.
151. J. Prinsep, 'Note or Inscriptions at Udayagiri and Khandagiri in Cut-

tack, in the lat character', *JASOB*, vol. VI, pp. 1077–8.
152. Ibid., p. 1073.
153. Ibid., pp. 1084–5.
154. K. Sitaramaiya, 'Hathigumpha Inscription', *PIHC*, 8th session, 1945, pp. 52–5.
155. *As. Res.*, vol. I, p. 278.
156. *JASOB*, vol. VI, p. 674.
156a. The basis of this assumption is not clear.
157. Ibid., p. 677.
158. Ibid., p. 678.
159. J. Prinsep, 'Note on the facsimiles of the various inscriptions on the ancient column at Allahabad, retaken by Captain Edward Smith', *JASOB*, vol. VI, p. 963.
160. Ibid., p. 964.
161. *PASOB*, 6 Sept. 1837.
162. Ibid., 4 Oct. 1837.
163. Ibid., 5 Jul. 1837.
164. Ibid.
165. J. Prinsep, 'Discovery of the name of Antiochus the Great, in two of the edicts of Asoka', *JASOB*, vol. VII, pp. 156–7.
166. Ibid., p. 166.
167. The first communication was presented at the Society's meeting of 7 Mar.; the present one on 4 Apr. 1838.
168. J. Prinsep, 'On the Edicts of Piyadasi, or Asoka, the Buddhist monarch of India, preserved on the Girnar rock in the Gujarat peninsula, and on the Dhauli rock in Cuttack, with the rediscovery of Ptolemy's name therein', *JASOB*, vol. VII, pt. I, p. 224.
169. Ibid., p. 226.
170. J. Prinsep, 'Examination of the separate edicts of the Aswatama inscription at Dhauli in Cuttack', *JASOB*, vol. VII, pt. I, p. 454.
171. William Taylor, 'Examination and Analysis of the Mackenzie Manuscripts deposited in the Madras College Library', *JASOB*, vol. VII, pt. I, pp. 105–31, 173–92, 317–414 and 469–521.
172. *JASOB*, vol. VII, pt. I, p. 38. It is not clear which inscription this refers to since there is no subsequent reference to any Skandagupta inscription having been found in Bhagalpur.
173. Dr A. Burns, 'Kaira Tamba Patra No. 1', *JASOB*, vol. VII. pt. 2, pp. 966–8.
174. *PASOB*, 14 Nov. 1838.
175. *JASOB*, vol. VII, pt. 2, p. 1047.
176. H. T. Prinsep, 'Memoir of the Author', *Essays in Indian Antiquities*, p. xvi.
177. Ibid.

Chapter 6. CONCLUSIONS

1. Frank Manuel, 'The Enlightenment and the History of Ideas', in N. Cantor, ed., *Perspectives on the European Past*, vol. II, Collier Macmillan, London, 1972, p. 30.
2. Ranjana Mukherjee, 'The History of the Andhra Region', Ph.D. thesis, SOAS, 1965, p. 425 fn.
3. Philips, *Historians of India*, p. 1
4. Some of these are: S. P. Sen (ed.), *Historians and Historiography in Modern India*, Institute of Historical Studies, Calcutta, 1973; J. S. Grewal, *Muslim Rule in India: The Assessment of British Historians*, O.U.P., Calcutta, 1970; R. C. Majumdar, *Historiography in Modern India*, Asia, Bombay, 1970; and Bhagvad Datta, *Western Indologists: A Study in Motives*, Itihas-Prakashana-Mandala, New Delhi, Samvat 2011. S. H. Hodivala in his *Studies in Indo-Muslim History*, Bombay, 1939–57, sought to provide a corrective to Elliot and Dowson's *History of India as told by its own Historians*. After going through Hodivala's book, the impression which remains is not that Elliot and Dowson deliberately distorted any passage to prove a specific point but that, in most cases, the passages admitted of a different translation or interpretation which was not necessarily or substantially different from that provided by the original authors.
5. Beside a large number of articles, there are full-length studies on Jones by Lord Teignmouth, A. J. Arberry, Garland Cannon, S. N. Mukherjee, Abu Taher Majumdar and Janardan Prasad Singh.
6. Colebrooke's biography was written by his son, and Hodgson's by W. W. Hunter.
7. R. S. Sharma, *Aspects of Political Ideas and Institutions in Ancient India*, Motilal Banarasidass, Delhi, 1959, p. 1.
8. Said, *Orientalism*, p. 3.
9. Ibid., p. 11.
10. From the booklet containing this address, p. 10.
11. Mukherjee, *Sir William Jones*, p. 2.
12. The Administration did encourage the compilation of Indian laws by Halhed, Jones and Colebrooke but this work was only an insignificant part of their overall scholarship.
13. It is difficult to accept Dilip Chakrabarti's view that the Society was founded to help the process of change in the role of the British in India 'from a trader to that of territorial rulers' (Dilip Chakrabarti, 'Indian Archaeology: The First Phase (1784–1861)', in *Towards a History of Archaeology* (ed.), p. 169.
14. *AEIM*, vol. III, 1832 (Jan.–Jun.), p. 537.
15. Daniel Ingalls, 'On the Study of the Past', *JAOS*, vol. 80, 1960, p. 191.
16. Bernard Lewis, *History—Remembered, Recovered, Invented*, Princeton University Press, 1975, pp. 87–8.
17. Ingalls, 'On the Study of the Past', *JAOS*, p. 191.
18. Sharma, *Aspects of Political Ideas*, p. 1.
19. The Preface covers pp. ix–xxviii. Page xi, from which the quotation is

taken, forms a part of the 'Program of a Translation'.
20. F. M. Max Müller, *The Sacred Books of the East*, reprint, Motilal Banarasidass, vol. I, pt. I, p. xi.
21. Ibid., pp. xxxvii–viii.
22. See the episode of Lady Welby narrated in Nirad Chaudhury, *Scholar Extraordinary*, O.U.P., London, 1974, p. 351.
23. Said, *Orientalism*, p. 18.
24. See the article on Joseph Boden in *DNB*.
25. Bhagavad Datta, *Western Indologists*, p. 4.
26. See 'Extract of a Letter from a Resident Fellow of Jesus College, dt. 24 February 1832', in IOL, MSS Eur. D. 930.
27. *Cal. Rev.*, vol. VI, 1846, p. 240.
28. Hunter, *Brian Houghton Hodgson*, p. 1.
29. Cannon, *Letters*, p. 766.
30. IOL, MSS Eur. D. 304 (Wilson Collection), vol.I, folio 1.
31. A. A. Macdonnell, *History of Sanskrit Literature*, London, 1917, p. 1.
32. Some of the important Societies are: the Asiatic Society of Paris (1822); the Royal Asiatic Society of Great Britain and Ireland (1823); the American Oriental Society (1851); the Vereenigung Von Vrienden der Aziatische Kunst, at the Hague (1918); the Verein der Freunde Asiatischer Kunst und Kultur, at Vienna (1920); the Association Française des Amis de l'Orient, at Paris (1920); and the Institut der Gesellschaft für Ostasiastische Kunst, at Berlin (1926). Societies for the study of eastern cultures were also established at Budapest, Oslo and Copenhagen.
33. Max Müller, *India, What Can it Teach Us*, p.6.
34. Quoted in Kopf, *Nineteenth Century Bengal*, Indian Committee for Cultural Freedom, Calcutta, 1963, p. 16.
35. A. L. Rowse, 'Welsh Orientalist: Sir William Jones', in *History Today*, vol. 21, Jan. 1971, p.59.
36. Surendra Gopal, 'James Mill', Ph.D. Thesis, University of Mysore, 1972.
37. Hemendra Ghose, 'Sanskrit Learning in India', *Cal. Rev.*, 1904, p. 179.

Select Bibliography

I. UNPUBLISHED RECORDS

Asiatic Society of Bengal, Calcutta
    Manuscript Proceedings,' 1784–1838
    Archival Material in the form of loose documents and letters
National Archives of India, New Delhi
    Documents in the Home Miscellaneous series upto 1838
Carey Library, Serampore'
    Analytical Index of articles on India published in various journals (2 vols.), 1873
India Office Library, London
    Mackenzie Papers (especially those relating to the Batavian Society)
    Orme Papers
    Eur. MSS D. 491 (two packets of loose letters)
    Wilson Correspondence (13 volumes)
Royal Asiatic Society of Great Britain, London
    Manuscript Proceedings, 1823–38
    Hodgson Papers

II. JOURNALS

Articles published in the Asiatic Society's publications, the *Asiatic Researches*, Volumes 1–20, and the *Journal of the Asiatic Society*, Volumes 1–7, form the main primary sources of this study. For considerations of space, however, these articles are not being separately listed.

Alexander's East India and Colonial Magazine, London
Asiatic Journal, London
Asiatic Researches, Calcutta
Bengal Annual, Calcutta
Bengal Past and Present, Calcutta
Blackwood's Edinburgh Magazine, London
British Critic, London
Bulletin of the School of Oriental and African Studies, London
Calcutta Review, Calcutta
Classical Journal, London
Columbia Forum, New York
East and West, Simla
Edinburgh Review, London

Friend of India, Serampore
Gentleman's Magazine, London
History Today, London
India Review, Calcutta
Indian Art and Letters, London
Indian Culture, Calcutta
Journal of All India Oriental Conference, Ahmedabad
Journal of American Oriental Society, Boston
Journal of Ancient Indian History, Calcutta
Journal of the Asiatic Society, Calcutta
Journal of Indian History, London
Journal of the Royal Asiatic Society of Great Britain and Ireland, London
Oriental Herald, London
Quarterly Review, London
Studies in History, Delhi

III. BOOKS

Anon., *The Nabob*, London, 1773
Arberry, A. J., *Asiatic Jones*, published for the British Council by Longmans, Green, London, 1946
——, *British Orientalists*, W. Collins, London, 1943
——, *Oriental Essays*, George Allen & Unwin, London, 1960
Aronson, A. , *Europe looks at India*, Bombay, 1946
Asiatic Society of Bengal, *Centenary Review (1784–1883)*, Calcutta, 1885
——, *150th Jubilee of the Royal Asiatic Society of Bengal (1784–1934) and the Bicentenary of Sir William Jones (1746–1946)*, Royal Asiatic Society of Bengal, Calcutta, 1946
——, *Sir William Jones: Bicentenary of His Birth, Commemoration Volume*, Royal Asiatic Society of Bengal, Calcutta, 1948
Basham, A. L., *A Cultural History of India*, Oxford, 1975
——, (ed.), *Papers on the date of Kanishka*, E. J. Brill, Leiden, 1968
——, *The Wonder that was India*, Sidgwick and Jackson, London, 1954
Bearce, G. D., *British Attitudes Towards India*, O. U. P., London, 1961
Becker, Carl, *The Heavenly City of Eighteenth Century Philosophers*, Yale University Press, New Haven, 1959
Burgess, James, *Archaeological Research in India*, E. J. Brill, Leiden, 1890
——, 'Notes on Hindu Astronomy and the History of our Knowledge of It, Hertford, 1893.' (Preserved as a tract in the Asutosh Collection of National Library, Calcutta)
Cannon, Garland, *Oriental Jones*, Asia Publishing House, Bombay, 1964
——, *Letters of Sir William Jones* (2 vols.), O.U.P., London, 1970
——, *Sir William Jones, an Annotated Bibliography of His Works*, University of Hawaii Press, Honolulu, 1952
Cantor, N., *Perspectives on the European Past*, Collier Macmillan, London, 1971
Chalmers, A., *The General Biographical Dictionary*, London, 1812–17

Chaudhuri, N., *Scholar Extraordinary*, O.U.P., London, 1974
Chaudhuri, S., *Index to the Publications of the Asiatic Society, 1888–1953*, Asiatic Society, Calcutta, 1956
Colebrooke, T. E., *Miscellaneous Essays of H. T. Colebrooke, with the life of the author* (3 vols.), Trubner & Co., London, 1873
Conant, M. P., *The Oriental Tale in England in the Eighteenth Century*, Columbia University Press, New York, 1908
Cunningham, A., *Archaeological Survey of India Reports* (23 vols.), Office of the Superintendent of Government Printing, Calcutta, 1871–1887
——, *The Bhilsa Topes*, Smith Elder & Co., London, 1854
Daniel, G., *Towards a History of Archaeology*, Thames and Hudson, London, 1981
Datta, Bhagavat, *Western Indologists: A Study in Motives*, Itihas Prakashana-Mandal, Delhi, 1954
Datta, K. K., *Dawn of Renaissant India*, University of Nagpur, 1959
——, *Survey of India's Social Life and Economic Conditions in the Eighteenth Century (1707–1813)*, Firma K. L. Mukhopadhyaya, Calcutta, 1961
Dictionary of National Biography, O.U.P., London, 1949–50
Drewery, Mary, *William Carey*, Hodder and Stoughton, London, 1978
Durant, Will and Ariel Durant, *The Age of Voltaire*, Simon & Schuster, New York, 1965
——, *Rousseau and Revolution*, Simon & Schuster, New York, 1967
Elphinstone, M., *An Account of the Kingdom of Kabul*, Richard Bentley, London, 1839
Fleet, J. F., *Corpus Inscriptionum Indicarum*, vol. III, Indological Book House, Varanasi, 1970
Francklin, W., *Inquiry Concerning the site of ancient Palibothra*, Black & Co., London, 1815–20
Goetz, Hermann, *The Crisis of Indian Civilization in the Eighteenth and Early Nineteenth Centuries*, Calcutta University, 1938
Grewal, J. S., *Muslim Rule in India*, O.U.P., Calcutta, 1970
Hodivala, S. H., *Studies in Indo-Muslim History*, published by the author, Bombay, 1939–57
Hunter, W. W., *Life of Brian H. Hodgson*, John Murray, London, 1896
Kaye, J. W., *Lives of Indian Officers*, J. J. Keliher & Co., London, 1904
Kopf, D., *British Orientalism and the Bengal Renaissance: The Dynamics of Indian Modernisation 1773–1835*, University of California, Berkeley, 1969
——, *Nineteenth Century Bengal*, Indian Committee for Cultural Freedom, Calcutta, 1963
Kulkarni, V. B., *British Statesmen in India*, Calcutta, 1961
Lach, D. F., *Asia in the Making of Europe*, University of Chicago Press, 1965
Laurie, Col. W. F. B., *Sketches of some Distinguished Anglo-Indians*, W. H. Allen & Co., London, 1887–8
Macdonell, A. A., *History of Sanskrit Literature*, Reprint, Munshiram Manoharlal, New Delhi, 1979
Mackenzie, W. C., *Colonel Colin Mackenzie*, London, 1952
Majumdar, R. C., *Ancient India*, Motilal Banarasidass, Delhi, 1960

———, *Ancient Indian Colonization in South East Asia, the Maharaja Sayajirao Gaekwad Honorarium Lecture, 1953-54*, Baroda Oriental Institute, 1955
———, *Hindu Colonies in the Far East*, General Printers and Publishers, Calcutta, 1944
———, *Historiography in Modern India*, Asia Publishing House, Bombay, 1970
———, (ed.), *History and Culture of the Indian People* (11 vols.), Bharatiya Vidya Bhavan, Bombay, 1951
Marshall, P. J., *The British Discovery of Hinduism in the Eighteenth Century*, Cambridge University Press, 1970
Masson, C., *Narrative of a Journey* (3 vols.), Oxford in Asia Historical Reprints, O.U.P., Karachi, 1975
Max-Müller, F. M., *Collected Works*, Longmans, Green & Co., London, 1910
———, *Chips from a German Workshop*, Longmans, Green & Co., London, 1867
———, *India—What Can it Teach Us*, Longmans, Green & Co., London, 1910
———, *My Autobiography*, Longmans, Green & Co., London, 1901
———, *On Ancient Hindu Astronomy and Chronology*, Oxford, London, 1868
———, (ed.), *The Sacred Books of the East*, vol. I, Reprint, Motilal Banarasidass, Delhi, 1969
Mill, James & H. H. Wilson, *The History of British India*, vol. I, James Madden & Co., London, 1840-6
Mirsky, J., *Sir Aurel Stein*, University of Chicago Press, 1977
Mitra, P. C., *Life of Dewan Ram Comul Sen*, I. C. Bose & Co., Calcutta, 1880
Mitra, S. K. , *East Indian Bronzes*, University of Calcutta, 1979
Mitter, P., *Much Maligned Monsters*, O.U.P., London, 1977
Monier-Williams, M., *Sakuntala*, 8th ed., London, 1898
———, *Two Addresses delivered before the International of Orientalists at Berlin on 14 September 1881* (see tract preserved in the Asutosh Collection of National Library, Calcutta)
Mukherjee, S. N., *Sir William Jones: A Study in Eighteenth Century British Attitudes to India*, Cambridge University Press, 1968
Natesan, G. A., *Eminent Orientalists*, G. A. Natesan & Co., Madras, 1922
Nehru, J., *The Discovery of India*, The Signet Press, Calcutta, 1947
Pandit, R. S. (tr.), *Rajatarangini*, Sahitya Academi, Delhi, 1968
Pedersen, Holger, *The Discovery of Language*, Indiana University Press, Bloomington, 1962
Philips, C. H., *Historians of India, Pakistan and Ceylon*, O.U.P., London, 1961
Pope, E. M., *India in Portuguese Literature*, Tipographia Range, Bastora, 1937
Potts, Daniel, *British Baptist Missionaries in India 1793-1837, The History of Serampore and its Missions*, Cambridge University Press, 1967
Prinsep, J., *Essays on Indian Antiquities*, John Murray, London, 1858
Ramachandran, K. S. and S. P. Gupta (ed.), *India and South-east Asia*, B. R. Publishing Corporation, Delhi, 1979
Ray, H. C., *The Dynastic History of Northern India*, Calcutta University Press, 1931
Rapson, E. J., *Indian Coins*, Karl J. Trubner, Strassburg, 1897
Rennell, James, *Memoir of a Map of Hindostan*, reprint, Calcutta, 1976

Robertson, W., *Historical Disquisition concerning ancient India*, reprint, Delhi, 1981

Rost, Reinhold (ed.), *Essays and Lectures on the Religion of the Hindus*, London, 1862

Roy, S., *The Story of Indian Archaeology, 1784–1947*, Archaeological Survey of India, New Delhi, 1961

Roychaudhuri, Durgaprasanna, *Sir William Jones and his Translation of Kalidasa's Sakuntala*, Calcutta, 1928

Said, Edward, *Orientalism*, Routledge and Kegan Paul, London, 1978

Sastri, Nilakanta, *A History of South India*, O.U.P., Madras, 1976

Sen, D. C., *History of Bengali Language and Literature*, Calcutta University Press, 1954

Sen, S. P., *Historians and Historiography in Modern India*, Institute of Historical Studies, Calcutta, 1973

Singh, J. P., *William Jones, His Mind and Art*, S. Chand & Co., Delhi, 1982

Sinha, N. K., *The History of Bengal*, Calcutta University Press, 1967

Shafaat Ahmad Khan, *The History and Historians of British India*, Srimant Sayaji Rao Lectures at Baroda, Kitabistan, Allahabad, 1938

Sharma, R. S., *Aspects of Political Ideas and Institutions in Ancient India*, Motilal Banarasidass, Delhi, 1959

Stein, Aurel, *Kalhana's Rajatarangini*, A. Constable & Co., London, 1900. Reprint, Motilal Banarasidass, Delhi, 1979

———, *Prospectus of a new edition of Kalhana's Rajatarangini* (tract in the Asutosh Collection of National Library, Calcutta)

Teignmouth, Lord, *The Works of Sir William Jones, with the Life of the Author* (13 vols.), London, 1799

Tennent, James Emerson, *Ceylon, An Account of the Island*, Longmans, Green, Longman and Roberts, London, 1860

Turnouv, G., *An Epitome of the History of Ceylon*, Church Mission Press, Ceylon, 1836

Voltaire, *An Essay on Universal History, the Manners and Spirit of Nations* (English trans.), Dublin, 1769

Ward, W., *A View of the History, Literature and Mythology of the Hindoos*, vol. I, Black, Kinsburg, Parbury & Allen, London, 1822

Wilson, H. H., *Ariana Antigua*, Reprint, Oriental Publishers, Delhi, 1971

———, *The Megha Dutt or. Cloud Messenger: A Poem in the Sanskrit Language by Calidasa Translated into English verse with notes and illustrations*, Published under the sanction of the College of Fort William, Calcutta, 1813

IV. UNPUBLISHED THESES

Datta, Rajat, 'Aspects of the Agrarian system of Bengal during the second half of the eighteenth century' (M.Phil. dissertation, Jawaharlal Nehru University), 1980

Mukherjee, Ranjana, 'The History of the Andhra Region, c. A.D. 75–350' (Ph.D. thesis, School of Oriental and African Studies, London), 1965

Shaukat Ullah Khan, 'Superior Zamindars in the Mughal Subah of Gujarat during the First Half of the Eighteenth Century' (M.Phil. dissertation, Jawaharlal Nehru University), 1977
Surendra Gopal, 'James Mill' (Ph.D. thesis, University of Mysore), 1972

Index

Seringapatam, 110, 133
Sevenska Argus 25
Sharma, R. S., 222, 225, 228
Shiva Lilarnava, 3
Shivapurana, 20
Shore, Sir John, 81, 93, 94, 137
Shujalpur Pargana, 197
Siddha Raja, 144
Siladitya I, 191
Siladitya II, 191
Siladitya III, 192
Siladitya Musalli IV, 192
Silhara, 52; Silhara dynasty, 51, 191, 223
Sindhuputra, see Sakambari Chauhans
Singhea, 185
Sinha, Ari, 144
Sinha, Maharaja Drona, 191
Sinha, Maharajadhiraja Varman, 199
Sirkar, D. C., 45
Sisac or Sacya, 58
Sital Singh, 129
Sitaramaiya, Dr K., 211
Sivananda, 4
Sivchundra Das, 152
Skandagupta, 203
Smith, Colonel, 150, 187
Smith, Captain Edward, 204, 212
Smith, Lewis Ferdinand, 96
Smith, Lewis, 71
Smith, Nathaniel, 24
Smith, Vincent, 189, 204, 209
Société Asiatique de Paris, 129, 195
Société d'Agriculture et de Commerce de la Ville de Caen, 122
Society of Antiquaries, in England, 110
Solo, Emperor of, 121
Soma, 63, 144
Sonnerat, Pierre, 18
Sotereagas, 178
Soul of India, 6
Speirs, Captain, 142, 188, 224
Spencer, Earl, 54, 63, 73
Spencer, Lady, 64
Sravana Belgola, 104
Sridhara Sena I, 191
Sridhara Sena II, 191
Stacy, Major, 175, 187, 189, 205
Stark, Harry, 46

Stein, Aurel, 128, 149
Steuart, J. R., 209
Stevens, Father Thomas, 14, 16
Stevenson, J., 174, 185
Stewart, Captain Charles, 104
Stirling, Andrew, 139, 140, 150, 173, 209
Strabo, 157, 194
Strachey, Edward, 112, 113, 114, 140, 227
Story, Justice, 31
(A) Study of History, 204
Subhatavarma, 197
Suddhitattwa, 79
Sudra rulers, 56
Sujyestha, 56
Sullivan, Richard Joseph, 13
Suma Oriental, 10
Sunga, kings, 56
'Supplement to the Essay on Indian Chronology', 62, 63
'(The) Supposed Vaidic Authority for the Burning of Hindu Widows' :(Wilson), 78
Surya Siddahanta, 62, 63, 69, 87, 88, 91
Suyasas, 56
Swai Jaisingh, Raja, 85
Swedish Royal Academy, 25
Swiney, Dr, 7, 166, 189, 199
Sydenham, Captain, 123, 224

Tagara, 51, 52
Tagore, Coloylal, 218
Tagore, Rabindranath, 232
Tamba Patra, 197
Tamil language (literature), 4, 95
Tanjore, 153
Tanna, 51
Tara Chand, 2
Tavernier, 13, 123
Taylor, William, 135, 217
Teja Pala, 145
Teignmouth, Lord, 30, 41, 74, 230
Teixeira, 16
'Telinga', 121
Terry, Edward, 13
Tewary, Suboor, 71
Thackeray, Dr, 30
Thaneshwar, 192